THERMODYNAMICS FOR ENGINEERS II

Kau-Fui Vincent Wong Ph.D., P.E.

University of Miami

Linus
Publications, Inc.

Published by Linus Publications, Inc.

Deer Park, NY 11729

Copyright © 2007 Kau-Fui Vincent Wong Ph.D., P.E.

All Right Reserved.

ISBN 1-934188-21-2

No part of this publications may be reproduced, stored in a retrieval system, or transmitted, in any form or by any means, electronic, mechanical, photocopying, recording, or otherwise, without the prior permission of the publisher.

Printed in the United States of America.

10 9 8 7 6 5 4 3 2 1

THERMODYNAMICS FOR ENGINEERS II

© 2007   Kau-Fui Vincent Wong, Ph.D., P.E.

PREFACE

In this third edition, the main objective is to present a comprehensive treatment of engineering thermodynamics from the classical aspect, so as to provide a foundation for all engineering students to prepare them to use thermodynamics in professional practice. The book is written for the second course in thermodynamics for undergraduates in engineering.

A prime difficulty of engineering undergraduates in studying thermodynamics is the use of thermodynamic tables, and finding the right properties of substances. This difficulty is removed by emphasizing the use of computer-aided thermodynamic tables from the onset.

In the spirit of simplicity, various thermodynamic systems are introduced; first, the refrigeration cycle, then the gas cycle, followed by thermodynamic relations and gas mixtures. After the gas mixtures, a detailed chapter on psychrometrics, a chapter on chemical reactions and combustion, a chapter on compressible fluid flow, ending with a chapter on sustainable energy systems.

The special features of the book are as follows:-

*   It is a print-on-demand book.

*   Lengthy treatise and unnecessary details have not been included. Only important facts and methods have been treated to make the work of the student easier.

*   Limit the manual interpolation of thermodynamic tables. Support the use of computer-aided thermodynamic tables. These tables are downloadable from the author's website.

* Allow expansion of the property tables by the reader.

* Minimize the differences between the ideal gas treatment and the vapor treatment, by referring to computer-aided thermodynamic tables for all properties.

* Unify the treatment of the conservation of energy, the creation of entropy, and the destruction of availability, by using a balance equation for each of them.

* The chapter on psychrometrics will give a very strong background for the student of air conditioning. If the student wants to develop an expertise in air conditioning, the material covered will be ideal. If the student just wants to have a general education in various thermodynamic systems, the chapter is more than adequate.

· The chapter on compressible flow will give an excellent introduction of the topic to the student. If the student intends to acquire an expertise in compressible flow, the topics covered will be ideal. If the student prefers to obtain a general education in compressible flow, the material covered is more than sufficient.

* The chapter on sustainable energy sources and applications focuses on fuel cells, wind turbines and tidal turbines. These topics are essential for the modern energy engineer.

The special features of the book are geared towards making thermodynamics a less difficult field for undergraduates in engineering. An electronic version of the thermodynamic tables is available at the author's website. One special feature is that students can add to the thermodynamic tables, either by using smaller intervals in the existing databases or increasing the ranges in the databases. This participatory nature of the textbook can be accomplished by any reader with excess to Excel. Adding to the databases is not only a good learning process but also provides a sense of accomplishment to students on completion.

As an assistance to the reader, an introductory section is provided to review the laws of thermodynamics.

THERMODYNAMICS FOR ENGINEERS II

© 2007, Kau-Fui Vincent Wong, Ph.D., P.E.

TABLE OF CONTENTS

Introduction	Laws of Thermodynamics		
Chapter 1	Refrigeration and Heat Pump Systems		
	1.1	The Reversed Carnot Vapor Cycle	1
	1.2	The Vapor-Compression Refrigeration Cycle	3
	1.3	Actual Vapor-Compression Refrigeration Cycle	6
	1.4	Heat Pump Systems	10
	1.5	Refrigerant Considerations	14
	1.6	Other Refrigeration Systems	15
	1.7	Gas Refrigeration Cycles	25
	1.8	Absorption Refrigeration System	30
Chapter 2	Gas Power Cycles		
	2.1	Basic Considerations	47
	2.2	Air Standard Cycles	48
	2.3	Preliminaries on Reciprocating Engines	49
	2.4	Air-Standard Otto Cycle	51
	2.5	Air-Standard Diesel Cycle	61
	2.6	Air-Standard Dual Cycle	68
	2.7	Stirling and Ericsson Cycles	74
	2.8	Gas Brayton Cycle	78
	2.9	Brayton Cycle with Regeneration	89
	2.10	Regenerative Gas Cycle with Reheat and Intercooling	93
	2.11	Jet Propulsion Cycles	99
	2.12	Second Law Analysis of Gas Power Cycles	105
Chapter 3	Thermodynamic Property Relations		
	3.1	The Maxwell Relations	111
	3.2	The Clapeyron Equation	117
	3.3	General Relations for Thermodynamic Properties	121
	3.4	The Joule-Thomson Coefficient	132
	3.5	The Enthalpy, Internal Energy, and Entropy Changes of Real Gases	137
Chapter 4	Gas Mixtures		
	4.1	Composition of a Gas Mixture	147
	4.2	P-v-T Relationships for Ideal and Real Gas Mixtures	149
	4.3	Properties of Ideal and Real Gas Mixtures	155

Chapter 5	Gas-Vapor Mixtures and Psychrometrics	
	5.1 Atmospheric Air and Dry Air	167
	5.2 Specific and Relative Humidity of Air	168
	5.3 Dew-Point Temperature	170
	5.4 Adiabatic Saturation Process and Wet-Bulb Temperatures	171
	5.5 The Psychrometric Chart	176
	5.6 Psychrometric Processes	179

Chapter 6	Chemical Reactions	
	6.1 Introduction	233
	6.2 Combustion Process	233
	6.3 First-Law Analysis of Reacting Systems	243
	6.4 Adiabatic Flame Temperature	250
	6.5 Third Law of Thermodynamics and Absolute Entropy	255

Chapter 7	Thermodynamics of Compressible Fluid Flow	
	7.1 Stagnation Properties	263
	7.2 Adiabatic, One-Dimensional, Steady-State, Steady Flow of an Incompressible Fluid through a Nozzle	265
	7.3 Velocity of Sound in an Ideal Gas	268
	7.4 Entropy Connection to Vorticity	270
	7.5. Reversible, Adiabatic, One-Dimensional Steady Flow of an Ideal Gas through a Nozzle	273
	7.6. Mass Rate of Flow of an Ideal Gas through an Isentropic Nozzle	277
	7.7. Nozzles	282
	7.8. Normal Shocks	287
	7.9. Supersonic Flow past Wedges and Cones	292
	7.10. Oblique Shocks	296

Chapter 8	Sustainable Energy Sources and Applications	
	8.1 Fuel Cells	311
	8.2 Wind Turbines	323
	8.3 Tidal Turbines	335

Appendices

DIMENSIONS	S.I./ENGLISH	ENGLISH/S.I.
Length	1 cm = 0.3937 in. 1 m = 3.2808 ft	1 in. = 2.54 cm 1 ft = 0.3048 m
Volume	1 c.c. = 0.061024 in.^{3} 1 m^3 = 35.315 ft^3 1 L = 10^{-3} m^3 1 L = 0.0353 ft^3	1 in.^{3} = 16.387 c.c. 1 ft^3 = 0.028317 m^3 1 gal = 0.13368 ft^3 1 gal = 0.0037854 m^3
Velocity	1 m/s = 3.2808 ft/s 1 km/h = 0.62137 mph	1 ft/s = 0.3048 m/s 1 mph = 1.6093 km/h
Mass and Density	1 kg = 2.2046 lb$_m$ 1 g/cm^3 = 62.428 lb/ft^3	1 lb$_m$ = 0.4536 kg 1 lb$_m$/ft^3 = 0.016018 g/cm^3 1 lb$_m$/ft^3 = 1.6018 kg/m^3
Force	1 N = 1 kg.m/s^2 1 N = 0.22481 lb$_f$	1 lb$_f$ = 32.174 lb$_m$.ft/s^2 1 lb$_f$ = 4.4482 N
Pressure	1 Pa = 1 N/m^2 = 1.4504x10^{-4} lb$_f$/in.^{2} 1 bar = 100 kPa = 10^5 N/m^2 1 atm = 1.01325 bars	1 lb$_f$/in.^{2} = 6894.8 Pa 1 atm = 14.696 lb$_f$/in.^{2} 1 lb$_f$/in.^{2} = 144 lb$_f$/ft^2
Energy and Specific Energy	1 J = 1 N.m = 0.73756 ft.lb$_f$ 1 kJ = 737.56 ft.lb$_f$ 1 kJ = 0.9478 Btu 1 kJ/kg = 0.42992 Btu/lb$_m$ 1 kcal = 4.1868 kJ	1 ft.lb$_f$ = 1.35582 J 1 Btu = 778.17 ft.lb$_f$ 1 Btu = 1.0551 kJ 1 Btu/lb$_m$ = 2.326 kJ/kg
Specific Heat	1 kJ/(kg.K) = 0.238846 Btu/(lb$_m$.°R) 1 kcal/(kg.K) = 1 Btu/(lb$_m$.°R)	1 Btu/(lb$_m$.°R) = 4.1868 kJ/(kg.K)
Rate of Energy Transfer	1 W = 1 J/s = 3.413 Btu/h 1 kW = 1.341 hp	1 Btu/h = 0.293 W 1 hp = 0.7457 kW 1 hp = 2545 Btu/h 1 hp = 550 ft.lb$_f$/s

Temperature Conversions	$T(°R) = 1.8 T(K)$
	$T(K) = T(°C) + 273.15$
	$T(°R) = T(°F) + 459.67$
Universal Gas Constant	$\bar{R} = 8.314 \text{ kJ/(kmol·K)}$
	$= 1.986 \text{ Btu/(lbmol·°R)}$
	$= 1545 \text{ (ft·lb}_f\text{)/(lbmol·°R)}$
Standard Atmospheric Pressure	$1 \text{ atm} = 1.01325 \text{ bars}$
	$= 14.696 \text{ lb}_f/\text{in.}^2$
Standard Acceleration of Gravity	$g = 32.174 \text{ ft/s}^2$
	$= 9.80665 \text{ m/s}^2$

INTRODUCTION. LAWS OF THERMODYNAMICS

There are four laws of thermodynamics, from the zeroth to the third law. All the laws are empirical, that is, they have been deduced from observations and practice. The zeroth law stipulates that if two bodies are in thermal equilibrium with a third, they are in thermal equilibrium with each other and therefore at the same temperature. This law forms the foundation of the temperature scale. One of the three bodies can be a thermometer. Hence, because of this law, the thermometer can be used to compare the temperatures of two bodies without the bodies being in touch with each other.

The first law of thermodynamics is the conservation of energy. It states that energy can neither be created nor destroyed. For the practice of engineering, it often means that whatever amount of energy one has at the beginning, one ends up with the same amount of energy, maybe transformed or distributed differently, but the same amount.

The second law of thermodynamics is also known as the creation of entropy. It states that entropy can be created, but not destroyed. In practice, it usually means that whatever amount of entropy one has at the beginning, one ends up with the same amount or more entropy.

The third law of thermodynamics states that the entropy of a pure crystalline substance is zero at the absolute zero temperature. This law forms the foundation of the absolute temperature scale.

The four laws of termodynamics are often used with the conservation of mass principle. This principle states that mass is neither created nor destroyed. For the engineer in the field, it generally means that whatever amount of mass one has at the beginning, one ends up with the exact amount of mass.

1. REFRIGERATION AND HEAT PUMP SYSTEMS

1.1 The Reversed Carnot Vapor Cycle

A T-s diagram of a reversed Carnot cycle operating as a heat pump or refrigerator is shown in Fig. 1.1. In the case of the refrigerator, a quantity of heat Q_L is transferred reversibly from a low temperature T_L to the cycle. The reversed Carnot cycle operates in a cycle during which net work W is added to the system and a quantity of heat is transferred reversibly to a higher temperature . From the first law, $Q_L + W = Q_H$. From the second law for a reversible process, $T_H / T_L = Q_H / Q_L$. The reverse Carnot vapor cycle is represented by a rectangle on a T-s diagram. It is a useful standard because it requires the minimum net work input for a given refrigeration effect.

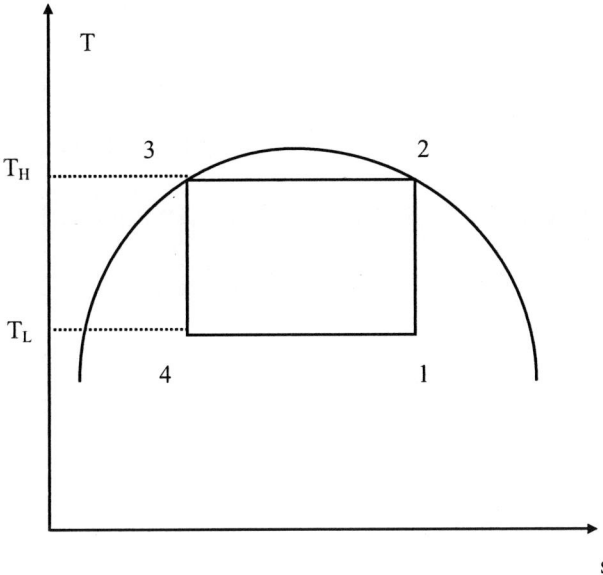

Figure 1.1 Reversed carnot cycle.

The performance of refrigeration processes is the coefficient of performance. The performance standard is defined as the ratio of the desired output to the costly input. The objective of the refrigerator is to remove heat from the low temperature space, and this is done by doing net work on the cycle. So the coefficient of performance (COP) for a refrigerator is defined as

$$\beta = \frac{Q_L}{W_{in}} \qquad (1.1)$$

Recall that the areas under the T_H and T_L lines in Fig. 1.1 represent Q_H and Q_L, respectively. Thus for a Carnot refrigerator,

$$\beta_{Carnot} = \frac{T_L}{T_H - T_L} \qquad (1.2)$$

Note that the value of the COP can exceed unity. The COP of the Carnot refrigerator is represented by the area under T_L divided by the area enclosed by the cycle. The performance is improved by increasing T_L and decreasing T_H. However, T_H cannot be lower than the environmental temperature because heat is rejected to it, and T_L cannot be higher than the temperature of the cold space from which heat is removed.

The objective of the heat pump is to add heat to the high temperature space from the low temperature space, and this is done by doing net work on the cycle. So the coefficient of performance (COP) for a heat pump is defined as

$$\gamma = \frac{Q_H}{W_{in}} \qquad (1.3)$$

Thus for a Carnot heat pump,

$$\gamma_{Carnot} = \frac{T_H}{T_H - T_L} \qquad (1.4)$$

The COP of the Carnot heat pump is represented by the area under T_H divided by the area enclosed by the cycle. The performance is improved by decreasing T_H and increasing T_L. However, T_L cannot be higher than the environmental temperature because heat is extracted from the environment, and T_H cannot be lower than the temperature of the warm space to which heat is added.

As before for the forward Carnot cycle, there are some impracticalities in the reversed Carnot cycle as described:

1. The isentropic compression process in the compressor is a problem because it is not practical to engineer a compressor that will handle two phases.

2. The expansion can be done easily in practice using an expansion valve, but the process will not be isentropic.

1.2   The Vapor-Compression Refrigeration Cycle

The impracticalities of the reversed Carnot cycle can be eliminated by compressing the working fluid entirely in the vapor region, and expanding the working fluid after the condenser through a valve or a capillary tube. The vapor-compression refrigeration cycle, shown in Fig. 1.2, does not have any internal irreversibilities except for the valve or capillary tube, and comprises the following processes:

1-2   Isentropic compression in a compressor

2-3   Heat is removed at constant pressure in the condenser

3-4   Adiabatic expansion in an expansion valve or capillary

4-1   Heat enters the evaporator at constant pressure.

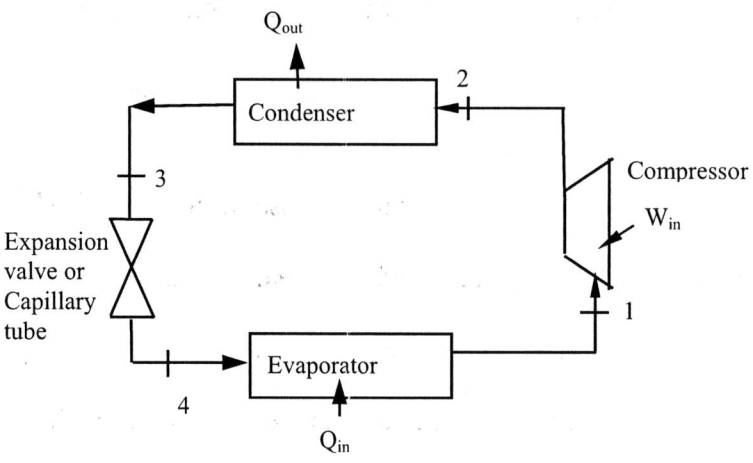

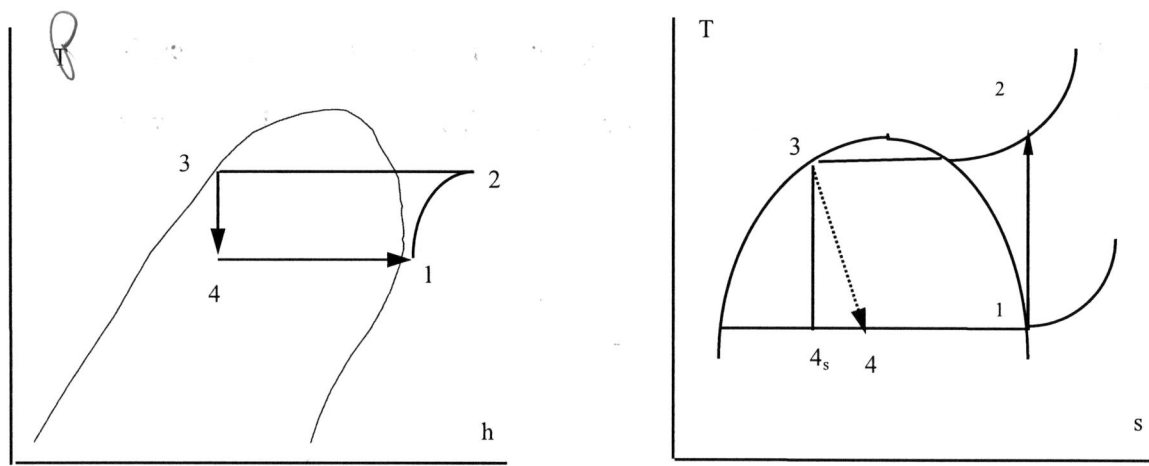

Figure 1.2 Vapor-compression refrigeration cycle.

Both the T-s diagram and the P-h diagram of the ideal vapor-compression refrigeration cycle are shown in Fig. 1.2. In the ideal cycle the working fluid leaves the evaporator at the saturated vapor state, and it leaves the condenser at the saturated liquid state. In the T-s diagram, the COP of the refrigeration cycle is represented by the area under process 4-1, divided by the area enclosed by the cycle. This can be expressed as

$$\beta = \frac{Q_L}{W_{in}} = \frac{h_1 - h_4}{h_2 - h_1} \qquad (1.5)$$

The P-h diagram is useful because three of the four processes appear as straight lines. In addition, the heat transfer in the evaporator and the condenser is proportional to the lengths of the corresponding process lines. The COP is the ratio of the length of the process 4-1 and the horizontal distance corresponding to the process curve 1-2.

Example 1.1

Problem

A refrigerator operates on an ideal vapor-compression refrigeration cycle between 0.15 and 0.6 MPa. Refrigerant-134a is the working fluid, and its flow rate in the cycle is 0.1 kg/s. Determine (i) the heat transfer rate from the refrigerated space, (ii) the power input, and (iii) the COP of the refrigerator.

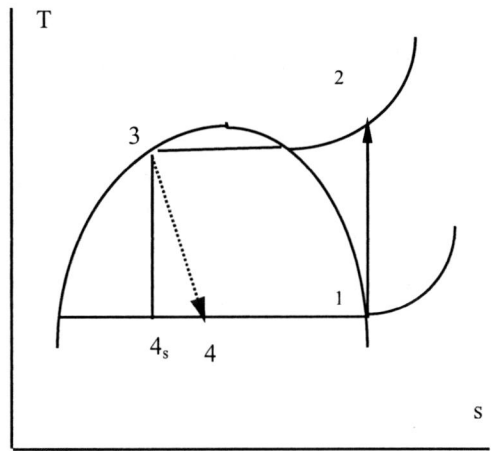

Solution

Assumptions: (i) K.E. and P.E. changes are negligible.

Analysis:

From $P_1 = 0.15$ MPa, $x_1 = 1.0$,

$$h_1 = 387.8 \text{ kJ/kg}, \qquad s_1 = 1.7372 \text{ kJ/(kg.K)}$$

From $P_2 = 0.6$ MPa, $s_2 = s_1$, $\qquad h_2 = 416.4$ kJ/kg,

From $P_3 = 0.6$ MPa, $x_3 = 0.0$, $\;h_3 = 229.6$ kJ/kg, $\qquad s_3 = 1.1035$ kJ/(kg.K)

From $P_4 = 0.15$ MPa, $h_4 = h_3$, $\qquad s_4 = 1.119$ kJ/(kg.K)

(i) From the first law applied to the evaporator,

$$\dot{Q}_L = \dot{m}(h_1 - h_4)$$

Hence, heat transfer rate from the refrigerated space is

(0.1 kg/s)(158.2 kJ/kg) = 15.82 kW

(ii) From the first law applied to the compressor,

$$\dot{W}_{in} = \dot{m}(h_2 - h_1)$$

Hence, the power input is

(0.1 kg/s) (28.6 kJ/kg) = 2.86 kW

(iii) The COP of the refrigerator is

$$\beta = \frac{\dot{Q}_L}{\dot{W}_{in}} = \frac{15.82}{2.86} = 5.53.$$

1.3 Actual Vapor-Compression Refrigeration Cycle

The actual vapor-compression refrigeration cycle differs from the ideal one in several ways because of the irreversibilities in the various components. Two of these irreversibilities are the viscosity of the working fluid, and heat interactions with the surroundings. The T-s diagram of the actual vapor-compression refrigeration cycle is shown in Fig. 1.3.

In the ideal cycle, the working fluid leaves the evaporator as a saturated vapor. Since it is not easy to control the state of the refrigerant, it is expedient to design the system so that the refrigerant is slightly superheated at the evaporator outlet. In addition, the pressure drop due to fluid viscosity and heat transfer from the surroundings to the refrigerant can be significant. The result of this is an increase in specific volume, thus an increase in the work input to the compressor because steady-flow work is proportional to the specific volume.

The actual compression process involves frictional effects, which increase the entropy, and heat interactions with the surroundings, which may increase or decrease the entropy, depending on the direction. Thus, the entropy of the refrigerant may increase (process 1-2) or decrease (process 1-3) during an actual compression process. The compression process 1-3 may be more desirable than the isentropic compression process (1-2_s) since the specific volume of the refrigerant and thus the work input are smaller for process 1-3. For this reason, the refrigerant is cooled during the compression process whenever practical.

In practice, some pressure drop does occur in the condenser and in the lines connecting the condenser to the other equipment. This is shown by state 4 being at a different pressure from state 3 in Fig.1.3. The condensation process cannot be controlled so precisely that the refrigerant leaves as a saturated liquid. Since it is undesirable to let the refrigerant enter the throttling valve as a two-phase fluid, the refrigerant is subcooled before it enters the throttling valve, state 4. This is desirable since the refrigerant enters the evaporator with a lower enthalpy and thus can absorb more heat from the refrigerated space. From state 4 to state 5, there are frictional losses in the connecting line.

Throttling lowers the pressure at state 5 to the pressure at state 6. The throttling valve is situated close to the evaporator to minimize the pressure drop in the connecting line.

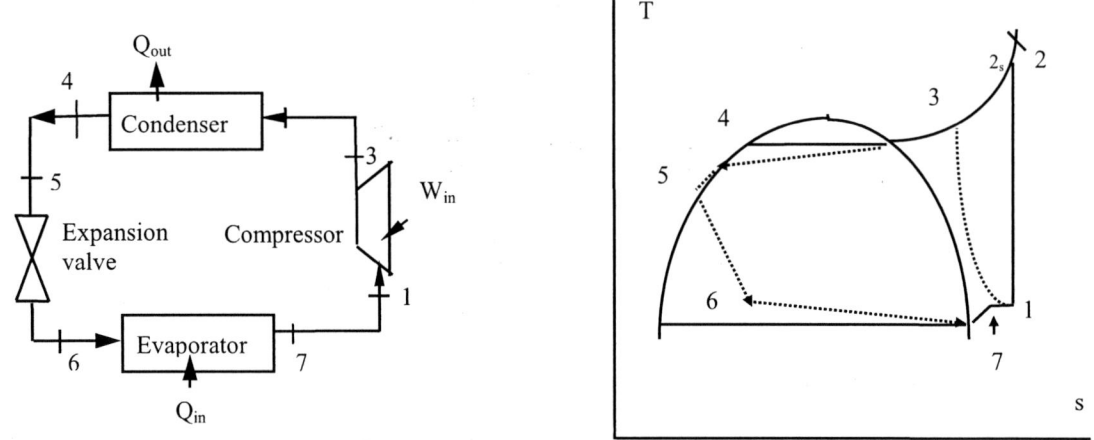

Figure 1.3   Actual vapor-compression refrigeration cycle.

Example 1.2

Problem

The inlet and outlet conditions of refrigerant-134a in the compressor of a refrigeration system are 0.15 MPa and -15°C and 0.6 MPa and 48°C, respectively. The mass flow rate is 0.1 kg/s. The refrigerant-134a is cooled to 18°C and 0.57 MPa in the condenser, and then throttled to 0.16 MPa. Calculate (a) the rate of heat transferred from the refrigerated space, (b) the isentropic efficiency of the compressor, (c) the compressor power input, and (d) the COP of the refrigeration system.

Solution

Assumptions: (i) Heat transfer in the connecting lines between the components are negligible.

(ii) Pressure drops in the connecting lines between the components are negligible.

Analysis:

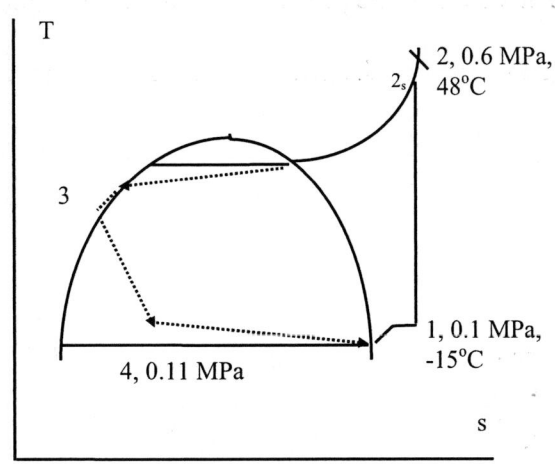

From $P_1 = 0.15$ MPa, $T_1 = -15°C$,

$h_1 = 389.7$ kJ/kg $\qquad s_1 = 1.7446$ kJ/(kg.K)

From $P_2 = 0.6$ MPa, $T_2 = 48°C$,

$h_2 = 436.7$ kJ/kg $\qquad s_2 = 1.8024$ kJ/(kg.K)

From $P_3 = 0.57$ MPa, $T_3 = 18°C$,

$h_3 = 224.7$ kJ/kg

$h_4 = h_3$

(a) From the first law equation applied to the evaporator,

$$\dot{Q}_L = \dot{m}(h_1 - h_4)$$

Rate of heat transferred from the refrigerated space is

(0.1 kg/s) (165 kJ/kg) = 16.5 kW

(b) Isentropic efficiency of the compressor is

$$\eta_c = \frac{h_{2s} - h_1}{h_2 - h_1}$$

$P_{2s} = 0.6$ MPa, $s_{2s} = s_1 = 1.7446$ kJ/(kg.K)

From the thermodynamic tables,

$h_{2s} = 418.6$ kJ/kg

Thus, $\eta_c = \dfrac{28.9}{47} = 0.615$

(c) From the first law equation applied to the compressor,

$$\dot{W}_{in} = \dot{m}(h_2 - h_1)$$

The compressor power input is

(0.1 kg/s) (47 kJ/kg) = 4.7 kW

(d) For the refrigeration system

$$\beta = \dfrac{\dot{Q}_L}{\dot{W}_{in}} = \dfrac{16.5}{4.7} = 3.51.$$

This example could be the actual cycle corresponding to the ideal cycle of Ex. 1.1. The heat transferred from the refrigerated space increases (by 4.3%), but the compressor power input increases by a larger percentage (64%). Hence, the COP of the refrigeration system decreases.

1.4 Heat Pump Systems

In spite of their relatively higher capital costs, heat pumps are increasingly popular. The most common energy source for heat pumps is atmospheric air, although water and soil have been used. The most serious problem is frost formation on the evaporator coils in humid climates (eastern U.S.A.) , when the temperature falls below about 5°C. The frost may be removed by reversing the heat pump cycle, that is, using it as an air conditioner. This obviously reduces the efficiency of the system.

Heat pumps and air conditioners have the same equipment. Thus, one system can be used as a heat pump in winter and an air conditioner in summer. This is done by adding a reversing valve to the cycle, Fig.1.4. The evaporator of the heat pump (located outdoors) acts as the condenser of the air conditioner in summer. The condenser of the heat pump (located indoors) acts as the evaporator of the air conditioner. Window units using this reversing principle are used in motels.

Heat pumps are most appropriate in regions that have a large cooling load in the summer and a relatively small heating load during the winter, as in the southern U.S.A. In these areas, the reversible heat pump systems can meet the entire heating and cooling requirements of the residential or commercial buildings. Heat pumps are less appropriate in areas where the heating load is significant and the cooling load is small, as in the northern U.S.A. Most air-source heat pumps need a supplementary heating system, such as electric resistance heaters when the heating load is large. This may not be needed for water-source or soil-source systems.

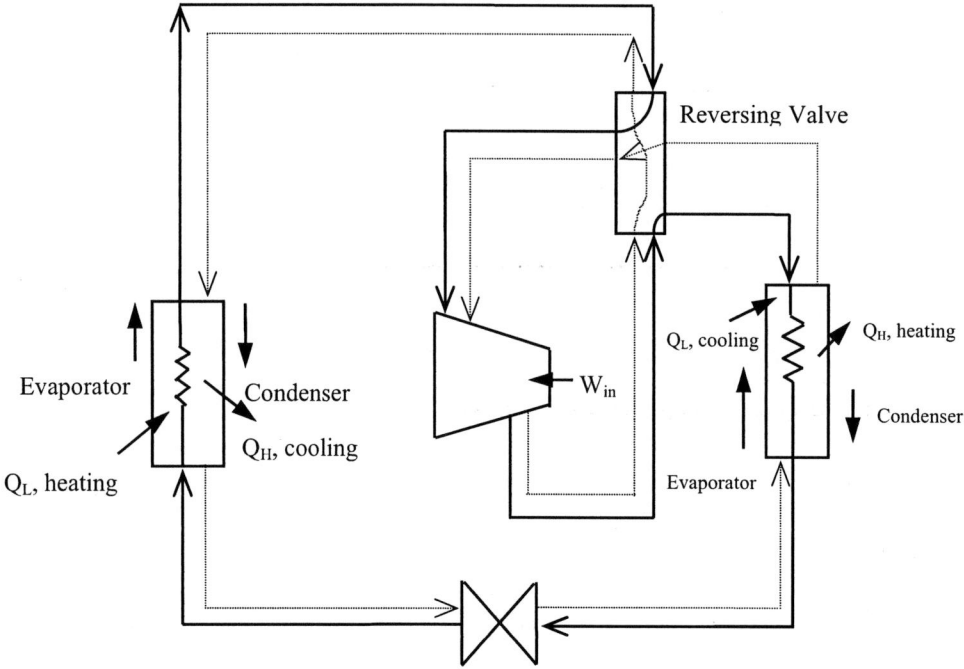

Figure 1.4 Heat pump system with reversing valve in heating mode (solid line) and cooling mode (dashed line)

Example 1.3

Problem

A refrigerant-134a heat pump is used for a residence with a design heating load of 200 Btu/s. The evaporator operates at 10°F and the condenser at 150 lb_f/in^2. Assume an ideal cycle. Determine (i) the mass flow rate of the refrigerant, (ii) the power input to the compressor, (iii) the COP of the heat pump.

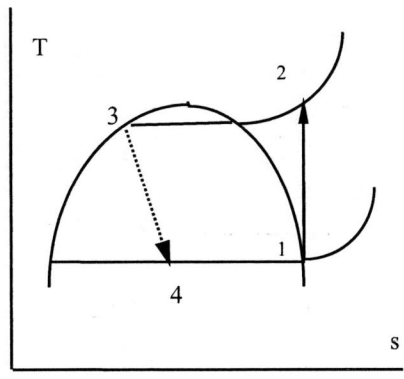

Solution

Assumptions: (I) K.E. and P.E. changes are negligible.

Analysis:

From $T_1 = 10°F$, $x_1 = 1.0$,

$P_1 = 26.79$ psia $h_1 = 168.06$ Btu/lb$_m$, $s_1 = 0.414$ Btu/(lb$_m$·°R)

From $P_2 = 150$ psia, $s_2 = s_1$, $h_2 = 183.5$ Btu/lb$_m$,

From $P_3 = 150$ psia, $x_3 = 0.0$, $h_3 = 110.7$ Btu/lb$_m$

(i) From the first law applied to the condenser,

$$\dot{Q}_H = \dot{m}(h_2 - h_3)$$

Hence, the heating load is

$\dot{m}(72.8 \text{ Btu/lbm}) = 200$ Btu/s

Mass flow rate of the refrigerant is 2.747 lb$_m$/s.

(ii) From the first law applied to the compressor,

$$\dot{W}_{in} = \dot{m}(h_2 - h_1)$$

Hence, the power input is

(2.747 lb$_m$/s) (15.44 Btu/lb$_m$) = 42.41 Btu/s

(iii) The COP of the heat pump is

$$\gamma = \frac{\dot{Q}_H}{\dot{W}_{in}} = \frac{200}{42.41} = 4.72.$$

1.5 Refrigerant Considerations

There are several refrigerants from which to select, such as chlorofluorocarbons (CFCs), ammonia, hydrocarbons (propane, ethane, ethylene,etc.), carbon dioxide, air (aircraft air-conditioning), and water (for applications above its freezing point). Of these, the CFCs make up the largest family of refrigerants.

Because of the concern about the effects of halogenated refrigerants on the earth's protective ozone layer, international agreements have been made to phase out their use. The halogenated refrigerants destroy the protective ozone layer, which regulates the ultraviolet radiation into the earth's atmosphere. The halogenated refrigerants also prevent the infrared radiation from escaping the earth and thus contribute to the greenhouse effects that causes global warming. Fully halogenated CFCs (such as R-11, R-12, and R-115) do the most damage to the ozone layer. The non-fully halogenated refrigerants such as R-22 have only a small percentage of the ozone-depleting capability of R-12. CFCs that do not deplete the ozone-layer and do not contribute to the greenhouse effect have been developed. At present, the chlorine-free R-134a is being used to replace R-12.

Ammonia is used in the industrial and commercial sectors with large loads. The advantages ammonia have over some of the other refrigerants are its low cost, the higher COPs of its absorption cycle, better transport properties, better heat transfer characteristics, greater detectability in the event of a leak, and no effect on the ozone layer. The major disadvantage of ammonia is its toxicity, which makes it unsuitable for domestic use.

The temperatures of the refrigerant in the evaporator and the condenser are respectively determined by the temperatures of the cold refrigerated space and the warm environment to which heat is rejected. Therefore, the choice of the refrigerant is in part based on its suitability of its pressure-temperature relationship in the range of the particular application. Because of leakage problems, it is best to avoid excessively high condenser pressures, and excessively low evaporator pressures. Other considerations in refrigerant choice include toxicity, chemical stability, corrosiveness, and cost. The compressor used also contributes to the selection of the refrigerant. Reciprocating compressors perform well over large pressure ranges and are suitable for handling low specific volume refrigerants. The centrifugal compressors are better for low evaporator pressures and refrigerants with large specific volumes.

1.6 Other Refrigeration Systems

For some large industrial applications, the simple vapor-compression refrigeration cycle is inadequate. A few modifications and improvements are discussed in the following sections.

1 Cascade Refrigeration Systems

A large temperature range requirement also means a large pressure range in the cycle and poor performance for a reciprocating compressor. One modification is to perform the refrigeration process in stages. In other words, two or more refrigeration cycles are made to operate in series. These refrigeration cycles are called cascade refrigeration cycles.

A two-stage cascade refrigeration cycle is shown in Fig. 1.4. The heat exchanger acts as the evaporator for the topping cycle and the condenser for the bottoming cycle. Under ideal conditions, the heat loss from the fluid in the topping cycle should equal the heat gain by the fluid in the bottoming cycle. The relationship of the mass flow rates in the cycles is obtained from this fact, that is

$$\dot{m}_a (h_5 - h_8) = \dot{m}_b (h_2 - h_3)$$

$$\dot{m}_a / \dot{m}_b = (h_2 - h_3) / (h_5 - h_8) \qquad (1.6)$$

Then,
$$\beta_{cascade} = \dot{Q}_{in} / \dot{W}_{net,in}$$

$$= \frac{\dot{m}_b (h_1 - h_4)}{\dot{m}_a (h_6 - h_5) + \dot{m}_b (h_2 - h_1)} \qquad (1.7)$$

In the cascade system shown in Figure 1.5, the refrigerant in the topping cycle is assumed to be the same as that in the bottoming cycle. However, this is not necessary since the heat exchanger is a closed kind and no mixing occurs. The refrigerants with more desirable characteristics can be used in each cycle. The saturation dome for each of the refrigerants will then be different.

From the T-s diagram of the figure, the compressor work decreases and the amount of heat removed from the refrigerated space increases as a result of cascading, as shown by the shaded areas in Fig 1.5. Thus the COP of the system is improved by cascading. Sometimes, three or four stages of cascading are used.

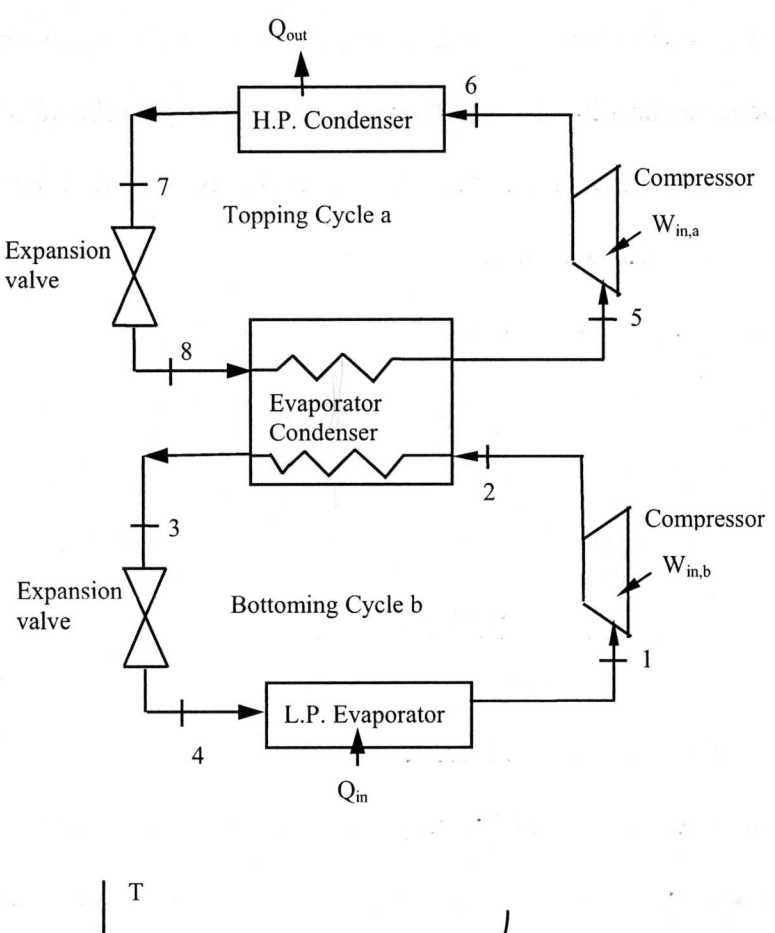

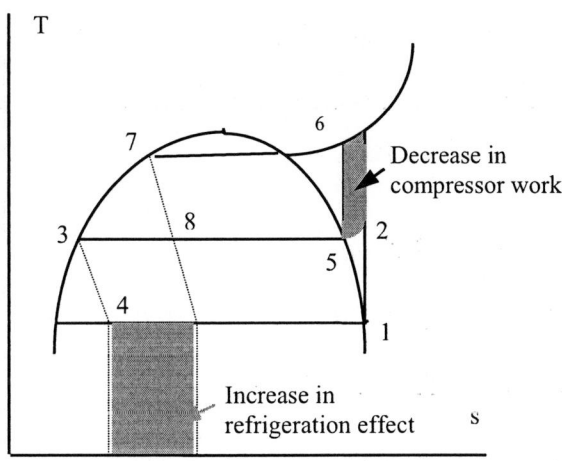

Figure 1.5 Cascade refrigeration cycle.

Example 1.4

Problem

A refrigerator operates on a two-stage cascade system between 0.15 MPa and 0.6 MPa. Refrigerant-134a is the working fluid in both cycles, and its flow rate in the topping cycle is 0.1 kg/s. The intermediate pressure of the adiabatic counterflow heat exchanger is 0.3 MPa, where heat is transferred from the bottoming cycle to the topping cycle. (Actually, the refrigerant in the bottoming cycle will be at a higher pressure and temperature in the heat exchanger for the heat transfer to take place.) Determine (i) the rate of heat transferred from the refrigerated space, (ii) the power input to the compressors, and (iii) the COP of the cascade refrigeration system.

Solution

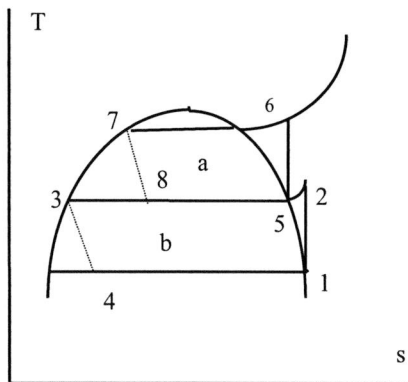

Assumptions: (i) The changes in K.E. and P.E. can be neglected.

(ii) Both compressors are isentropic.

(iii) The refrigerant enters both compressors as saturated vapor.

(iv) The refrigerant leaves both condensers as saturated liquid.

Analysis:

Cycle a is the topping cycle, and cycle b is the bottoming cycle.

From $P_5 = 0.3$ MPa, $x_5 = 1.0$,

$$h_5 = 398.7 \text{ kJ/kg}, \quad s_5 = 1.7259 \text{ kJ/(kg.K)}$$

From $P_6 = 0.6$ MPa, $s_6 = s_5$, $\quad h_6 = 413$ kJ/kg

From $P_7 = 0.6$ MPa, $x_7 = 0.0$, $\quad h_7 = 229.6$ kJ/kg

$$P_8 = 0.3 \text{ MPa and } h_8 = h_7$$

From $P_1 = 0.15$ MPa, $x_1 = 1.0$,

$$h_1 = 387.8 \text{ kJ/kg}, \quad s_1 = 1.7372 \text{ kJ/(kg.K)}$$

From $P_2 = 0.3$ MPa, $s_2 = s_1$, $\quad h_2 = 401.8$ kJ/kg

From $P_3 = 0.3$ MPa, $x_3 = 0.0$, $\quad h_3 = 200.8$ kJ/kg

$$P_4 = 0.15 \text{ MPa and } h_4 = h_3$$

(i) To obtain the mass flow rate of the refrigerant in the bottoming cycle, the first law equation is applied to the counterflow heat exchanger.

$$\dot{m}_a (h_5 - h_8) = \dot{m}_b (h_2 - h_3)$$

$$(0.1 \text{ kg/s})(169.1 \text{ kJ/kg}) = \dot{m}_b (201 \text{ kJ/kg})$$

Hence, the mass of refrigerant flow in the bottoming cycle is 0.08413 kg/s.

From the first law equation applied to the evaporator,

$$\dot{Q}_L = \dot{m}_b (h_1 - h_4)$$

Rate of heat transferred from the refrigerated space is

$$(0.08413 \text{ kg/s})(187 \text{ kJ/kg}) = 15.73 \text{ kJ/s}.$$

(ii) Power input to the compressors is

$$\dot{m}_a (h_6 - h_5) + \dot{m}_b (h_2 - h_1)$$

$$= 1.43 + 1.178 = 2.608 \text{ kW}$$

(iii) The COP of the cascade refrigeration system is

$$\beta = \frac{\dot{Q}_L}{\dot{W}_{in}} = \frac{15.73}{2.608} = 6.03.$$

2 Multistage Compression Refrigeration Systems

A multistage compression refrigeration system is one where there is more than one stage of compression and the working fluid in all the stages are the same. Since the refrigerant is the same, the heat exchanger in the cascade system can be replaced by a mixing chamber (called a flash chamber) which has better heat transfer characteristics. A two-stage compression refrigeration system is shown in Fig. 1.6.

In Fig. 1.6, it can be seen that the saturated refrigerant vapor at state 1 is first compressed to the interstage pressure at state 2. Here, it is mixed with the saturated vapor leaving the flash chamber at state 3 to produce a mixture at state 9. The second stage of compression brings the pressure of the refrigerant up to the condenser pressure at state 4. After giving up heat to the warm environment in the condenser, the liquid refrigerant expands in the first expansion valve to the flash chamber pressure, which is at the compressor interstage pressure. Part of the liquid vaporizes and at state 3, is mixed with the superheated vapor from state 2 as stated above. The saturated liquid at state 7 expands through the second expansion valve into the evaporator, where it removes heat from the refrigerated space.

The compression process in this system is essentially a two-stage compression with intercooling, since the superheated vapor at state 2 is cooled to state 9 before the next stage of compression. As such, the specific volume of the vapor is decreased and the overall compressor work decreases. The mass flow rates are not the same in all parts of the cycle.

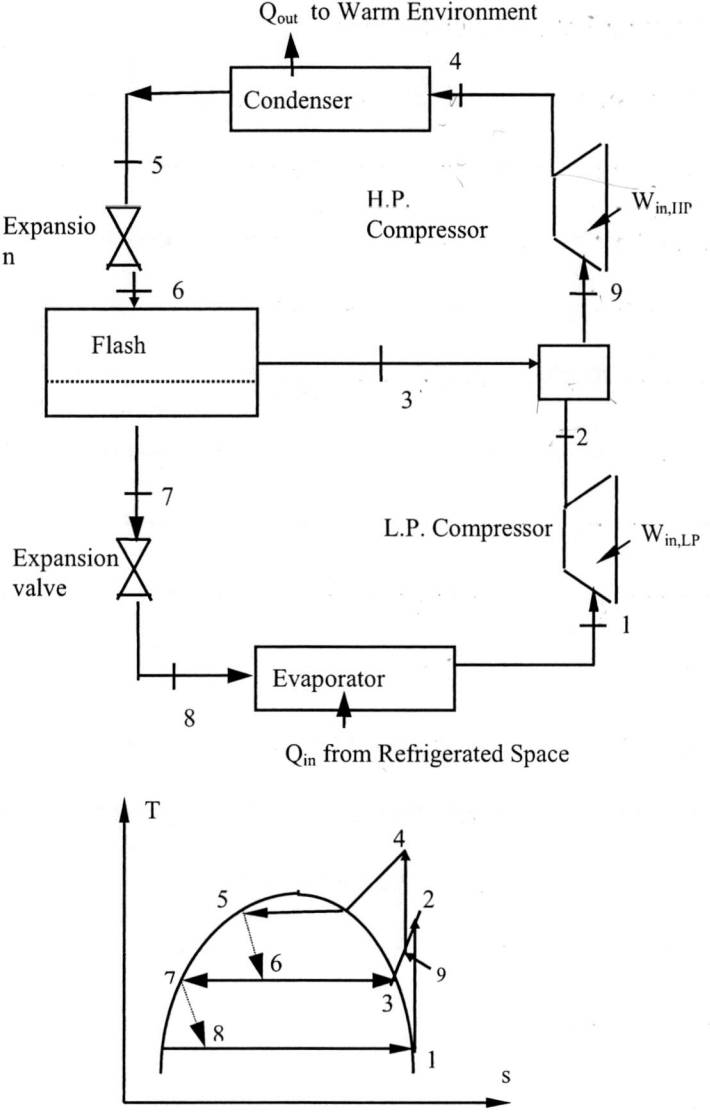

Figure 1.6 Two-stage compression refrigeration system with a flash chamber.

3 Multievaporators with One Compressor

One compressor may be used to compress the refrigerant from several evaporators operating at different pressures, hence temperatures. A cycle with a compressor with two evaporators is shown in Fig. 1.7.

An example of the two-evaporator refrigeration cycle is the household refrigerator-freezer unit. Such units are mostly used for foods, which generally have a high water content. The refrigerated space must be maintained above the ice point to prevent freezing. The freezer compartment, on the other hand, is maintained at about -18°C. This means that the refrigerant should enter the freezer at about -25°C to facilitate heat transfer. If a single evaporator were used, the refrigerant would have to circulate in both the refrigerated space and the freezer at about -25°C, which would cause ice formation near and around the evaporator coils and dehydration of the produce. This is not acceptable. This problem is overcome by throttling the refrigerant to a higher pressure (hence temperature) for use in the refrigerated space and then throttling it to the minimum pressure for use in the freezer. A single compressor is used to compress the refrigerant to the condenser pressure.

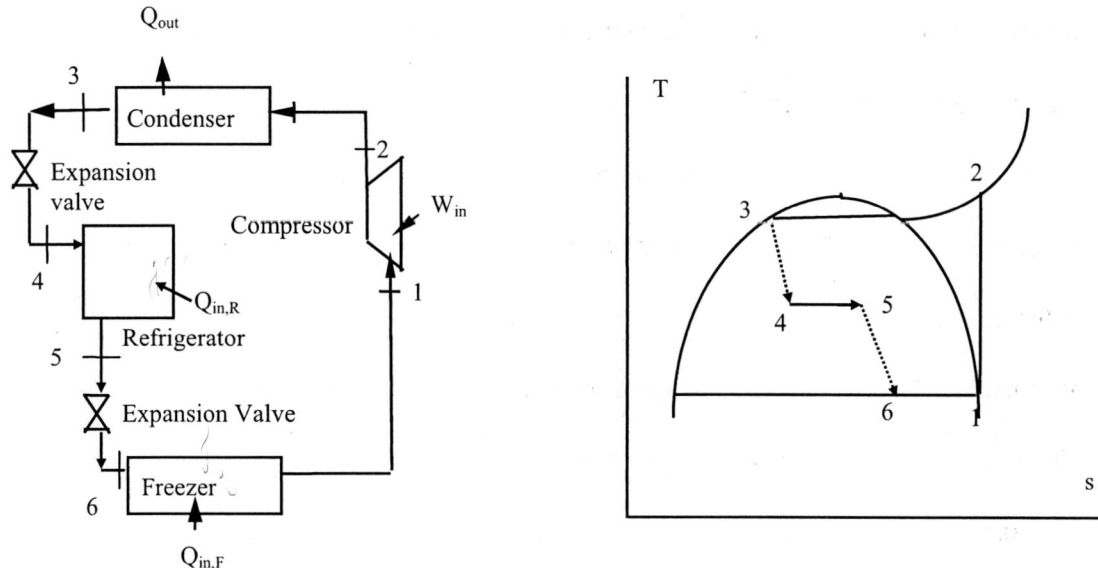

Figure 1.7 Two-evaporator with one compressor refrigeration cycle.

Example 1.5

Problem

A refrigerator operates on a two-evaporator with one compressor cycle, using refrigerant-134a as the working fluid. The flow rate of the refrigerant is 0.1 kg/s. The pressure of the freezer evaporator is 0.15 MPa, and that of the refrigerator evaporator is 0.3 MPa; the condenser pressure is 0.6 MPa. The rate of heat transfer from the refrigerator space is 10 kJ/s. Determine (i) the rate of heat transferred from the freezer space, (ii) the power input to the compressor, and (iii) the COP of the system.

Solution

Assumptions: (i) The changes in K.E. and P.E. can be neglected.

(ii) The compressor is isentropic.

(iii) The refrigerant enters the compressor as saturated vapor.

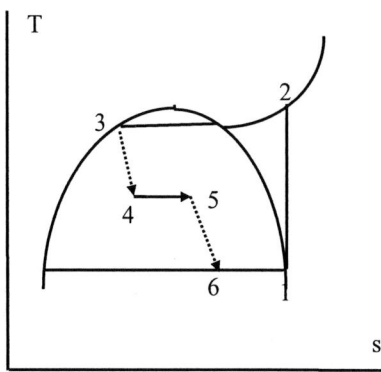

(iv) The refrigerant leaves the condenser as saturated liquid.

Analysis:

From $P_1 = 0.15$ MPa, $x_1 = 1.0$,

$$h_1 = 387.8 \text{ kJ/kg}, \qquad s_1 = 1.7372 \text{ kJ/(kg.K)}$$

From $P_2 = 0.6$ MPa, $s_2 = s_1$, $\qquad h_2 = 416.4$ kJ/kg

From $P_3 = 0.6$ MPa, $x_3 = 0.0$,

$$h_3 = 229.6 \text{ kJ/kg}, \qquad s_3 = 1.1035 \text{ kJ/(kg.K)}$$

Also, $P_4 = 0.3$ MPa, $h_4 = h_3$

Apply the first law to the refrigerator evaporator,

$$\dot{Q} + \dot{m}h_4 = \dot{m}h_5$$

$$10 + (0.1)(229.6) = 0.1h_5$$

Thus, $h_5 = 329.6$ kJ/kg.

Also, $P_6 = 0.15$ MPa, $h_6 = h_5$

(i) Apply the first law to the freezer evaporator,

$$\dot{Q} + \dot{m}h_6 = \dot{m}h_1$$

$$\dot{Q} = \dot{m}(h_1 - h_6)$$

The rate of heat transfer from the freezer evaporator is

$$(0.1 \text{ kg/s})(58.2 \text{ kJ/kg}) = 5.82 \text{ kW}.$$

(ii) Apply first law to the compressor,

$$\dot{m} h_1 = \dot{m} h_2 - \dot{W}_c$$

$$\dot{W}_c = -\dot{m}(h_2 - h_1)$$

The power input to the compressor is

$$(0.1 \text{ kg/s})(28.6 \text{ kJ/kg}) = 2.86 \text{ kW}.$$

(iii) COP of the system is

$$\beta = \frac{\text{Rate of heat removed by both evaporators}}{\dot{W}_c} = \frac{10 + 5.82}{2.86} = 5.53.$$

Note that the COP of the system does not change from that of the corresponding ideal refrigeration cycle with one evaporator, as worked out in Ex. 1.1.

1.7 Gas Refrigeration Cycles

The vapor compression cycles considered this far involve changes in phase. This allowed the heat transfer at the evaporator and at the condenser to take place at constant temperature, as in the reversed Carnot cycle. In gas refrigeration cycles, the working fluid remains a gas throughout the cycle. Since the heat transfer at the evaporator and at the condenser then do not take place at constant temperature, the cycle deviates more than the vapor compression cycle from the reversed Carnot cycle, thus giving up performance. However, gas cycles are used for a number of important applications. They are used for specialized applications like aircraft cabin cooling, and for the liquefaction of air and other gases where very low temperatures are required.

The simple gas refrigeration cycle is shown in Fig. 1.8. The gas is compressed during process 1-2_s. The high-temperature gas then rejects heat to the surroundings in process 2_s-3. The gas is then expanded in a turbine, where the pressure drops to P_4. The cool gas removes heat from the refrigerated space in process 4_s-1. The ideal cycle is shown by 1-2_s-3-4_s-1. The actual cycle would be 1-2-3-4-1, which takes into account the irreversibilities during adiabatic compression and expansion. Pressure drops due to fluid viscosity have not been considered.

The coefficient of performance for the gas refrigeration cycle is

$$\beta = \frac{q_L}{W_{net,in}} \qquad (1.8)$$

where $\quad q_L = h_1 - h_4$

$W_{net,in} = W_{compressor,in} - W_{turbine,out} = (h_2 - h_1) - (h_3 - h_4)$

Even though they have relatively low COPs, the gas refrigeration cycles have two desirable characteristics. They involve simple, lighter components, which is a good feature for aircraft cooling. Gas cycles can include regeneration, which makes them suitable for liquefaction of gases and cryogenic applications.

The regenerative gas cycle is shown in Fig. 1.9. In the cycle, a counterflow heat exchanger is added. Without regeneration, the lowest turbine inlet temperature is T_o, the temperature of the surroundings or any other cooling medium. With regeneration, the high-pressure gas is cooled further to T_4 before expanding in the turbine. By lowering the turbine inlet temperature, the turbine exit temperature is correspondingly lowered. The turbine exit temperature is the lowest temperature in the cycle. Very low temperatures can be obtained by repeating this process.

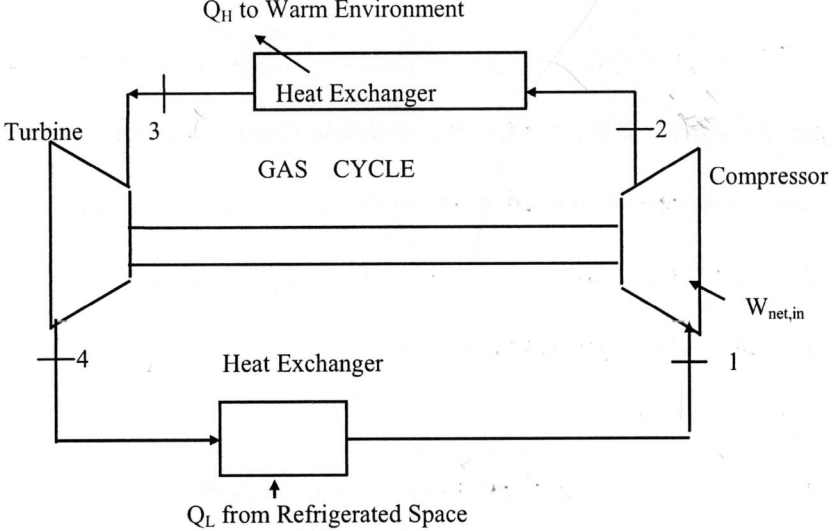

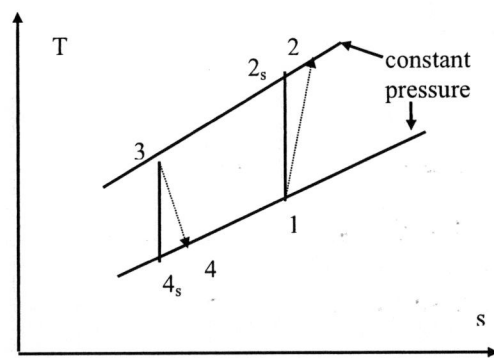

Figure 1.8 Simple gas refrigeration cycle.

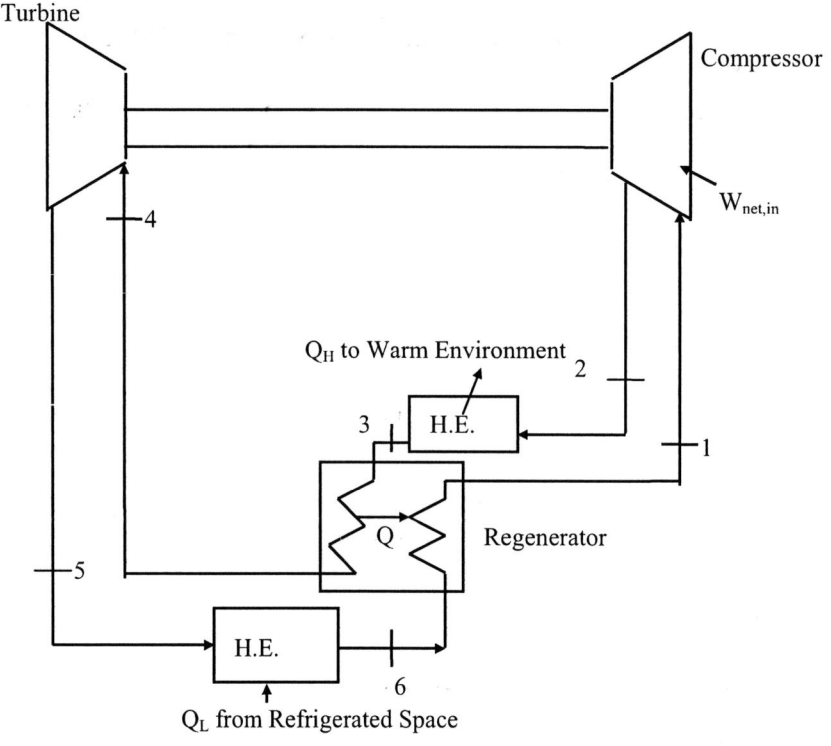

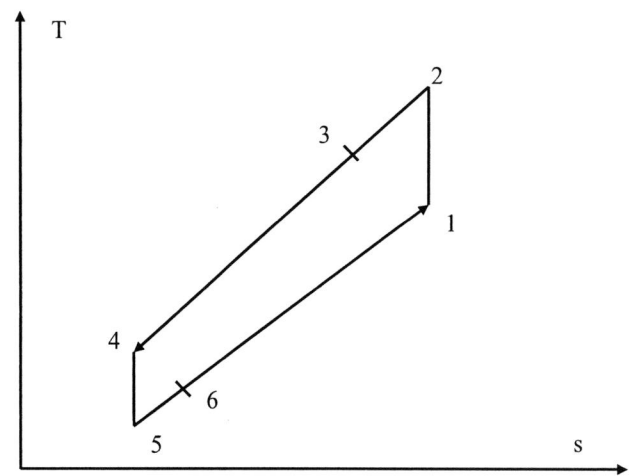

Figure 1.9 Gas refrigeration cycle with regeneration.

Example 1.6

Problem

An air-refrigeration ideal cycle keeps the refrigerated space at -13°C, and rejects heat to the environment at 22°C. The compressor pressure ratio is 3. Calculate (i) the temperature range of the cycle, (ii) the COP.

Solution

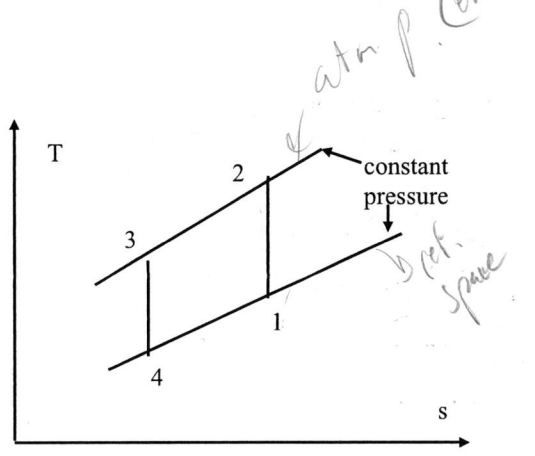

Assumptions: (i) Neglect K.E. and P.E. changes.

(ii) Both turbine and compressor are isentropic.

Analysis:

(i)   From the tables,

$T_1 = 260$ K $h_1 = 260.09$ kJ/kg   and $P_{r1} = 0.8405$

$$P_{r2} = \frac{P_2}{P_1} P_{r1} = (3)(0.8405) = 2.5215$$

Hence, $h_2 = 356.5$ kJ/kg   and $T_2 = 356$ K

$T_3 = 295$ K $h_3 = 295.17$ kJ/kg   and $P_{r3} = 1.3068$

$$P_{r4} = \frac{P_4}{P_3} P_{r3} = \left(\frac{1}{3}\right)(1.3068) = 0.4356$$

Hence, $h_4 = 214.97$ kJ/kg   and $T_4 = 215$ K

The temperature range of the cycle is (356 - 215) K = 141 K.

(ii) Apply first law equation to the evaporator,

$$q_L = h_1 - h_4 = 45.12 \text{kJ/kg}$$

Apply first law equation to the turbine,

$$w_t = h_3 - h_4 = 80.2 \text{kJ/kg}$$

Apply first law equation to the compressor,

$$w_c = h_1 - h_2 = -96.4 \text{kJ/kg}$$

$$COP = \frac{q_L}{\text{net work input}} = \frac{45.12}{16.2} = 2.79.$$

1.8 Absorption Refrigeration System

Absorption refrigeration is a form of refrigeration that becomes financially attractive when there is a rather inexpensive source of energy at about 100 to 200°C. These sources include solar energy, geothermal energy, waste heat from process heat or cogeneration, and inexpensive natural gas.

Absorption refrigeration cycles are similar to vapor compression cycles, except in two aspects. The first is that instead of the refrigerant being compressed between the evaporator and the condenser, the refrigerant of an absorption system is absorbed by a secondary fluid (called an absorbent) to form a liquid solution. The liquid solution is pumped to the higher pressure. Since the average specific volume of the liquid solution is a lot less than that of the refrigerant vapor, much less work is required. Consequently, there is a relatively small work input in such cycles compared to vapor-compression cycles.

The second difference is that an energy source mentioned above is needed as input to a means that retrieves the refrigerant vapor from the liquid solution before the refrigerant enters the condenser.

The schematic of the simple ammonia-water absorption refrigeration system is shown in Fig. 1.10. After picking up heat from the cold refrigerated space in the evaporator, the ammonia vapor enters the absorber where it dissolves and reacts with water. The formation of this liquid solution is exothermic. Since the quantity of ammonia that is soluble in water increases as the solution temperature decreases, it is necessary to cool the absorber to maintain its temperature as low as possible, hence to maximize the amount of ammonia dissolved in water. The strong ammonia-water solution leaves the absorber and enters the pump, where its pressure is increased to that of the generator. Heat is transferred to the solution from a source to vaporize some of the solution. The vapor, which is rich in ammonia, passes through a rectifier where the water is separated and returned to the generator. The high-pressure pure ammonia vapor then continues through the rest of the cycle , by next entering the condenser. The hot ammonia and water solution, which is weak in ammonia, then goes through a regenerator, where it gives up some heat to the rich solution leaving the pump, and is throttled to the absorber pressure.

Absorption refrigeration systems are more complex and thus more expensive than vapor-compression systems. They occupy more space,and tend to be less efficient thus requiring much larger cooling towers to reject the waste heat. They are less popular and thus it is more difficult to find help to service them. However, interests in ammonia as a refrigerant has grown with the awareness of the poor environmental qualities of refrigerants like the chlorofluorocarbons (CFCs). Absorption refrigeration systems are primarily used in large commercial and industrial installations.

The COP of absorption refrigeration systems is defined as

$$\beta = \frac{\text{Desired output}}{\text{Required input}}$$

$$= \frac{Q_{in}}{Q_{gen} + W_{pump,in}} \cong \frac{Q_{in}}{Q_{gen}} \qquad (1.9)$$

Another kind of absorption system uses lithium bromide as the absorbent and water as the refrigerant. Basically, the operation principle is the same as the ammonia-water systems. To improve the low temperature characteristics of the lithium-water absorption system, it may be combined with an ammonia cycle to form a cascade refrigeration system.

The maximum COP of an absorption refrigeration system will be lower than the COP of the corresponding heat operated Carnot refrigeration cycle shown in Fig. 1.11. In such a system, the heat from the source is transferred to a Carnot heat engine, and the work output of this heat engine ($W = \eta_{th,rev} Q_{gen}$) is used to power a Carnot refrigerator to remove heat from the refrigerated space. Since $Q_L = W \times \beta_{rev} = \eta_{th,rev} Q_{gen} \beta_{rev}$, then the overall COP of the reversible absorption refrigeration system is

$$\beta_{\text{Heated Carnot}} = \frac{Q_{in}}{Q_{gen}} = \eta_{th,rev} \beta_{rev} = \left(1 - \frac{T_o}{T_s}\right)\left(\frac{T_L}{T_o - T_L}\right). \qquad (1.10)$$

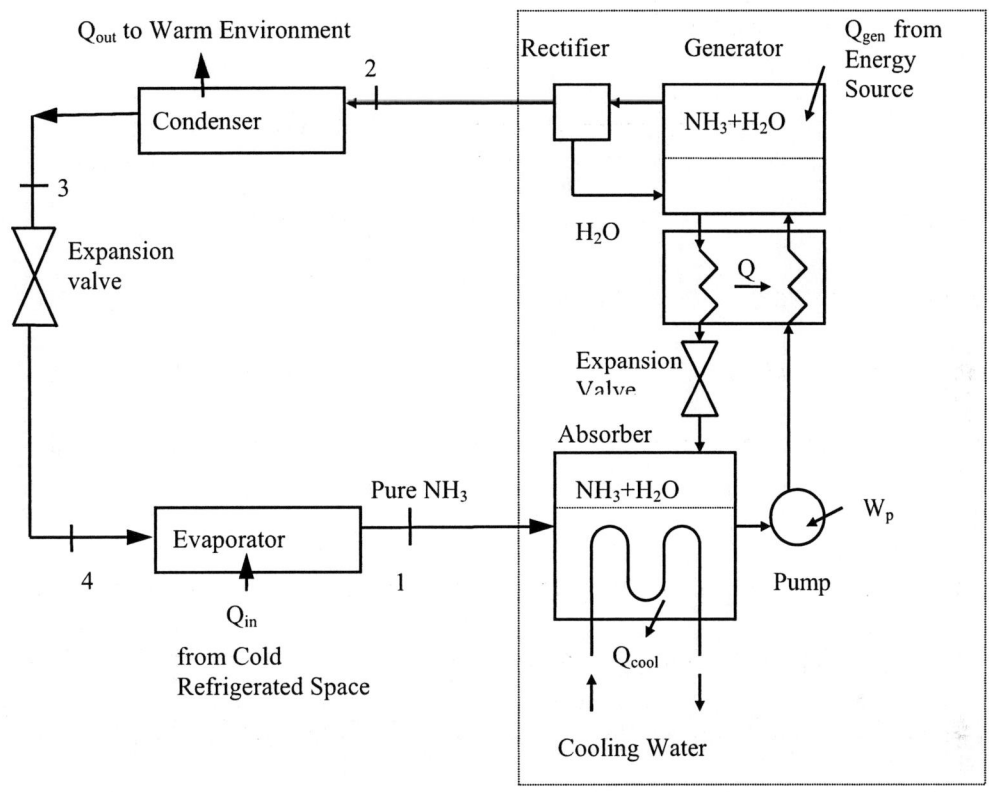

Figure 1.10 Ammonia absorption refrigeration cycle.

T_s, T_o, and T_L are the absolute temperatures of the heat source, environment, and refrigerated space, respectively. Any absorption refrigeration system operating between a temperature of T_s and T_L, in an environment of T_o, will not have a COP higher than that given by Eq. (1.10).

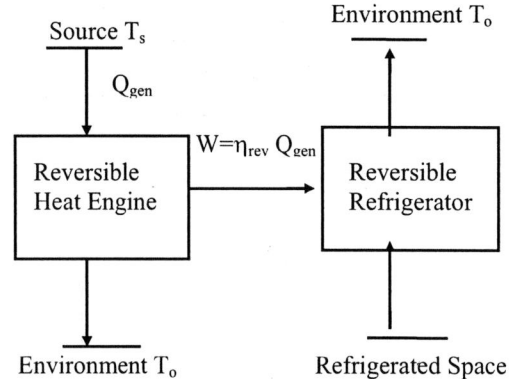

$$W = \eta_{th,rev} Q_{gen} = (1 - \frac{T_o}{T_s}) Q_{gen}$$

$$Q_L = \beta_{rev} W = (\frac{T_L}{T_o - T_L}) W$$

$$\beta_{\text{Heated Carnot}} = \frac{Q_{in}}{Q_{gen}} = (1 - \frac{T_o}{T_s})(\frac{T_L}{T_o - T_L})$$

Figure 1.11   Maximum COP of an heat operated Carnot refrigeration system.

Example 1.7

Problem

An absorption refrigeration system requires 40 Btu/s from a geothermal source at 260°F to remove heat at 25 Btu/s from the refrigerated space. The condenser rejects heat at 20 Btu/s to the environment at 80°F, and the cooling water removes heat at 35 Btu/s from the absorber. Determine the power supplied to the pump. Determine the temperature of the refrigerated space.

Solution

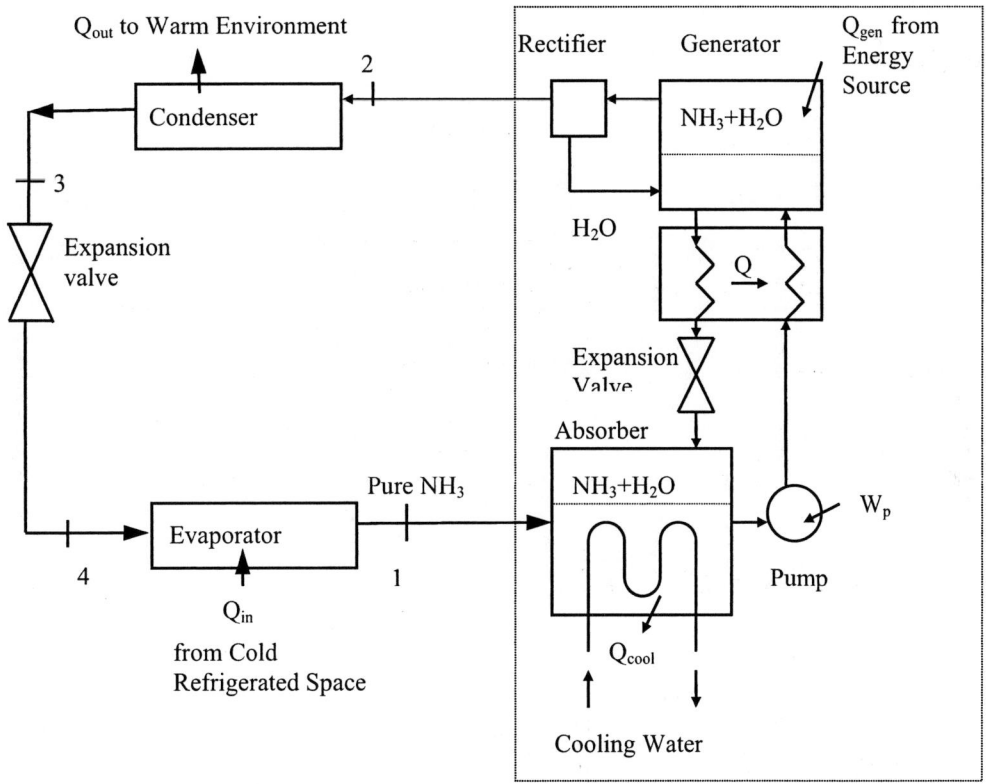

Apply the first law to the whole cycle,

$Q_{gen} + Q_{in} - Q_{cool} - Q_{out} = W_p$

Hence, $W_p = 40+25-35-20 = 10$ Btu/s.

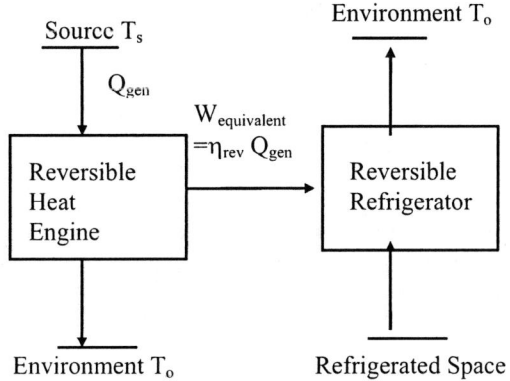

But $\beta_{\text{Heated Carnot}} = \dfrac{\dot{Q}_{in}}{\dot{Q}_{gen}} = \left(1 - \dfrac{T_o}{T_s}\right)\left(\dfrac{T_L}{T_o - T_L}\right)$

Thus, $\dfrac{25}{40} = (0.222)\left(\dfrac{T_L}{T_o - T_L}\right)$

$\dfrac{T_o}{T_L} - 1 = 0.355$

$T_L = 413°R.$

PROBLEMS

Vapor-Compression Refrigeration Cycle

1.1. A refrigerator operates on an ideal vapor-compression refrigeration cycle between 0.12 and 0.7 MPa. Refrigerant-134a is the working fluid, and its flow rate in the cycle is 0.15 kg/s. Determine (i) the heat transfer rate from the refrigerated space, (ii) the power input, and (iii) the COP of the refrigerator.

1.2. A refrigerator operates on an ideal vapor-compression refrigeration cycle between 20 and 90 lb_f/in^2. Refrigerant-134a is the working fluid, and its flow rate in the cycle is 0.06 lb_m/s. Determine (i) the heat transfer rate from the refrigerated space, (ii) the power input, and (iii) the COP of the refrigerator.

1.3. A refrigerator operates on an ideal vapor-compression refrigeration cycle between 0.12 and 0.7 MPa. Refrigerant 12 is the working fluid, and its flow rate in the cycle is 0.15 kg/s. Determine (i) the heat transfer rate from the refrigerated space, (ii) the power input, and (iii) the COP of the refrigerator.

1.4. A refrigerator operates on an ideal vapor-compression refrigeration cycle between 20 and 90 lb_f/in^2. Refrigerant 12 is the working fluid, and its flow rate in the cycle is 0.06 lb$_m$/s. Determine (i) the heat transfer rate from the refrigerated space, (ii) the power input, and (iii) the COP of the refrigerator.

Actual Vapor-Compression Refrigeration Cycle

1.5. The inlet and outlet conditions of refrigerant-134a in the compressor of a refrigeration system are 0.1 MPa and -15°C and 0.75 MPa and 55°C, respectively. The mass flow rate is 0.08 kg/s. The refrigerant-134a is cooled to 25°C and 0.70 MPa in the condenser, and then throttled to 0.11 MPa. Calculate (a) the rate of heat transferred from the refrigerated space, (b) the isentropic efficiency of the compressor, (c) the compressor power input, and (d) the COP of the refrigeration system.

1.6. The inlet and outlet conditions of refrigerant-134a in the compressor of a refrigeration system are 14.7 lb$_f$/in^2 and 0°F and 110 lb$_f$/in^2 and 145°F, respectively. The mass flow rate is 0.18 lb$_m$/s. The refrigerant-134a is cooled to 77°F and 103 lb$_f$/in^2 in the condenser, and then throttled to 16 lb$_f$/in^2. Calculate (a) the rate of heat transferred from the refrigerated space, (b) the isentropic efficiency of the compressor, (c) the compressor power input, and (d) the COP of the refrigeration system.

1.7. The inlet and outlet conditions of refrigerant 12 in the compressor of a refrigeration system are 0.1 MPa and -15°C and 0.75 MPa and 60°C, respectively. The mass flow rate is 0.08 kg/s. The refrigerant 12 is cooled to 25°C and 0.70 MPa in the condenser, and then throttled to 0.11 MPa. Calculate (a) the rate of heat transferred from the refrigerated space, (b) the isentropic efficiency of the compressor, (c) the compressor power input, and (d) the COP of the refrigeration system.

1.8. The inlet and outlet conditions of refrigerant 12 in the compressor of a refrigeration system are 14.7 lb$_f$/in^2 and 0°F and 110 lb$_f$/in^2 and 150°F, respectively. The mass flow rate is 0.18 lb$_m$/s. The refrigerant 12 is cooled to 77°F and 103 lb$_f$/in^2 in the condenser, and then throttled to 16 lb$_f$/in^2. Calculate (a) the rate of heat transferred from the refrigerated space, (b) the isentropic efficiency of the compressor, (c) the compressor power input, and (d) the COP of the refrigeration system.

Heat Pump Systems

1.9. A refrigerant-134a heat pump is used for a residence with a design heating load of 250 kW. The evaporator operates at -12°C and the condenser at 1 MPa. Assume an ideal cycle. Determine (i) the mass flow rate of the refrigerant, (ii) the power input to the compressor, (iii) the COP of the heat pump.

1.10. A refrigerant-134a heat pump is used for a residence with a design heating load of 300 kW. The evaporator operates at -10°C and the condenser at 0.9 MPa. Assume an ideal cycle. Determine (i) the mass flow rate of the refrigerant, (ii) the power input to the compressor, (iii) the COP of the heat pump.

1.11. A refrigerant 12 heat pump is used for a residence with a design heating load of 280 kW. The evaporator operates at -18°C and the condenser at 1 MPa. Assume an ideal cycle. Determine (i) the mass flow rate of the refrigerant, (ii) the power input to the compressor, (iii) the COP of the heat pump.

1.12. A refrigerant 12 heat pump is used for a residence with a design heating load of 260 Btu/s. The evaporator operates at 0°F and the condenser at 150 lb$_f$/in^2. Assume an ideal cycle. Determine (i) the mass flow rate of the refrigerant, (ii) the power input to the compressor, (iii) the COP of the heat pump.

Other Refrigeration Systems

1.13. A refrigerator operates on a two-stage cascade system between 0.12 MPa and 0.7 MPa. Refrigerant-134a is the working fluid in both cycles, and its flow rate in the topping cycle is 0.15 kg/s. The intermediate pressure of the adiabatic counterflow heat exchanger is 0.35 MPa, where heat is transferred from the bottoming cycle to the topping cycle. (Actually, the refrigerant in the bottoming cycle will be at a higher pressure and temperature in the heat exchanger for the heat transfer to take place.) Determine (i) the rate of heat transferred from the refrigerated space, (ii) the power input to the compressors, and (iii) the COP of the cascade refrigeration system.

1.14. A refrigerator operates on a two-stage cascade system between 20 $lb_f/in.^2$ and 90 $lb_f/in.^2$. Refrigerant-134a is the working fluid in both cycles, and its flow rate in the topping cycle is 0.06 lb_m/s. The intermediate pressure of the adiabatic counterflow heat exchanger is 55 $lb_f/in.^2$, where heat is transferred from the bottoming cycle to the topping cycle. (Actually, the refrigerant in the bottoming cycle will be at a higher pressure and temperature in the heat exchanger for the heat transfer to take place.) Determine (i) the rate of heat transferred from the refrigerated space, (ii) the power input to the compressors, and (iii) the COP of the cascade refrigeration system.

1.15. A refrigerator operates on a two-stage cascade system between 0.12 MPa and 0.7 MPa. Refrigerant 12 is the working fluid in both cycles, and its flow rate in the topping cycle is 0.15 kg/s. The intermediate pressure of the adiabatic counterflow heat exchanger is 0.35 MPa, where heat is transferred from the bottoming cycle to the topping cycle. (Actually, the refrigerant in the bottoming cycle will be at a higher pressure and temperature in the heat exchanger for the heat transfer to take place.) Determine (i) the rate of heat transferred from the refrigerated space, (ii) the power input to the compressors, and (iii) the COP of the cascade refrigeration system.

1.16. A refrigerator operates on a two-stage cascade system between 20 $lb_f/in.^2$ and 90 $lb_f/in.^2$. Refrigerant 12 is the working fluid in both cycles, and its flow rate in the topping cycle is 0.06 lb_m/s. The intermediate pressure of the adiabatic counterflow heat exchanger is 55 $lb_f/in.^2$, where heat is transferred from the bottoming cycle to the topping cycle. (Actually, the refrigerant in the bottoming cycle will be at a higher pressure and temperature in the heat exchanger for the heat transfer to take place.) Determine (i) the rate of heat transferred from the refrigerated space, (ii) the power input to the compressors, and (iii) the COP of the cascade refrigeration system.

1.17. A refrigerator operates on a two-evaporator with one compressor cycle, using refrigerant-134a as the working fluid. The flow rate of the refrigerant is 0.15 kg/s. The pressure of the freezer evaporator is 0.12 MPa, and that of the refrigerator evaporator is 0.35 MPa; the condenser pressure is 0.7 MPa. The rate of heat transfer from the refrigerator space is 10 kW. Determine (i) the rate of heat transferred from the freezer space, (ii) the power input to the compressor, and (iii) the COP of the system.

1.18. A refrigerator operates on a two-evaporator with one compressor cycle, using refrigerant-134a as the working fluid. The flow rate of the refrigerant is 0.06 lb_m/s. The pressure of the freezer evaporator is 20 $lb_f/in.^2$, and that of the refrigerator evaporator is 55 $lb_f/in.^2$; the condenser pressure is 90 $lb_f/in.^2$. The rate of heat transfer from the refrigerator space is 1 Btu/s. Determine (i) the rate of heat transferred from the freezer space, (ii) the power input to the compressor, and (iii) the COP of the system.

1.19. A refrigerator operates on a two-evaporator with one compressor cycle, using refrigerant 12 as the working fluid. The pressure of the freezer evaporator is 0.12 MPa, and that of the refrigerator evaporator is 0.35 MPa; the condenser pressure is 0.7 MPa. The rate of heat transfer from the freezer space and the refrigerator space together are 20 kW. Determine the mass flow rate of the refrigerant.

1.20. A refrigerator operates on a two-evaporator with one compressor cycle, using refrigerant 12 as the working fluid. The pressure of the freezer evaporator is 20 $lb_f/in.^2$, and that of the refrigerator evaporator is 55 $lb_f/in.^2$; the condenser pressure is 90 $lb_f/in.^2$ The rate of heat transfer from the freezer space and the refrigerator space together are 20 Btu/s. Determine the mass flow rate of the refrigerant.

Gas Refrigeration Cycles

1.21. An air-refrigeration ideal cycle keeps the refrigerated space at -18°C, and rejects heat to the environment at 27°C. The compressor pressure ratio is 3.5. Calculate (i) the temperature range of the cycle, (ii) the COP.

1.22. An air-refrigeration ideal cycle keeps the refrigerated space at -20°F, and rejects heat to the environment at 80°F. The compressor pressure ratio is 3.5. Calculate (i) the temperature range of the cycle, (ii) the COP.

1.23. An air-refrigeration ideal cycle keeps the refrigerated space at -23°C, and rejects heat to the environment at 32°C. The compressor pressure ratio is 4.5. Calculate (i) the temperature range of the cycle, (ii) the COP.

1.24. An air-refrigeration ideal cycle keeps the refrigerated space at -10°F, and rejects heat to the environment at 90°F. The compressor pressure ratio is 4.5. Calculate (i) the temperature range of the cycle, (ii) the COP.

1.25. An air-refrigeration cycle keeps the refrigerated space at -18°C, and rejects heat to the environment at 27°C. The compressor pressure ratio is 3.5. The isentropic efficiencies of the compressor and the turbine are respectively 0.75, 0.9. Calculate (i) the temperature range of the cycle, (ii) the COP.

1.26. An air-refrigeration ideal cycle keeps the refrigerated space at -20°F, and rejects heat to the environment at 80°F. The compressor pressure ratio is 3.5. The isentropic efficiencies of the compressor and the turbine are respectively 0.8, 0.85. Calculate (i) the temperature range of the cycle, (ii) the COP.

Absorption Refrigeration System

1.27. An absorption refrigeration system requires 40 kW from a geothermal source at 127°C to remove heat at 25 kW from the refrigerated space. The condenser rejects heat at 20 kW to the environment at 25°C, and the cooling water removes heat at 35 kW from the absorber. Determine the power supplied to the pump. Determine also the temperature of the refrigerated space.

1.28. A solar source supplies heat to an absorption refrigeration system at 107°C at a rate of 30 kW. The refrigerated space is kept at -13°C, and the environment is at 25°C. Calculate the best rate at which the system can remove heat from the refrigerated space.

1.29. A solar source supplies heat to an absorption refrigeration system at 220°F at a rate of 30 Btu/s. The refrigerated space is kept at 4°F, and the environment is at 85°F. Calculate the best rate at which the system can remove heat from the refrigerated space.

1.30. An absorption refrigeration system requires heat at 117°C at a rate of 25 kW. Its COP is 0.8. Calculate the rate at which the system removes heat from the refrigerated space.

1.31. An absorption refrigeration system requires heat at 230°F at a rate of 25 Btu/s. Its COP is 0.75. Calculate the rate at which the system removes heat from the refrigerated space.

COMPUTER, DESIGN AND GENERAL PROBLEMS

1.32. Discuss the use of fans with the condenser and the evaporator. What are the factors that are taken into consideration in selecting the fans? How is the COP of the system affected by the use of these fans?

1.33. Discuss when water-cooled condensers are used, instead of air-cooled ones. What are the factors that should be considered in selecting the kind and size of heat exchanger for this type of condenser?

1.33. A forced-draft cooling tower is used to cool the water from a water-cooled condenser. The heat removed from the condenser is 40 kW. Describe the design procedure for the cooling tower.

1.34. It is proposed to use water as the working fluid for a refrigerator where the refrigerated space needs to be less than the average environmental temperature that does not go below 72°F, but can be above 32°F. Discuss the possibilities of this proposal.

1.35. What other fluids besides the chlorofluorocarbons, ammonia, and water could be used as the working fluid in a refrigeration cycle? Discuss each fluid, with the appropriate temperature range of operation.

1.36. Discuss the different design possibilities for the rectifier in an absorption refrigeration system.

1.37. Write an essay on the types of compressors used in refrigeration systems.

1.38. Research and write about the vortex tube (also called the Hirsch or Ranque tube). It produces a refrigeration effect by expanding pressurized gas in a tube.

1.39. A refrigeration system maintains a space at -10°C in an environment at 25°C. It was previously using refrigerant 12, but has to be converted to use the environmentally-friendly refrigerant-134a. Determine the possible pressure levels for the converted system. Use the COP as one of the factors in selecting the final pressure levels.

1.40. The important qualities of refrigerants to consider include the following:- performance, efficiency, stability, toxicity, flammability, compatability, lubrication, leak tendency, lifetime of the refrigerant and price. Since restrictions have been placed on the use of many of the common refrigerants, the refrigerant manufacturers have been spending a lot of resources to find suitable alternates that are suitable. Research and write about the new refrigerants.

2. GAS POWER CYCLES

2.1 Basic Considerations

Heat engines are devices that transform energy (usually heat) into work. Their performance is expressed in terms of the thermal efficiency, η_{th}, which is the ratio of the net work done to the total heat input.

$$\eta_{th} = \frac{W_{net}}{Q_{in}} \qquad (2.1)$$

Previously it has been pointed out that the Carnot cycle has the highest thermal efficiency of all heat engines operating between the same temperature levels.

The Carnot cycle comprises four reversible processes: isothermal heat addition, isentropic expansion, isothermal heat rejection, and isentropic compression. The Carnot cycle phase diagrams, T-s and P-v are shown in Fig. 2.1. The Carnot cycle can be executed in a steady-flow system (using two turbines and two compressors) or in a closed system (a piston-cylinder device), and either with a gas or a vapor as the working fluid. It is the most efficient of cycles that operate between the temperature levels of T_H and T_L, and its thermal efficiency is expressed as

$$\eta_{th} = 1 - \frac{T_L}{T_H} \qquad (2.2)$$

The Carnot cycle is a useful standard against which actual and ideal cycles can be compared. From Eq.(2.2), it is clear that the thermal efficiency is improved by an increase in the average temperature at which heat is added to the system or by a decrease in the average temperature at which heat is thrown out from the system.

There are limitations on the highest and lowest temperatures in the cycle. The lowest temperature is limited by the temperature of the cooling fluid such as atmospheric air, or water from a lake or river. The highest temperature is limited by the material tolerance of the piston or the turbine blades.

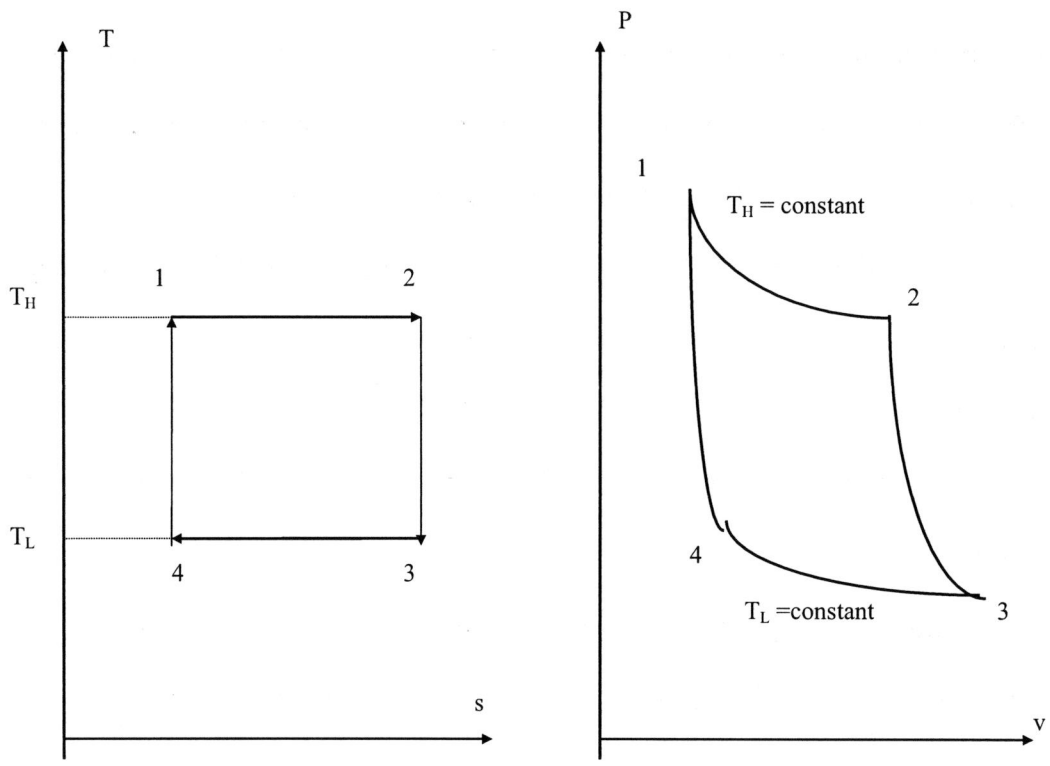

Figure 2.1 T-s and P-v diagrams of a Carnot cycle.

2.2 Air Standard Cycles

Common examples of machines that operate on gas cycles are the spark-ignition automobile engines, diesel engines, and gas turbines. These are all internal combustion engines, since energy is supplied by combusting a fuel within the system boundaries. The composition of the working fluid changes from air and fuel to combustion products during the cycle. Since air is mostly nitrogen that does not undergo much change in the combustion chamber, the working fluid is like air throughout the cycle.

The working fluid in internal combustion engines does not undergo a complete thermodynamic cycle, although the engines themselves operate on a mechanical cycle (the piston returns to the same position at the end of each cycle). Since the working fluid is exhausted, it undergoes an open cycle. This is characteristic of all internal combustion engines.

The actual gas power cycles are rather complex. The following assumptions are made to simplify the analyses, also known as the **air-standard assumptions**:

1. All the processes are internally reversible.

2. The working fluid is air, which behaves like an ideal gas.

3. The combustion process is replaced by a heat-addition process from an external source.

4. The exhaust process is replaced by heat removal that restores the air to its initial state.

Sometimes for further simplification, the air is assumed to have constant specific heats whose values are selected at room temperature (25°C or 77°F). When this assumption is used, the above are called the **cold-air-standard assumptions**.

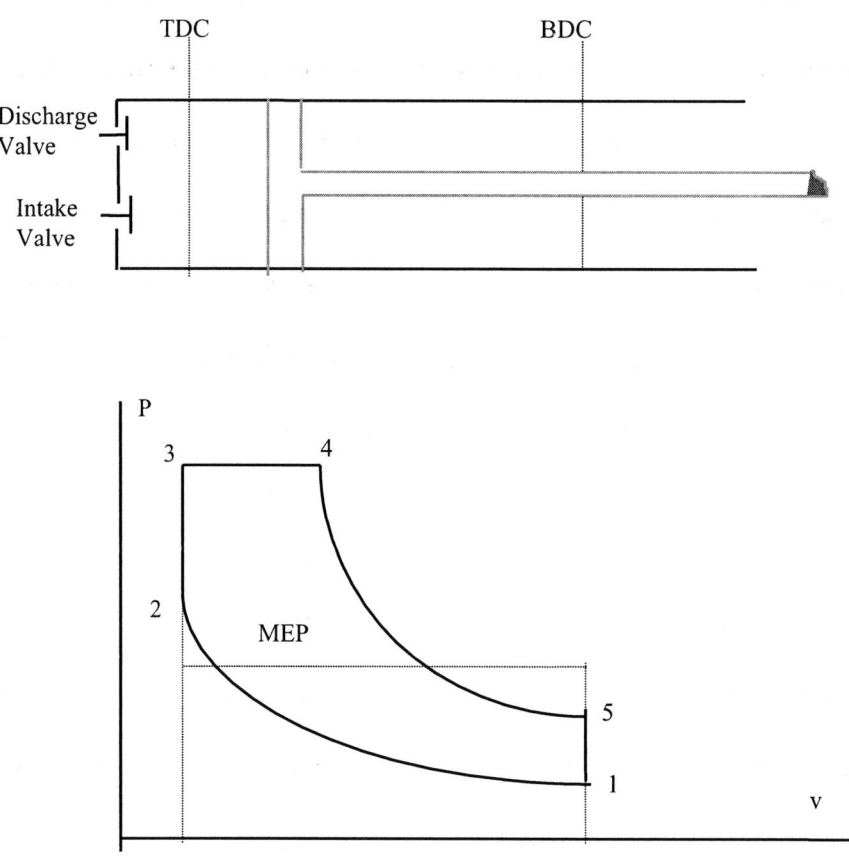

Figure 2.2   Mean effective pressure on a P-v diagram.

2.3   Preliminaries on Reciprocating Engines

The piston-cylinder arrangement is used in several internal combustion engines. This section discusses the terminology used for this piston-cylinder devices. The piston diameter is called its bore, and the stroke is the distance moved by the piston in one direction. The top dead center (TDC) is the position the piston has moved to such that a minimum fluid volume is left in the cylinder. This minimum volume is also called the clearance volume. The bottom-dead-center (BDC) is the position of the piston when it has moved its stroke, or the position corresponding to the maximum volume of the fluid. The displacement volume is the volume displaced by the piston as it moves from the TDC to the BDC or vice versa. The clearance volume is often quoted in terms of the percentage of clearance, which is the percentage of the piston displacement equal to the clearance volume. The compression ratio r of a reciprocating device is defined as the volume of the fluid at BDC divided by the volume of the fluid at TDC:

$$r = \frac{V_{BDC}}{V_{TDC}} = \frac{\text{clearance volume + displacement volume}}{\text{clearance volume}} \quad (2.3)$$

The compression ratio is expressed in terms of a volume ratio.

The mean effective pressure (MEP) is defined as an average pressure which, if acted on the piston during the entire power stroke, would produce the same work output as the net work output for the actual cyclic process. The work per cycle is given by

$$W_{cycle} = (MEP)(\text{piston area})(\text{stroke})$$
$$= (MEP)(\text{displacement volume}) \quad (2.4)$$

For reciprocating devices of the same bore, a larger MEP means a better power output at the same rated speed. In Fig. 2.2, the net work produced is represented by the enclosed area 1-2-3-4-5-1. The MEP of the cycle is as shown, and the area under this horizontal line equals the enclosed area 1-2-3-4-5-1.

2.4 Air-Standard Otto Cycle

The air-standard Otto cycle is an ideal cycle for spark-ignition reciprocating engines; the P-v and T-s diagrams are shown in Fig. 2.3. It comprises the following four internally reversible processes:

1-2   Isentropic compression

2-3   Constant volume heat addition

3-4   Isentropic expansion

4-1   Constant volume heat rejection

On the P-v diagram, area 1-2-a-b-1 represents the work input per unit of mass during the compression process and area 3-4-b-a-3 the work done per unit of mass in the expansion process. On the T-s diagram, area 2-3-a-b-2 represents the heat added per unit mass and area 1-4-a-b-1 is the heat rejected per unit of mass. The enclosed area in the P-v diagram is the net work output. The enclosed area in the T-s diagram is the net heat added. Since the cycle is ideal, both these quantities are equal.

The air in the Otto cycle is a closed system. Work is done in processes 1-2 and 3-4; heat transfer occurs in processes 2-3 and 4-1. Neglecting potential and kinetic energy, the expressions for the work and heat are

$$\frac{W_{12}}{m} = u_2 - u_1, \qquad \frac{W_{34}}{m} = u_3 - u_4$$

$$\frac{Q_{23}}{m} = u_3 - u_2, \qquad \frac{Q_{41}}{m} = u_4 - u_1 \qquad (2.5)$$

Note that we have written all work and heat transfers as positive quantities; this is usually done in analyzing cycles. The net work of the cycle is

$$\frac{W_{cycle}}{m} = \frac{W_{34}}{m} - \frac{W_{12}}{m} = (u_3 - u_4) - (u_2 - u_1) \qquad (2.6)$$

In addition, the net work is equal to the net heat added, which is

$$\frac{W_{cycle}}{m} = \frac{Q_{net}}{m} = \frac{Q_{23}}{m} - \frac{Q_{41}}{m} = (u_3 - u_2) - (u_4 - u_1) \qquad (2.7)$$

The thermal efficiency is the ratio of the net work of the cycle to the heat added,

$$\eta_{th} = 1 - \frac{u_4 - u_1}{u_3 - u_2} \qquad (2.8)$$

The following relationships apply for the isentropic processes 1-2 and 3-4:

$$v_{r2} = v_{r1} \left(\frac{V_2}{V_1}\right) = \frac{v_{r1}}{r} \qquad (2.9)$$

$$v_{r4} = v_{r3} \left(\frac{V_4}{V_3}\right) = r v_{r3} \qquad (2.10)$$

where r is the compression ratio. Note that $r = V_1/V_2 = V_4/V_3$.

When the Otto cycle is analyzed on a cold air-standard basis, the following expressions introduced earlier would be used for the isentropic processes in place of Eqs. (2.9) and (2.10) respectively:

$$\frac{T_2}{T_1} = \left(\frac{V_1}{V_2}\right)^{k-1} = r^{k-1} \quad \text{(constant k)} \qquad (2.11)$$

$$\frac{T_4}{T_3} = \left(\frac{V_3}{V_4}\right)^{k-1} = r^{k-1} \quad \text{(constant k)} \qquad (2.12)$$

where k is the specific heat ratio, $k = c_P/c_V$.

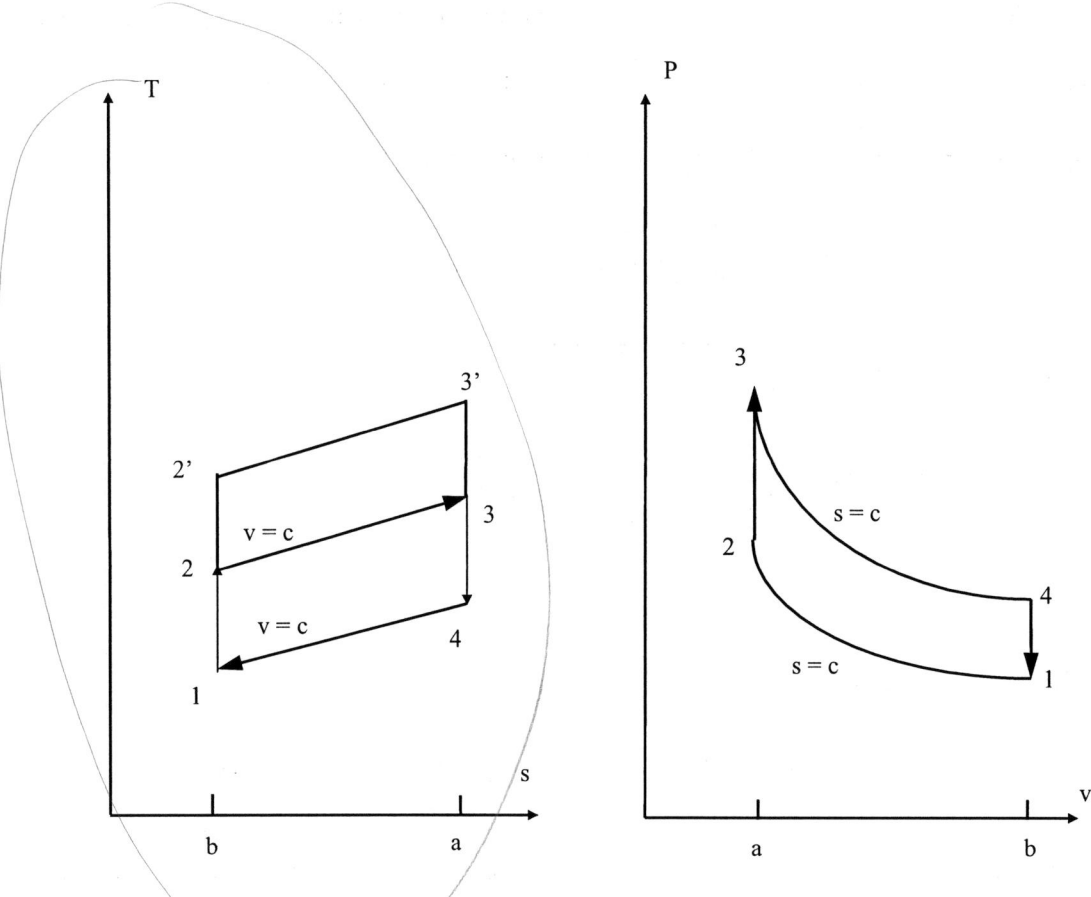

Figure 2.3 T-s and P-v diagrams of the air-standard Otto cycle.

From Fig. 2.3 we can see that with an increase in compression ratio, the cycle changes from 1-2-3-4-1 to 1-2'-3'-4-1. Since the net work performed has increased and the ratio of net work to heat added has increased, the thermal efficiency has increased with compression ratio. This conclusion can also be seen by the following derivation based on a cold air-standard basis. For constant c_v, Eq. (2.8) becomes

$$\eta = 1 - \frac{c_v(T_4 - T_1)}{c_v(T_3 - T_2)}$$

which gives

$$\eta = 1 - \frac{T_1(T_4/T_1 - 1)}{T_2(T_3/T_2 - 1)}$$

From Eqs. (2.11) and (2.12) above, $T_4/T_1 = T_3/T_2$, thus

$$\eta = 1 - \frac{T_1}{T_2}$$

Using Eq. (2.11) again,

$$\eta = 1 - \frac{1}{r^{k-1}} \qquad \text{(constant k)} \qquad (2.13)$$

This equation states that the cold air-standard Otto cycle thermal efficiency is a function of the compression ratio and the specific heat ratio. This is shown graphically in Fig. 2.4 for k =1.4.

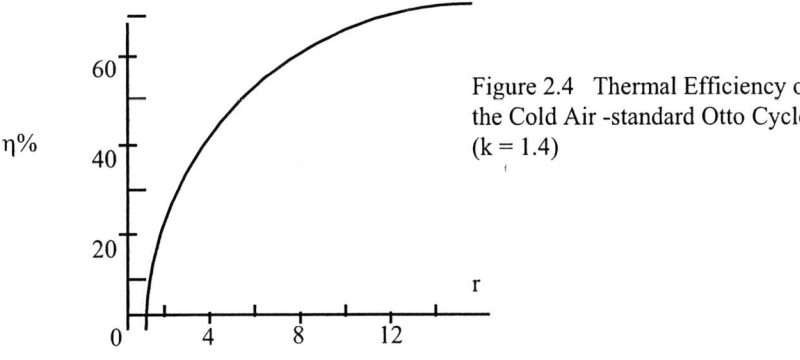

Figure 2.4 Thermal Efficiency of the Cold Air-standard Otto Cycle (k = 1.4)

An increase in compression ratio increases the thermal efficiency of internal combustion engines. The premature ignition of fuel, called **autoignition**, produces an audible noise, which is called **engine knock**; this places an upper limit on the compression ratio of spark-ignition engines. Since the temperature of the air-fuel mixture during the compression stroke increases as the compression ratio increases, the possibility of auto-ignition occurring increases with the compression ratio. Fuels with tetraethyl lead retard autoignition and so permit relatively high compression ratios, up to about 12. The unleaded gasoline in use today because of environmental concerns about pollution from lead, limits the compression ratios of spark-ignition engines. As a result of decreased compression ratios, the thermal efficiency of spark-ignition car engines has decreased somewhat. However, cars today have better fuel economy because of improvements in other areas (improved aerodynamic design, reduction in car weight, etc.)

In compression-ignition engines, higher compression ratios can be used because air alone is compressed. Compression ratios from 12 to 20 are commonplace. Less refined fuels having higher ignition temperatures can also be used in compression-ignition engines unlike in spark-ignition engines where more volatile fuels are required.

The actual and ideal P-v diagram with wide-open throttle for a four-stroke spark-ignition engine is shown in Fig. 2.5. It can clearly be seen that in general the four reversible processes are just approximations, and in particular that the constant volume processes are idealizations.

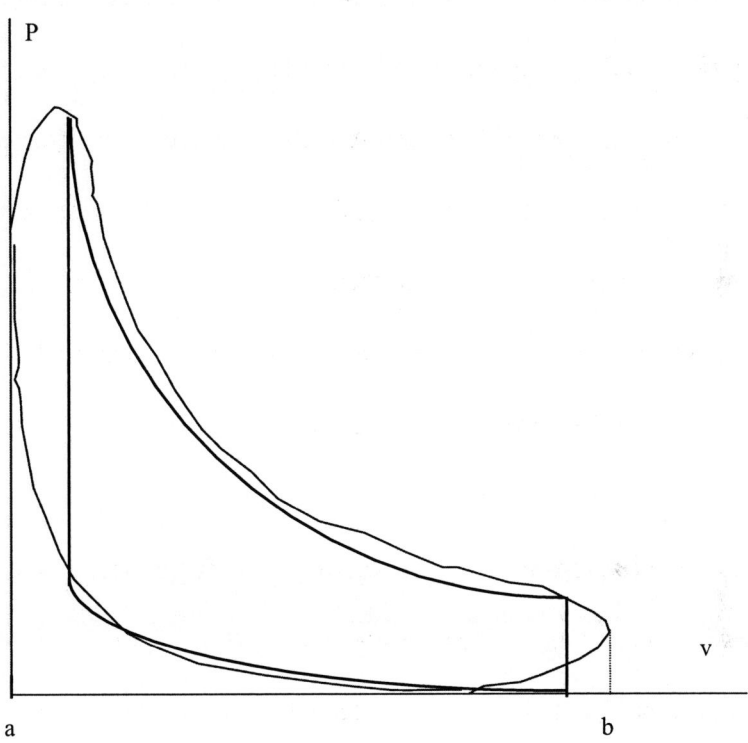

Figure 2.5 Actual and ideal P-v diagram for wide-open throttle for a four-stroke spark-ignition engine.

Example 2.1

Problem

An ideal Otto cycle uses air as the working fluid. At the start of the compression process, the air is at 22°C and 100 kPa. The compression ratio of the cycle is 9, and the cylinder volume is 600 c.c. The maximum temperature of the cycle is 1827°C. Determine (a) the end states of each process, (b) the thermal efficiency, and (c) the mean effective pressure.

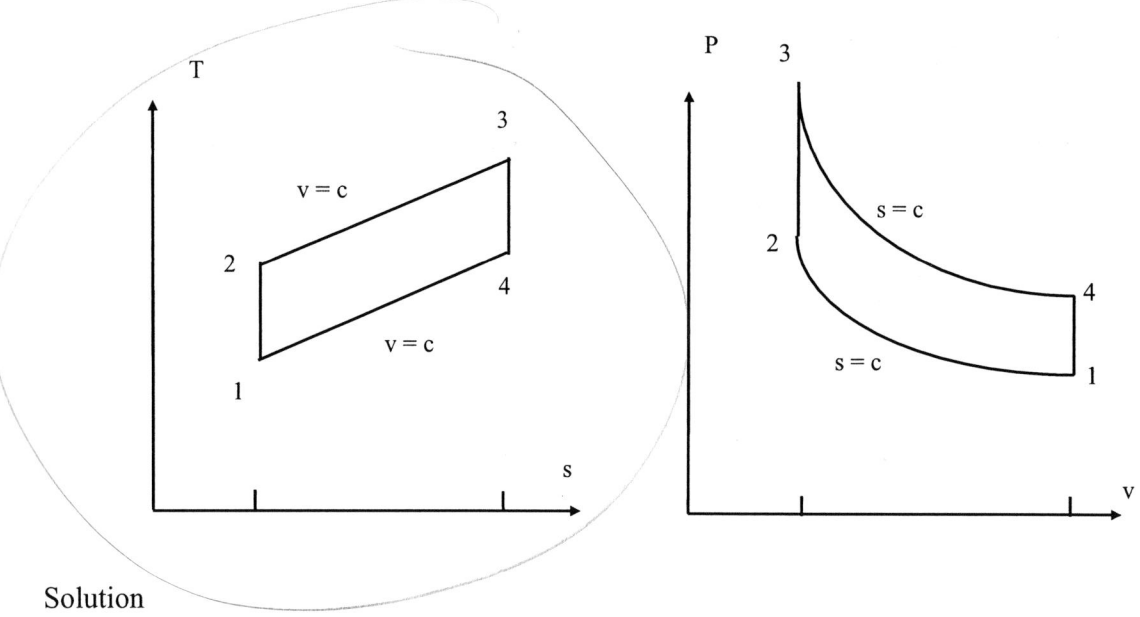

Solution

Assumptions:

(1) All processes are internally reversible.

(2) The compression and expansion processes are adiabatic.

(3) Changes in K.E. and P.E. are negligible.

(4) The air behaves like an ideal gas.

Analysis:

(a)   From the thermodynamic tables,

when $T_1 = 295$ K, $u_1 = 210.49$ kJ/kg, $v_{r1} = 187.3$, $P_{r1} = 1.052$

For the isentropic compression process 1-2,

$$v_{r2} = \frac{V_2}{V_1} v_{r1} = \frac{v_{r1}}{r} = \frac{647.9}{9} = 20.81.$$

Interpolating from the tables, $T_2 = 692$ K,

$u_2 = 506.0$ kJ/kg, $P_{r2} = 22.19$

The pressure at state 2 is then found from

$$P_2 = P_1 \left(\frac{P_{r2}}{P_{r1}}\right) = (100 \text{ kPa})\left(\frac{22.19}{1.052}\right) = 2110 \text{ kPa}.$$

This pressure at state 2 may also be computed by using the ideal gas equation of state,

$$P_2 = P_1 \left(\frac{T_2}{T_1}\right)\left(\frac{V_1}{V_2}\right).$$

Process 2-3 is a constant volume process. The ideal gas equation of state gives

$$P_3 = P_2 \left(\frac{T_3}{T_2}\right) = (2111 \text{ kPa})\left(\frac{2100}{692}\right) = 6406 \text{ kPa}.$$

From the thermodynamic tables,

when $T_3 = 2100$ K, $u_3 = 1775.3$ kJ/kg, $v_{r3} = 0.6824$, $P_{r3} = 2052$

For the isentropic expansion process 3-4,

$$v_{r4} = \frac{V_4}{V_3} v_{r3} = r v_{r3} = 9(0.6824) = 6.142.$$

Interpolating from the tables, $T_4 = 1059$ K,

$u_4 = 809.8$ kJ/kg, $P_{r4} = 115.2$

The pressure at state 4 is then found from

$$P_4 = P_3\left(\frac{P_{r4}}{P_{r3}}\right) = (6406 \text{ kPa})\left(\frac{143.37}{2559}\right) = 358.9 \text{ kPa}.$$

This pressure at state 4 may also be computed by using the ideal gas equation of state,

$$P_4 = P_3\left(\frac{T_4}{T_3}\right)\left(\frac{V_3}{V_4}\right).$$

(b) The thermal efficiency is

$$\eta = 1 - \frac{Q_{41}/m}{Q_{23}/m} = 1 - \frac{u_4 - u_1}{u_3 - u_2}$$

$$= 1 - \frac{809.8 - 210.49}{1775.3 - 506.0} = 0.5278.$$

(c) The net work per cycle is needed to calculate the mean effective pressure.

$$W_{cycle} = m[(u_3 - u_4) - (u_2 - u_1)]$$

where the mass of air, m, is computed from the ideal gas equation of state.

$$m = \frac{P_1 V_1}{(\overline{R}/M)T_1}$$

$$= \frac{100(0.0006)(28.97)}{8.314 \times 295} \frac{\text{kN}}{\text{m}^2} \cdot \frac{\text{kgmol.K}}{\text{kJ}} \cdot \frac{\text{kg}}{\text{kgmol}} \cdot \text{m}^3 \cdot \frac{1}{\text{K}} \cdot \frac{\text{kJ}}{\text{kN.m}}$$

$$= 0.00071 \text{ kg}$$

Hence, $W_{cycle} = 0.00071[(1775.3 - 809.8) - (506.0 - 210.49)]$ kJ $= 0.4757$ kJ.

Since the displacement volume is V_1-V_2, the mean effective pressure is

$$mep = \frac{W_{cycle}}{V_1 - V_2} = \frac{W_{cycle}}{V_1(1 - V_2/V_1)}$$

$$= \frac{0.4757 \text{ kJ}}{(0.0006 \text{ m}^3)(1 - 1/9)} = 892 \text{ kPa}.$$

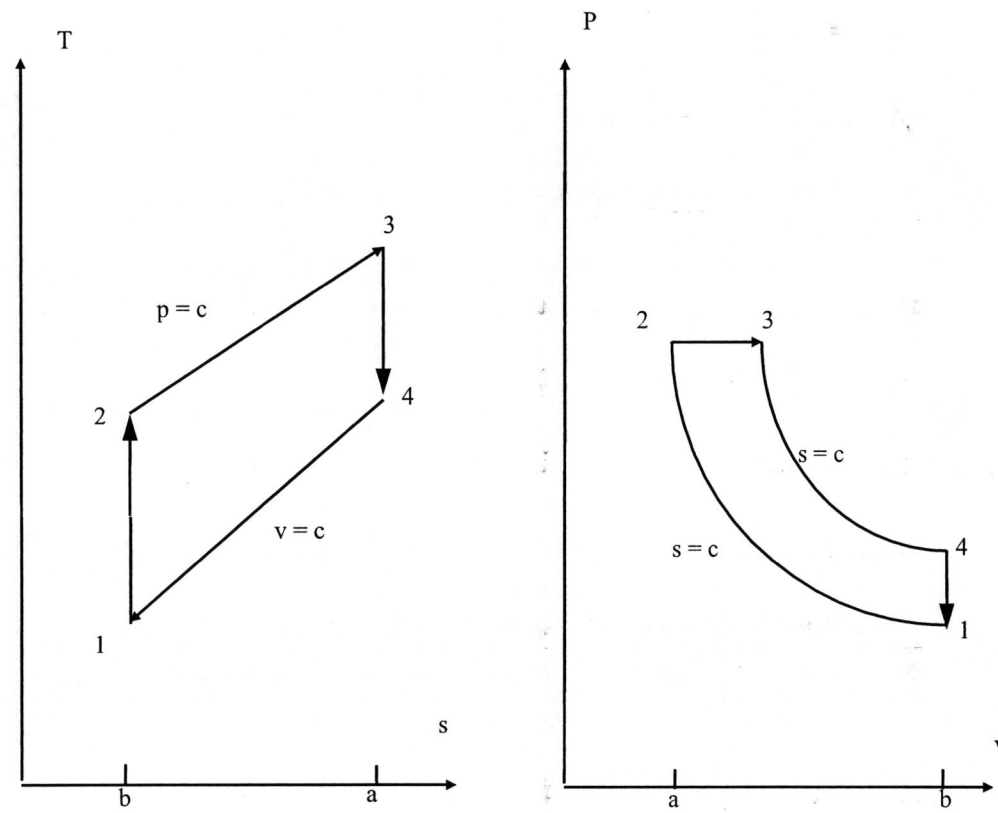

Figure 2.6 T-s and P-v diagrams of the air-standard diesel cycle.

2.5 Air-Standard Diesel Cycle

The air-standard Diesel cycle is an ideal cycle for compression-ignition reciprocating engines; the P-v and T-s diagrams are shown in Fig. 2.6. It comprises the following four internally reversible processes:

- 1-2 Isentropic compression
- 2-3 Constant pressure heat addition
- 3-4 Isentropic expansion
- 4-1 Constant volume heat rejection

Note that process 2-3 makes up the first part of the power stroke. The second part of the power stroke is process 3-4. On the P-v diagram, area 1-2-a-b-1 represents the work input per unit of mass during the compression process. As the piston moves from top dead center to bottom dead center, the work done per unit of mass is the area 2-3-4-b-a-2. On the T-s diagram, area 2-3-a-b-2 represents the heat added per unit of mass and area 1-4-a-b-1 is the heat rejected per unit of mass. The enclosed area in the P-v diagram is the net work output. The enclosed area in the T-s diagram is the net heat added. Since the cycle is ideal, both these quantities are equal.

Heat addition takes place at constant pressure. Thus, process 2-3 involves both work and heat. The work is calculated as

$$\frac{W_{23}}{m} = \int_2^3 p \, dv = p_2(v_3 - v_2) \qquad (2.14)$$

By applying the closed system energy balance,

$$Q_{23} - W_{23} = mu_1 - mu_2$$

Using Eq. (2.14),

$$\frac{Q_{23}}{m} = (u_3 - u_2) + p_2(v_3 - v_2) = (u_3 + p_3v_3) - (u_2 + p_2v_2) \qquad (p_3 = p_2)$$

$$= h_3 - h_2 \qquad (2.15)$$

The heat rejected in process 4-1, as in the Otto cycle, is given by

$$\frac{Q_{41}}{m} = u_4 - u_1$$

The thermal efficiency is the ratio of the net work output to the heat added

$$\eta = \frac{W_{net}/m}{Q_{23}/m} = 1 - \frac{Q_{41}/m}{Q_{23}/m} = 1 - \frac{u_4 - u_1}{h_3 - h_2} \qquad (2.16)$$

This thermal efficiency increases with the compression ratio, as in the Otto cycle.

Let us now discuss how a typical cycle is evaluated. For an initial temperature T_1 and compression ratio r, the conditions at state 2 can be calculated using the following isentropic relationship:

$$v_{r2} = \frac{V_2}{V_1} v_{r1} = \frac{1}{r} v_{r1} \qquad (2.17)$$

To find state 3, use the ideal gas equation of state with $p_3 = p_2$ to give

$$T_3 = \frac{V_3}{V_2} T_2 = r_c T_2$$

where $r_c = V_3/V_2$ is called the cutoff ratio. The **cutoff ratio** is the ratio of the cylinder volumes after and before the combustion process.

Since $V_4 = V_1$, the volume ratio for the isentropic process 3-4 can be expressed as

$$\frac{V_4}{V_3} = \frac{V_4}{V_2}\frac{V_2}{V_3} = \frac{V_1}{V_2}\frac{V_2}{V_3} = \frac{r}{r_c} \qquad (2.18)$$

State 4 can be determined from the isentropic relationship

$$v_{r4} = \frac{V_4}{V_3} v_{r3} = \frac{r}{r_c} v_{r3} \qquad (2.19)$$

In the cold air-standard analysis, the temperature at state 2 can be evaluated by

$$\frac{T_2}{T_1} = \left(\frac{V_1}{V_2}\right)^{k-1} = r^{k-1} \quad \text{(constant k)} \qquad (2.20)$$

$$\frac{T_4}{T_3} = \left(\frac{V_3}{V_4}\right)^{k-1} = \left(\frac{r_c}{r}\right)^{k-1} \quad \text{(constant k)} \qquad (2.21)$$

where Eq. (2.18) has been used to substitute for the volume ratio.

On a cold air-standard basis, the thermal efficiency of the Diesel cycle is

$$\eta = 1 - \frac{1}{r^{k-1}} \left[\frac{r_c^k - 1}{k(r_c - 1)}\right] \quad \text{(constant k)} \qquad (2.22)$$

This relationship is shown graphically in Fig. 2.7 for k = 1.4. Equation (2.22) for the Diesel cycle should be compared to Eq. (2.13) for the Otto cycle. The difference is the term within brackets. For $r_c > 1$, this term is greater than one. When the compression ratio r is the same, the thermal efficiency of the cold air-standard Otto cycle is greater than that of the cold air-standard Diesel cycle. However, as has been discussed previously, it is possible to reach much higher compression ratios in the Diesel cycle, typically from 12 to 20.

The actual and ideal P-v diagram for a compression-ignition engine is shown in Fig. 2.8. It can clearly be seen that in general the four reversible processes are just approximations, and in particular that the constant pressure and constant volume processes are idealizations.

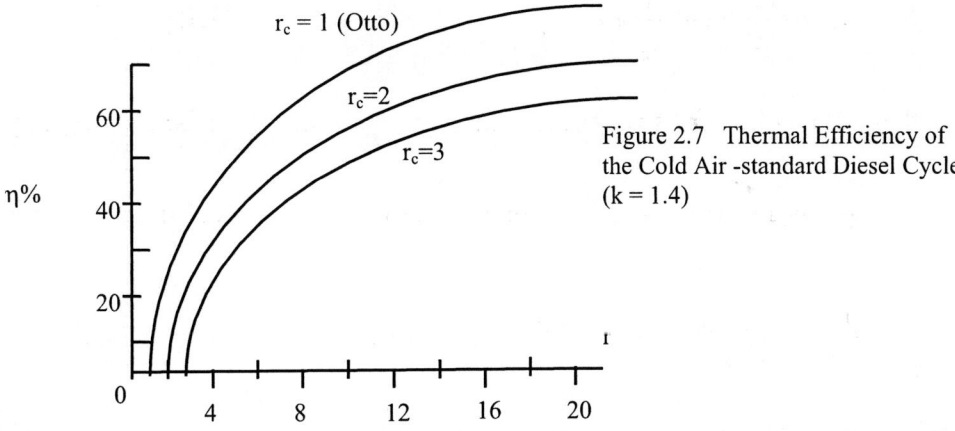

Figure 2.7 Thermal Efficiency of the Cold Air-standard Diesel Cycle (k = 1.4)

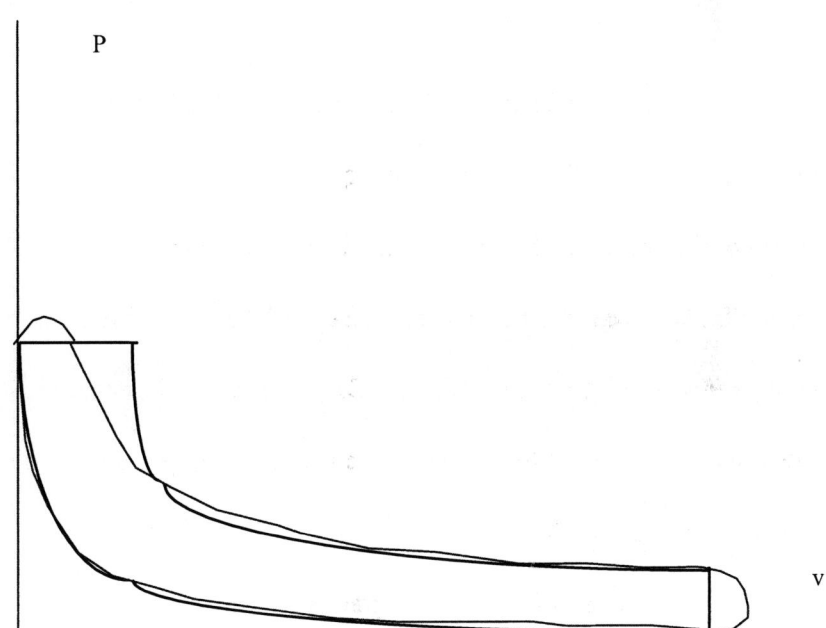

Figure 2.8 Actual and ideal P-v diagram for a compression-ignition engine.

Example 2.2

Problem

Air is the working fluid in an ideal Diesel cycle with a compression ratio of 16 and a cut-off ratio of 2. The air at the beginning of the compression process is at 77°F, and 1 atm. Calculate (a) the end states of each process, (b) the thermal efficiency, and (c) the mean effective pressure.

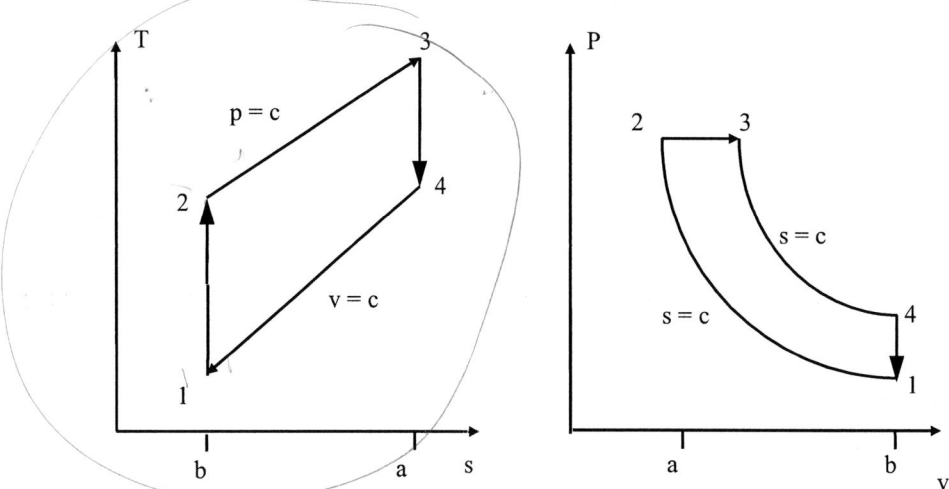

Solution

Assumptions:

(1) All processes are internally reversible.

(2) The compression and expansion processes are adiabatic.

(3) Changes in K.E. and P.E. are negligible.

(4) The air behaves like an ideal gas.

Analysis:

(a)   From the thermodynamic tables,

when $T_1 = 537°R$, $u_1 = 91.64$ Btu/lb$_m$, $v_{r1} = 182.0$, $P_{r1} = 1.093$

For the isentropic compression process 1-2,

$$v_{r2} = \frac{v_2}{v_1} v_{r1} = \frac{v_{r1}}{r} = \frac{182.0}{16} = 11.375.$$

Interpolating from the tables, $T_2 = 1545°R$,

$h_2 = 381.1$ Btu/lb$_m$, $P_{r2} = 50.34$

The pressure at state 2 is found from the ideal gas equation of state,

$$P_2 = P_1 \left(\frac{T_2}{T_1}\right)\left(\frac{v_1}{v_2}\right) = (1 \text{ atm})\left(\frac{1545}{537}\right)16 = 46.0 \text{ atm.}$$

This pressure at state 2 may also be computed by using the isentropic relationship,

$$P_2 = P_1 \left(\frac{P_{r2}}{P_{r1}}\right)$$

Process 2-3 is a constant pressure process. The ideal gas equation of state gives

$$T_3 = T_2 \left(\frac{v_3}{v_2}\right)$$

Since the cutoff ratio $r_c = v_3/v_2$,

$$T_3 = r_c T_2 = 2(1545) = 3090°R$$

From the thermodynamic tables,

when $T_3 = 3090°R$, $h_3 = 817.1$ Btu/lb$_m$, $v_{r3} = 1.335$, $P_{r3} = 857.4$

For the isentropic expansion process 3-4,

$$v_{r4} = \frac{r}{r_c} v_{r3} = \frac{16}{2}(1.335) = 10.68.$$

Interpolating from the tables, $T_4 = 1580°R$,

$u_4 = 282$ Btu/lb$_m$, $P_{r4} = 54.9$

The pressure at state 4 is then found from

$$P_4 = P_1\left(\frac{T_4}{T_1}\right)\left(\frac{V_1}{V_4}\right) = P_1\left(\frac{T_4}{T_1}\right) = (1 \text{ atm.})\left(\frac{1580}{537}\right) = 2.94 \text{ atm.}$$

This pressure at state 4 may also be computed by using the isentropic relationship,

$$P_4 = P_3\left(\frac{P_{r4}}{P_{r3}}\right).$$

(b) The thermal efficiency is

$$\eta = 1 - \frac{Q_{41}/m}{Q_{23}/m} = 1 - \frac{u_4 - u_1}{h_3 - h_2}$$

$$= 1 - \frac{282 - 91.64}{817.1 - 381.1} = 0.56.$$

(c) The net work per cycle is needed to calculate the mean effective pressure.

$$W_{cycle} = [(h_3 - h_2) - (u_4 - u_1)] = 436 - 190.36 = 245.64 \text{ Btu/lb}_m$$

The specific volume at state 1 is

$$v_1 = \frac{(\overline{R}/M)T_1}{P_1}$$

$$= \frac{1545(537)}{28.97 \times 14.7 \times 144} \frac{\text{ft.lb}_f}{\text{lbmol.}^\circ R} \cdot \frac{\text{lbmol}}{\text{lbm}} \cdot \frac{\text{in}^2}{\text{lb}_f} \cdot {}^\circ R \cdot \frac{\text{ft}^2}{\text{in}^2}$$

$$= 13.53 \text{ ft}^3/\text{lb}_m$$

Hence, the mean effective pressure is

$$\text{mep} = \frac{W_{cycle}}{V_1 - V_2} = \frac{W_{cycle}}{V_1(1 - 1/r)}$$

$$= \frac{244.39 \times 778}{(13.53)(1 - 1/16)} \frac{\text{Btu}}{\text{lb}_m} \cdot \frac{\text{lb}_m}{\text{ft}^3} \cdot \frac{\text{ft.lb}_f}{\text{Btu}} = 15,066 \frac{\text{lb}_f}{\text{ft}^2} = 7.1 \text{ atm.}$$

2.6 Air-Standard Dual Cycle

As has been shown, the P-v diagrams of actual spark-ignition and compression-ignition engines are not well represented by the Otto and Diesel cycles. The air-standard dual cycle makes a better approximation of the pressure variations. The P-v and T-s diagrams are shown in Fig. 2.9. It comprises the following five internally reversible processes:

1-2   Isentropic compression

2-3   Constant volume heat addition

3-4   Constant pressure heat addition

4-5   Isentropic expansion

5-1   Constant volume heat rejection

Note that the heat addition is done in two processes, rather than one as in the Otto and Diesel cycles. The process 3-4 makes up the first part of the power stroke. The second part of the power stroke is process 4-5. The enclosed area in the P-v diagram is the net work output. The enclosed area in the T-s diagram is the net heat added. Since the cycle is ideal, both these quantities are equal.

Work is done in processes 1-2, 3-4 and 4-5; heat transfer occurs in processes 2-3, 3-4 and 5-1. Neglecting potential and kinetic energy, the expressions for the work and heat are

$$\frac{W_{12}}{m} = u_2 - u_1, \qquad \frac{W_{34}}{m} = u_4 - u_3 = P(v_4 - v_3), \qquad \frac{W_{45}}{m} = u_4 - u_5$$

$$\frac{Q_{23}}{m} = u_3 - u_2, \qquad \frac{Q_{34}}{m} = h_4 - h_3, \qquad \frac{Q_{51}}{m} = u_5 - u_1 \qquad (2.23)$$

Process 3-4 is the only one with both work and heat, so its derivation is the same as the corresponding process in the Diesel cycle.

The thermal efficiency is the ratio of the net work of the cycle to the total heat added

$$\eta = \frac{W_{net}/m}{Q_{23}/m + Q_{34}/m} = 1 - \frac{Q_{51}/m}{Q_{23}/m + Q_{34}/m}$$

$$= 1 - \frac{(u_5 - u_1)}{(u_3 - u_2) + (h_4 - h_3)} \qquad (2.24)$$

Both the Otto and the Diesel cycles can be obtained as special cases of the dual cycle.

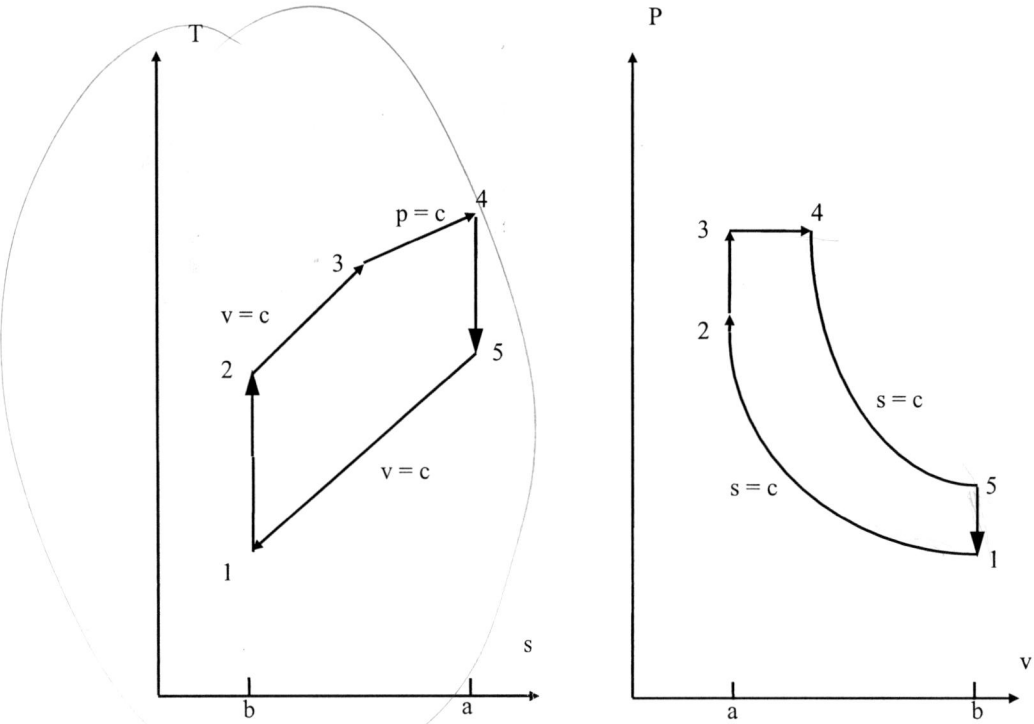

Figure 2.9 T-s and P-v diagrams of the air-standard dual cycle.

Example 2.3

The air at the start of the compression process of an air-choked dual cycle with a compression ratio of 16, is at 77°F, and 1 atm. The pressure ratio for the isochoric portion of the heating process is 1.6:1, and the volume ratio for the isobaric portion of that heating process is 1.1:1. Calculate (a) the end states of each process, (b) the thermal efficiency, and (c) the mean effective pressure.

Solution

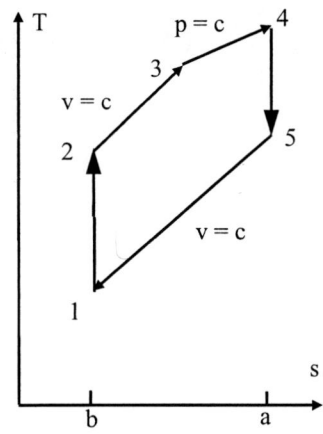
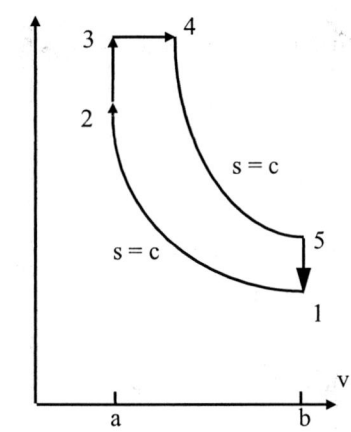

Assumptions:

(1) All processes are internally reversible.

(2) The compression and expansion processes are adiabatic.

(3) Changes in K.E. and P.E. are negligible.

(4) The air behaves like an ideal gas.

Analysis:

(a) The end states of process 1-2 are the same as in Example 2.2. Hence,

u_1 = ~~90.39~~ Btu/lb$_m$, v_{r1}= 182.0
     91.64

u_2 = 275.18 Btu/lb$_m$, v_{r2}= 11.375

Process 2-3 is a constant volume one, so the ideal gas equation of state gives

$$T_3 = \frac{P_3}{P_2} T_2 = (1.6)(1545°R) = 2472°R$$

Interpolating from the tables,

$h_3 = 637.8$ Btu/lb$_m$, $u_3 = 468.3$ Btu/lb$_m$

Process 3-4 is an isobaric one, so the ideal gas equation of state gives

$$T_4 = \frac{V_4}{V_3} T_3 = (1.1)(2472°R) = 2719°R$$

Interpolating from the tables,

$h_4 = 708.85$ Btu/lb$_m$, $v_{r4} = 2.02$

The air expands isentropically in process 4-5, hence

$$v_{r5} = v_{r4} \frac{V_5}{V_4}$$

The volume ratio

$$\frac{V_5}{V_4} = \frac{V_5}{V_3} \cdot \frac{V_3}{V_4}$$

$$= \frac{V_1}{V_2} \cdot \frac{V_3}{V_4} \text{ since } V_5 = V_1 \text{ and } V_2 = V_3$$

$$= 16\left(\frac{1}{1.6}\right) = 10 \quad 14.55$$
$$\phantom{= 16\left(\frac{1}{}\right)}1.1$$

Thus, $v_{r5} = (2.02)(10) = 20.2.$
$\phantom{Thus, v_{r5} = (2.02)(}14.55$
$\phantom{Thus, v_{r5} = (2.02)(10) = }29.4$

Interpolating from the tables,

$T_5 = 1259°R$, $u_5 = 220.1$ Btu/lb$_m$
$1090°R$ 190

(b)   The thermal efficiency is

$$\eta = 1 - \frac{Q_{51}/m}{(Q_{23}/m + Q_{34}/m)}$$

$$= 1 - \frac{(u_5 - u_1)}{(u_3 - u_2) + (h_4 - h_3)}$$

$$= 1 - \frac{129.71}{193.12 + 71.05} = 0.51 \quad .63$$

(with handwritten: 98.3)

(c) The mean effective pressure is

$$mep = \frac{W_{cycle}}{V_1 - V_2} = \frac{W_{cycle}}{V_1(1 - 1/r)} = \frac{W_{cycle}/m}{v_1(1 - 1/r)}$$

Since $W_{cycle} = Q_{cycle}$,

$$mep = \frac{(u_3 - u_2) + (h_4 - h_3) - (u_5 - u_1)}{v_1(1 - 1/r)}$$

$v_1 = 13.53$ ft³/lb_m from Example 2.2.

Hence,

$$mep = \frac{(193.12 + 71.05 - 129.71) \times 778}{(13.53)(1 - 1/16)} \frac{Btu}{lb_m} \cdot \frac{lb_m}{ft^3} \cdot \frac{ft \cdot lb_f}{Btu} = 8,247.15 \frac{lb_f}{ft^2} = 3.90 \text{ atm.}$$

(handwritten annotations: 98.3; 10,124; 4.8)

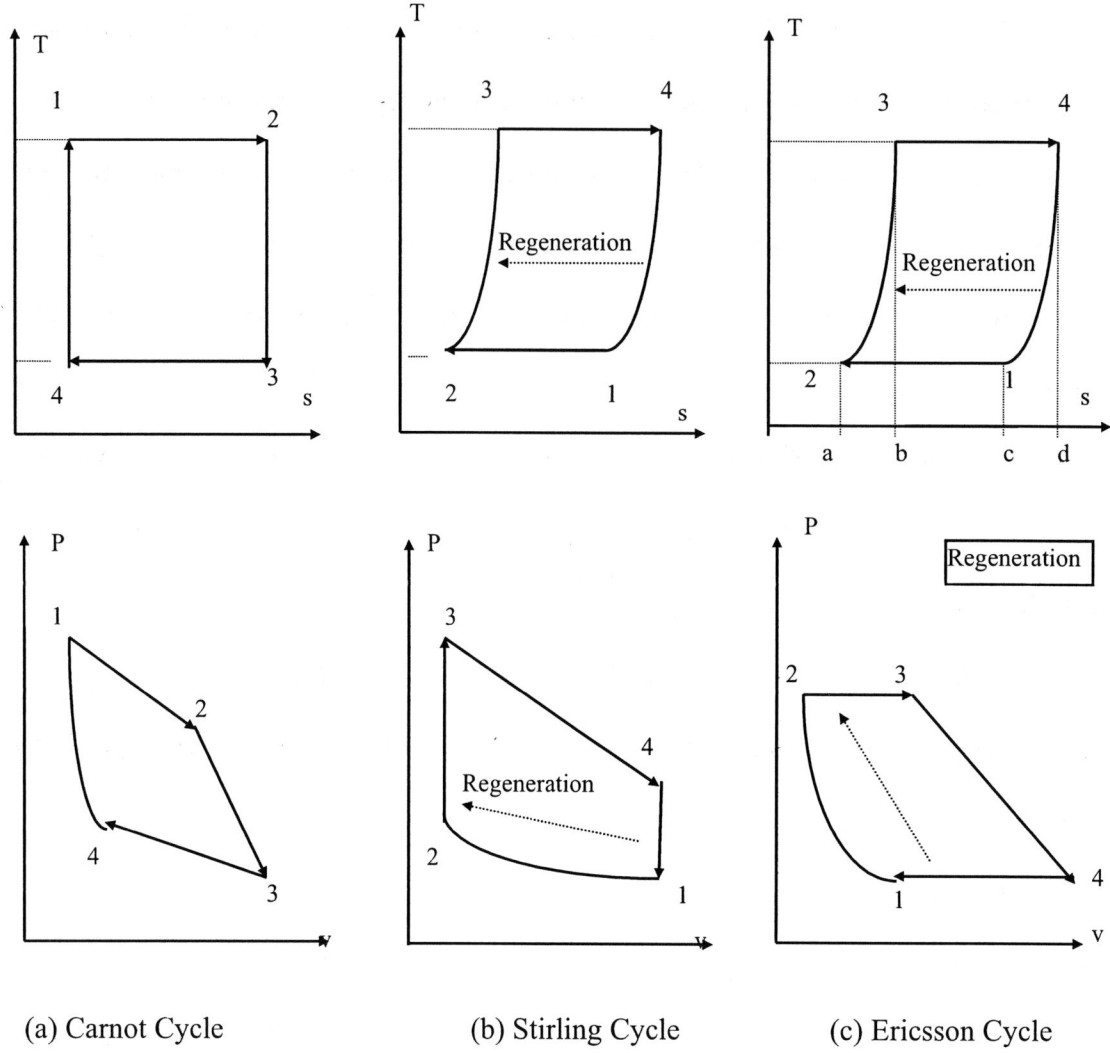

Figure 2.10 T-s and P-v diagrams of Carnot, Stirling, and Ericsson cycles.

2.7 Stirling and Ericsson Cycles

The ideal Otto and Diesel cycles are composed of internally reversible processes, but are not totally reversible. This is because they incorporate heat transfer through a finite temperature difference during the nonisothermal heat addition and rejection processes, which are irreversible. It follows that the thermal efficiency of the Otto or Diesel engine is less than that of a Carnot engine operating between the same temperature range.

The Stirling and Ericsson cycles serve to show how a regenerator can be used in a cycle to give a significant increase in efficiency. The Stirling cycle is shown in Fig. 2.10(b). It comprises the following four totally reversible processes:

1-2 Isothermal expansion (heat is added from an external source)

2-3 Constant volume regeneration (internal heat transfer from the working fluid to the

      regenerator)

3-4 Isothermal compression (heat is rejected to the external sink)

4-1 Constant volume regeneration (internal heat transfer from the regenerator back to

      the working fluid)

The execution of this cycle with a regenerator is discussed after the Ericsson cycle is introduced.

The Ericsson cycle is shown in 2.10(c). It comprises the following four totally reversible processes:

1-2 Isothermal expansion (heat is added from an external source)

2-3 Isobaric regeneration (internal heat transfer from the working fluid to the regenerator)

3-4 Isothermal compression (heat is rejected to the external sink)

4-1 Isobaric regeneration (internal heat transfer from the regenerator back to the working fluid)

Because of the inclusion of a regenerator, the air-standard Stirling and Ericsson cycles may have an efficiency equal to that of a Carnot cycle operating between the same temperatures. This can be shown by studying Fig. 2.11, in which the Ericsson cycle is followed by a gas turbine with a regenerator. If we assume an ideal heat transfer process in the regenerator, i.e., no pressure drop and an infinitesimal temperature difference between the two streams, and reversible expansion and compression processes, the cycle shown is the Ericsson cycle.

Note that the heat transfer to the gas between states 2 and 3, area 23ba2, is equal to the heat transfer from the gas between states 4 and 1, area 14dc1. As the heat is supplied and rejected isothermally, the efficiency of this cycle is equal to that of a Carnot cycle operating in the same temperature range. A similar cycle could be created that operate on the Stirling cycle.

In practice, there are some difficulties. It is difficult to have isothermal compression or expansion in a device operating at a reasonable speed. There will be a temperature difference between the two streams flowing through the regenerator and pressure drops in the regenerator. The gas turbine with intercooling and regenerators, discussed in a later section, is an attempt to approach the Ericsson cycle. Similar attempts have been made to approach the Stirling cycle.

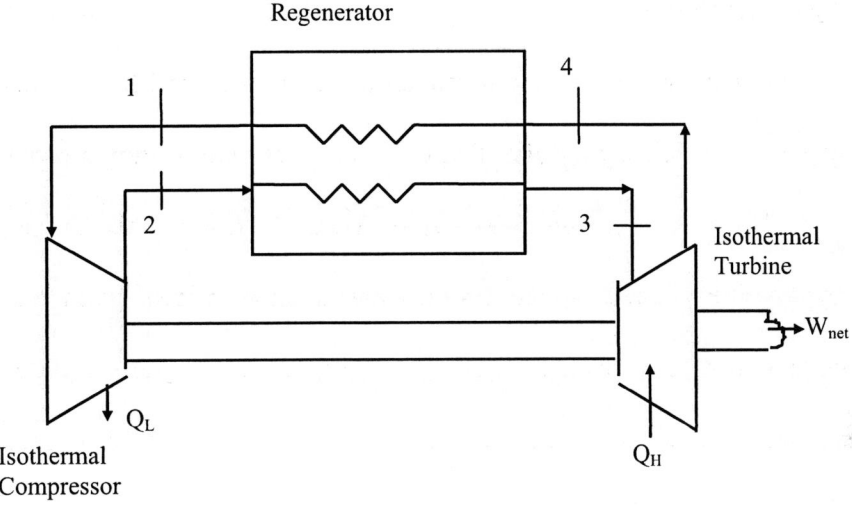

Figure 2.11   An engine using a regenerator to operate on the Ericsson cycle.

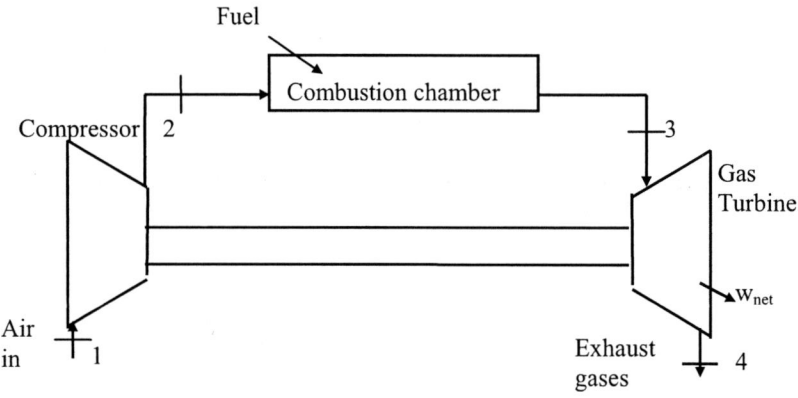

(a) Open Cycle

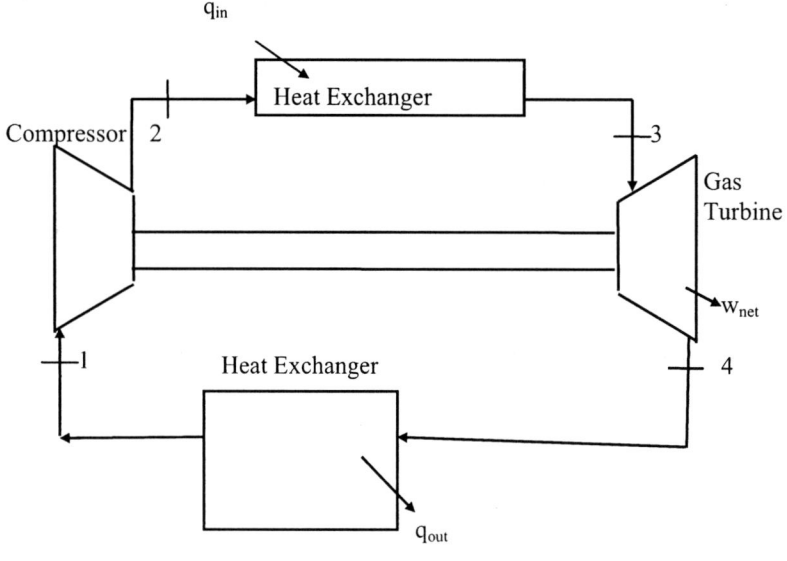

(b) Closed Cycle

Figure 2.12 Gas turbine systems.

2.8 Gas Brayton Cycle

Gas turbines usually operate on an open cycle, as shown in Fig.2.12(a). Air is drawn from the surroundings into the compressor, where its pressure and temperature are increased. The high pressure air then goes into the combustor where the fuel is burned at constant pressure. The high-temperature gases then enter the turbine where they are expanded to atmospheric pressure, thus producing work. The spent gases are exhausted to the surroundings; thus the cycle is an open cycle.

By using the air-standard assumptions, the open gas-turbine cycle can be modeled as a closed cycle, shown in Fig. 2.12(b). The isobaric heat-addition process from an external source replaces the combustion process, and an isobaric heat-rejection process replaces the exhaust process. Both the compression and expansion processes remain the same as before. The ideal closed cycle that the working fluid undergoes is called the Brayton cycle. The cycle comprises the following four internally reversible processes:

1-2   Isentropic compression

2-3   Isobaric heat addition

3-4   Isentropic expansion

4-1   Isobaric heat rejection

The P-v and T-s diagrams of the ideal Brayton cycle are shown in Fig. 2.13. Since all four processes are performed in steady-flow equipment, they are analyzed as steady-flow processes. When changes in kinetic and potential energies are neglected, the heat transfers to and from the working fluid are

$$q_{in} = h_3 - h_2 \qquad (2.25)$$

$$q_{out} = h_4 - h_1 \qquad (2.26)$$

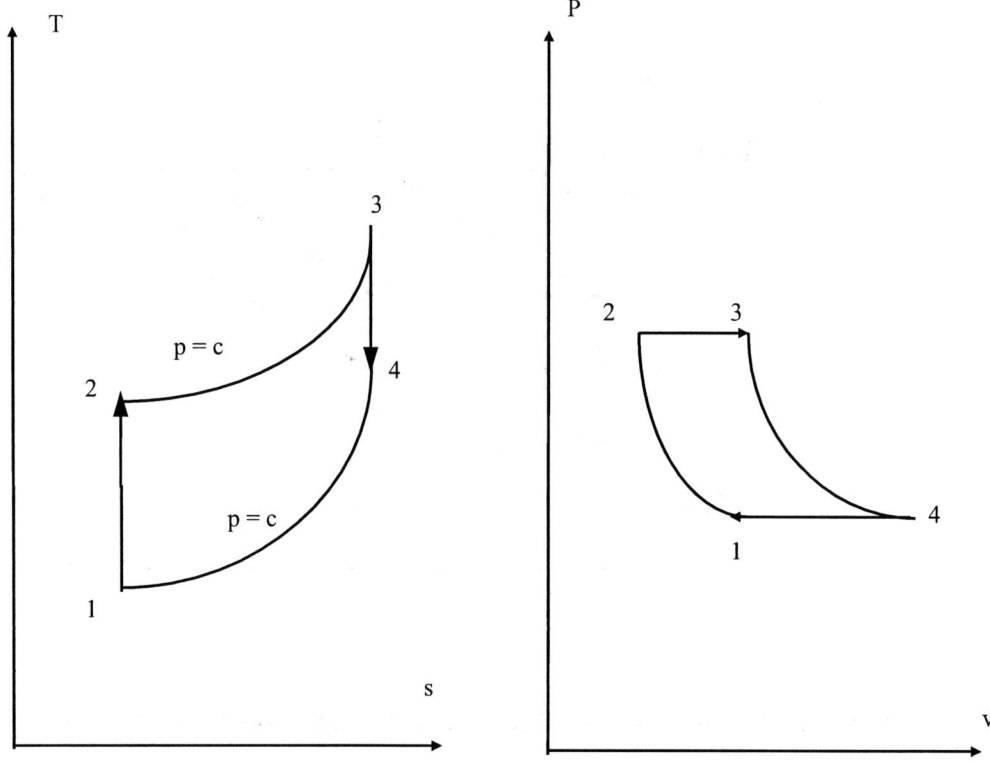

Figure 2.13   T-s and P-v diagrams for the ideal Brayton cycle.

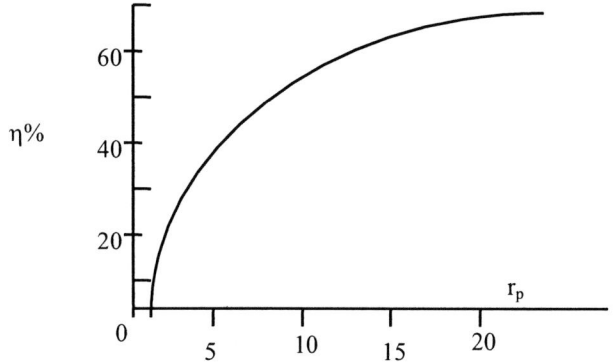

Figure 2.14   Thermal efficiency of the ideal Brayton cycle as a function of the pressure ratio.

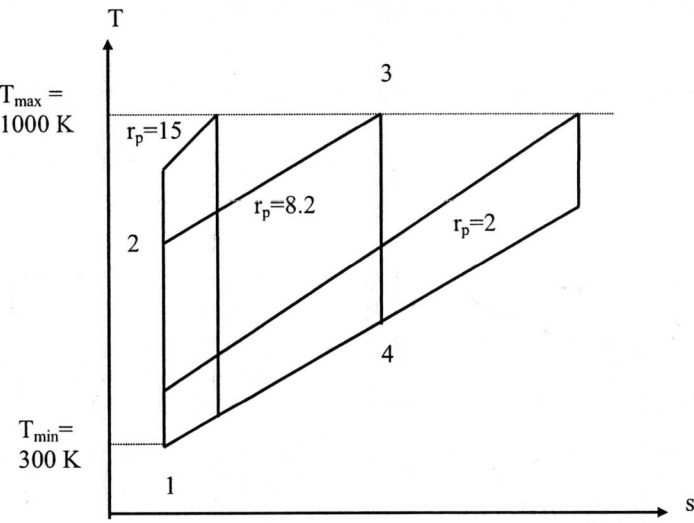

Figure 2.15 The net work of the Brayton cycle has an optimum value.

When the air data are used for analysis, the following relationships apply for the isentropic processes 1-2 and 3-4:

$$P_{r2} = P_{r1}\frac{P_2}{P_1}$$

$$P_{r4} = P_{r3}\frac{P_4}{P_3} = P_{r3}\frac{P_1}{P_2}$$

The thermal efficiency of the ideal Brayton cycle is

$$\eta_{th,Brayton} = \frac{w_{net}}{q_{in}} = \frac{w_t - w_c}{q_{in}} = \frac{(h_3 - h_4) - (h_2 - h_1)}{(h_3 - h_2)} \quad (2.27)$$

The back work ratio of the cycle is

$$bwr = \frac{w_c}{w_t} = \frac{(h_2 - h_1)}{(h_3 - h_4)} \quad (2.28)$$

The ratio of the compressor work to the turbine work is called the **back work ratio (bwr)**. Typical bwr's are from 40% to 80%. The typical bwr's for vapor power plants are 1 to 2%. The work used to drive the pumps in the vapor power plants are much smaller than that used to drive the compressors in the gas cycle because the specific volume of the gas is much bigger than that of the liquid in the vapor power cycle.

Under the cold air-standard assumptions, the above analysis becomes as follows:

$$q_{in} = h_3 - h_2 = c_p(T_3 - T_2) \quad (2.29)$$

$$q_{out} = h_4 - h_1 = c_p(T_4 - T_1) \quad (2.30)$$

The thermal efficiency of the ideal Brayton cycle is

$$\eta_{th,Brayton} = \frac{(h_3 - h_4) - (h_2 - h_1)}{(h_3 - h_2)} = 1 - \frac{c_p(T_4 - T_1)}{c_p(T_3 - T_2)} = 1 - \frac{T_1(T_4/T_1 - 1)}{T_2(T_3/T_2 - 1)} \quad (2.31)$$

The back work ratio of the cycle is

$$\text{bwr} = \frac{w_c}{w_t} = \frac{(h_2 - h_1)}{(h_3 - h_4)} = \frac{T_1(T_2/T_1 - 1)}{T_4(T_3/T_4 - 1)} \qquad (2.32)$$

Processes 1-2 and 3-4 are isentropic, and $P_2 = P_3$ and $P_4 = P_1$. Thus,

$$\frac{T_2}{T_1} = \left(\frac{P_2}{P_1}\right)^{(k-1)/k} = \left(\frac{P_3}{P_4}\right)^{(k-1)/k} = \frac{T_3}{T_4} \qquad (2.33)$$

Substituting these equations and simplifying for the thermal efficiency gives

$$\eta_{th,Brayton} = 1 - \frac{1}{r_p^{(k-1)/k}} \qquad (2.34)$$

where

$$r_p = \frac{P_2}{P_1} \qquad (2.35)$$

is the **pressure ratio** and k is the ratio of specific heats. Under cold air-standard assumptions, the thermal efficiency of an ideal Brayton cycle depends on the pressure ratio and the specific heat ratio. The thermal efficiency increases with both these parameters, which is found to be the case for actual gas turbines. Figure 2.14 is a plot of thermal efficiency as a function of the pressure ratio, for k=1.4 which is the value for air at room temperature.

There is a limit of about 1700 K (3060°R) on the maximum temperature at the turbine inlet because of metallurgical considerations regarding the turbine blades. This in turn limits the pressure ratios that can be used. For a fixed turbine inlet temperature T_3, the net work output per cycle increases with the pressure ratio, hits a maximum, and then decreases, as shown in Fig. 2.15. In practice, there is compromise between the pressure ratio (thus the thermal efficiency) and the net work output. If the work output per cycle is less, a larger mass flow rate (concomitantly a larger system) is needed to maintain the same power output which may not be economical. In practice, the pressure ratio of gas turbines can range from 10 to 20. It can be shown that the pressure ratio $P_2/P_1 = (T_3/T_1)^{k/[2(k-1)]}$ corresponds to the maximum net work output per unit of mass flow.

Example 2.4

Problem

An on-land power plant operating on an ideal Brayton cycle has a pressure ratio of 10. The compressor inlet state of the air is 298 K, 100 kPa. The turbine inlet temperature is 1350 K. Determine (a) the states at the end of each process, (b) the back work ratio, (c) the thermal efficiency.

Solution

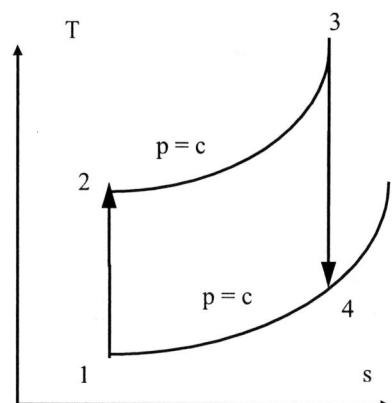

Assumptions: (1) Each of the four components of the cycle is analyzed as a control volume at steady state.

(2) Pressure drops across the heat exchangers are neglected.

(3) Changes in K.E. and P.E. are negligible.

(4) The expansion and compression processes are isentropic.

(5) The air is modeled as an ideal gas.

Analysis:

From the thermodynamic tables,

$h_1 = 298.61$ kJ/kg, $s_1 = 6.8631$ kJ/kg.K,   relative pressure ratio $P_{r1} = 1.0907$

Since $P_2 = 1000$ kPa, $s_2 = s_1$, relative pressure ratio $P_{r2} = 10 \times 1.0907 = 10.907$

$h_2 = 576.64$ kJ/kg

Since $T_3 = 1350$ K, $P_3 = 1000$ kPa,

$h_3 = 1455.61$ kJ/kg, $s_3 = 7.8246$ kJ/kg.K,

Since $P_4 = 100$ kPa, $s_4 = s_3$

$h_4 = 775.52$ kJ/kg

(b) The back work ratio is

$$\text{bwr} = \frac{w_c}{w_t} = \frac{h_2 - h_1}{h_3 - h_4} = \frac{278.03}{680.09} = 0.409.$$

(c) The thermal efficiency is

$$\eta = \frac{w_t - w_c}{q_{in}} = \frac{(h_3 - h_4) - (h_2 - h_1)}{h_3 - h_2} = \frac{680.09 - 278.03}{878.97} = 0.457.$$

With the cold-air-standard assumptions, that is, constant specific heats, values at room temperature, the thermal efficiency would be

$$\eta_{th,\text{Brayton}} = 1 - \frac{1}{r_p^{(k-1)/k}} = 1 - \frac{1}{10^{(1.4-1)/1.4}} = 0.48.$$

The comparison shows that the cold-air-standard gives a reasonably close approximation to the actual efficiency.

2.8.1 Major Irreversibilities and Losses

The actual gas turbine cycle differs from the ideal Brayton cycle on several points, as shown in Fig.2.16. Some pressure drop during the heat addition and heat rejection processes should be expected. The actual work input to the compressor will be more, and the actual work output from the turbine will be less because of irreversibilities. The actual cycle is illustrated in Fig. 2.16(a). In Fig. 2.16(b), the pressure drops are neglected and only the irreversibilities in the turbine and in the compressor are considered. In practice, the effect of the pressure drops are small compared to that of the turbine and compressor irreversibilities. Under this assumption, the isentropic efficiencies of the turbine and compressor are :

$$\eta_{isen,t} = \frac{W_{isen}}{W_{actual}} = \frac{h_3 - h_4}{h_3 - h_{4s}} \qquad (2.36)$$

$$\eta_{isen,c} = \frac{W_{actual}}{W_{isen}} = \frac{h_{2s} - h_1}{h_2 - h_1} \qquad (2.37)$$

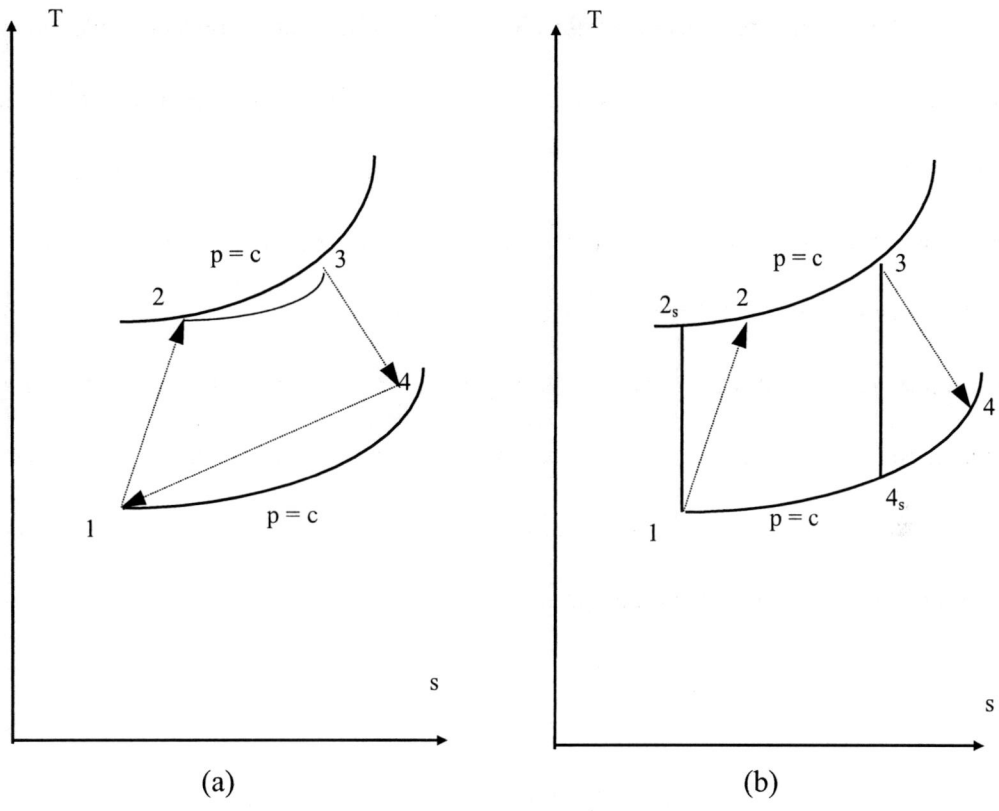

Figure 2.16 Irreversibilities and losses on the closed gas turbine cycle.

Example 2.5

Problem

In Ex. 2.4, the turbine and the compressor have isentropic efficiencies of 86% and 82% respectively. Determine (a) the states at the end of each process, (b) the back work ratio, (c) the thermal efficiency, and (d) the irreversibility rates in the turbine and in the compressor. Take $T_o = 25°C$, $P_o = 100$ kPa.

Solution

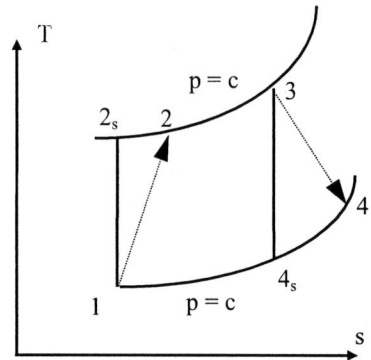

Assumptions: (1) Each of the four components of the cycle is analyzed as a control volume at steady state.

(2) Pressure drops across the heat exchangers are neglected.

(3) Changes in K.E. and P.E. are negligible.

(4) The air is modeled as an ideal gas.

Analysis:

From Ex. 2.4,

$h_1 = 298.61$ kJ/kg, $s_1 = 6.8631$ kJ/kg.K

Isentropic compressor efficiency is

$$\eta_{isen,c} = \frac{h_{2s} - h_1}{h_2 - h_1}$$

Hence, $0.82 = \dfrac{576.64 - 298.61}{h_2 - 298.61}$

$h_2 = 637.67$ kJ/kg

From the tables, $s_2 = 6.9649$ kJ/(kg.K)

From Ex. 2.4,

$h_3 = 1455.61$ kJ/kg, $s_3 = 7.8246$ kJ/kg.K

Isentropic turbine efficiency is

$$\eta_{isen,t} = \frac{h_3 - h_4}{h_3 - h_{4s}}$$

Hence, $0.86 = \dfrac{1455.61 - h_4}{1455.61 - 775.52}$

$h_4 = 870.73$ kJ/kg

From the tables, $s_4 = 7.9442$ kJ/(kg.K)

(b) The back work ratio is

$$bwr = \frac{w_c}{w_t} = \frac{h_2 - h_1}{h_3 - h_4} = \frac{339.06}{584.88} = 0.58.$$

(c) The thermal efficiency is

$$\eta = \frac{w_t - w_c}{q_{in}} = \frac{(h_3 - h_4) - (h_2 - h_1)}{h_3 - h_2} = \frac{584.88 - 339.06}{817.94} = 0.30.$$

Note that the back work ratio has increased, and the thermal efficiency has decreased in the actual cycle, as compared to the corresponding ideal cycle.

(d) The irreversibility rate in the compressor is

$T_o(s_2 - s_{2s}) = 298.15(0.1018) = 30.35$ kJ/kg.

The irreversibility rate in the turbine is

$T_o(s_4 - s_{4s}) = 298.15(0.1196) = 35.65$ kJ/kg.

2.9 Brayton Cycle with Regeneration

In gas turbines, the gas temperature at the turbine exit is often much higher than the temperature of the air leaving the compressor. It is possible to heat the air leaving the compressor with the hot exhaust gases in a counter-flow heat exchanger, which is called a regenerator or recuperator. A schematic of the gas turbine cycle with a regenerator and the T-s diagram are shown in Fig.2.17.

The air leaves the regenerator at T_5, which is normally below T_4, the temperature of the exhaust gases leaving the turbine. In the ideal situation, the temperature T_5 may be made to approach T_4. As a measure of the performance of the regenerator, an effectiveness η_{reg} is defined such that

$$\eta_{reg} = \frac{q_{reg,\,actual}}{q_{reg,\,ideal}} = \frac{h_5 - h_2}{h_{5'} - h_2} \tag{2.38}$$

With the cold-air-standard assumptions, the above expression reduces to

$$\eta_{reg} = \frac{T_5 - T_2}{T_{5'} - T_2} = \frac{T_5 - T_2}{T_4 - T_2} \tag{2.39}$$

Under the same cold-air-standard assumptions, the thermal efficiency of an ideal Brayton cycle with regeneration is

$$\eta_{th,reg} = 1 - (\frac{T_1}{T_3})(r_p)^{(k-1)/k} \tag{2.40}$$

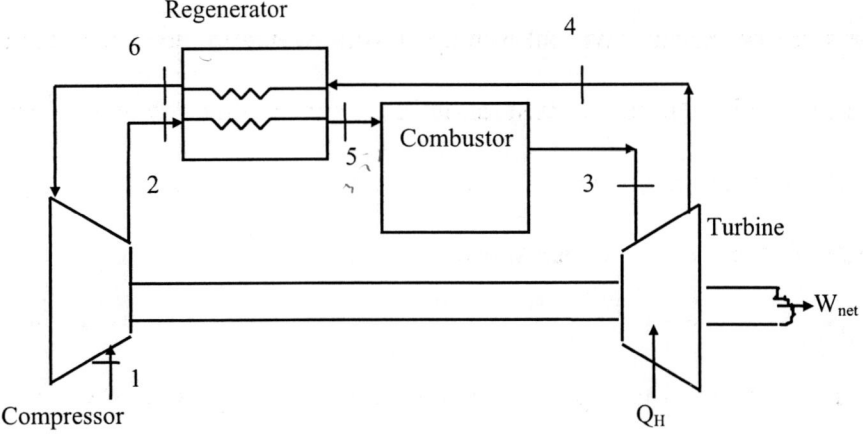

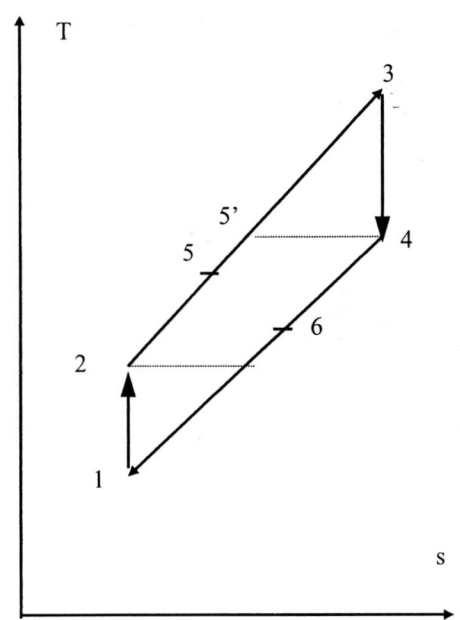

Figure 2.17 Gas turbine with regenerator.

It can be seen that the thermal efficiency depends on the ratio of the minimum to maximum temperatures in addition to the pressure ratio. The plot of thermal efficiency versus pressure ratio, with different minimum-to-maximum temperature ratios, is given in Fig. 2.18. Regeneration is best at lower pressure ratios and low minimum-to-maximum temperature ratios.

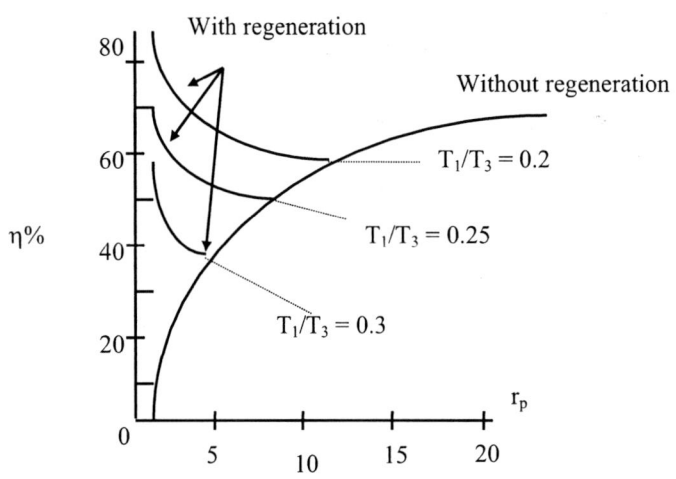

Figure 2.18   Thermal efficiency of the ideal Brayton cycle with and without regeneration.

Example 2.6

Problem

A regenerator of effectiveness 75 percent is installed in the gas-turbine plant of Ex. 2.5. Determine its thermal efficiency.

Solution

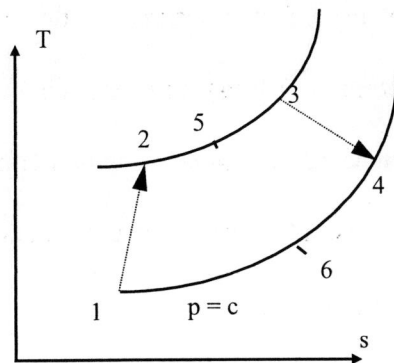

Assumptions: (1) Each component is analyzed as a control volume at steady state.

(2) Pressure drops across the heat exchangers are neglected.

(3) Changes in K.E. and P.E. are negligible.

(4) The air is modeled as an ideal gas.

Analysis:

From the definition of effectiveness,

$$\eta_{reg} = \frac{h_5 - h_2}{h_4 - h_2}$$

$$0.75 = \frac{(h_5 - 637.67)}{870.73 - 637.67}$$

$$h_5 = 812.47 \text{ kJ/kg}$$

Thus, $q_{in} = h_3 - h_5 = (1455.61 - 812.47)$ kJ/kg $= 643.14$ kJ/kg.

The net work output is not affected by the regenerator. The thermal efficiency

$$\eta = \frac{w_{net}}{q_{in}} = \frac{245.82}{643.14} = 0.38.$$

The thermal efficiency of the gas power plant has been increased to 38 percent with the inclusion of a regenerator.

2.10   Regenerative Gas Cycle with Reheat and Intercooling

It was pointed out in a previous section that when an ideal regenerator is included in the Ericsson cycle, the efficiency may be made to approach that of the corresponding Carnot cycle. It is practically impossible to achieve the isothermal compression and expansion in the Ericsson cycle. The practical approach to this cycle is to have a regenerator using multistage compression with intercooling between stages, and multistage expansion with reheat between stages.

A cycle with two stages of compression and two stages of expansion is shown in Fig. 2.19. The air-standard cycle is also shown on the T-s diagram. The maximum efficiency for this cycle is achieved if equal pressure ratios are kept across the two compressors and two turbines. In the ideal cycle it is assumed that the temperature of the air leaving the intercooler, T_3, is the same as the temperature of the air entering the first stage of compression, T_1. It is also assumed that the temperature after reheating, T_8, is the same as that entering the first turbine, T_6. In addition, it is assumed that the temperature of the high-pressure air leaving the regenerator, T_5, is the same as that of the low-pressure air leaving the turbine, T_9. The Ericsson cycle is approached if a large number of stages of compression and expansion are used. This is shown in Fig. 2.20. In practice the economical limit is two or three stages. There are losses and pressure drops in the turbine and compressor stages.

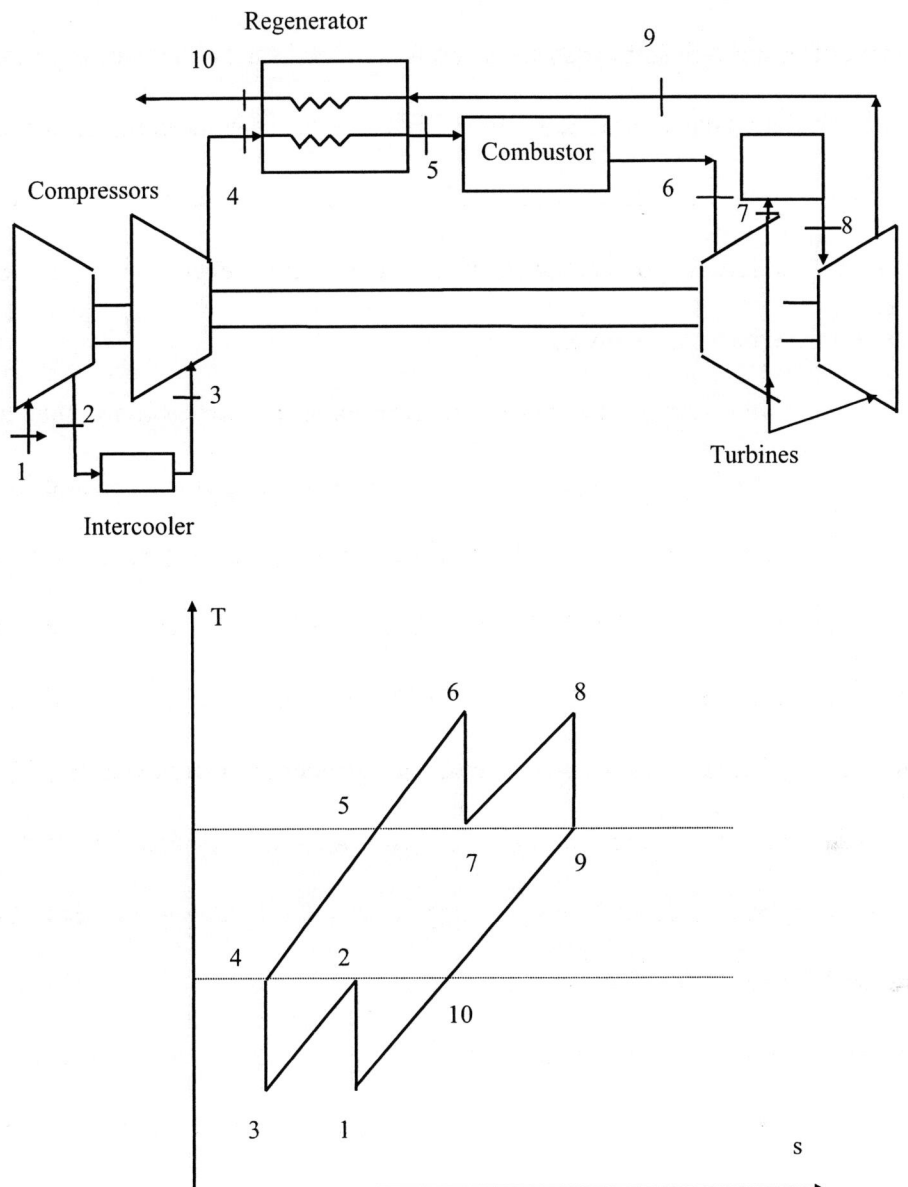

Figure 2.19 Ideal regenerative Brayton cycle with reheat and intercooling.

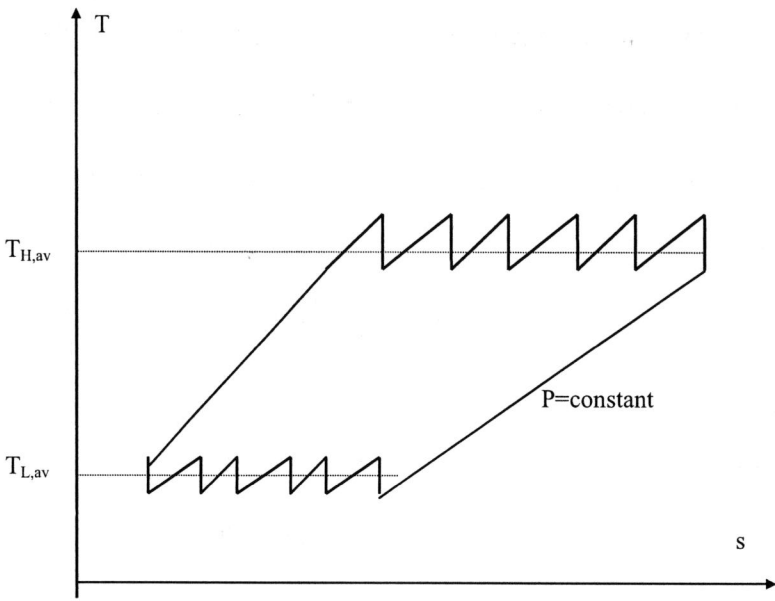

Figure 2.20 Gas-turbine with many stages approaches the Ericsson cycle.

Example 2.7

Problem

An ideal gas-turbine cycle with an overall pressure ratio of 10, has 2 stages of compression and two stages of expansion. At each stage of the compressor, air enters at 298 K. At each stage of the turbine, air enters at 1350 K. Determine the back work ratio and the thermal efficiency of the cycle. If an ideal regenerator with 100 percent effectiveness is added, compute the thermal efficiency.

Solution

Assumptions: (1) Each component is analyzed as a control volume at steady state.

(2) Pressure drops across the heat exchangers are neglected.

(3) Changes in K.E. and P.E. are negligible.

(4) The air is modeled as an ideal gas.

(5) For a two-stage compression and expansion gas-turbine cycle, the work input is minimized and the work output is maximized when both stages of the compressor and the turbine have the same pressure ratio.

Analysis:

$$\frac{P_2}{P_1} = \frac{P_4}{P_3} = \sqrt{10} = 3.16 \text{ and } \frac{P_6}{P_7} = \frac{P_8}{P_9} = \sqrt{10} = 3.16$$

Since the air enters each stage of the compressor at the same temperature, and each stage has a hundred percent adiabatic efficiency, the temperature (and hence enthalpy) of the air at the outlet of each compression stage will be identical. A similar deduction is true for the turbine.

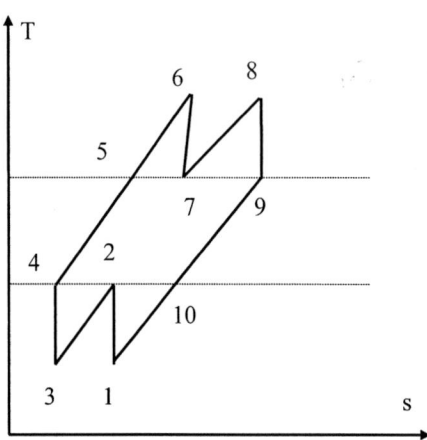

Inlets: $T_1 = T_3$, $h_1 = h_3$ and $T_6 = T_8$, $h_6 = h_8$

Outlets: $T_2 = T_4$, $h_2 = h_4$ and $T_7 = T_9$, $h_7 = h_9$

The work input at each stage of the compressor will be the same, and the work output from each stage of the turbine will be the same.

Since $T_1 = 298$ K, $h_1 = 298.61$ kJ/kg, $P_{r1} = 1.0907$

$$P_{r2} = \frac{P_2}{P_1} P_{r1} = \sqrt{10}(1.0907) = 3.449$$

Hence, $T_2 = 413.6$ K, $h_2 = 415.23$ kJ/kg

Since $T_6 = 1350$ K, $h_6 = 1455.61$ kJ/kg, $P_{r6} = 310.89$

$$P_{r7} = \frac{P_7}{P_6} P_{r6} = \frac{1}{\sqrt{10}}(310.89) = 98.3$$

Hence, $T_7 = 1017.6$ K, $h_7 = 1066.5$ kJ/kg

The compressor work and turbine work are

$$w_c = 2(h_2 - h_1) = 2(116.62) = 233.2 \text{ kJ/kg}$$

$$w_t = 2(h_6 - h_7) = 2(389.11) = 778.2 \text{ kJ/kg}$$

The net work is $w_{net} = w_t - w_c = 545$ kJ/kg.

The heat input is $q_{in} = (h_6 - h_4) - (h_8 - h_7)$

$$= (1455.61 - 415.23) + (1455.61 - 1066.5)$$

$$= 1429.49 \text{ kJ/kg}.$$

Thus, $\text{bwr} = \dfrac{w_c}{w_t} = \dfrac{233.2}{778.2} = 0.30.$

The thermal efficiency is

$$\eta = \frac{w_{net}}{q_{in}} = \frac{545}{1429.49} = 0.38.$$

Comparing these figures with those in Ex. 2.4, the back work ratio is decreased but the thermal efficiency is decreased as well. The multistage compression with intercooling and multistage expansion with reheating helps the back work ratio, but is not good for the thermal efficiency.

When an ideal regenerator is added, the turbine work and the compressor work are not affected. In the ideal regenerator, the compressed air is heated to the turbine exit temperature T_9 before entry into the combustion chamber. Hence,

$h_5 = h_7 = h_9.$

The heat input is $q_{in} = (h_6 - h_5) + (h_8 - h_7)$

$$= 389.11 + 389.11 = 778.22 \text{ kJ/kg}.$$

The thermal efficiency is

$$\eta = \frac{w_{net}}{q_{in}} = \frac{545}{778.22} = 0.70.$$

The thermal efficiency is increased greatly by regeneration. Hence, intercooling and reheating should be used in conjunction with regeneration for best effect.

If more stages are added, the capital costs will increase and there will be more pressure losses at each stage. The ultimate efficiency achievable is the efficiency of the corresponding Ericsson cycle, which is

$$\eta_{th,Ericsson} = \eta_{th,Carnot} = 1 - \frac{T_L}{T_H} = 1 - \frac{298}{1350} = 0.779.$$

The efficiency does not increase that much beyond the second stage of compression and expansion, hence in practice no more than two stages are used.

2.11 Jet Propulsion Cycles

In jet propulsion cycles, the work done by the turbine is just enough to drive the compressor. The gases expanding in the turbine perform just enough work to equal the compressor work. The exhaust pressure of the turbine is above that of the surroundings, so the gas is expanded in a nozzle to the pressure of the surroundings. As the gases leave at a high velocity, the change in momentum of the gases undergo results in a thrust upon the aircraft into which the engine has been installed. The pressures at the inlet and the exit of a turbojet engine are identical (surrounding pressure), so the net thrust developed by the engine is

$$F = (\dot{m}V)_{exit} - (\dot{m}V)_{inlet} = \dot{m}(V_{exit} - V_{inlet}) \qquad (N) \qquad (2.41)$$

where V_{inlet} is the inlet velocity of the air and V_{exit} is the exit velocity of the exhaust gases, both relative to the aircraft.

The propulsive power $\dot{W}_p$, is the propulsive force (thrust) multiplied by the distance this thrust acts on the aircraft per unit time. In other words, this is the thrust times the aircraft velocity:

$$\dot{W}_p = (F)V_{aircraft} = \dot{m}(V_{exit} - V_{inlet})V_{aircraft} \quad (kW) \qquad (2.42)$$

The net work developed by a turbojet engine is zero; thus, we cannot evaluate it the same way as we do a stationary gas turbine. Instead, we define a propulsive efficiency as an evaluation parameter. This is defined in the general method of defining efficiency, which is the ratio of the desired output to the required input. The desired output is the power produced to propel the aircraft $\dot{W}_p$, and the required input is the thermal energy of the fuel released in the combustion process $\dot{Q}_{in}$. The propulsive efficiency is thus

$$\eta_p = \frac{\text{Propulsive power}}{\text{Energy input rate}} = \frac{\dot{W}_p}{\dot{Q}_{in}} \qquad (2.43)$$

The propulsive efficiency is to compare the propulsive energy with the energy input during the combustion process. The schematic and T-s diagram of the ideal jet-propulsion cycle is shown in Fig. 2.21.

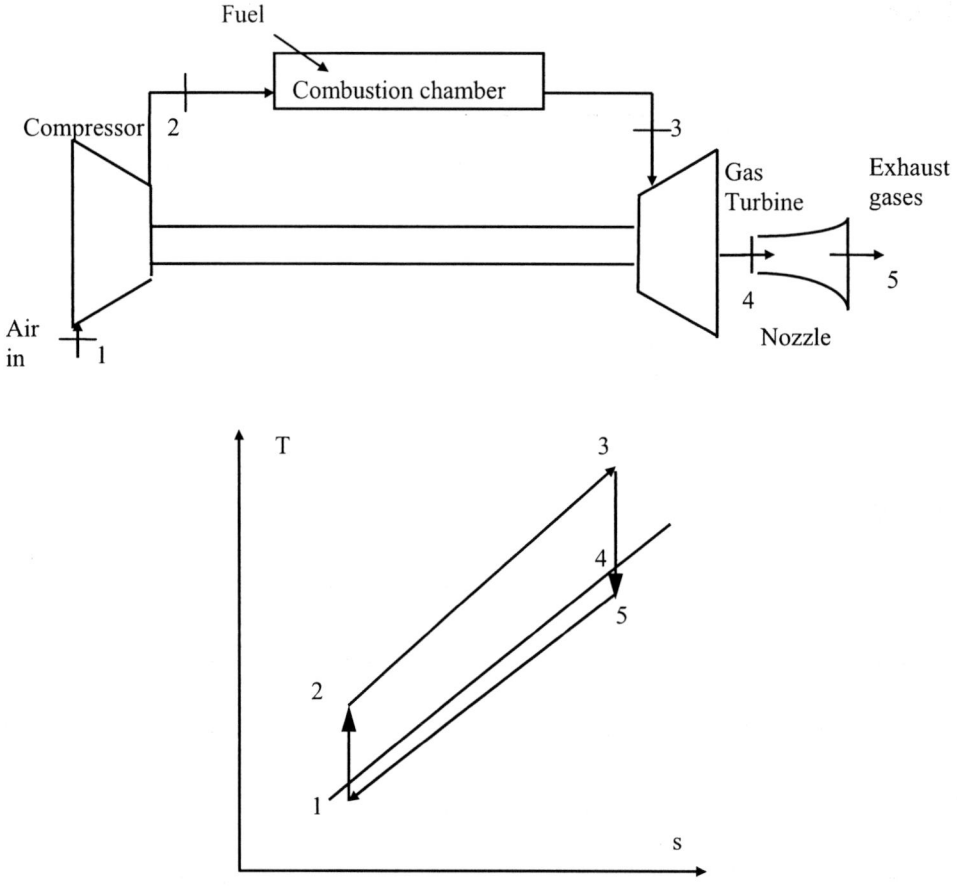

Figure 2.21   Ideal jet propulsion cycle.

Example 2.8

Problem

An aircraft with a turbojet engine flies with a speed of 540 mph (792 ft/s) at an altitude where the air enters the engine at 12 lb$_f$/in.^{2}, 440°R. The compressor has a pressure ratio of 9, and the temperature of the gases at the turbine inlet is 2300°R. The compressor, turbine, diffuser, and nozzle processes are isentropic, and the gases undergo an isobaric process in the combustor. Determine the principal states of the gas before and after each system component. Hence, calculate (a) the velocity of the gases at the nozzle exit, and (b) the propulsive efficiency of the cycle.

Solution

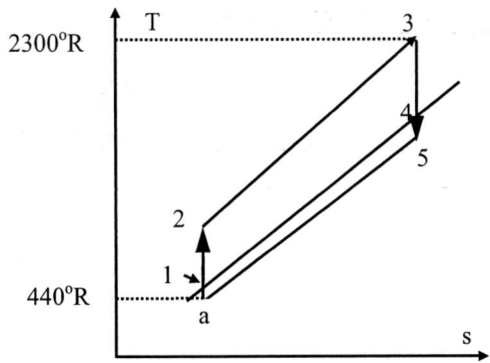

Assumptions:

(1) Each component is analyzed as a control volume at steady state.

(2) The turbine work output is just enough to drive the compressor.

(3) Kinetic energy effects are negligible, except at the inlet and outlet of the engine. Potential energy effects are negligible throughout.

(4) The working fluid is modeled as air behaving like an ideal gas.

Analysis:

<u>Process a-1</u>.

We can consider the air as moving towards a stationary aircraft at a velocity of V_1 = 792 ft/s. In the ideal case, the air will leave the diffuser with a very small velocity ($V_2 \approx 0$). Applying the first law to the diffuser,

$$q_{a1} - w_{a1} = h_1 - h_a + \frac{V_1^2 - V_a^2}{2}$$

$$h_1 = h_a + \frac{V_a^2}{2}$$

With h_a from the thermodynamic tables and the given value of V_a,

$$h_1 = 105.2 \text{ Btu/lb}_m + \left[\frac{(792)^2}{2}\right]\left(\frac{\text{ft}^2}{\text{s}^2}\right)\left(\frac{1 \text{ lb}_f}{32.2 \text{ lb.ft/s}^2}\right)\left(\frac{1 \text{ Btu}}{778 \text{ ft.lb}_f}\right)$$

$$= 105.2 + 12.5 = 117.7 \text{ Btu/lb}_m$$

From the thermodynamic tables, $P_{r1} = 0.8712$. The flow through the diffuser is isentropic. The pressure P_1 is hence

$$P_1 = \frac{P_{r1}}{P_{ra}} P_a$$

Since $P_{ra} = 0.6776$,

$$P_1 = \frac{0.8712}{0.6776}(12 \text{ lb}_f/\text{in}^2) = 15.43 \text{ lb}_f/\text{in}^2$$

Process 1-2.

The compressor pressure ratio is 9, hence the pressure at state 2 is

$$P_2 = 9(15.43 \text{ lb}_f/\text{in.}^2) = 138.87 \text{ lb}_f/\text{in.}^2$$

The flow through the compressor is isentropic. Thus

$$P_{r2} = P_{r1}\frac{P_2}{P_1} = 0.8712(9) = 7.841$$

From the thermodynamic tables, we obtain $h_2 = 225.7 \text{ Btu/lb}_m$.

Process 2-3.

At state 3, the temperature is known to be at $2300°R$. From the thermodynamic tables, $h_3 = 588.82 \text{ Btu/lb}_m$. It is given that $P_3 = P_2$. It is also given that

$$\frac{\dot{W}_t}{\dot{m}} = \frac{\dot{W}_c}{\dot{m}}$$

$$h_3 - h_4 = h_2 - h_1$$

Process 3-4.

Solving for h_4,

$$h_4 = h_3 + h_1 - h_2$$

$$= 588.82 + 117.7 - 225.7$$

$$= 480.82 \text{ Btu/lb}_m$$

From the thermodynamic tables, $P_{r4} = 117$.

The turbine expansion is isentropic, hence

$$P_4 = P_3 \frac{P_{r4}}{P_{r3}}$$

With $P_3 = P_2$ and P_r value from the thermodynamic tables,

$$P_4 = (138.87 \text{ lb}_f/\text{in.}^2)\frac{117}{247.4} = 65.67 \text{ lb}_f/\text{in}^2$$

Process 4-5.

The nozzle expansion is isentropic to $P_5 = 12 \text{ lb}_f/\text{in.}^2$

Thus, $P_{r5} = P_{r4}\dfrac{P_5}{P_4} = (117)\dfrac{12}{65.67} = 21.38$

From the thermodynamic tables, $h_5 = 299.86 \text{ Btu/lb}_m$.

(a) For the nozzle,

$$q_{45} - w_{45} = h_4 - h_5 + \frac{V_4^2 - V_5^2}{2}$$

$V_4 = 0$ by assumption (3). Hence,

$$V_5 = \sqrt{2(h_4 - h_5)}$$

$$= \sqrt{2(480.82 - 299.86)\frac{\text{Btu}}{\text{lb}}\left(\frac{32.2 \text{ lb.ft/s}^2}{1 \text{ lb}_f}\right)\left(\frac{778 \text{ ft.lb}_f}{1 \text{ Btu}}\right)}$$

$$= 3011 \text{ ft/s } (2053 \text{ mph}).$$

(b) To find the propulsive efficiency of the engine, we need the propulsive power and the heat transfer rate.

$$\dot{W}_p = \dot{m}(V_{outlet} - V_{inlet})V_{aircraft}$$
$$= \dot{m}[(3011-792)\text{ft/s}](792\text{ ft/s})\left(\frac{1\text{ Btu/lb}_m}{25,037\text{ ft}^2/\text{s}^2}\right)$$
$$= 70.19\,\dot{m}\text{ Btu/lb}_m$$

$$\dot{Q}_{in} = \dot{m}(h_3 - h_2)$$
$$= (588.82 - 225.7)\,\dot{m}\,\frac{\text{Btu}}{\text{lb}_m}$$
$$= 363.12\,\dot{m}\,\frac{\text{Btu}}{\text{lb}_m}$$

Substituting in the above expression,

$$\eta_p = \frac{70.19}{363.12} = 19.3\%$$

It can be seen that only 19.3 percent of the energy input is used to move the aircraft. The rest of the energy has served to increase the energy of the gases leaving the aircraft.

2.12 Second Law Analysis of Gas Power Cycles

The ideal Carnot, Ericsson, and Stirling cycles are totally reversible, and so they act as the ultimate standards for comparison. There are no irreversibilities in these cycles. The ideal Otto, Diesel, Dual and Brayton cycles are internally reversible, and they do include irreversibilities external to the system. These irreversibilities include combustion irreversibilities, irreversible heat transfer, etc.

The relations for availability (exergy) and irreversibility were developed in the first book on thermodynamics by the author. The irreversibility for a closed system may be expressed as

$$I = T_o S_{gen} = T_o(\Delta S_{sys} - S_{in} + S_{out}) = T_o\left[(S_2 - S_1)_{sys} - \frac{Q_{in}}{T_{b,in}} + \frac{Q_{out}}{T_{b,out}}\right] \quad (kJ)$$

(2.44)

where $T_{b,in}$ and $T_{b,out}$ are the temperatures of the system boundary where heat is entering into and going out of the system, respectively.

The irreversibility of a cycle is the sum of the irreversibilities of the processes that make up that cycle. In addition, the irreversibility of the whole cycle may be found by considering the whole cycle as a single process. For a cycle, the initial and final states are the same; so $s_e = s_i$. Therefore, the irreversibility of a cycle is dependent on the heat transfer with the high- and low-temperature reservoirs and the magnitude of the temperatures. On a per unit mass basis, it may be expressed as

$$i = T_o\left[\sum \frac{q_{out}}{T_{b,out}} - \sum \frac{q_{in}}{T_{b,in}}\right] \quad (kJ/kg) \quad (2.45)$$

When there is only one source at T_H and one sink at T_L, the irreversibility is

$$i = T_o\left[\frac{q_{out}}{T_L} - \frac{q_{in}}{T_H}\right] \quad (kJ/kg) \quad (2.46)$$

The specific availability of a closed system and the flow availability of a fluid stream have been previously defined as

$a = (u - u_o) + P_o(v - v_o) - T_o(s - s_o) + V^2/2 + gz \quad (kJ/kg)$

$a_f = (h - h_o) - T_o(s - s_o) + V^2/2 + gz \quad (kJ/kg) \quad (2.47)$

where P_o and T_o are conditions of the reference state. By finding the availability change of the working fluid in any process, the reversible work for that process can be determined.

PROBLEMS

Air Standard Otto, Diesel and Dual Cycles

2.1. An ideal Otto cycle uses air as the working fluid. At the start of the compression process, the air is at 17°C and 100 kPa. The compression ratio of the cycle is 7, and the cylinder volume is 600 c.c. The maximum temperature of the cycle is 1777°C. Determine (a) the end states of each process, (b) the thermal efficiency, and (c) the mean effective pressure.

2.2. An ideal Otto cycle uses air as the working fluid. At the start of the compression process, the air is at 60°F and 1 atm. The compression ratio of the cycle is 7, and the cylinder volume is 0.018 ft^3. The maximum temperature of the cycle is 3240°F. Determine (a) the end states of each process, (b) the thermal efficiency, and (c) the mean effective pressure.

2.3. Air is the working fluid in an ideal Diesel cycle with a compression ratio of 20 and a cut-off ratio of 2. The air at the beginning of the compression process is at 27°C, and 100kPa. Calculate (a) the end states of each process, (b) the thermal efficiency, and (c) the mean effective pressure.

2.4. Air is the working fluid in an ideal Diesel cycle with a compression ratio of 20 and a cut-off ratio of 2. The air at the beginning of the compression process is at 80°F, and 1 atm. Calculate (a) the end states of each process, (b) the thermal efficiency, and (c) the mean effective pressure.

2.5. The air at the start of the compression process of an air-choked dual cycle with a compression ratio of 20, is at 27°C, and 100 kPa. The pressure ratio for the isochoric portion of the heating process is 2.0:1, and the volume ratio for the isobaric portion of that heating process is 1.1:1. Calculate (a) the end states of each process, (b) the thermal efficiency, and (c) the mean effective pressure.

2.6. The air at the start of the compression process of an air-choked dual cycle with a compression ratio of 20, is at 80°F, and 1 atm. The pressure ratio for the isochoric portion of the heating process is 2.0:1, and the volume ratio for the isobaric portion of that heating process is 1.1:1. Calculate (a) the end states of each process, (b) the thermal efficiency, and (c) the mean effective pressure.

Gas Brayton Cycle

2.7. An on-land power plant operating on an ideal Brayton cycle has a pressure ratio of 8. The compressor inlet state of the air is 303 K, 100 kPa. The turbine inlet temperature is 1380 K. Determine (a) the states at the end of each process, (b) the back work ratio, (c) the thermal efficiency.

2.8. An on-land power plant operating on an ideal Brayton cycle has a pressure ratio of 8. The compressor inlet state of the air is 550°R, 1atm. The turbine inlet temperature is 2500°R. Determine (a) the states at the end of each process, (b) the back work ratio, (c) the thermal efficiency.

2.9. In Problem 2.7, the turbine and the compressor have isentropic efficiencies of 85% and 80% respectively. Determine (a) the states at the end of each process, (b) the back work ratio, (c) the thermal efficiency, and (d) the irreversibility rates in the turbine and in the compressor. Take $T_o = 25°C$, $P_o = 100$ kPa.

2.10. In Problem 2.8, the turbine and the compressor have isentropic efficiencies of 85% and 80% respectively. Determine (a) the states at the end of each process,

(b) the back work ratio, (c) the thermal efficiency, and (d) the irreversibility rates in the turbine and in the compressor. Take $T_o = 77°F$, $P_o = 1$ atm.

2.11. A regenerator of effectiveness 72 percent is installed in the gas-turbine plant of Problem 2.7. Determine the thermal efficiency of the plant.

2.12. A regenerator of effectiveness 82 percent is installed in the gas-turbine plant of Problem 2.8. Determine the thermal efficiency of the plant.

2.13. An ideal gas-turbine cycle with an overall pressure ratio of 8, has 2 stages of compression and two stages of expansion. At each stage of the compressor, air enters at 303 K. At each stage of the turbine, air enters at 1380 K. Determine the back work ratio and the thermal efficiency of the cycle. If an ideal regenerator with 100 percent effectiveness is added, compute the thermal efficiency.

2.14. An ideal gas-turbine cycle with an overall pressure ratio of 8, has 2 stages of compression and two stages of expansion. At each stage of the compressor, air enters at 550°R. At each stage of the turbine, air enters at 2500°R. Determine the back work ratio and the thermal efficiency of the cycle. If an ideal regenerator with 100 percent effectiveness is added, compute the thermal efficiency.

3. THERMODYNAMIC PROPERTY RELATIONS

3.1 The Maxwell Relations

The Maxwell relations are the equations that relate the partial derivatives of properties P, v, T, and s of a simple compressible system to each other. They are derived from the four Gibbs equations.

If z is a function of x and y, then

$$dz = \left(\frac{\partial z}{\partial x}\right)_y dx + \left(\frac{\partial z}{\partial y}\right)_x dy \qquad (3.1)$$

or

$$dz = Mdx + Ndy \qquad (3.2)$$

But

$$\left(\frac{\partial M}{\partial y}\right)_x = \frac{\partial^2 z}{\partial x\, \partial y} \quad \text{and} \quad \left(\frac{\partial N}{\partial x}\right)_y = \frac{\partial^2 z}{\partial y\, \partial x}$$

so

$$\left(\frac{\partial M}{\partial y}\right)_x = \left(\frac{\partial N}{\partial x}\right)_y \qquad (3.3)$$

Two of the Gibbs relations are expressed as

$$du = Tds - Pdv \qquad (3.4)$$

$$dh = Tds + vdP \qquad (3.5)$$

The other two Gibbs relations are based on two new combination properties. The Helmholtz function b and the Gibbs function g, are defined as

$$b = u - Ts \qquad (3.6)$$

$$g = h - Ts \qquad (3.7)$$

Differentiating, we obtain

$$db = du - Tds - sdT$$

$$dg = dh - Tds - sdT$$

From these relations and Eqs. (3.4) and (3.5), we obtain the other two Gibbs relations for simple compressible systems:

$$db = -sdT - Pdv \quad (3.8)$$

$$dg = -sdT + vdP \quad (3.9)$$

It can be seen that the four Gibbs relations are of the form of Eq. (3.2), so the relation in Eq. (3.3) is true. Since u,h,b,and g are properties and thus have exact differentials, we apply Eq. (3.3) to each of them, to obtain

$$\left(\frac{\partial T}{\partial v}\right)_s = -\left(\frac{\partial P}{\partial s}\right)_v \quad (3.10)$$

$$\left(\frac{\partial T}{\partial P}\right)_s = \left(\frac{\partial v}{\partial s}\right)_P \quad (3.11)$$

$$\left(\frac{\partial s}{\partial v}\right)_T = \left(\frac{\partial P}{\partial T}\right)_v \quad (3.12)$$

$$\left(\frac{\partial s}{\partial P}\right)_T = -\left(\frac{\partial v}{\partial T}\right)_P \quad (3.13)$$

These are called the Maxwell relations. They are very valuable in thermodynamics because they allow the change of entropy to be determined, which cannot be measured directly, by simply measuring the changes in properties P, v, and T.

Example 3.1

Problem

Consider air as an ideal gas with molecular weight of 28.97, and at a state characterized by T = 400 K and v = 1.0 m³/kg. Estimate the change in pressure of the gas if the state of the gas changes to 403 K and 1.01 m³/kg. Use two methods, to evaluate the change.

Solution

One method of estimation is to use the ideal gas equation. The other method is to use Eq. (3.1).

(a) For an ideal gas, $Pv = RT$

$$P = \frac{RT}{v} \qquad (a)$$

Initially, $P_1 = 0.287 \dfrac{kPa.m^3}{kg.K} \times 400\,K \times \dfrac{kg}{1\,m^3} = 114.8\,kPa$

Finally, $P_2 = 0.287 \dfrac{kPa.m^3}{kg.K} \times 403\,K \times \dfrac{kg}{1.01\,m^3} = 114.5\,kPa$

Change in pressure = (114.5 - 114.8) kPa = -0.3 kPa.

(b) Apply Eq. (3.1) to Eq. (a) above, and use average values for T and v.

Then, $dP = \left(\dfrac{\partial P}{\partial T}\right)_v dT + \left(\dfrac{\partial P}{\partial v}\right)_T dv = \dfrac{R\,dT}{v} - \dfrac{RT\,dv}{v^2} \qquad (b)$

$$dP = \left(0.287 \dfrac{kPa.m^3}{kg.K}\right)\left(\dfrac{3\,K}{1.005\,m^3/kg} - \dfrac{(401.5\,K)(0.01\,m^3/kg)}{(1.005\,m^3/kg)^2}\right)$$

$dP = (0.287)(-0.99007)\,kPa = -0.28\,kPa.$

Note that the changes in pressure estimated by both methods are approximately the same.

Example 3.2

Problem

Show that $\left(\dfrac{\partial T}{\partial v}\right)_s = -\left(\dfrac{\partial P}{\partial s}\right)_v$ is valid for steam at 6.7 kJ/(kg.K) and 0.2 m³/kg.

Solution

$$\left(\frac{\Delta T}{\Delta v}\right)_s = -\left(\frac{\Delta P}{\Delta s}\right)_v \text{ is an approximation of } \left(\frac{\partial T}{\partial v}\right)_s = -\left(\frac{\partial P}{\partial s}\right)_v$$

We can use the computerized thermodynamic property tables to show the validity of the approximate equation.

Left-hand-side, LHS $= \left(\dfrac{\Delta T}{\Delta v}\right)_{s=6.7\frac{kJ}{kg.k}}$

$$= \left(\frac{(T_{v=0.21} - T_{v=0.19})K}{(0.21 - 0.19)\dfrac{m^3}{kg}}\right)_{s=6.7\frac{kJ}{kg.K}}$$

$$= \left(\frac{(199 - 213)K}{0.02\dfrac{m^3}{kg}}\right) = -700\frac{kg.K}{m^3}$$

Right-hand-side, RHS $= -\left(\dfrac{\Delta P}{\Delta s}\right)_{v=0.2\frac{m^3}{kg}}$

$$= -\left[\frac{P_{s=6.8} - P_{s=6.6}}{(6.8 - 6.6)\dfrac{kJ}{kg.K}}\right]_{v=0.2\frac{m^3}{kg}}$$

$$= -\left(\frac{(1118 - 973)kPa}{0.2\dfrac{kJ}{kg.K}}\right) = -725\frac{kg.K}{m^3}$$

The two values are within 3 % of each other, and the difference is due to the approximate equation used. The difference may also be decreased by using smaller intervals for Δs

and Δv. Since the difference is small, it may be said that the first Maxwell relation is valid for steam at the state specified.

Example 3.3

Problem

Show that $\left(\dfrac{\partial T}{\partial P}\right)_s = -\left(\dfrac{\partial v}{\partial s}\right)_P$ is valid for steam at 6.7 kJ/(kg.K) and 1000 kPa.

Solution

$\left(\dfrac{\Delta T}{\Delta P}\right)_s = -\left(\dfrac{\Delta v}{\Delta s}\right)_P$ is an approximation of $\left(\dfrac{\partial T}{\partial P}\right)_s = -\left(\dfrac{\partial v}{\partial s}\right)_P$

We can use the computerized thermodynamic property tables to show the validity of the approximate equation.

Left-hand-side, LHS $= \left(\dfrac{\Delta T}{\Delta P}\right)_{s=6.7\,\frac{kJ}{kg.K}}$

$= \left(\dfrac{(T_{P=1050} - T_{P=950})K}{(1050-950)\,kPa}\right)_{s=6.7\,\frac{kJ}{kg.K}}$

$= \left(\dfrac{(206.6 - 195.6)K}{100\,kPa}\right) = 0.11\,\dfrac{K}{kPa}$

Right-hand-side, RHS $= \left(\dfrac{\Delta v}{\Delta s}\right)_{P=1000kPa}$

$= -\left[\dfrac{v_{s=6.8} - v_{s=6.6}}{(6.8-6.6)\,\dfrac{kJ}{kg.K}}\right]_{P=1000kPa}$

$$= \left(\frac{(0.2179 - 0.19587)\frac{m^3}{kg}}{0.2 \frac{kJ}{kg \cdot K}} \right) = 0.11 \frac{K}{kPa}$$

Since there is no difference between the LHS and the RHS, it may be said that the second Maxwell relation is valid for steam at the state specified.

Example 3.4

Problem

Show that $\left(\frac{\partial s}{\partial v}\right)_T = \left(\frac{\partial P}{\partial T}\right)_v$ is valid for steam at 200°C and 0.2 m³/kg.

Solution

$\left(\frac{\Delta s}{\Delta v}\right)_T = \left(\frac{\Delta P}{\Delta T}\right)_v$ is an approximation of $\left(\frac{\partial s}{\partial v}\right)_T = \left(\frac{\partial P}{\partial T}\right)_v$.

We can use the computerized thermodynamic property tables to show the validity of the approximate equation.

Left-hand-side, LHS $= \left(\frac{\Delta s}{\Delta v}\right)_{T=200°C}$

$$= \left(\frac{(s_{v=0.21} - s_{v=0.19})K}{(0.21 - 0.19)\frac{m^3}{kg}} \right)_{T=200°C}$$

$$= \left(\frac{(6.704 - 6.651)\frac{kJ}{kg \cdot K}}{0.02 \frac{m^3}{kg}} \right) = 2.65 \frac{kJ}{m^3 \cdot K}$$

Right-hand-side, RHS $= \left(\frac{\Delta P}{\Delta T}\right)_{v=0.2 \frac{m^3}{kg}}$

$$= \left[\frac{P_{T=201°C} - P_{T=199°C}}{(201-199)°C}\right]_{v=0.2\frac{m^3}{kg}}$$

$$= \left(\frac{(1030.5 - 1025.2)\text{kPa}}{2\text{ K}}\right) = 2.65\frac{\text{kJ}}{\text{m}^3\cdot\text{K}}$$

Since there is no difference between the LHS and the RHS, it may be said that the third Maxwell relation is valid for steam at the state specified.

Example 3.5

Problem

Problem

Show that $\left(\frac{\partial s}{\partial P}\right)_T = -\left(\frac{\partial v}{\partial T}\right)_P$ is valid for steam at 200°C and 1000 kPa.

Solution

$\left(\frac{\Delta s}{\Delta P}\right)_T = -\left(\frac{\Delta v}{\Delta T}\right)_P$ is an approximation of $\left(\frac{\partial s}{\partial P}\right)_T = -\left(\frac{\partial v}{\partial T}\right)_P$

We can use the computerized thermodynamic property tables to show the validity of the approximate equation.

Left-hand-side, LHS $= \left(\frac{\Delta s}{\Delta P}\right)_{T=200°C}$

$$= \left(\frac{(s_{P=1050} - s_{P=950})\frac{\text{kJ}}{\text{kg.K}}}{(1050-950)\text{kPa}}\right)_{T=200°C}$$

$$= \left(\frac{(6.667 - 6.722)\frac{\text{kJ}}{\text{kg.K}}}{100\text{ kPa}}\right) = -0.00055\frac{\text{m}^3}{\text{kg.K}}$$

Right-hand-side, $\text{RHS} = -\left(\dfrac{\Delta v}{\Delta T}\right)_{P=1000\text{kPa}}$

$$= -\left[\dfrac{v_{T=201°C} - v_{T=199°C}}{(201-199)°C}\right]_{P=1000\text{kPa}}$$

$$= -\left(\dfrac{(0.2065 - 0.2054)\dfrac{m^3}{kg}}{2\text{ K}}\right) = -0.00055\,\dfrac{m^3}{kg\cdot K}$$

Since there is no difference between the LHS and the RHS, it may be said that the fourth Maxwell relation is valid for steam at the state specified.

3.2 The Clapeyron Equation

The Maxwell relations are important because they may be used to derive other useful thermodynamic relations. The Clapeyron equation, which may be so derived, allows the enthalpy change associated with a phase change to be determined from the values of P, v, and T.

Look at the third Maxwell relation, Eq. (3.12),

$$\left(\dfrac{\partial P}{\partial T}\right)_v = \left(\dfrac{\partial s}{\partial v}\right)_T$$

During a phase-change process, the pressure is the saturation pressure, which depends on the temperature only and not dependent on the specific volume. In other words, the partial derivative $(\partial P/\partial T)_v$ is the total derivative $(dP/dT)_{sat}$, which is the slope of the saturation curve on a P-T diagram. This slope or gradient is not dependent on the specific volume, and thus it can be treated as a constant during the integration of Eq. (3.12) between two saturation states at the same temperature. For example, in an isothermal liquid-vapor phase-change process, integration of Eq. (3.12) gives

$$s_g - s_f = \left(\frac{dP}{dT}\right)_{sat} (v_g - v_f) \qquad (3.14)$$

or
$$\left(\frac{dP}{dT}\right)_{sat} = \frac{s_{fg}}{v_{fg}} \qquad (3.15)$$

The pressure remains constant during this process. Thus, from Eq. (3.5),

$$dh = Tds$$

$$\int_f^g dh = \int_f^g Tds$$

$$h_{fg} = Ts_{fg}$$

Substituting this in Eq. (3.15), we get

$$\left(\frac{dP}{dT}\right)_{sat} = \frac{h_{fg}}{Tv_{fg}} \qquad (3.16)$$

which is the Clapeyron equation, named after the French engineer and physicist E. Clapeyron (1799-1864). This relation allows us to determine the enthalpy of vaporization h_{fg} at a given temperature by measuring the slope of the saturation curve on a P-T diagram and the specific volume of saturated vapor and of saturated liquid at that given temperature.

The Clapeyron equation is valid for any phase-change process that takes place at constant temperature and pressure. It may be expressed in a general form as follows, where the subscripts 1 and 2 indicate the two phases:

$$\left(\frac{dP}{dT}\right)_{sat} = \frac{h_{12}}{Tv_{12}} \qquad (3.17)$$

Example 3.6

Problem

Estimate the enthalpy of vaporization for ammonia at 10°C, and compare the value with that in the property tables.

Solution

Use the Clapeyron equation,

$$h_{fg} = T v_{fg} \left(\frac{dP}{dT} \right)_{sat}$$

From the tables, $v_{fg} = (v_g - v_f)_{at\ 10°C}$

$$= (0.2055 - 0.0016005) \frac{m^3}{kg} = 0.2039 \frac{m^3}{kg}$$

$$\left(\frac{dP}{dT} \right)_{sat, 10°C} \approx \left(\frac{\Delta P}{\Delta T} \right)_{sat, 10°C} = \frac{P_{sat\ at\ 11°C} - P_{sat\ at\ 9°C}}{11°C - 9°C}$$

$$= \frac{(636.4 - 593.9)\,kPa}{2°C}$$

$$= 21.25 \frac{kPa}{K}$$

$$h_{fg} = (283K)\left(0.2039 \frac{m^3}{kg} \right)\left(21.25 \frac{kPa}{K} \right)\left(\frac{1\,kJ}{1\,kPa.m^3} \right) = 1226.2 \frac{kJ}{kg}$$

The property tables give h_{fg} at 10°C as 1225.1 kJ/kg. The difference is the result of using the approximation for the slope of the saturation curve at 10°C.

The Clapeyron equation can be made simple for liquid-vapor and solid-vapor phase changes by using some approximations. At low pressures $v_g \gg v_f$, so $v_{fg} \approx v_g$. If the vapor may be treated as an ideal gas, $v_g = RT/P$. Putting these approximations into Eq. (3.16),

$$\left(\frac{dP}{dT} \right)_{sat} = \frac{P h_{fg}}{RT^2} \qquad (3.18)$$

or
$$\left(\frac{dP}{P}\right)_{sat} = \frac{h_{fg}}{R}\left(\frac{dT}{T^2}\right)_{sat} \qquad (3.19)$$

When temperature intervals are small, h_{fg} can be taken as a constant at some mean value. Integrating this equation between two saturation states gives

$$\ln\left(\frac{P_2}{P_1}\right)_{sat} \approx \frac{h_{fg}}{R}\left(\frac{1}{T_1} - \frac{1}{T_2}\right)_{sat} \qquad (3.20)$$

This relation is named the Clausius-Clapeyron equation. It can be utilized in finding the variation of saturation pressure with temperature. In addition, it can be used in the solid-vapor region by replacing h_{fg} by h_{ig} (the enthalpy of sublimation) of the substance.

Example 3.7

Problem

The property tables show that for ammonia, at -50°C, h_{fg}=1416.20 kJ/kg, P_{sat} = 40.86 kPa. Estimate the saturation pressure of ammonia at -60°C.

Solution

The Clausius-Clapeyron equation gives

$$\ln\left(\frac{P_2}{P_1}\right)_{sat} \approx \frac{h_{fg}}{R}\left(\frac{1}{T_1} - \frac{1}{T_2}\right)_{sat}$$

For ammonia, $R = \dfrac{8.314}{17}\dfrac{kJ}{kg.K} = 0.489\dfrac{kJ}{kg.K}$

$$\ln\left(\frac{P_2}{40.86\,kPa}\right) \approx \frac{1416.20\,\frac{kJ}{kg}}{0.489\,\frac{kJ}{kg.K}}\left(\frac{1}{223\,K} - \frac{1}{213\,K}\right) = -0.6097$$

$P_2 \approx 22.2\,kPa$

The actual value of the saturation pressure, obtained from another reliable source, is 21.9 kPa. The error is about 1.4%, which is acceptable for many practical situations. With linear extrapolation, one gets 13.5 kPa, which has an error of 38.3%.

3.3 General Relations for Thermodynamic Properties

The state of a simple compressible system is completely specified by two independent, intensive properties. This means that in theory, we can calculate all the properties of a system at any state if two independent, intensive properties are known. The internal energy, enthalpy, and entropy cannot be measured directly. These properties have to be calculated from the measurable properties. This in turn depends on relations between the two groups. In this section, general relations for changes in internal energy, enthalpy, and entropy are developed in terms of pressure, specific volume, temperature, and specific heats. Some general relations involving specific heats are also developed. The relations are for the changes in these properties. The property values at specified state can be determined after the choice of a reference state, which is arbitrary.

3.3.1 Internal Energy Changes

Choose the internal energy to be a function of T and v, i.e. $u = u(T,v)$ and its total differential is thus

$$du = \left(\frac{\partial u}{\partial T}\right)_v dT + \left(\frac{\partial u}{\partial v}\right)_T dv$$

Using the definition of C_v,

$$du = C_v dT + \left(\frac{\partial u}{\partial v}\right)_T dv \qquad (3.21)$$

Choose the entropy to be a function of T and v, i.e. s = s(T,v) and its total differential is thus

$$ds = \left(\frac{\partial s}{\partial T}\right)_v dT + \left(\frac{\partial s}{\partial v}\right)_T dv \qquad (3.22)$$

Substituting this into the Tds relation du = Tds - Pdv gives

$$du = T\left(\frac{\partial s}{\partial T}\right)_v dT + \left[T\left(\frac{\partial s}{\partial v}\right)_T - P\right]dv \qquad (3.23)$$

Comparing the coefficients of dT and dv in Eqs. (3.21) and (3.23) yields

$$\left(\frac{\partial s}{\partial T}\right)_v = \frac{C_v}{T} \qquad (3.24)$$

$$\left(\frac{\partial u}{\partial T}\right)_v = T\left(\frac{\partial s}{\partial v}\right)_T - P$$

Using the third Maxwell relation, Eq.(3.12), we obtain

$$\left(\frac{\partial u}{\partial v}\right)_T = T\left(\frac{\partial P}{\partial T}\right)_v - P$$

Substituting this into Eq. (3.21), we have the desired relation for du:

$$du = C_v dT + \left[T\left(\frac{\partial P}{\partial T}\right)_v - P\right]dv \qquad (3.25)$$

The change in internal energy of a simple compressible system from state 1 to state 2 when the temperatures and specific volumes are known, is calculated by integration:

$$u_2 - u_1 = \int_{T_1}^{T_2} C_v dT + \int_{v_1}^{v_2} \left[T\left(\frac{\partial P}{\partial T}\right)_v - P\right]dv \qquad (3.26)$$

3.3.2 Enthalpy Changes

The general relation for dh is determined in the same manner. Choose the enthalpy to be a function of T and P, i.e. h = h(T,P), and its total differential is thus

$$dh = \left(\frac{\partial h}{\partial T}\right)_P dT + \left(\frac{\partial h}{\partial P}\right)_T dP$$

Using the definition of C_p,

$$dh = C_p dT + \left(\frac{\partial h}{\partial P}\right)_T dP \qquad (3.27)$$

Choose the entropy to be a function of T and P, i.e. $s = s(T,P)$ and its total differential is thus

$$ds = \left(\frac{\partial s}{\partial T}\right)_P dT + \left(\frac{\partial s}{\partial P}\right)_T dP \qquad (3.28)$$

Substituting this into the Tds relation $dh = Tds + vdP$ yields

$$dh = T\left(\frac{\partial s}{\partial T}\right)_P dT + \left[v + T\left(\frac{\partial s}{\partial P}\right)_T\right] dP \qquad (3.29)$$

Comparing the coefficients of dT and dP in Eqs. (3.27) and (3.29) gives

$$\left(\frac{\partial s}{\partial T}\right)_P = \frac{C_P}{T} \qquad (3.30)$$

$$\left(\frac{\partial h}{\partial P}\right)_T = v + T\left(\frac{\partial s}{\partial P}\right)_T \qquad (3.31)$$

Using the fourth Maxwell relation, Eq. (3.13), we obtain

$$\left(\frac{\partial h}{\partial P}\right)_T = v - T\left(\frac{\partial v}{\partial T}\right)_P \qquad (3.32)$$

Substituting this into Eq. (3.27), we have the desired relation for dh:

$$dh = C_p dT + \left[v - T\left(\frac{\partial v}{\partial T}\right)_P\right] dP \qquad (3.33)$$

The change in enthalpy of a simple compressible system from state 1 to state 2 when the temperatures and pressures are known, is calculated by integration:

$$h_2 - h_1 = \int_{T_1}^{T_2} C_p dT + \int_{P_1}^{P_2} \left[v - T \left(\frac{\partial v}{\partial T} \right)_P \right] dP \qquad (3.34)$$

In practice, we need only to determine either $h_2 - h_1$ from Eq. (3.34) or $u_2 - u_1$ from Eq. (3.26), depending on which data is available. The other can then be calculated from the definition of enthalpy $h = u + Pv$:

$$h_2 - h_1 = u_2 - u_1 + (P_2 v_2 - P_1 v_1) \qquad (3.35)$$

3.3.3 Entropy Changes

We develop two general relations for the entropy change of a simple compressible system. The first relation is derived by substituting the first partial derivative in the total differential ds {Eq. (3.22)} by Eq. (3.24) and the second partial derivative by the third Maxwell relation {Eq. (3.12)}, giving

$$ds = \frac{C_v}{T} dT + \left(\frac{\partial P}{\partial T} \right)_v dv \qquad (3.36)$$

and

$$s_2 - s_1 = \int_{T_1}^{T_2} \frac{C_v}{T} dT + \int_{v_1}^{v_2} \left(\frac{\partial P}{\partial T} \right)_v dv \qquad (3.37)$$

The second relation is derived by substituting the first partial derivative in the total differential of ds {Eq. (3.28)} by Eq. (3.30), and the second partial derivative by the fourth Maxwell relation {Eq. (3.13)}, giving

$$ds = \frac{C_p}{T} dT - \left(\frac{\partial v}{\partial T} \right)_P dP \qquad (3.38)$$

$$s_2 - s_1 = \int_{T_1}^{T_2} \frac{C_P}{T} dT - \int_{P_1}^{P_2} \left(\frac{\partial v}{\partial T}\right)_P dP \qquad (3.39)$$

Depending on the available data, the entropy change may be calculated from either relation.

Example 3.8

Problem

Using the van der Waals equation of state, develop an expression for the enthalpy, $\{h(v_2,T_1)-h(v_1,T_1)\}$.

Solution

From Eq. (3.33), $\quad dh = C_P dT + \left[v - T\left(\frac{\partial v}{\partial T}\right)_P\right] dP$

van der Waals equation is $\left(P + \frac{a}{v^2}\right)(v-b) = RT$

Hence, $\left(\frac{\partial P}{\partial T}\right)_v (v-b) = R \quad$ or $\quad \left(\frac{\partial P}{\partial T}\right)_v = \frac{R}{v-b} \qquad (a)$

Also by rearranging the van der Waals equation,

$$P = \frac{RT}{v-b} - \frac{a}{v^2}$$

So, $\quad \left(\frac{\partial P}{\partial v}\right)_T = \frac{-RT}{(v-b)^2} + \frac{2a}{v^3} \qquad (b)$

But $\quad dP = \left(\frac{\partial P}{\partial T}\right)_v dT + \left(\frac{\partial P}{\partial v}\right)_T dv$

Substituting for dP in Eq. (3.33)

$$dh = C_P dT + \left[v - T\left(\frac{\partial v}{\partial T}\right)_P\right]\left[\left(\frac{R}{v-b}\right) dT + \left\{\frac{2a}{v^3} - \frac{RT}{(v-b)^2}\right\} dv\right]$$

From van der Waals eq., $P\left(\dfrac{\partial v}{\partial T}\right)_P - \dfrac{a}{v^2}\left(\dfrac{\partial v}{\partial T}\right)_P + \dfrac{2ab}{v^3}\left(\dfrac{\partial v}{\partial T}\right)_P = R$

Rearranging, $\left(\dfrac{\partial v}{\partial T}\right)_P = \dfrac{R}{P - \dfrac{a}{v^2} + \dfrac{2ab}{v^3}}$

Substituting for P, $\left(\dfrac{\partial v}{\partial T}\right)_P = \dfrac{R}{\dfrac{RT}{v-b} - \dfrac{2a}{v^2} + \dfrac{2ab}{v^3}}$

Hence, $h(v_2, T_1) - h(v_1, T_1) = \displaystyle\int_{v_1}^{v_2}\left[v - \dfrac{RT_1}{\dfrac{RT_1}{v-b} - \dfrac{2a}{v^2} + \dfrac{2ab}{v^3}}\right]\left\{\dfrac{2a}{v^3} - \dfrac{RT_1}{(v-b)^2}\right\}dv$

Example 3.9

Problem

Using the van der Waals equation of state, develop an expression for the entropy $\{s(v_2,T_1) - s(v_1,T_1)\}$.

Solution

From Eq. (3.36), $ds = \dfrac{C_v}{T}dT + \left(\dfrac{\partial P}{\partial T}\right)_v dv$

Van der Waal's equation is $\left(P + \dfrac{a}{v^2}\right)(v-b) = RT$

Hence, $\left(\dfrac{\partial P}{\partial T}\right)_v (v-b) = R$ or $\left(\dfrac{\partial P}{\partial T}\right)_v = \dfrac{R}{v-b}$ \hfill (a)

Substituting Eq. (a) in Eq. (3.36),

$$ds = \dfrac{C_v}{T}dT + \dfrac{R}{v-b}dv$$

Hence, $s(v_2, T_1) - s(v_1, T_1) = \displaystyle\int_{v_1}^{v_2}\dfrac{R}{v-b}dv = R\ln\dfrac{v_2 - b}{v_1 - b}.$

3.3.4 Specific Heats C_V and C_P

At low pressures gases behave like ideal gases and their specific heats depend on temperature mostly. These specific heats are named zero pressure, or ideal-gas specific heats (denoted by C_{v0} and C_{P0}). It is desirable to have some general relations to calculate the specific heats at higher pressures from a knowledge of C_{v0} and C_{P0} and the P-v-T behavior of the substance. We apply the test of exactness {Eq. (3.3)} on Eqs. (3.36) and (3.38), which gives

$$\left(\frac{\partial C_v}{\partial v}\right)_T = T\left(\frac{\partial^2 P}{\partial T^2}\right)_v \tag{3.40}$$

and

$$\left(\frac{\partial C_P}{\partial P}\right)_T = -T\left(\frac{\partial^2 v}{\partial T^2}\right)_P \tag{3.41}$$

For instance, the deviation of C_P from C_{P0} with increasing pressure, is found by integrating Eq. (3.41) from zero pressure to any pressure P along an isothermal path:

$$\left(C_P - C_{P0}\right)_T = -T\int_0^P \left(\frac{\partial^2 v}{\partial T^2}\right)_P dP \tag{3.42}$$

The integration on the right side of the equation requires information of the P-v-T behavior of the substance only.

Another useful relation is one that relates the two specific heats. If one specific heat (usually C_P) is known, the other may be calculated using this relation and the P-v-T data of the substance. We get this relation by equating the two ds relations {Eqs. (3.36) and (3.38)} and solving for dT:

$$dT = \frac{T(\partial P/\partial T)_v}{C_P - C_v}dv + \frac{T(\partial v/\partial T)_P}{C_P - C_v}dP$$

Selecting $T = T(v,P)$ and differentiating, we obtain

$$dT = \left(\frac{\partial T}{\partial v}\right)_P dv + \left(\frac{\partial T}{\partial P}\right)_v dP$$

Equating the coefficient of either dP or dv of the above two equations provides the desired result:

$\frac{C_p}{C_v} = k \qquad C_p - C_v = R$

$$C_P - C_v = T\left(\frac{\partial v}{\partial T}\right)_P \left(\frac{\partial P}{\partial T}\right)_v \qquad (3.43)$$

An alternative form of this relation is provided by using the relation:

$$\left(\frac{\partial P}{\partial T}\right)_v \left(\frac{\partial T}{\partial v}\right)_P \left(\frac{\partial v}{\partial P}\right)_T = -1$$

so

$$\left(\frac{\partial P}{\partial T}\right)_v = -\left(\frac{\partial v}{\partial T}\right)_P \left(\frac{\partial P}{\partial v}\right)_T$$

Putting the result into Eq. (3.43) results in

$$C_P - C_v = T\left(\frac{\partial v}{\partial T}\right)_P^2 \left(\frac{\partial P}{\partial v}\right)_T \qquad (3.44)$$

This relation may be expressed in terms of two other thermodynamic properties called the volume expansivity β and the isothermal compressibility α, which are defined as

$$\beta = \frac{1}{v}\left(\frac{\partial v}{\partial T}\right)_P \qquad (3.45)$$

and

$$\alpha = -\frac{1}{v}\left(\frac{\partial v}{\partial P}\right)_T \qquad (3.46)$$

Putting these two relations into Eq. (3.44), we have a third general relation for $C_P - C_v$:

$$C_p - C_v = \frac{vT\beta^2}{\alpha} = R \quad (3.47)$$

It is named the Mayer relation after the German physician and physicist J.R. Mayer (1814-1878). We can make several deductions from this relation:

1. The isothermal compressibility α is a positive quantity for all substances in all phases. The volume expansivity could be negative for some substances (e.g. liquid water below 4°C), but its square is always positive or zero. The absolute temperature T is also positive. Thus we deduce that the constant-pressure specific heat is always greater than or equal to the constant-volume specific heat.

2. The difference $C_P - C_V$ approaches zero as the absolute temperature approaches zero.

3. The two specific heats are the same for incompressible substances since v = constant. For almost incompressible substances, like liquids and solids, the difference $C_P - C_V$ is very small and thus negligible.

Example 3.10

Problem

(a) For a reversible adiabatic compression or expansion process, show that Pv^k = constant, where k is the isentropic exponent defined as

$$k = -\frac{v}{P}\left(\frac{\partial P}{\partial v}\right)_s$$

Start with s = s(P,v) and employ the Maxwell relations.

(b) For the special case of an ideal gas, show that $k = C_p/C_v$.

(a) In general, the entropy s may be expressed as

$$s = s(P,v)$$

Thus,
$$ds = \left(\frac{\partial s}{\partial P}\right)_v dP + \left(\frac{\partial s}{\partial v}\right)_P dv \qquad (a)$$

Employ the Maxwell relations

$$\left(\frac{\partial s}{\partial v}\right)_P = \left(\frac{\partial P}{\partial T}\right)_s \quad \text{and} \quad \left(\frac{\partial s}{\partial P}\right)_v = -\left(\frac{\partial v}{\partial T}\right)_s$$

For an isentropic process, ds = 0, so equation (a) becomes

$$-\left(\frac{\partial v}{\partial T}\right)_s dP + \left(\frac{\partial P}{\partial T}\right)_s dv = 0$$

Rearranging, $\quad dP - \left(\frac{\partial T}{\partial v}\right)_s \left(\frac{\partial P}{\partial T}\right)_s dv = 0$

$$dP - \left(\frac{\partial P}{\partial v}\right)_s = 0$$

Dividing by P, $\quad \dfrac{dP}{P} - \dfrac{1}{P}\left(\dfrac{\partial P}{\partial v}\right)_s dv = 0 \qquad (b)$

The isentropic exponent k is defined as

$$k = -\frac{v}{P}\left(\frac{\partial P}{\partial v}\right)_s$$

Employing this definition in Eq. (b),

$$\frac{dP}{P} + k\frac{dv}{v} = 0$$

Take k to be a constant and integrate,

$$\ln P + k \ln v = \text{constant}$$

$$\ln Pv^k = \text{constant}$$

Hence, $\quad Pv^k = \text{constant}$

(b) Write the cyclic relations for the group of variables (s,T,P)

$$\left(\frac{\partial s}{\partial T}\right)_P \left(\frac{\partial P}{\partial s}\right)_T \left(\frac{\partial T}{\partial P}\right)_s = -1$$

Since $C_P = T\left(\frac{\partial s}{\partial T}\right)_P$,

$$\frac{C_P}{T}\left(\frac{\partial P}{\partial s}\right)_T \left(\frac{\partial T}{\partial P}\right)_s = -1 \qquad (c)$$

Write the cyclic relations for the group of variables (s,T,v)

$$\left(\frac{\partial s}{\partial T}\right)_v \left(\frac{\partial v}{\partial s}\right)_T \left(\frac{\partial T}{\partial v}\right)_s = -1$$

Since $C_v = T\left(\frac{\partial s}{\partial T}\right)_v$,

$$\frac{C_v}{T}\left(\frac{\partial v}{\partial s}\right)_T \left(\frac{\partial T}{\partial v}\right)_s = -1 \qquad (d)$$

Equating Eqs. (c) and (d),

$$\frac{C_P}{T}\left(\frac{\partial P}{\partial s}\right)_T \left(\frac{\partial T}{\partial P}\right)_s = \frac{C_v}{T}\left(\frac{\partial v}{\partial s}\right)_T \left(\frac{\partial T}{\partial v}\right)_s$$

Hence, $\dfrac{C_P}{C_v} = \left(\dfrac{\partial s}{\partial P}\right)_T \left(\dfrac{\partial P}{\partial T}\right)_s \left(\dfrac{\partial v}{\partial s}\right)_T \left(\dfrac{\partial T}{\partial v}\right)_s$

$$\frac{C_P}{C_v} = \left(\frac{\partial s}{\partial P}\frac{\partial v}{\partial s}\right)_T \left(\frac{\partial P}{\partial T}\frac{\partial T}{\partial v}\right)_s = \left(\frac{\partial v}{\partial P}\right)_T \left(\frac{\partial P}{\partial v}\right)_s \qquad (e)$$

But for an ideal gas, $\left(\dfrac{\partial v}{\partial P}\right)_T = \left(\dfrac{\partial (RT/P)}{\partial P}\right)_T = -\dfrac{v}{P}$

Substituting in Eq. (e),

$$\frac{C_P}{C_v} = -\frac{v}{P}\left(\frac{\partial P}{\partial v}\right)_s = k$$

3.4 The Joule-Thomson Coefficient

The temperature behavior of a fluid during a throttling (h = constant) process is revealed by the Joule-Thomson coefficient, defined as

$$\mu = \left(\frac{\partial T}{\partial P}\right)_h \tag{3.49}$$

The Joule-Thomson coefficient is a measure of the change in temperature with pressure during an isenthalpic process. Note that in a throttling process if

$$\mu_{JT} \begin{cases} < 0 & \text{temperature increases} \\ = 0 & \text{temperature remains constant} \\ > 0 & \text{temperature decreases.} \end{cases}$$

An examination of Eq. (3.49) shows that the Joule-Thomson coefficient represents the slope of h = constant lines on a T-P diagram. Such diagrams can be drawn from temperature and pressure measurements alone during throttling processes. A fluid at a fixed temperature and pressure T_1 and P_1 (thus fixed enthalpy) is forced through a porous plug, and its temperature and pressure downstream (T_2 and P_2) are measured. The experiment is carried out for different types of porous plugs, each giving a different set of T_2 and P_2. Plotting the temperatures against the pressures gives an h = constant line on a T-P diagram. Doing the experiment for different sets of inlet pressure and temperature and plotting the results, a T-P diagram for a substance with several h = constant lines can be obtained, as shown in Fig. (3.1).

Some isenthalpic lines on the T-P diagram show a maximum value or zero slope (zero Joule-Thomson coefficient). The curve that passes through these maximum points is called the inversion line, and the temperature at a point where an isenthalpic line intersects the inversion line is called the inversion temperature. The temperature at the intersection of the upper portion of the inversion curve with the P = 0 line (ordinate) is the maximum inversion temperature.

A throttling process proceeds along an isenthalpic line in the direction of decreasing pressure, that is, from right to left. Therefore, the temperature of a fluid will increase during a throttling process that occurs on the right-hand side of the inversion curve. The fluid temperature will decrease during a throttling process that occurs on the left-hand side of the inversion curve. It can be seen from the diagram that a cooling effect cannot be achieved by throttling unless the fluid is below its maximum inversion temperature. Note that throttling is used in the operation of refrigerators and air conditioners to create cooling in the fluid. For certain substances this is not possible since their maximum inversion temperature is well below atmospheric temperature. For example, hydrogen has a maximum inversion temperature of -68°C. Therefore, the temperature of the hydrogen has to be reduced to below this temperature in order to achieve any further cooling by throttling.

Next we will develop a relation for the Joule-Thomson coefficient in terms of the specific heats, pressure, specific volume, and temperature. This can be done by looking at the isenthalpic case of the generalized relation for enthalpy change, Eq. (3.33),

$$dh = C_P \, dT + \left[v - T \left(\frac{\partial v}{\partial T} \right)_P \right] dP$$

For an isenthalpic process, dh = 0. Then this equation may be written as

$$-\frac{1}{C_P}\left[v - T \left(\frac{\partial v}{\partial T} \right)_P \right] = \left(\frac{\partial v}{\partial P} \right)_h = \mu_{JT} \qquad (3.50)$$

which is the desired relation. Therefore, the Joule-Thomson coefficient can be determined from data of the constant-pressure specific heat and the P-v-T behavior of the substance. Conversely, the constant-pressure specific heat of a substance can be computed from the Joule-Thomson coefficient and the P-v-T data.

Example 3.11

Problem

The compressiblity factor $Z = Z(P,T)$ is such that $Pv = ZRT$ for real gases. Use Eq. (3.50) to show that the Joule-Thomson coefficient inversion curve on the T-P plane is described by the equation $\left(\dfrac{\partial Z}{\partial T}\right)_P = 0$.

Solution

The inversion curve is the configuration of points at which the the Joule-Thompson coefficient has zero value. From Eq. (3.50),

$$-\frac{1}{C_P}\left[v - T\left(\frac{\partial v}{\partial T}\right)_P\right] = \left(\frac{\partial T}{\partial P}\right)_h = \mu_{JT} = 0$$

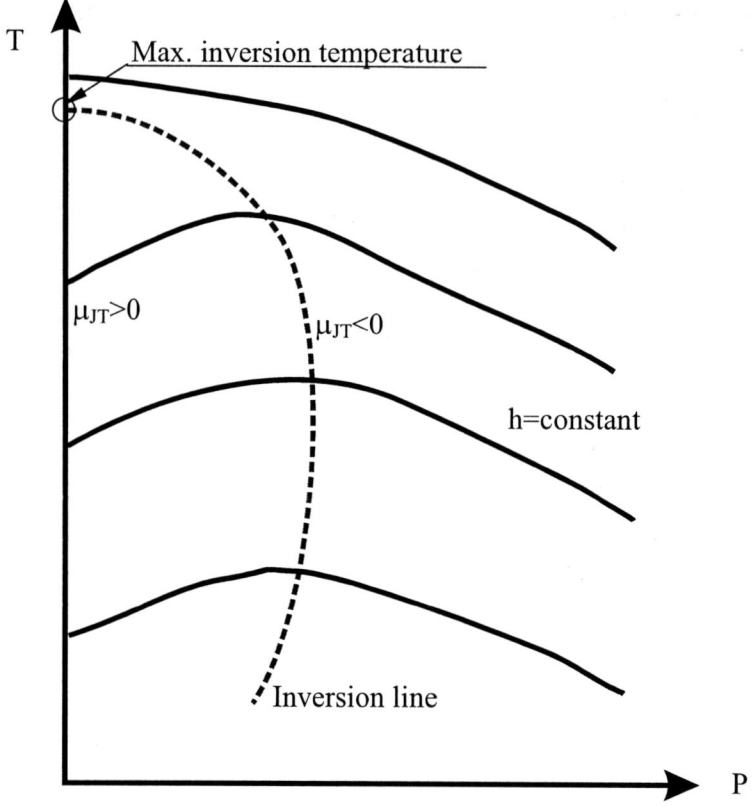

Figure 3.1 Isenthalpic lines on a T-P diagram for a substance.

Since $v = \dfrac{ZRT}{P}$ and rearranging,

$$T\left(\dfrac{\partial v}{\partial T}\right)_P - \dfrac{ZRT}{P} = 0 \qquad (a)$$

Keep P constant and take the derivative with respect to T,

$$\left(\dfrac{\partial v}{\partial T}\right)_P = \left[\dfrac{\partial(ZRT/P)}{\partial T}\right]_P = \dfrac{R}{P}\left[T\left(\dfrac{\partial Z}{\partial T}\right)_P + Z\right]$$

Substitute in Eq. (a),

$$\dfrac{TR}{P}\left[T\left(\dfrac{\partial Z}{\partial T}\right)_P + Z\right] - \dfrac{ZRT}{P} = 0$$

$$\dfrac{TR}{P}\left[T\left(\dfrac{\partial Z}{\partial T}\right)_P + Z - Z\right] = 0$$

Hence, $\left(\dfrac{\partial Z}{\partial T}\right)_P = 0$.

3.5 The Enthalpy, Internal Energy, and Entropy Changes of Real Gases

Gases at low pressures behave like ideal gases which follow the relation Pv=RT. At higher pressures, gases deviate from the relation and these deviations have to be taken into account.

3.5.1 Enthalpy Changes of Real Gases

The enthalpy of real gases generally depends on the temperature and pressure, as contrasted to ideal gases whose enthalpies are dependent on temperature only. From Eq. (3.34), the enthalpy change of a simple compressible system from state 1 to state 2 is given by

$$h_2 - h_1 = \int_{T_1}^{T_2} C_p dT + \int_{P_1}^{P_2} \left[v - T \left(\frac{\partial v}{\partial T} \right)_P \right] dP$$

When the process is isobaric, the second term is zero. When the process is isothermal, the first term is zero.

The enthalpy change of a real gas during a process 1-2 may be expressed as

$$h_2 - h_1 = (h_2 - h_{2,ideal}) + (h_{2,ideal} - h_{1,ideal}) + (h_{1,ideal} - h_1) \qquad (3.51)$$

which is essentially breaking up the process 1-2 to three processes.

From Eq. (3.34),

$$h_2 - h_{2,ideal} = 0 + \int_{P_{2,ideal1}}^{P_2} \left[v - T \left(\frac{\partial v}{\partial T} \right)_P \right]_{T=T_2} dP$$

$$(3.52)$$

$$h_{2,ideal} - h_{1,ideal} = \int_{T_1}^{T_2} C_p T + 0 = \int_{T_1}^{T_2} C_{P0}(T) dT \qquad (3.53)$$

$$h_1 - h_{1,ideal} = 0 + \int_{P_1}^{P_{1,ideal}} \left[v - T \left(\frac{\partial v}{\partial T} \right)_P \right]_{T=T_2} dP$$

$$= -\int_0^{P_1} \left[v - T \left(\frac{\partial v}{\partial T} \right)_P \right]_{T=T_2} dP \qquad (3.54)$$

The pressure P0 can be chosen to be very low or zero (as done above), so the gas is treated as an ideal gas in the P0 = constant process.

The difference $(h - h_{ideal})$ is called the *enthalpy departure*. This accounts for the variation of the gas enthalpy with pressure at a constant temperature. The computation of enthalpy departure needs the P-v-T data of the gas. When such data is not available, we can use the relation Pv=ZRT, where Z is the compressiblity factor. When we substitute v = ZRT/P into Eq. (3.54) and simplify, we obtain

$$(h_{ideal} - h)_T = -RT^2 \int_0^P \left(\frac{\partial Z}{\partial T}\right)_P \frac{dP}{P}$$

The equation may be made more general by expressing it in terms of the reduced properties, that is, $T = T_{cr}T_R$ and $P = P_{cr}P_R$. After manipulation, the nondimensionalized form of the equation is

$$Z_h = \frac{(\overline{h}_{ideal} - \overline{h})_T}{R_u T_{cr}} = T_R^2 \int_0^{P_R} \left(\frac{\partial Z}{\partial T_R}\right)_{P_R} d(\ln P_R) \qquad (3.55)$$

where Z_h is the *enthalpy departure factor*. The integral may be done graphically or numerically by using data from the compressibility charts for various values of T_R and P_R. The graph representing Z_h as a function of P_R and T_R is the *generalized enthalpy departure chart*. This chart is used to determine the difference of the enthalpy of a gas at a given T and P from the enthalpy of an ideal gas at the same temperature T. The enthalpy change of a gas during a process 1-2, Eq. (3.51), may be written as

$$h_2 - h_1 = RT_{cr}(Z_{h_1} - Z_{h_2}) + (h_2 - h_1)_{ideal} \qquad (3.56)$$

or $\quad \overline{h}_2 - \overline{h}_1 = RT_{cr}(Z_{h_1} - Z_{h_2}) + (\overline{h}_2 - \overline{h}_1)_{ideal} \qquad (3.57)$

$(h_2 - h_1)_{ideal}$ is found from the ideal-gas tables, and Z_h is found from the generalized enthalpy chart. For ideal gases, the first terms on the right-hand side are zero.

3.5.2 Internal Energy Changes of Real Gases

The internal energy change of a real gas can be determined by its relationship to the enthalpy change. Since $\overline{h} = \overline{u} + P\overline{v} = \overline{u} + ZR_u T$,

$$\overline{u}_2 - \overline{u}_1 = (\overline{h}_2 - \overline{h}_1) - R_u(Z_2 T_2 - Z_1 T_1) \qquad (3.58)$$

3.5.3 Entropy Changes for Real Gases

The approach used for entropy change is similar to that for the enthalpy change. In general, the relation for ds, Eq. (3.39),

$$s_2 - s_1 = \int_{T_1}^{T_2} \frac{C_P}{T} dT - \int_{P_1}^{P_2} \left(\frac{\partial v}{\partial T}\right)_P dP$$

The entropy change of a real gas during a process 1-2 may be expressed as

$$s_2 - s_1 = (s_2 - s_{b,ideal}) + (s_{b,ideal} - s_{2,ideal}) + (s_{2,ideal} - s_{1,ideal}) + (s_{1,ideal} - s_{a,ideal})$$
$$+ (s_{a,ideal} - s_1) \quad (3.59)$$

which is essentially breaking up the process 1-2 to component processes. States 1 and 1,ideal are identical $(T_1 = T_{1,ideal}$ and $P_1 = P_{1,ideal})$, so are states 2 and 2,ideal. The gas is assumed to behave ideally at states 1,ideal and 2,ideal, as well as at the states between them, including states a and b. Thus, the entropy change for process 1,ideal-2,ideal may be determined from the entropy-change relations for ideal gases. The entropy change between an actual state and the corresponding imaginary ideal-gas state is more complicated, and needs the use of generalized entropy charts, as discussed below.

Let us look at a gas at pressure P and temperature T. To find the deviation of the entropy of this gas with respect to that of an ideal gas at the same temperature and pressure, consider an isothermal process from the actual state P,T to zero (or near zero) pressure and back to the imaginary ideal-gas state P_{ideal}, T_{ideal}, Fig. 3.2. The entropy change during this isothermal process is

$$(s_P - s_{P,ideal})_T = -\int_P^0 \left(\frac{\partial v}{\partial T}\right)_P dP - \int_0^P \left(\frac{\partial v_{ideal}}{\partial T}\right)_P dP$$

where $v = ZRT/P$ and $v_{ideal} = RT/P$. Differentiating and rearranging,

$$(s_P - s_{P,ideal})_T = \int_0^P \left[\frac{(1-Z)R}{P} - \frac{RT}{P}\left(\frac{\partial Z}{\partial T}\right)_P\right] dP$$

The equation may be made more general by expressing it in terms of the reduced properties, that is, $T = T_{cr}T_R$ and $P = P_{cr}P_R$. After manipulation, the nondimensionalized form of the equation is

$$Z_s = \frac{(\bar{s}_{ideal} - \bar{s})_{T,P}}{R_u} = \int_0^{P_R} Z - 1 + T_R \left(\frac{\partial Z}{\partial T_R}\right)_{P_R} d(\ln P_R) \qquad (3.60)$$

where $(\bar{s}_{ideal} - \bar{s})_{T,P}$ is called the *entropy departure* and Z_s is the *entropy departure factor*.

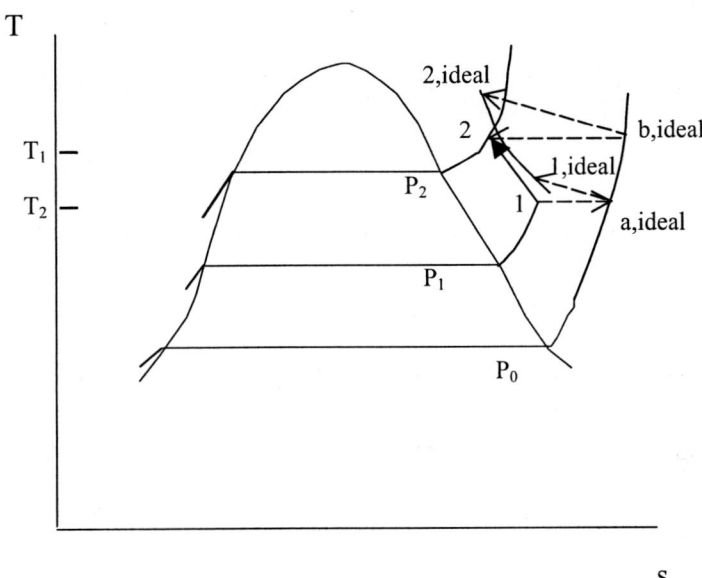

Figure 3.2 The process path of ideal states used to evaluate the entropy changes of real gases during process 1-2.

The integral may be done graphically or numerically by using data from the compressibility charts for various values of T_R and P_R. The graph representing Z_s as a function of P_R and T_R is the *generalized entropy departure chart.* This chart is used to determine the difference of the entropy of a gas at a given T and P from the entropy of an ideal gas at the same T and P. The entropy change of a gas during a process 1-2, Eq. (3.59), may be written as

$$s_2 - s_1 = R(Z_{s_1} - Z_{s_2}) + (s_2 - s_1)_{ideal} \qquad (3.61)$$

or

$$\bar{s}_2 - \bar{s}_1 = R_u(Z_{s_1} - Z_{s_2}) + (\bar{s}_2 - \bar{s}_1)_{ideal} \qquad (3.62)$$

$(s_2 - s_1)_{ideal}$ is found from the ideal-gas tables, and Z_s is found from the generalized entropy chart. For ideal gases, the first terms on the right-hand side are zero.

PROBLEMS

The Maxwell Relations

3.1. Consider air as an ideal gas with molecular weight of 28.97, and at a state characterized by T = 500 K and v = 1.2 m³/kg. Estimate the change in pressure of the gas if the state of the gas changes to 498 K and 1.198 m³/kg. Use two methods, to evaluate the change.

3.2. Consider air as an ideal gas with molecular weight of 28.97, and at a state characterized by T = 440°F and v = 20 ft³/lb$_m$. Estimate the change in pressure of the gas if the state of the gas changes to 438°F and 19.8 ft³/lb$_m$. Use two methods, to evaluate the change.

3.3. Show that $\left(\dfrac{\partial T}{\partial v}\right)_s = +\left(\dfrac{\partial P}{\partial s}\right)_v$ is valid for steam at 8.0 kJ/(kg.K) and 0.3 m³/kg.

3.4. Show that $\left(\dfrac{\partial T}{\partial P}\right)_s = +\left(\dfrac{\partial v}{\partial s}\right)_P$ is valid for steam at 8.0 kJ/(kg.K) and 1500 kPa.

3.5. Show that $\left(\dfrac{\partial s}{\partial v}\right)_T = \left(\dfrac{\partial P}{\partial T}\right)_v$ is valid for steam at 700°C and 0.3 m³/kg.

3.6. Show that $\left(\dfrac{\partial s}{\partial P}\right)_T = -\left(\dfrac{\partial v}{\partial T}\right)_P$ is valid for steam at 700°C and 1500 kPa.

3.7. Show that $\left(\dfrac{\partial T}{\partial v}\right)_s = -\left(\dfrac{\partial P}{\partial s}\right)_v$ is valid for steam at 2.1 Btu/(lb$_m$.°R) and 75 ft³/lb$_m$.

3.8. Show that $\left(\dfrac{\partial T}{\partial P}\right)_s = +\left(\dfrac{\partial v}{\partial s}\right)_P$ is valid for steam at 2.1 Btu/(lb$_m$.°R) and 10 lb$_f$/in².

3.9. Show that $\left(\dfrac{\partial s}{\partial v}\right)_T = \left(\dfrac{\partial P}{\partial T}\right)_v$ is valid for steam at 800°F and 75 ft³/lb$_m$.

3.10. Show that $\left(\dfrac{\partial s}{\partial P}\right)_T = -\left(\dfrac{\partial v}{\partial T}\right)_P$ is valid for steam at 800°F and 10 lb$_f$/in^2.

The Clapeyron Equation

3.11. Estimate the enthalpy of vaporization for ammonia at 50°C, and compare the value with that in the property tables.

3.12. Estimate the enthalpy of vaporization for refrigerant-12 at 0°C, and compare the value with that in the property tables.

3.13. The property tables show that for ammonia, at -60°F, h_{fg}=610.56 Btu/lb$_m$, P_{sat} = 5.548 lb$_f$/in.^{2} Estimate the saturation pressure of ammonia at -70°F.

3.14. The property tables show that for ammonia, at -10°C, h_{fg}=1296.4 kJ/kg, P_{sat} = 0.2907 MPa. Estimate the saturation pressure of ammonia at -20°C.

3.15. The property tables show that for ammonia, at -65, h_{fg}=1442.65 kJ/kg, P_{sat} = 0.219 MPa. Estimate the saturation pressure of ammonia at -75°C.

General Relations for Thermodynamic Properties

3.16. Using the Beattie-Bridgeman equation of state, develop an expression for the enthalpy, $\{h(v_2,T_1)-h(v_1,T_1)\}$.

3.17. Using the Beattie-Bridgeman equation of state, develop an expression for the entropy $\{s(v_2,T_1)-s(v_1,T_1)\}$.

3.18. The compressibility factor of a gas is given by

$$Z = 1 + \dfrac{DP}{RT}$$

where D is a function of temperature. Develop expressions for the enthalpy $\{h(P_2,T_1)-h(P_1,T_1)\}$ and the entropy $\{s(P_2,T_1)-s(P_1,T_1)\}$.

3.19. The compressibility factor of a gas is given by

$$Z = 1 + \frac{D_1}{v} + \frac{D_2}{v^2}$$

where D_1 and D_2 are functions of temperature. Develop an expression for the entropy $\{s(v_2,T_1)-s(v_1,T_1)\}$.

3.20. The compressibility factor of a gas is given by

$$Z = 1 - \frac{DP}{T^4}$$

where D is a constant. Obtain an expression for the difference in specific heats, $C_P - C_V$.

The Joule Thomson Coefficient

3.21. Estimate the Joule-Thomson coefficient of nitrogen at (a) 7 MPa and 300 K and (b) 6.5 MPa and 300K.

3.22. Estimate the Joule-Thomson coefficient of ammonia at (a) 3 MPa and 300.15 K and (b) 3.3 MPa and 295.14 K.

COMPUTER, DESIGN AND GENERAL PROBLEMS

3.23. The following data are available for water:

(i) Saturated pressures and temperatures are known

(ii) Pressure, specific volume, and temperature data in the vapor region.

(iii) Zero-pressure specific heat for the vapor.

(iv) Density of the saturated liquid and the critical pressure and temperature.

Research the literature, and obtain the vapor-pressure equation for water, and the equation of state for water vapor. Write a computer program to compute the values for the pressure, temperature, specific volume, enthalpy, entropy, and internal energy of saturated liquid, saturated vapor, and superheated vapor over a wide range.

3.24. Problem 3.23. applies to ammonia. Write the corresponding program for ammonia.

3.25. Problem 3.23. applies to refrigerant 12 and refrigerant 134a. Write the corresponding programs for the two refrigerants.

3.26. Problem 3.23. applies to methane. Write the corresponding programs for methane.

4. GAS MIXTURES

4.1 Composition of a Gas Mixture

In order to know the properties of a mixture, the composition of the mixture and the properties of the components have to be known. The composition can either be expressed in terms of the number of moles of each component, called **molar analysis**, or in terms of the mass of each component, called **gravimetric analysis**.

Let a mixture have k components. The mass of the mixture m_m is the sum of the masses of the components, and the total number of moles of the mixture N_m is the sum of the number of moles of the components. In equation form,

$$m_m = \sum_{i=1}^{k} m_i \quad \text{and} \quad N_m = \sum_{i=1}^{k} N_i \qquad (4.1)$$

The percentage of a component in the mixture in terms of mass is called the **mass fraction**, mf. The percentage of a component in the mixture in terms of moles is called the **mole fraction** y.

$$mf_i = \frac{m_i}{m_m} \quad \text{and} \quad y_i = \frac{N_i}{N_m} \qquad (4.2)$$

It is obvious that the sum of the mass fractions and mole fractions for a mixture is equal to unity.

$$\sum_{i=1}^{k} mf_i = 1 \quad \text{and} \quad \sum_{i=1}^{k} y_i = 1 \qquad (4.3)$$

The mass of a substance is related to its molar mass m by

$$m = NM \qquad (4.4)$$

where N is the number of moles of the substance. The average molar mass of a mixture is

$$M_m = \frac{m_m}{N_m} = \frac{\sum m_i}{N_m} = \frac{\sum N_i M_i}{N_m} = \sum_{i=1}^{k} y_i M_i \quad (kg/kmol) \quad (4.5)$$

The average (or apparent) gas constant of the mixture is

$$R_m = \frac{\sum_{i=1}^{k} y_i R_i}{M_m} = \frac{R_{universal}}{M_m} \quad [kJ/(kg.K)] \quad (4.6)$$

Example 4.1

Problem

The gaseous products of combustion in a certain process are CO_2, H_2O, O_2 and N_2. Their corresponding mass fractions are 0.30, 0.10, 0.05, and 0.55, respectively. Calculate (a) the composition in mole fractions, and (b) the apparent molecular weight of the mixture.

Solution

(a) Equations (4.2) and (4.3) are used for the calculations. Consider any convenient amount of the mixture, say 100 lb_m. Set up the table as shown below. Column (b) gives the mass of each component. Column (c) gives the molecular weight of each component, and column (d) is the evaluated mole fraction. Finally, column (e) is the column (d) divided by the total number of moles, i.e., 3.36.

(a)	(b)		(c)		(d)	(e)
Component	mf_i	÷	M_i	=	n_i	y_i (%)
CO_2	30		44		0.68	20.2
H_2O	10		18		0.56	16.7
O_2	5		32		0.16	4.8

| N₂ | 55 | 28 | 1.96 | 58.3 |

Σ= 100   Σ= 3.36

(b) 100 lb$_m$ of mixture is considered. This gives 3.36 moles of the mixture. The apparent molecular weight of the mixture is thus

$$M = \frac{m}{n} = \frac{100 \text{ lb}_m}{3.36 \text{ lbmol}} = 29.8 \frac{\text{lb}_m}{\text{lbmol}} = 29.8 \frac{\text{kg}}{\text{kgmol}}$$

4.2 P-v-T Relationships for Ideal and Real Gas Mixtures

Real gases approximate the behavior of ideal gases at low densities, that is, at a low pressure or high temperature relative to their critical-point values. The P-v-T relationship of an ideal gas is $Pv = RT$. The P-v-T relationship of real gases is expressed by $Pv = ZRT$, where Z is the compressibility factor.

When two or more nonreacting ideal gases are mixed, the mixture also behaves as an ideal gas. For example, air is treated as an ideal gas in the range of temperature and pressure where nitrogen and oxygen behave as ideal gases. The behavior of real (nonideal) gases is more involved.

The behavior of gas mixtures is usually based on two models: Dalton's law of additive pressures and Amagat's law of additive volumes.

Dalton's law of additive pressures: The pressure of a gas mixture is equal to the sum of the pressures each gas would exert if it existed alone at the mixture temperature and volume, Fig. (4.1).

Amagat's law of additive volumes: The volume of a gas mixture is equal to the sum of the volumes each gas would occupy if it existed alone at the mixture temperature and pressure, Fig. (4.2).

```
┌─────────┐     ┌─────────┐     ┌──────────┐
│ Gas A   │     │ Gas B   │     │Gas Mixture│
│ V , T   │  +  │ V , T   │  ≡  │  A + B   │
│         │     │         │     │  V , T   │
│  P_A    │     │  P_B    │     │ P_A + P_B│
└─────────┘     └─────────┘     └──────────┘
```

Figure 4.1   Dalton's Law of additive pressures for two ideal gases.

```
┌─────────┐     ┌─────────┐     ┌──────────┐
│ Gas A   │     │ Gas B   │     │Gas Mixture│
│ P , T   │  +  │ P , T   │  ≡  │  A + B   │
│         │     │         │     │  P , T   │
│  V_A    │     │  V_B    │     │ V_A + V_B│
└─────────┘     └─────────┘     └──────────┘
```

Figure 4.2   Amagat's Law of additive volumes for two ideal gases.

Dalton's and Amagat's laws are exact for ideal-gas mixtures, but only approximate for real-gas mixtures. The reason is that intermolecular forces are significant for real gases at high densities. For ideal gases, these two laws give the same results. Dalton's and Amagat's laws can be expressed as follows:

$$\text{Dalton's law: } P_m = \sum_{i=1}^{k} P_i(T_m, V_m) \quad (4.7)$$

exact for ideal gases, approximate for real gases

$$\text{Amagat's law: } V_m = \sum_{i=1}^{k} V_i(T_m, P_m) \quad (4.8)$$

P_i is called the **component pressure** or **partial pressure** of component i, and V_i is the **component volume** or **partial volume** of component i. The volume V_i is the volume a component would occupy if it existed by itself at T_m and P_m; this is not the actual volume occupied by the component in the mixture. Note that in a gas mixture contained in a vessel, the volume of each component is equal to the volume of the vessel. The ratio P_i/P_m is called the **pressure fraction** and the ratio V_i/V_m is called the **volume fraction** of component i.

1. Ideal-Gas Mixtures

For ideal gases, P_i and V_i may be related accordingly:

$$\frac{P_i(T_m, V_m)}{P_m} = \frac{N_i R_u T_m / V_m}{N_m R_u T_m / V_m} = \frac{N_i}{N_m} = y_i$$

$$\frac{V_i(T_m, P_m)}{V_m} = \frac{N_i R_u T_m / P_m}{N_m R_u T_m / P_m} = \frac{N_i}{N_m} = y_i$$

Thus
$$\frac{P_i}{P_m} = \frac{V_i}{V_m} = \frac{N_i}{N_m} = y_i \qquad (4.9)$$

The component $y_i P_m$ is the partial pressure (identical to component pressure for ideal gases), and the quantity $y_i V_m$ is the partial volume (identical to the component volume for ideal gases). For an ideal-gas mixture, the mole fraction, the pressure fraction, and the volume fraction of a component are all equal.

2. Real-Gas Mixtures

Dalton's law and Amagat's law may be used for real gases, with reasonable accuracy. The component pressures or component volumes should be calculated from relationships that take into consideration the nonideal behavior. One method is to use the equations of state for real gases (van der Waals, Beattie-Bridgeman, etc.). Another method is to use the compressibility factor as

$$PV = ZNR_uT \tag{4.10}$$

The compressibility factor of the mixture Z_m can be found from the compressibility factors of the components Z_i by applying Eq. (4.10) to both sides of Dalton's law or Amagat's law expression and simplifying. Thus,

$$Z_m = \sum_{i=1}^{k} y_i Z_i \tag{4.11}$$

where Z_i is determined either at T_m and V_m (Dalton's law) or at T_m and P_m (Amagat's law) for each component. Using either law does not yield the same result. Dalton's law yield better results at low pressures; Amagat's law yields better results at high pressures.

One other approach for predicting the P-v-T behavior of a gas mixture is to treat the gas mixture as a pseudopure substance. The **Kay's rule** (1936) involves the use of a pseudocritical pressure $P'_{cr,m}$ and pseudocritical temperature $T'_{cr,m}$ for the mixture, defined in terms of the critical pressures and temperatures of the components as

$$P'_{cr,m} = \sum_{i=1}^{k} y_i P_{cr,i} \quad \text{and} \quad T'_{cr,m} = \sum_{i=1}^{k} y_i T_{cr,i} \tag{4.12}$$

The compressibility factor of the mixture Z_m can then be determined by using these pseudocritical properties. The result obtained by using Kay's rule is accurate over a wide range of temperatures and pressures, to within 10 percent.

Another approach is to treat the gas mixture as a pseudopure substance with the use of an equation of state such as the van der Waals, or the Beattie-Bridgeman equation. The constant coefficients have to be determined in terms of the coefficients of the components. For example, the two constants in the van der Waals equation, for the mixture can be determined from

$$a_m = \left(\sum_{i=1}^{k} y_i a_i^{1/2}\right)^2 \quad \text{and} \quad b_m = \sum_{i=1}^{k} y_i b_i \quad (4.13)$$

where a_i and b_i are constants.

Example 4.2

Problem

A tank of fixed volume contains 1 kmol of nitrogen and 4 kmol of methane gases at 310K and 10 MPa. Estimate the volume of the tank using (a) the ideal gas equation of state, (b) compressiblity factors and Amagat's law, and (c) Kay's rule.

Solution

For an ideal gas, $\quad V = \dfrac{N R_u T}{P}$

For the mixture, $\quad N = N_{N_2} + N_{CH_4} = (1+4) \text{ kmol} = 5 \text{ kmol}$

$$V_m = \frac{(5 \text{ kmol})[8.314 \text{ kPa.m}^3/(\text{kmol.K})](310 \text{ K})}{10,000 \text{ kPa}} = 1.289 \text{m}^3$$

(b) When using compressiblity factors and Amagat's law, Eq. (4.11) is employed. Use the thermodynamic tables to find the critical properties of the gases.

For nitrogen, $T_{cr} = 126.2$ K, $\qquad P_{cr} = 3.39$ MPa

For methane, $T_{cr} = 191.1$ K, $\qquad P_{cr} = 4.64$ MPa

For nitrogen, $T_R = \dfrac{T}{T_{cr}} = \dfrac{310}{126.2} = 2.456$

$$P_R = \frac{P}{P_{cr}} = \frac{10 \text{MPa}}{3.39 \text{MPa}} = 2.95$$

From the Nelson-Obert compressibility chart, $Z_{N_2} = 1.00$

For methane, $T_R = \dfrac{T}{T_{cr}} = \dfrac{310}{191.1} = 1.622$

$P_R = \dfrac{P}{P_{cr}} = \dfrac{10 \text{ MPa}}{4.64 \text{ MPa}} = 2.155$

From the Nelson-Obert compressibility chart, $Z_{CH_4} = 0.67$

For the mixture,
$$Z_m = \sum_i y_i Z_i$$
$$= y_{N_2} Z_{N_2} + y_{CH_4} Z_{CH_4}$$
$$= (0.20)(1.00) + (0.80)(0.67)$$
$$= 0.736$$

Hence, $V_m = \dfrac{Z_m N R_u T}{P_m}$

$$V_m = \dfrac{(0.736)(5 \text{ kmol})[8.314 \text{ kPa.m}^3/(\text{kmol.K})](310 \text{ K})}{10{,}000 \text{ kPa}} = 0.948 \text{ m}^3$$

(c) When using Kay's rule, one needs to find the pseudocritical temperature and pseudocritical pressure of the mixture.

From Eq. (4.12),
$$T'_{cr,i} = \sum_{i=1}^{k} y_i T_{cr,i}$$
$$= (0.20)(126.2\text{K}) + (0.80)(191.1\text{K})$$
$$= 178.1 \text{K}$$

From Eq. (4.12),
$$P'_{cr,i} = \sum_{i=1}^{k} y_i P_{cr,i}$$
$$= (0.20)(3.39 \text{MPa}) + (0.80)(4.64 \text{MPa})$$
$$= 4.39 \text{MPa}$$

For the mixture, $T_R = \dfrac{T_m}{T'_{cr,m}} = \dfrac{310}{178.1} = 1.74$

$$P_R = \frac{P_m}{P'_{cr,m}} = \frac{10\text{MPa}}{4.39\text{MPa}} = 2.28$$

From the Nelson-Obert compressibility chart, $Z_m = 0.77$

Hence, $$v_m = \frac{Z_m N R_u T}{P_m}$$

$$v_m = \frac{(0.777)(5\,\text{kmol})[8.314\,\text{kPa.m}^3/(\text{kmol.K})](310\,\text{K})}{10{,}000\,\text{kPa}} = 0.992\,\text{m}^3$$

Note that the ideal-gas assumption is rather poor in this case.

4.3 Properties of Ideal and Real Gas Mixtures

To compute the extensive properties of a nonreacting ideal- or real-gas mixture, add the contributions of each component of the mixture. The total internal energy, enthalpy, and entropy of a gas mixture are respectively,

$$U_m = \sum_{i=1}^{k} U_i = \sum_{i=1}^{k} m_i u_i = \sum_{i=1}^{k} N_i \overline{u}_i \quad (\text{kJ}) \quad (4.14)$$

$$H_m = \sum_{i=1}^{k} H_i = \sum_{i=1}^{k} m_i h_i = \sum_{i=1}^{k} N_i \overline{h}_i \quad (\text{kJ}) \quad (4.15)$$

$$S_m = \sum_{i=1}^{k} S_i = \sum_{i=1}^{k} m_i s_i = \sum_{i=1}^{k} N_i \overline{s}_i \quad (\text{kJ/K}) \quad (4.16)$$

It follows that the changes in internal energy, enthalpy, and entropy of a gas mixture during a process are respectively,

$$\Delta U_m = \sum_{i=1}^{k} \Delta U_i = \sum_{i=1}^{k} m_i \Delta u_i = \sum_{i=1}^{k} N_i \Delta \overline{u}_i \quad (\text{kJ}) \quad (4.17)$$

$$\Delta H_m = \sum_{i=1}^{k} \Delta H_i = \sum_{i=1}^{k} m_i \Delta h_i = \sum_{i=1}^{k} N_i \Delta \overline{h}_i \quad (\text{kJ}) \quad (4.18)$$

$$\Delta S_m = \sum_{i=1}^{k} \Delta S_i = \sum_{i=1}^{k} m_i \Delta s_i = \sum_{i=1}^{k} N_i \Delta \overline{s}_i \quad (\text{kJ/K}) \quad (4.19)$$

The internal energy, enthalpy, and entropy of a gas mixture per unit mass or per unit mole of the mixture, are intensive properties. They may be determined from the equations above by dividing the equations by the mass or the number of moles of the mixture (m_m or N_m).

$$u_m = \sum_{i=1}^{k} mf_i u_i \quad \text{and} \quad \overline{u}_m = \sum_{i=1}^{k} y_i \overline{u}_i \quad \text{(kJ/kg or kJ/kmol)} \quad (4.20)$$

$$h_m = \sum_{i=1}^{k} mf_i h_i \quad \text{and} \quad \overline{h}_m = \sum_{i=1}^{k} y_i \overline{h}_i \quad \text{(kJ/kg or kJ/kmol)} \quad (4.21)$$

$$s_m = \sum_{i=1}^{k} mf_i s_i \quad \text{and} \quad \overline{s}_m = \sum_{i=1}^{k} y_i \overline{s}_i \quad [\text{(kJ/kg.K) or kJ/(kmol.K)}] (4.22)$$

In like manner, the specific heats of a gas mixture are

$$C_{v,m} = \sum_{i=1}^{k} mf_i C_{v,i} \quad \text{and} \quad \overline{C}_{v,m} = \sum_{i=1}^{k} y_i \overline{C}_{v,i} \quad [\text{(kJ/kg.°C) or kJ/(kmol. °C)}]$$

$$(4.23)$$

$$C_{p,m} = \sum_{i=1}^{k} mf_i C_{p,i} \quad \text{and} \quad \overline{C}_{p,m} = \sum_{i=1}^{k} y_i \overline{C}_{p,i} \quad [\text{(kJ/kg.°C) or kJ/(kmol. °C)}]$$

$$(4.24)$$

Note that the properties per unit mass involve mass fractions and the properties per unit mole involve mole fractions.

The relationships developed thus far are applicable to both ideal- and real-gas mixtures. They are also applicable to nonreacting liquid and solid solutions. The main difficulty is to determine the properties for each component in the mixture. The ideal-gas model provides simplification.

1. Ideal-Gas Mixtures

Under the ideal-gas assumption, the properties of a gas are not affected by the presence of other gases, and each gas component in the mixture behaves as if it exists by itself at the mixture temperature T_m and mixture volume V_m. The principle used is called the **Gibbs-Dalton law**, which is an extension of Dalton's law of additive pressures. In addition, the u, h, C_v, and C_p of an ideal gas is a function of temperature only and independent of the pressure or the volume of the ideal-gas mixture. The partial pressure of a component is given by $P_i = y_i P_m$, where P_m is the mixture pressure.

Computation of Δu or Δh requires only a knowledge of the initial and final temperatures. Computation of Δs, however, requires care since the entropy of an ideal gas depends on the pressure or volume of the component in addition to its temperature. The entropy change of individual gases in an ideal-gas during a process can be computed from

$$\Delta s_i = s^o_{i,2} - s^o_{i,1} - R_i \ln \frac{P_{i,2}}{P_{i,1}} \cong C_{p,i} \ln \frac{T_{i,2}}{T_{i,1}} - R_i \ln \frac{P_{i,2}}{P_{i,1}} \qquad (4.25)$$

or

$$\Delta \bar{s}_i = \bar{s}^o_{i,2} - \bar{s}^o_{i,1} - R_u \ln \frac{P_{i,2}}{P_{i,1}} \cong \bar{C}_{p,i} \ln \frac{T_{i,2}}{T_{i,1}} - R_u \ln \frac{P_{i,2}}{P_{i,1}} \qquad (4.26)$$

where $P_{i,2} = y_{i,2} P_{m,2}$ and $P_{i,1} = y_{i,1} P_{m,1}$. Note that the partial pressure P_i of each component is used in the calculation of the entropy change.

Example 4.3

Problem

A tank of fixed volume has two sections separated by a thin wall. One section has 10 kg of oxygen at 30°C and 120 kPa, and the other has 2 kg of carbon dioxide at 45°C and 200 kPa. Then the thin wall is removed so that the gases can mix. Assume that there is no heat transferred, and equilibrium is reached. Determine the mixture temperature and pressure.

Solution

Apply the first law to the system containing both the oxygen and the carbon dioxide.

$$-W = \Delta U = \Delta U_{O_2} + \Delta U_{CO_2}$$

$$[mC_v(T_m - T_1)]_{O_2} + [mC_v(T_m - T_1)]_{CO_2} = 0$$

Using the C_v values at room temperature (from the thermodynamic property tables), the equilibrium temperature of the mixture is found to be

$$(10\text{kg})\left[0.658\frac{\text{kJ}}{(\text{kg.K})}\right](T_m - 30)(K) +$$

$$(2\text{kg})\left[0.657\frac{\text{kJ}}{(\text{kg.K})}\right](T_m - 45)(K) = 0$$

Hence, $\quad 6.58(T_m - 30) + 4.32(T_m - 45) = 0$

$$T_m = 35.9°C$$

(b) The equilibrium pressure of the mixture is found from the ideal-gas relationship,

$$P_m V_m = N_m R_u T_m$$

Calculating the number of molecules,

$$N_{O_2} = \frac{m}{M} = \frac{10}{32} = 0.3125 \text{ kmol}$$

$$N_{CO_2} = \frac{m}{M} = \frac{2}{44} = 0.0455 \text{ kmol}$$

$$N_m = N_{O_2} + N_{CO_2} = 0.358 \text{ kmol}$$

$$V_{O_2} = \left(\frac{NR_u T_1}{P_1}\right)_{O_2} = \frac{(0.3125 \text{ kmol})[8.314 \text{ kPa.m}^3/(\text{kmol.K})](303 \text{ K})}{120 \text{ kPa}} = 6.56 \text{m}^3$$

$$V_{CO_2} = \left(\frac{NR_u T_1}{P_1}\right)_{CO_2} = \frac{(0.0455 \text{ kmol})[8.314 \text{ kPa.m}^3/(\text{kmol.K})](318 \text{ K})}{200 \text{ kPa}} = 0.60 \text{ m}^3$$

Hence, $P_m = \left(\frac{N_m R_u T_m}{V_{1m}}\right) = \frac{(0.358 \text{ kmol})[8.314 \text{ kPa.m}^3/(\text{kmol.K})](308.9 \text{ K})}{7.16 \text{ m}^3} = 128 \text{ kPa}$

Example 4.4

Problem

A tank of fixed volume has two sections separated by a thin wall. One section holds 8 kmol of nitrogen and the other section holds 2 kmol of oxygen. Initially, both gases are at 20°C and 150 kPa. Then the thin wall is removed so that the gases can mix. Assume the process is adiabatic. The surrounding environment is at 20°C and both gases behave like ideal gases. Evaluate the entropy change and the irreversibility of the process.

Solution

Since the gases are initially at the same temperature and pressure, and it is assumed that the two gases will not react at that temperature and pressure, the mixture will be at the same temperature and pressure. (These are the components of air, and the temperature and pressure are in the normal range, so the assumption is valid.) The entropy change of each gas can be found by using Eqs. (4.19) and (4.26).

$$\Delta S_m = \sum_{i=1}^k \Delta S_i = \sum_{i=1}^k N_i \Delta \bar{s}_i = \sum_{i=1}^2 N_i \left(\bar{C}_{P,i} \ln \frac{T_{i,2}}{T_{i,1}} - R_u \ln \frac{P_{i,2}}{P_{i,1}} \right) \quad \text{(a)}$$

$$= -R_u \sum_{i=1}^2 N_i \ln \frac{y_i P_{m,2}}{P_{i,1}} = -R_u \sum_{i=1}^2 N_i \ln y_i$$

since $P_{m,2} = P_{i,1} = 150$ kPa.

Calculating the parameters,

$$N_m = N_{N_2} + N_{O_2} = (8+2) \text{ kmol} = 10 \text{ kmol}$$

$$y_{N_2} = \frac{N_{N_2}}{N_m} = \frac{8 \text{ kmol}}{10 \text{ kmol}} = 0.8$$

$$y_{O_2} = \frac{N_{O_2}}{N_m} = \frac{2 \text{ kmol}}{10 \text{ kmol}} = 0.2$$

$$\Delta S_m = -R_u \left(N_{N_2} \ln y_{N_2} + N_{O_2} \ln y_{O_2} \right)$$

$$= -[8.314 \text{ kJ/(kmol.K)}]\{(8 \text{ kmol})(\ln 0.8) + (2 \text{ kmol})(\ln 0.2)\}$$

$$= 41.6 \text{ kJ/K}$$

The irreversibility of the process is

$$I = T_o S_{gen} = T_o (\Delta S_m) = (293 \text{K})(41.6 \text{ kJ/K}) = 12,189 \text{ kJ}$$

The value of the irreversibility indicates that mixing processes are irreversible to a large extent.

2. Real-Gas Mixtures

When the components of a gas mixture do not behave like ideal gases, the analysis is more complex. The properties of real (nonideal) gases such as u, h, C_v, and C_p depend on the pressure (or specific volume) as well as on the temperature.

One way of accounting for nonideal behavior, is to use compressibility factors in conjunction with generalized equations and charts. Consider the following Tds equation for a gas mixture:

$$dh_m = T_m ds_m + v_m dP_m$$

This can also be expressed as

$$d\left(\sum mf_i h_i\right) = T_m d\left(\sum mf_i s_i\right) + \left(\sum mf_i v_i\right) dP_m$$

or $\quad \sum mf_i (dh_i - T_m ds_i - v_i dP_m) = 0$

which gives $\quad dh_i = T_m ds_i + v_i dP_m \quad\quad\quad (4.27)$

This is an important equation because it is a starting equation in the development of the generalized relationships and charts for enthalpy and entropy. The approach just described is somewhat similar to Amagat's law of additive volumes (computing mixture properties at the mixture pressure and temperature), which is exact for ideal-gas mixtures and only approximate for real-gas mixtures. Thus, the mixture properties determined with this approach will not be exact.

If the mixture volume and temperature are known instead of the mixture pressure and temperature, just evaluate the mixture pressure, using Dalton's law of additive pressures. Use this value as an approximation of the mixture pressure.

Another approach to compute the properties of a real-gas mixture is to consider the mixture as a pseudopure substance having pseudocritical properties. These pseudocritical properties can be determined in terms of the critical properties of the components by using Kay's rule. The method is rather simple.

Example 4.5

Problem

A gaseous mixture is made up of nitrogen and carbon dioxide in the mole fractions 0.70, 0.30, respectively. The mixture is cooled from 400 K and 310 K at a constant pressure of 8 MPa, in a steady-flow process. Find the heat transferred per kmol of the mixture for the process, by employing (a) the ideal-gas model, and (b) Kay's rule.

Solution

Assumption: (1) Changes in K.E. and P.E. are negligible.

Analysis:

Use the thermodynamic tables to find the critical properties of the gases.

For nitrogen, $T_{cr} = 126.2$ K, $P_{cr} = 3.39$ MPa

For carbon dioxide, $T_{cr} = 304.2$ K, $P_{cr} = 7.39$ MPa

Apply the first law to the system, on a unit-mole basis,

$$\bar{q} - \cancel{\bar{w}}^{0} = \Delta\bar{h} = \sum_{i=1}^{2} y_i \bar{h}_i$$

$$\bar{q} = y_{N_2}(\bar{h}_2 - \bar{h}_1)_{N_2} + y_{CO_2}(\bar{h}_2 - \bar{h}_1)_{CO_2} \qquad (a)$$

(a) Using the ideal-gas model, the enthalpy of the mixture will be a function of temperature only. The initial and final enthalpies of the individual gases may be found from the ideal-gas tables of nitrogen and carbon dioxide.

When $T_1 = 400$ K, $\bar{h}_{1,N_2} = 11{,}436$ kJ/kmol $\bar{h}_{1,CO_2} = 4002.5$ kJ/kmol

When $T_2 = 310$ K, $\bar{h}_{2,N_2} = 8598$ kJ/kmol $\bar{h}_{2,CO_2} = 443$ kJ/kmol

From Eq. (a), $\bar{q} = (0.7)(8598 - 11{,}436)$ kJ/kmol $+ (0.30)(443 - 4002.5)$ kJ/kmol

$= -3054.45$ kJ/kmol

(b) Using Kay's rule, the gaseous mixture is treated as a pseudopure substance, the pseudocritical temperature and pressure of which has to be found.

From Eq. (4.12),
$$T'_{cr,i} = \sum_{i=1}^{k} y_i T_{cr,i}$$
$$= (0.70)(126.2\text{K}) + (0.30)(304.2\text{K})$$
$$= 179.6\text{K}$$

From Eq. (4.12),
$$P'_{cr,i} = \sum_{i=1}^{k} y_i P_{cr,i}$$
$$= (0.70)(3.39\text{MPa}) + (0.30)(7.39\text{MPa})$$
$$= 4.59\text{MPa}$$

For the mixture,
$$T_{R,1} = \frac{T_{m,1}}{T'_{cr,m}} = \frac{400\text{K}}{179.6\text{K}} = 2.23$$

$$P_R = \frac{P_m}{P'_{cr,m}} = \frac{8\text{MPa}}{4.59\text{MPa}} = 1.74$$

$$T_{R,2} = \frac{T_{m,2}}{T'_{cr,m}} = \frac{310\text{K}}{179.6\text{K}} = 1.73$$

From $T_{R,1}$, P_R and the Nelson-Obert compressibility chart, $Z_{h_1,m} = 0.84$

From $T_{R,2}$, P_R and the Nelson-Obert compressibility chart, $Z_{h_2,m} = 0.67$

In addition,

$$\bar{h}_{m1,ideal} = y_{N_2} \bar{h}_{1,ideal,N_2} + y_{CO_2} \bar{h}_{1,ideal,CO_2}$$
$$= (0.7)(11{,}436 \text{ kJ/kmol}) + (0.3)(4002.5 \text{ kJ/kmol})$$
$$= 9206 \text{ kJ/kmol}$$

$$\bar{h}_{m2,ideal} = y_{N_2} \bar{h}_{2,ideal,N_2} + y_{CO_2} \bar{h}_{2,ideal,CO_2}$$
$$= (0.7)(8598 \text{ kJ/kmol}) + (0.3)(443 \text{ kJ/kmol})$$
$$= 6152 \text{ kJ/kmol}$$

$$\bar{q} = R_u T_{cr} \left(Z_{h_1} - Z_{h_2}\right)_m + \left(\bar{h}_{m2,ideal} - \bar{h}_{m1,ideal}\right)$$

$$= \left[8.314 \frac{kJ}{(kmol.K)} \right] (179.6K)(0.84 - 0.67) + (6152 - 9206) \frac{kJ}{kmol} = -2800 \text{ kJ/kmol}$$

The difference in results is about 9%.

PROBLEMS

Composition of a Gas Mixture

4.1. The gaseous products of combustion in a certain process are CO_2, H_2O, O_2 and N_2. Their corresponding mass fractions are 0.20, 0.15, 0.10, and 0.65, respectively. Calculate (a) the composition in mole fractions, and (b) the apparent molecular weight of the mixture.

4.2. The gaseous products of combustion in a certain process are CO_2, H_2O, O_2 and N_2. Their corresponding mass fractions are 0.15, 0.05, 0.05, and 0.75, respectively. Calculate (a) the composition in mole fractions, and (b) the apparent molecular weight of the mixture.

4.3. A gas mixture composition of CO_2, H_2O and N_2 expressed in mole fractions are 0.25, 0.15, and 0.60, respectively. Calculate (a) the apparent molecular weight of the mixture, (b) the composition in mass fractions.

4.4. A gas mixture composition of CO_2, H_2O, N_2 and CH_4 expressed in mole fractions are 0.10, 0.05, 0.50 and 0.35, respectively. Calculate (a) the apparent molecular weight of the mixture, (b) the composition in mass fractions.

P-v-T Relationships for Ideal and Real Gas Mixtures

4.5. A tank of fixed volume contains 1 kmol of nitrogen and 2 kmol of methane gases at 330K and 20 MPa. Estimate the volume of the tank using (a) the ideal gas equation of state, (b) compressiblity factors and Amagat's law, and (c) Kay's rule.

4.6. A tank of fixed volume contains 1 kmol of nitrogen and 2 kmol of ammonia gases at 420K and 20 MPa. Estimate the volume of the tank using (a) the ideal gas equation of state, (b) compressiblity factors and Amagat's law, and (c) Kay's rule.

Properties of Ideal and Real Gas Mixtures

4.7. A tank of fixed volume has two sections separated by a thin wall. One section has 10 kg of oxygen at 20°C and 100 kPa, and the other has 5 kg of carbon dioxide at 40°C and 250 kPa. Then the thin wall is removed so that the gases can mix. Assume that there is no heat transferred, and equilibrium is reached. Determine the mixture temperature and pressure.

4.8. A tank of fixed volume has two sections separated by a thin wall. One section has 10 kg of methane at 20°C and 100 kPa, and the other has 5 kg of oxygen at 40°C and 250 kPa. Then the thin wall is removed so that the gases can mix. Assume that there is no heat transferred, and equilibrium is reached. Determine the mixture temperature and pressure.

4.9. A tank of fixed volume has two sections separated by a thin wall. One section holds 2.5 kmol of nitrogen and the other section holds 7.5 kmol of oxygen.

Initially, both gases are at 25°C and 180 kPa. Then the thin wall is removed so that the gases can mix. Assume the process is adiabatic. The surrounding environment is at 25°C and both gases behave like ideal gases. Evaluate the entropy change and the irreversibility of the process.

4.10. A tank of fixed volume has two sections separated by a thin wall. One section holds 2.5 kmol of oxygen and the other section holds 7.5 kmol of methane. Initially, both gases are at 20°C and 180 kPa. Then the thin wall is removed so that the gases can mix. Assume the process is adiabatic. The surrounding environment is at 20°C and both gases behave like ideal gases. Evaluate the entropy change and the irreversibility of the process.

4.11. A gaseous mixture is made up of nitrogen and carbon dioxide in the mole fractions 0.55, 0.45, respectively. The mixture is cooled from 500 K and 400 K at a constant pressure of 9 MPa, in a steady-flow process. Find the heat transferred per kmol of the mixture for the process, by employing (a) the ideal-gas model, and (b) Kay's rule.

4.12. A gaseous mixture is made up of oxygen and carbon dioxide in the mole fractions 0.65, 0.35, respectively. The mixture is cooled from 440 K and 350 K at a constant pressure of 10 MPa, in a steady-flow process. Find the heat transferred per kmol of the mixture for the process, by employing (a) the ideal-gas model, and (b) Kay's rule.

5. GAS-VAPOR MIXTURES AND PSYCHROMETRICS

5.1 Atmospheric Air and Dry Air

Air is a mixture of nitrogen, oxygen, small but important amounts of carbon dioxide, and about one percent of rare gases (argon, helium, neon, krypton, xenon). The air in actuality contains some water vapor (or moisture) and is called **atmospheric air**. The air that does not contain any moisture is called **dry air**. It is sometimes easier to treat atmospheric air as a combination of dry air and water vapor, since the composition of dry air is fairly constant but the amount of water vapor changes quite frequently.

The temperature range in most air-conditioning applications is -10 to 50°C. The dry air in this temperature range can be treated as an ideal gas with a constant C_p value without significant error. Using 0°C as the reference temperature, the enthalpy and enthalpy change of dry air can be evaluated from

$$h_{dry\ air} = C_p T = [1.005 \text{ kJ/kg.°C}]T \qquad \text{(kJ/kg)} \qquad (5.1)$$

and

$$\Delta h_{dry\ air} = C_p \Delta T = [1.005 \text{ kJ/kg.°C}]\Delta T \qquad \text{(kJ/kg)} \qquad (5.2)$$

The atmospheric air may be treated as an ideal-gas mixture whose pressure is the sum of the partial pressure of dry air P_a and that of the water vapor P_v:

$$P = P_a + P_v \qquad (5.3)$$

The partial pressure of the water vapor is also called the **vapor pressure**. This is pressure exerted by the water vapor if it existed by itself at the temperature and volume of the mixture.

In the air conditioning temperature range, the enthalpy of water vapor in air can be taken to be the same as the enthalpy of the saturated vapor at the same temperature. In other words,

$$h_v(T, \text{low } P) \cong h_g(T) \qquad (5.4)$$

The enthalpy of water vapor at 0°C is 2501.3 kJ/kg. The average C_p value of water vapor in the air-conditioning temperature range is about 1.82 kJ/(kg.°C). Hence, a good approximation of the enthalpy of water vapor is

$$h_g(T) \cong 2501.3 + 1.82T \qquad (\text{kJ/kg}) \qquad T \text{ in } °C \qquad (5.5)$$

5.2 Specific and Relative Humidity of Air

The amount of water vapor in a unit mass of dry air may be expressed by the **specific humidity** or **absolute humidity** (also called the **humidity ratio**). This is designated by ω:

$$\omega = \frac{m_v}{m_a} \qquad (5.6)$$

The specific humidity can also be expressed as

$$\omega = \frac{m_v}{m_a} = \frac{P_v V / (R_v T)}{P_a V / (R_a T)} = \frac{P_v / R_v}{P_a / R_a} = 0.622 \frac{P_v}{P_a} \qquad (5.7)$$

or

$$\omega = \frac{0.622 P_v}{P - P_v} \qquad (\text{kg water vapor/kg dry air}) \qquad (5.8)$$

Dry air contains no water vapor, and by definition, its specific humidity is zero. As we introduce water vapor or moisture to this dry air, its specific humidity will increase. This will continue until the air can no longer hold any more moisture, and it is said to be **saturated**. The quantity of moisture in saturated air at a specified temperature and pressure can be calculated from Eq. (5.8) by putting P_g in place of P_v, where P_g is the saturation pressure of water at that temperature. At atmospheric pressure, this saturation pressure of water is a function only of temperature.

The amount of moisture in the air m_v relative to the maximum amount of moisture the air can hold at the same temperature (m_g), is its relative humidity ϕ:

$$\phi = \frac{m_v}{m_g} = \frac{P_v V/(R_v T)}{P_g V/(R_v T)} = \frac{P_v}{P_g} \quad (5.9)$$

where
$$P_g = P_{sat@T} \quad (5.10)$$

Combining Eqs. (5.8) and (5.9), the relative humidity can be expressed as

$$\phi = \frac{\omega P}{(0.622 + \omega) P_g} \quad \text{and} \quad \omega = \frac{0.622 \phi P_g}{P - \phi P_g} \quad (5.11)$$

The amount of moisture atmospheric air can hold depends on its temperature. Even if the specific humidity of the air were kept constant, the relative humidity can change with temperature. The relative humidity ranges from zero for dry air to one for saturated air.

The enthalpy of atmospheric air is expressed per unit mass of dry air, not in terms of per unit mass of the air-moisture mixture. The total enthalpy of atmospheric air is the sum of the enthalpies of the dry air and the water vapor:

$$H = H_a + H_v = m_a h_a + m_v h_v$$

Thus,
$$h = \frac{H}{m_a} = h_a + \frac{m_v}{m_a} h_v = h_a + \omega h_v$$

or
$$h = h_a + \omega h_g \quad (5.12)$$

since $h_v \cong h_g$.

5.3 Dew-Point Temperature

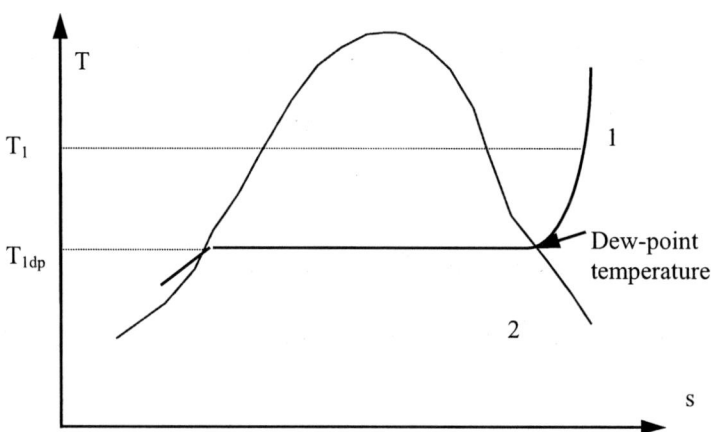

Figure 5.1   Constant pressure cooling and the dew-point temperature.

The temperature of the atmospheric air measured by an ordinary thermometer (e.g. mercury thermometer) is normally referred to as the **dry-bulb temperature** to differentiate it from other forms of temperatures.

The **dew-point temperature** T_{dp} is defined as the temperature at which condensation starts when the air is cooled at constant pressure. T_{dp} is the saturation temperature of water corresponding to the vapor pressure P_v:

$$T_{dp} = T_{sat@Pv} \tag{5.13}$$

This is shown in Fig. 5.1. As the air is cooled at constant pressure, the vapor pressure P_v remains constant. The vapor in the air (state 1) undergoes an isobaric cooling process until it reaches the saturated vapor line (state 2). The temperature at this point is T_{dp}, and if the temperature is lowered any further, some moisture condenses out. In that case, the amount of vapor in the air decreases, which results in P_v decreasing. The dry bulb temperature and the dew-point temperature of the saturated air are the same.

The dew-point temperature of atmospheric air can be found simply. Put water in a cup. Add ice to the water and stir to maintain a well-mixed condition. The temperature of the outer surface of the cup at which dew starts to form is the dew-point temperature of the surrounding air.

5.4 Adiabatic Saturation Process and Wet-Bulb Temperatures

In the last section, it was discussed how to measure the dew-point temperature of atmospheric air. Knowing this temperature, the vapor pressure P_v can be calculated and subsequently, the relative humidity.

Another method of determining the absolute or relative humidity is the adiabatic saturation process. This is shown schematically and on a T-s diagram in Fig. 5.2. The apparatus comprises a long insulated chamber that contains liquid water. Unsaturated air that has a specific humidity of ω_1 (unknown) and temperature T_1 is passed through this chamber. In this process, the moisture content of the air will increase and its temperature will decrease, since part of the latent heat of vaporization for the liquid water will come from the air. When the chamber is long enough, the air will exit as saturated air (ϕ=100%) at temperature T_2, which is called the **adiabatic saturation temperature**.

When makeup water is supplied to the chamber at the rate of evaporation and at temperature T_2, the adiabatic saturation process can be analyzed as a steady-state steady-flow process. Neglecting potential and kinetic energy terms, the mass and energy conservation equations are as follows:

Mass conservation:

$$\dot{m}_{a,1} = \dot{m}_{a,2} = \dot{m}_a$$

$$\dot{m}_{w,1} + \dot{m}_f = \dot{m}_{w,2}$$

or

$$\dot{m}_a \omega_1 + \dot{m}_f = \dot{m}_a \omega_2$$

Thus,

$$\dot{m}_f = \dot{m}_a (\omega_2 - \omega_1)$$

Energy balance:

$$\dot{m}_{a,1} h_1 + \dot{m}_f h_{f,2} = \dot{m}_{a,2} h_2$$

or $\quad \dot{m}_a h_1 + \dot{m}_a (\omega_2 - \omega_1) h_{f,2} = \dot{m}_a h_2$

Dividing by $\dot{m}_a$,

$$h_1 + (\omega_2 - \omega_1) h_{f,2} = h_2$$

or $\quad (C_p T_1 + \omega_1 h_{g,1}) + (\omega_2 - \omega_1) h_{f,2} = (C_p T_2 + \omega_2 h_{g,2})$

which gives

$$\omega_1 = \frac{C_p (T_2 - T_1) + \omega_2 h_{fg,2}}{h_{g,1} - h_{f,2}} \tag{5.14}$$

where, from Eq. (5.11),

$$\omega_2 = \frac{0.622 \phi P_{g,2}}{P_2 - \phi P_{g,2}} \tag{5.15}$$

since $\phi_2 = 100\%$. Thus the specific humidity (and relative humidity) of the air can be determined from Eqs.(5.14) and (5.15) by measuring the pressure and temperature of the air at the inlet and exit of an adiabatic saturation chamber.

The adiabatic saturation chamber is a rather long device. A more practical approach is to use an ordinary thermometer whose bulb is covered with a cotton wick saturated with water and to allow air to flow over the wick, as shown in Fig. 5.3. The temperature thus measured is called the wet-bulb temperature T_{wb}, and is normally used in air-conditioning. The wet-bulb temperature may also be measured by placing the wet-wicked thermometer in a holder with a handle and rotating the holder, that is, by moving the thermometer instead of the air. Normally a dry-bulb thermometer is also mounted on the frame so that both the wet- and dry-bulb temperatures can be read together. This device is called a sling psychrometer.

The adiabatic saturation temperature is generally not the same as the wet-bulb temperature. But for air-water-vapor mixtures at atmospheric pressure, the two temperatures are pretty close to each other. Thus, the wet-bulb temperature T_{wb} can be used in Eq. (5.14) instead of T_2 to determine ω of the air. The wet-bulb temperature may also be taken to be the dew-point temperature.

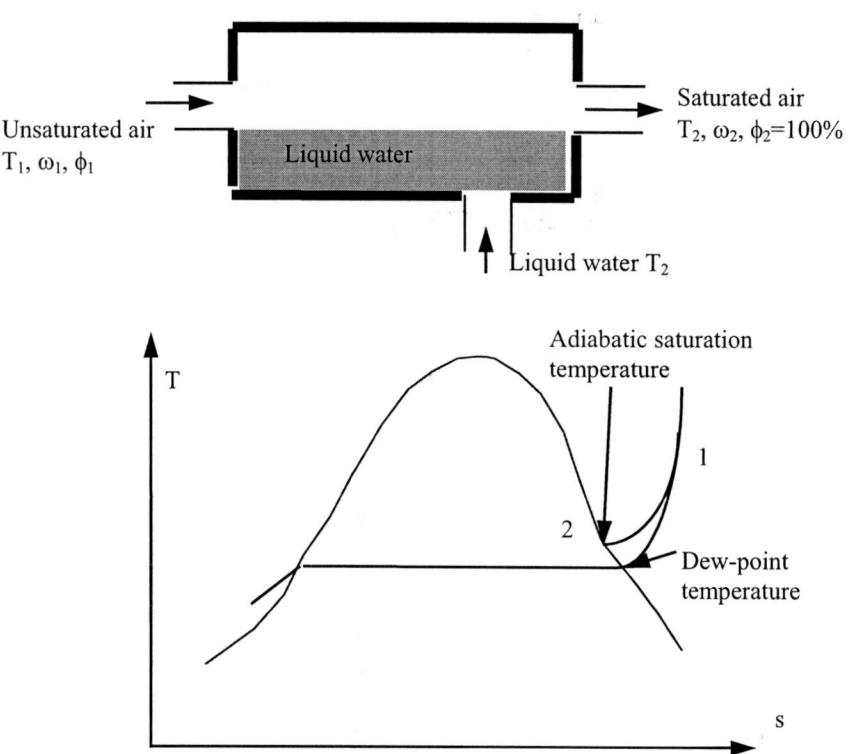

Figure 5.2   Adiabatic saturation process.

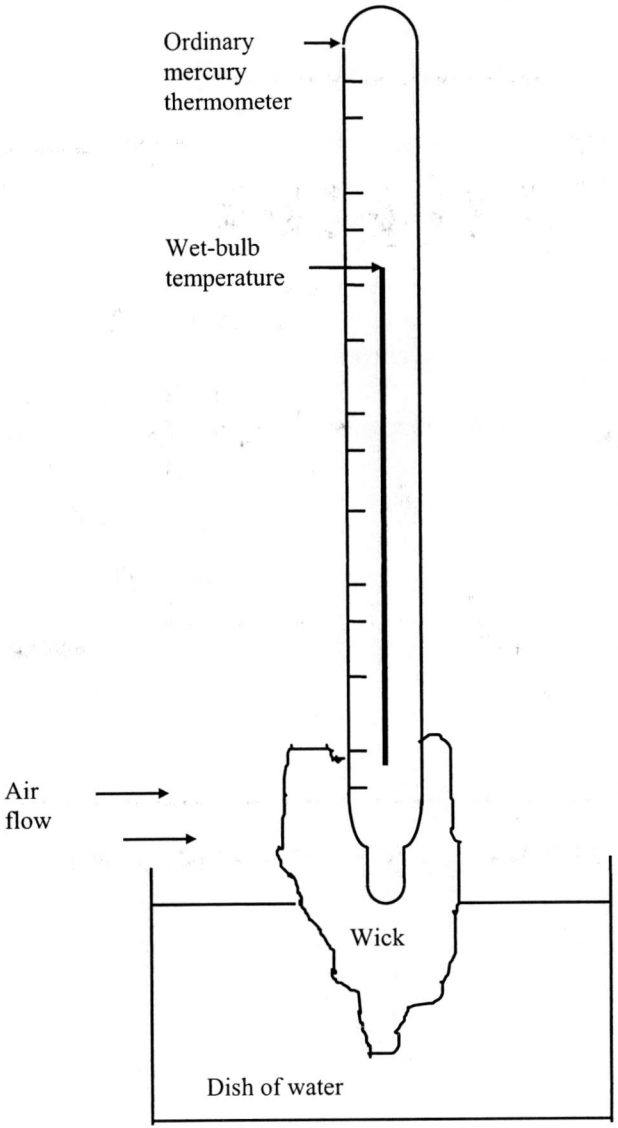

Figure 5.3 A simple set-up to measure the wet-bulb temperature.

5.5 The Psychrometric Chart

The state of atmospheric air at a specified pressure is specified completely by two independent intensive properties. The other properties can be calculated from the equations developed in the previous sections. However, since a large number of these calculations are involved in air-conditioning system design, psychrometric charts have been developed to make these calculations easier.

The main features of the psychrometric chart are illustrated in Fig. 5.4. The horizontal axis is the dry bulb temperature and the vertical axis is the specific humidity or humidity ratio. All the saturated air states are located on the saturation curve (or line) situated on the left end of the chart. This saturation curve is also the curve of one hundred percent relative humidity. Other relative humidity curves have a similar shape.

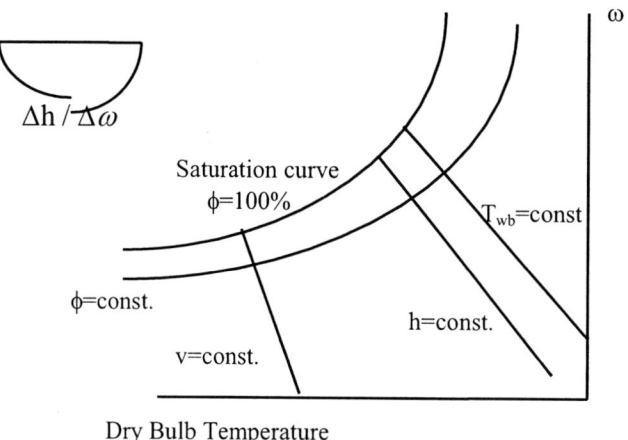

Figure 5.4   Schematic of a psychrometric chart.

Lines of constant wet-bulb temperature have a descending gradient to the right. Lines of constant specific volume (in m^3/kg dry air) have a steeper descending gradient to the right. Isenthalpic lines (in kJ/kg dry air) lie nearly parallel to the lines of constant wet-bulb temperature. There is also a protractor on the upper left-hand corner of the chart. One scale usually shows the ratio of enthalpy difference to specific humidity difference, $\Delta h/\Delta \omega$.

For saturated air, the dry-bulb, wet-bulb, and dew-point temperatures are the same. Thus, the dew-point temperature of atmospheric air at any point on the chart can be found by drawing a horizontal line (a line of constant ω) from that point to the saturation curve. The temperature at the point of intersection is the dew-point temperature.

The purpose of air-conditioning is to maintain a living space or a commercial facility at the desired temperature and humidity. The human body continuously rejects heat and moisture to the surrounding environment. The amount of heat and moisture is dependent on the activity level. The objective is to allow both the human heat and moisture to be removed from the body without discomfort. Air-conditioning processes are employed to keep the temperature and humidity at the desired level.

Air-conditioning processes or psychrometric processes are easily visualized with the use of a psychrometric chart. These processes include sensible heating (raising the dry bulb temperature only), sensible cooling (lowering the dry bulb temperature only), humidification (adding moisture), and dehumidification (removing moisture). These psychrometric processes are illustrated on the psychrometric chart in Fig. 5.5. It may take two or more processes to bring the air to the desired temperature and humidity level.

Note that the sensible heating or sensible cooling process appear as horizontal lines on the chart. Any deviation from a horizontal line shows that the moisture content of the air is changed during the process.

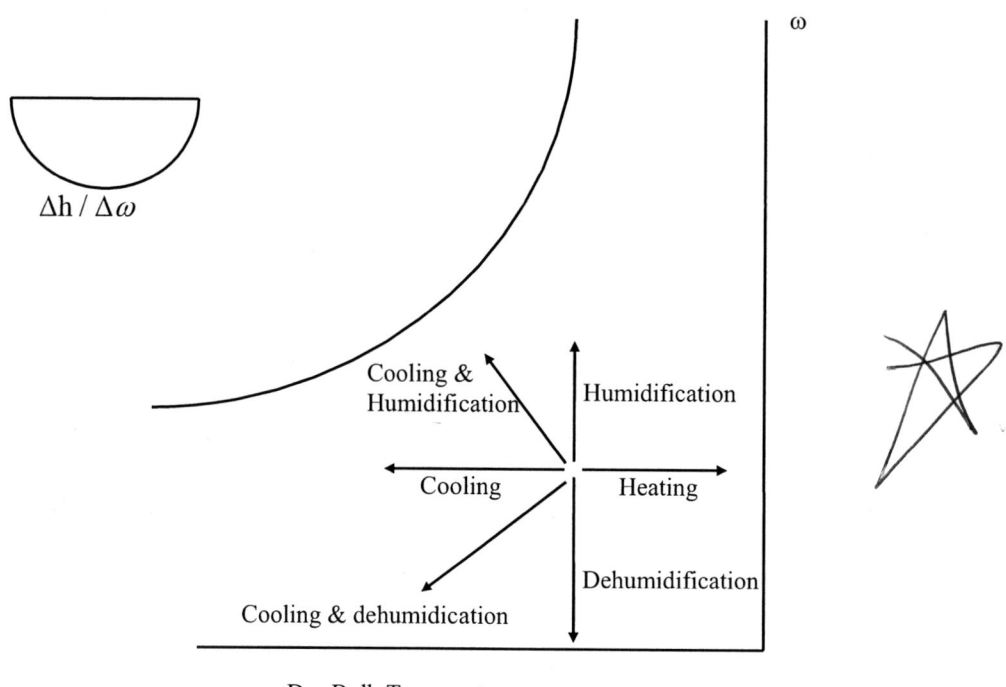

Figure 5.5   Air-conditioning or psychrometric processes.

5.6 Psychrometric Processes

The analysis of psychrometric processes is done by considering a control volume and then applying the principles of the conservation of mass and of energy (first law) to the control volume. All the processes are steady-flow processes with negligible changes in potential and kinetic energy. Generally no shaft work is involved. Thus the steady-state energy equation gives

$$\sum_{in} \dot{m}h + \dot{Q} = \sum_{out} \dot{m}h \qquad (5.16)$$

The sign convention used is that $\dot{Q}$ is positive when heat is added to the control volume. In psychrometric applications, the control volume chosen will often be a volume of moist air that is present in the air-conditioning apparatus.

Commercial air conditioning equipment such as centrifugal fans, heating coils, etc., are usually rated in terms of volume flow of standard air. In addition, the units used in air conditioning is often the British units. Standard air may be defined as moist air having a specific density of 0.075 lb/ft³. In general,

$$\rho \text{ (lb/ft}^3\text{)} = \frac{1+\omega}{v}, \quad \omega = [lb_w/lb_a], \quad v = [ft^3/lb_a]$$

EXAMPLE 5.1

Convert supply volume of 10,650 ft³/min at $v_1 = 13.27$ ft³/lb$_a$, $\omega = 0.00842$ lb$_w$/lb$_a$ to standard air.

Solution

$$\rho_1 = \frac{1+\omega_1}{v_1} = \frac{1+0.00842}{13.27} = 0.0760 \text{ lb}/\text{ft}^3$$

$$\text{Supply volume} = \frac{\rho_1 V_1}{0.075} \text{ ft}^3/\text{min standard air}$$

$$= \frac{(0.0760)(10{,}650)}{0.075}$$

$$= 10{,}790 \text{ ft}^3/\text{min standard air}$$

1.   Simple Heating and Cooling (ω = constant)

If heat is added to moist air with no addition of moisture, then the process is one of sensible heating. The process could occur if moist air is passed across a heated surface, like a bundle of finned tubes, where a working fluid such as hot water or steam circulates inside the tubes.

Sensible cooling is the reverse of sensible heating. It could occur if air is passed across a cool surface. To restrict the process to only sensible cooling, the surface temperature must be higher than the air dew-point temperature. In Figure 5.6 is shown a schematic for a device to heat air, and also a sketch of the process on a psychrometric chart. Note that the humidity ratio (ω) remains constant.

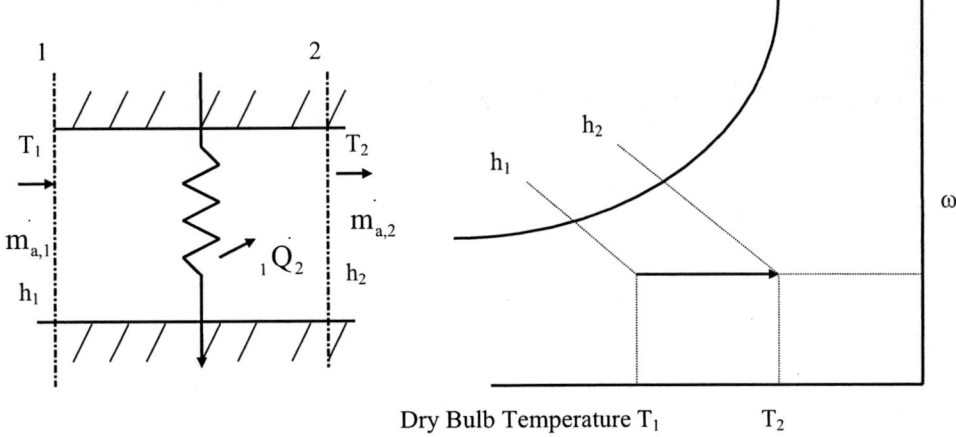

Figure 5.6   Schematic illustration of sensible heating of moist air.

The steady-state steady-flow energy and mass balance equations are

$$m_{a,1} h_1 + {}_1\dot{Q}_2 = m_{a,2} h_2 \tag{5.17}$$

$$\dot{m}_{a,1} = \dot{m}_{a,2} \tag{5.18}$$

$$\dot{m}_{a,1} \omega_1 = \dot{m}_{a,2} \omega_2 \tag{5.19}$$

where h_1 and h_2 are enthalpies per unit mass of dry air at the inlet and the exit of the heating or cooling section, respectively. Equation (5.18) states that the mass of dry air entering and exiting are the same. It follows that ω_1 and ω_2 are the same in Eq. (5.19)

EXAMPLE 5.2

200 cfm of air at 70°F, 60% R.H. are heated to 100°F. Find the required heat transfer. The total pressure is 1 atm.

Solution

The first law of thermodynamics or energy conservation equation gives

$$_1\dot{Q}_2 = \dot{m}_{a,2} h_2 - \dot{m}_{a,1} h_1$$

The inlet state is completely specified. Since the absolute humidity does not change in the process, the process is a horizontal line on the psychrometric chart. Thus, both the inlet and the exit states of the air can be determined and the properties read from the psychrometric chart.

$h_1 = 27.2$ Btu/lb of dry air

$v_1 = 13.53$ ft^3/lb of dry air

$h_2 = 34.5$ Btu/lb of dry air

Mass flow rate is $\dot{m}_{a,1} = \dfrac{V_1}{v_1} = \dfrac{200 \text{ ft}^3/\text{min}}{13.53 \text{ ft}^3/\text{lb}} = 14.78$ lb/min

$_1\dot{Q}_2 = 14.78$ lb/min $(34.5 - 27.2)$ Btu/lb $= 107.9$ Btu/min

2. Humidification of Moist Air

A psychrometric process used frequently is that of adding only moisture to air passing through a chamber. The moisture may either be in vapor or liquid form, and no other energy is added. A device for humidifying the moist air in steady flow is shown in Fig. 5.7. The steady-state steady-flow mass balance for water and the energy equation are

$$\dot{m}_w = \dot{m}_a (\omega_2 - \omega_1) \tag{5.20}$$

$$\dot{m}_w h_w = \dot{m}_a (h_2 - h_1) \tag{5.21}$$

Thus

$$q' = \frac{h_2 - h_1}{\omega_2 - \omega_1} = h_\omega \qquad (5.22)$$

The direction of the condition line connecting states 1 and 2 depends on the enthalpy of the moisture added. Several humidification condition lines are shown in Fig. 5.8. The constant dry-bulb temperature line divides the processes into two categories. If $h_w > h_g$, the air will be sensibly heated and humidified with the moisture spray. If $h_w < h_g$, the air will be sensibly cooled and humidified. When $h_w = h_g$, the air will just be humidified, its dry bulb temperature remaining unchanged. The $\Delta h / \Delta \omega$ value can be read directly off the psychrometric chart for the straight line connecting states 1 and 2.

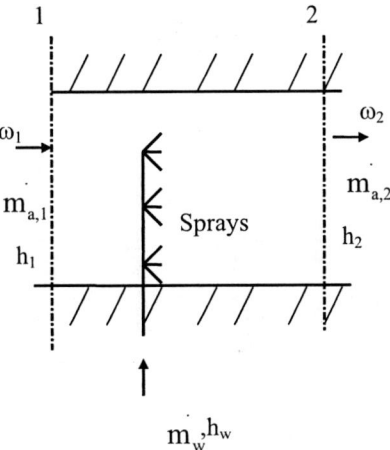

Figure 5.7   Schematic of humidification by the injection of water.

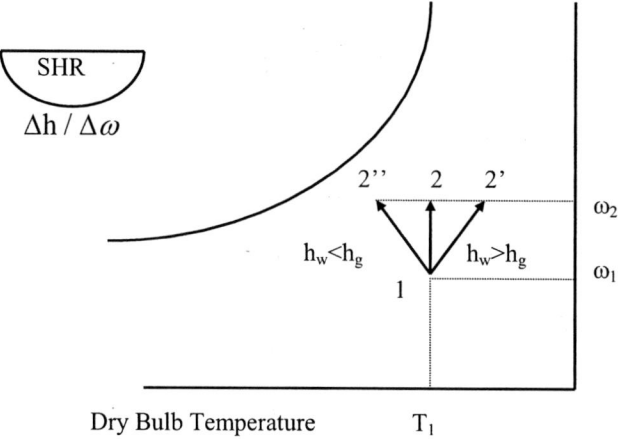

Figure 5.8   Humidification processes on psychrometric chart.

Example 5.3

An air conditioning system is to take in outdoor air at 55°F and 30% relative humidity at a steady rate of 300 cfm and to condition it to 72°F and 60% relative humidity. The outdoor air is sprayed with steam to accomplish this process. Assuming the whole process takes place at atmospheric pressure, calculate (a) the rate of heat added and (b) the mass flow rate of moisture added.

Solution

Since both the inlet and the exit states of the air are completely specified, the properties can be read from the psychrometric chart.

h_1 = 16.4 Btu/lb of dry air

v_1 = 13.05 ft³/lb of dry air

ω_1 = 0.0028 lb$_w$/lb of dry air

h_2 = 28.2 Btu/lb of dry air

$\omega_2 = 0.010$ lb$_w$/lb of dry air

Mass flow rate is $\dot{m}_a = \dot{m}_{a,1} = \dfrac{\dot{V}_1}{v_1} = \dfrac{300 \text{ ft}^3/\text{min}}{13.05 \text{ ft}^3/\text{lb}} = 22.99$ lb/min

(a) The rate of heat added is

$$\dot{Q} = \dot{m}_a (h_2 - h_1) = 22.99 \text{ lb/min} \, (28.2 - 16.4) \text{ Btu/lb} = 271.3 \text{ Btu/min}$$

(b) The mass rate of moisture added is

$$\dot{m}_w = \dot{m}_a (\omega_2 - \omega_1) = 22.99 \text{ lb/min} \, (0.010 - 0.0028) \text{ lb}_w/\text{lb} = 0.166 \text{ lb}_w/\text{min}$$

3. Dehumidification of Moist Air by Cooling

When moist air is cooled below its dew point, condensation will take place. A schematic of the cooling device is shown in Fig. 5.9. The process is shown in Fig. 5.10. The ideal process is one in which the air is uniformly and perfectly contacted by the cooling coil. No condensation occurs until the average or bulk temperature of the air reaches the dew-point temperature. As the temperature is decreased, the process goes along the saturation line to the final state.

The dry air and the water mass balances are thus

$$\dot{m}_{a,1} = \dot{m}_{a,2} = \dot{m}_a \qquad (5.23)$$

$$\dot{m}_{a,1} \omega_1 = \dot{m}_{a,2} \omega_2 + \dot{m}_w \Rightarrow \dot{m}_w = \dot{m}_a (\omega_1 - \omega_2) \qquad (5.24)$$

The first law of thermodynamics (energy balance) gives

$$\dot{m}_{a,1} h_1 + {}_1\dot{Q}_2 = \dot{m}_{a,2} h_2 + \dot{m}_w h_{w,2} \qquad (5.25)$$

The condensate can leave the apparatus at various temperatures ranging from the initial dew point to the final temperature T_2. It is normally assumed that the condensate leaves at the final temperature T_2.

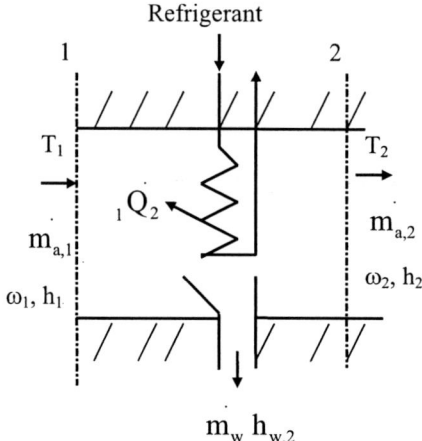

Figure 5.9   Schematic illustration of dehumidification by cooling.

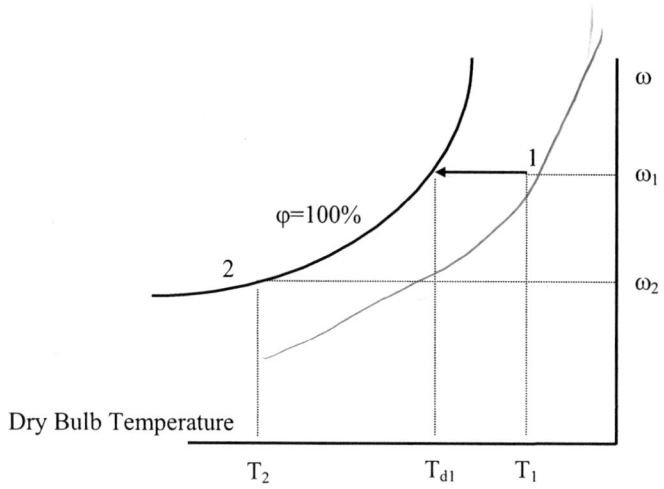

Figure 5.10   Dehumidification by cooling on psychrometric chart.

Example 5.4

500 cfm of air at 80°F, 70% R.H. are cooled to 60°F ideally. Find the mass of water condensed and the required heat transfer. Do not neglect the energy in the condensate.

Solution

Both states are completely defined, so that the properties may be read off the psychrometric chart.

$h_1 = 36.2$ Btu/lb of dry air

$v_1 = 13.94$ ft³/lb of dry air

$\omega_1 = 0.0154$ lb$_w$/lb of dry air

$h_2 = 26.6$ Btu/lb of dry air

$\omega_2 = 0.0112$ lb$_w$/lb of dry air   R.H. at state 2 is 100%

Mass flow rate is $\dot{m}_a = \dot{m}_{a,1} = \dfrac{\dot{V}_1}{v_1} = \dfrac{500 \text{ ft}^3/\text{min}}{13.94 \text{ ft}^3/\text{lb}} = 35.87$ lb/min

(a) The water mass balance is thus

$\dot{m}_w = \dot{m}_a(\omega_2 - \omega_1) = 35.87$ lb/min $(0.0112 - 0.0154)$ lb$_w$/lb $= -0.15$ lb/min

The mass of water condensed is 0.15 lb/min or 9 lb/hr.

(b) The first law of thermodynamics (energy balance) gives

$_1\dot{Q}_2 = \dot{m}_a(h_2 - h_1) + \dot{m}_w h_{w,2}$

$_1\dot{Q}_2 = 2152.2$ lb/hr$(26.6 - 36.2)$ Btu/lb $+ 9$ lb/.hr$(28.08$ Btu/lb$)$
       $= -20{,}408$ Btu/hr

The amount of heat removed is 20,408 Btu/hr. The enthalpy of the condensate is the enthalpy of saturated liquid water at 60°F.

4. Evaporative Cooling of Moist Air

Evaporative cooling may be used in hot and arid climates. It is based on a simple principle. When water evaporates, the latent heat of vaporization is absorbed from the water body and the surrounding air. Both the water and the air are cooled as a result.

The evaporative cooling process is the same as the adiabatic saturation process since the heat transfer between the airstream and the surroundings is generally negligible. Hence, the evaporative cooling process follows a line of constant wet-bulb temperature on the psychrometic chart. This is exactly the case only if the liquid water is supplied at a temperature that is the same as the exit temperature of the airstream. Since the constant-wet-bulb-temperature lines are almost coincidental with the isenthalpic lines, the enthalpy of the airstream may also be assumed to remain constant. Thus,

$$T_{wb} \cong \text{constant} \qquad (5.26)$$

$$h \cong \text{constant} \qquad (5.27)$$

This is a reasonably accurate approximation. Note that this is a special case of the humidification of moist air. A schematic of the evaporative cooling process is shown in Fig. 5.11. The process is shown on a psychrometric chart in Fig. 5.12.

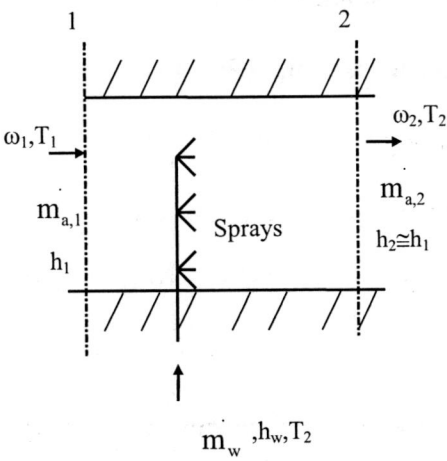

Figure 5.11   Schematic of evaporative cooling.

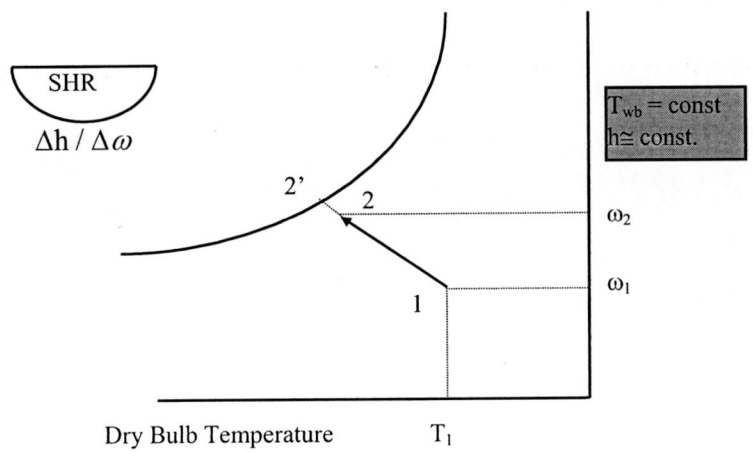

Figure 5.12   Evaporative cooling process on psychrometric chart.

Example 5.5

Outside air at 90°F and 20% R.H. in a small town in Arizona is cooled evaporatively to 65% R.H. Determine the dry-bulb temperature of the processed air.

Solution

The process line follows approximately the constant-wet-bulb-temperature line. Hence, from the psychrometric chart, it may be read that

$T_2 = 70.5°F$.

5. Adiabatic Mixing of Two Streams of Moist Air

Mixing of two or more air streams is a very common occurrence in air conditioning systems. Normally, such mixing processes occur under adiabatic conditions. The mixing of two airstreams is shown in Fig. 5.13. The governing equations are

$$\dot{m}_{a,1} h_1 + \dot{m}_{a,2} h_2 = \dot{m}_{a,3} h_3$$

$$\dot{m}_{a,1} + \dot{m}_{a,2} = \dot{m}_{a,3}$$

$$\dot{m}_{a,1} \omega_1 + \dot{m}_{a,2} \omega_2 = \dot{m}_{a,3} \omega_3 \qquad (5.28)$$

By eliminating $\dot{m}_{a,3}$ between the equations, we obtain

$$\frac{\dot{m}_{a,1}}{\dot{m}_{a,2}} = \frac{h_2 - h_3}{h_3 - h_1} = \frac{\omega_2 - \omega_3}{\omega_3 - \omega_1} \qquad (5.29)$$

From Eq. (5.29), we know that the resulting state 3 must lie on a straight line connecting states 1 and 2 on the psychrometric chart. In addition, segments of this line are proportional to the masses of dry air mixed. In Fig. 5.14, we may write

$$\frac{\dot{m}_{a,1}}{\dot{m}_{a,2}} = \frac{\overline{32}}{\overline{13}} \quad \text{or} \quad \frac{\dot{m}_{a,1}}{\dot{m}_{a,3}} = \frac{\overline{32}}{\overline{12}} \quad \text{or} \quad \frac{\dot{m}_{a,2}}{\dot{m}_{a,3}} = \frac{\overline{13}}{\overline{12}} \quad (5.30)$$

(Physical length)

where $\overline{32}$ and $\overline{13}$ are the physical lengths of the lines joining 3 to 2, and 1 to 3, etc. When states 1 and 2 are situated close to the saturation curve, the straight line joining the two states will cross the saturation curve, and state 3 may be situated left of the saturation curve. This is not physically possible. In actuality, some water will condense during the mixing process. State 3 is located by drawing the constant wet-bulb temperature line through the point to the left of the saturation curve and finding the point of intersection with the saturation curve.

Example 5.6

320 cfm of air at 90°F, 60% R.H. are mixed with 500 cfm of air at 75°F, 45% R.H. Find the dbt, wbt and R.H. of the mixed air. Calculate the cfm of the mixed air from the state of the mixed air.

Solution

Both initial states are completely defined, so their properties may be read from the psychrometric chart.

$v_1 = 14.26$ ft³/lb of dry air

$v_2 = 13.65$ ft³/lb of dry air

$$\dot{m}_{a,1} = \frac{\dot{V}_1}{v_1} = \frac{320 \text{ ft}^3 / \text{min}}{14.26 \text{ ft}^3 / \text{lb}} = 22.44 \text{ lb} / \text{min}$$

$$\dot{m}_{a,2} = \frac{\dot{V}_2}{v_2} = \frac{500 \text{ ft}^3/\text{min}}{13.65 \text{ ft}^3/\text{lb}} = 36.63 \text{ lb/min}$$

The final state 3 can be found on the psychrometric chart, on the line joining 1 to 2, such that

$$\frac{\dot{m}_{a,1}}{\dot{m}_{a,2}} = \frac{22.44}{36.63} = 0.613$$

Thus, $T_3 = 80.8°F$, $T_{3wb} = 68.7°F$, R.H. at 3 = 54%, $v_3 = 13.89$ ft³/lb of dry air

Volume of air at final state = (22.44+36.63) lb/min × 13.89 ft³/lb = 820.3 cfm.

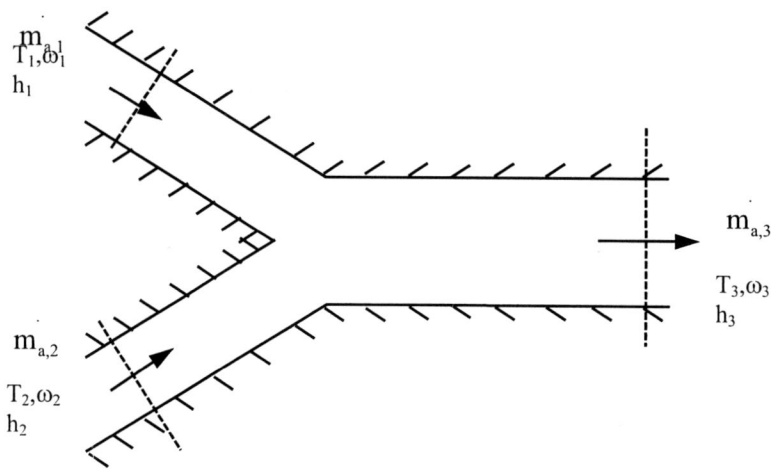

Figure 5.13   Schematic illustration of adiabatic mixing of two streams of moist air.

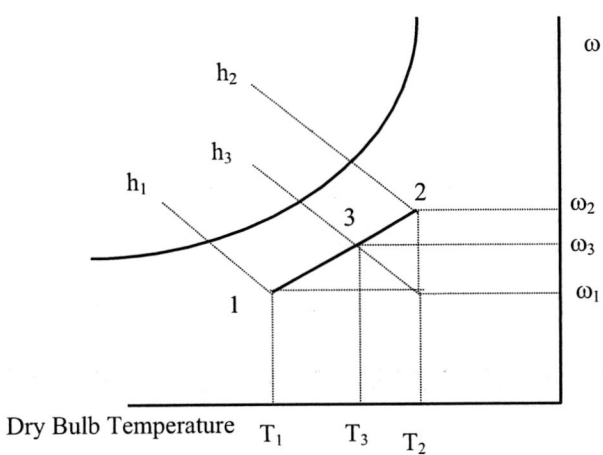

Figure 5.14   Adiabatic mixing process on psychrometric chart.

Example 5.7

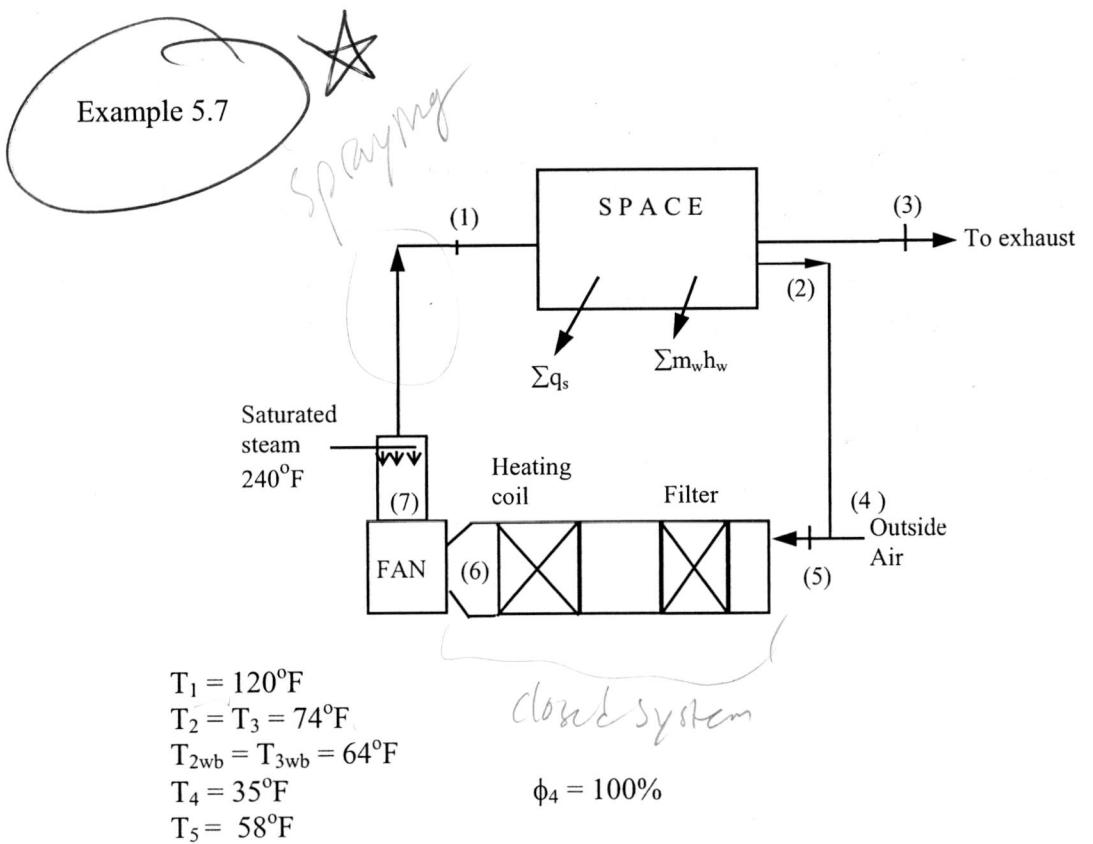

$T_1 = 120°F$
$T_2 = T_3 = 74°F$
$T_{2wb} = T_{3wb} = 64°F$
$T_4 = 35°F$ $\phi_4 = 100\%$
$T_5 = 58°F$

In winter, an indoor space is conditioned by a system with schematic as shown. The rate of sensible heat loss from the space is 135,000 Btu per hr and the rate of moisture loss (average h_w = 1150 Btu per lb_w) is 16.0 lb per hr. The pressure is 14.696 psia. (a) Locate all statepoints on the psychrometric chart and read values of T_{1wb}, T_{5wb}, T_7, and T_{7wb}. (b) Find the required volume of air supplied to the space in cu ft per min. (c) Calculate the lb per hr of steam required for the humidifier.

Solution

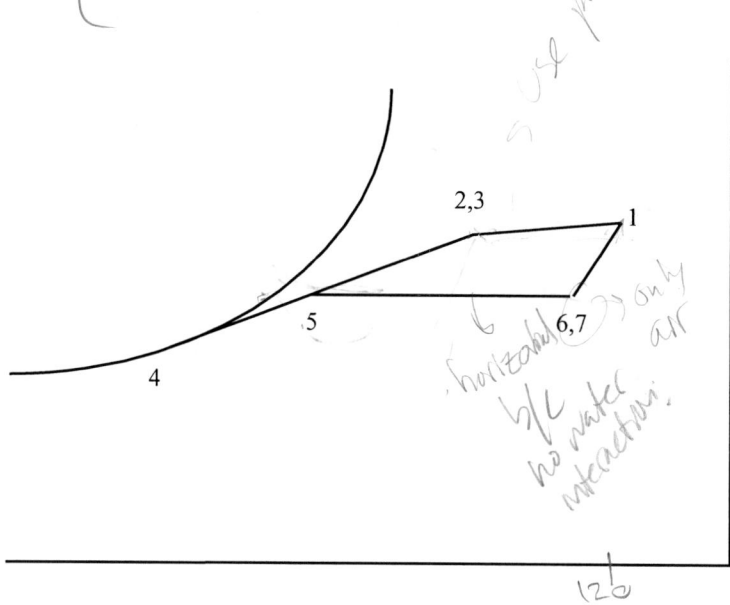

The schematic of the psychrometric chart of the processes are shown above.

(a) First, locate states 2 (3) and 4.

$$\Sigma q_s + \Sigma m_w h_w = -135{,}000 - (16)(1150)$$

$$= -153{,}400 \text{ Btu/hr}$$

$$q' = \frac{\text{sensible heat}}{\text{total heat}} = \frac{-135{,}000}{-153{,}400} = 0.88$$

Use the protractor to aid the drawing of the space condition line and locate state 1.

$T_{1wb} = 79°F$

For the mixing process, locate state 5 as lying on the line 4-2, at $T_5 = 58°F$.

$T_{5wb} = 54°F$

Alternatively, ω_5 may be calculated as follows:

$$\frac{m_{a,2}}{m_{a,5}} = \frac{T_5 - T_4}{T_2 - T_4} = \frac{\omega_5 - \omega_4}{\omega_2 - \omega_4}$$

$$\omega_5 = \omega_4 + (\omega_2 - \omega_4)\frac{T_5 - T_4}{T_2 - T_4}$$

$$= 0.0043 + (0.0104 - 0.0043)\frac{(58 - 35)}{(74 - 35)}$$

$$= 0.0079 \, lb_w/lb_a$$

For the humidifier,

$$\frac{\text{enthalpy}}{\text{humidity ratio}} = 1161 \, Btu/lb_w$$

Use the chart protractor to locate state 6 (7).

$T_7 = 118.3°F$, $T_{7wb} = 74°F$.

The first law of thermodynamics give $Q = m_a(h_2 - h_1)$

$$m_{a,1} = \frac{\sum q_s + \sum m_w h_w}{h_2 - h_1}$$

$$= \frac{-153,400}{29.4 - 42.6} = 11,621 \, lb_a/hr$$

Supply volume $= m_{a,1} v_1 = (11,621)(14.72)/(60) = 2851$ cu ft/min.

(c) For the humidifier,

$$m_w = m_{a,1}(\omega_1 - \omega_7) = 11,621(0.012 - 0.008) = 46.5 \, lb_w/hr.$$

Example 5.8

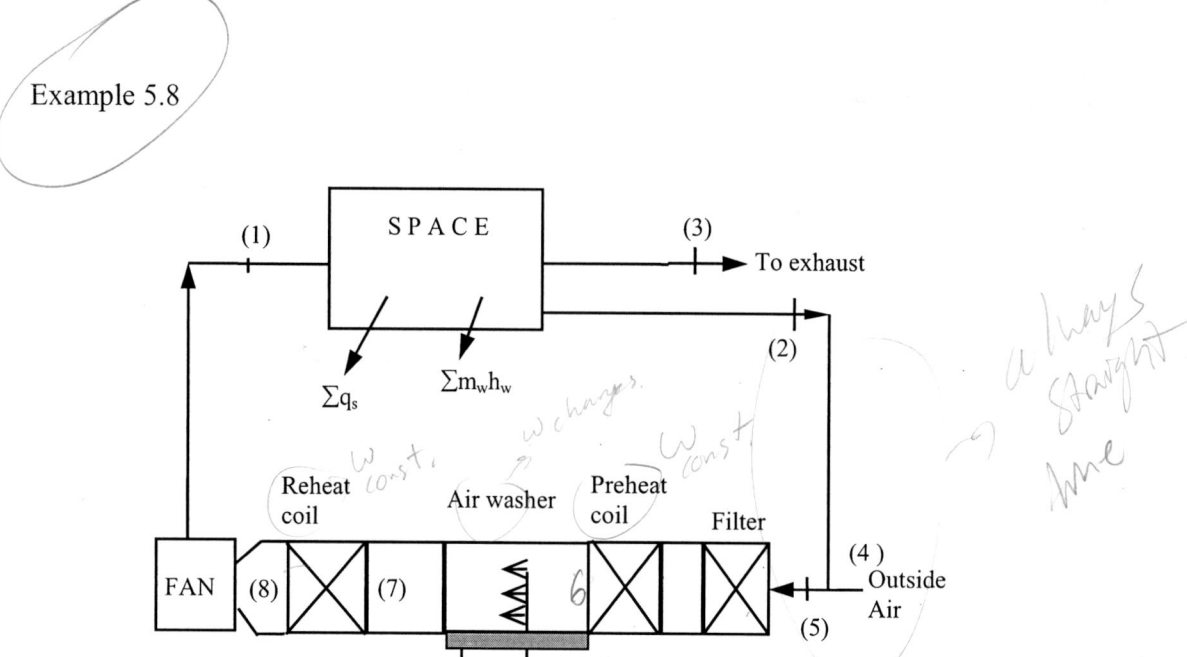

In winter, a space is conditioned as shown. The sensible heat loss is 200,000 Btu per hr and the rate of moisture loss (average h_w = 1090 Btu per lb_w) of 18 lb_w per hr. Moist air is withdrawn from the space at 68°F dry-bulb temperature and 55°F wet-bulb temperature. Barometric pressure is atmospheric. Moist air is supplied to the space at 102°F dry-bulb temperature. Outdoor air is saturated at 36°F. The dry-air flow rate of outdoor air let into the system is 50% of the dry-air flow rate of the air supplied to the space. The air washer has an efficiency of 45%. Find (a) the volume of air supplied to the space in cu ft per min of standard air, (b) the spray water temperature, (c) the lb per hr of make-up water required for the air washer, and (d) the rate of heat added to the air by each heating coil in Btu per hr.

Solution

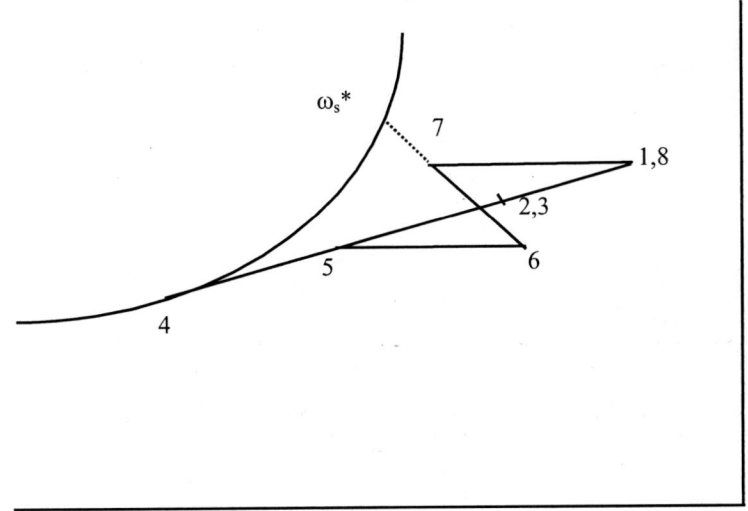

Locate states 2 and 4 from the conditions given.

$$\Sigma q_s + \Sigma m_w h_w = -200{,}000 - (18)(1090)$$

$$= -219{,}620 \text{ Btu/hr}$$

$$q' = \frac{\text{sensible heat}}{\text{total heat}} = \frac{-200{,}000}{-219{,}620} = 0.91$$

Draw the space condition line and locate state 1.

Mixing outdoor air and recirculated air,

$$\frac{m_{a,4}}{m_{a,5}} = \frac{52}{42} = 0.5$$

→ measure length and divide by 2.

Locate state 5 to be in the middle of the line $\overline{42}$.

$\omega_5 = \omega_6 = 0.0054 \text{ lb}_w/\text{lb}_a$

$\omega_7 = \omega_8 = \omega_1 = 0.008 \text{ lb}_w/\text{lb}_a$

States 6 and 7 have the same wet bulb temperature, $T_6^* = T_7^*$. Let ω_s^* be the specific humidity at $T_6^* = T_7^*$. The air washer efficiency is defined as

$$\eta_w = \frac{\omega_7 - \omega_6}{\omega_s^* - \omega_6}$$

$$\omega_s^* = \omega_6 + \frac{(\omega_7 - \omega_6)}{\eta_w}$$

$$= 0.0054 + \frac{(0.008 - 0.0054)}{0.45}$$

$$= 0.0112 \text{ lb}_w/\text{lb}_a$$

Locate states 6 and 7.

The first law of thermodynamics give $Q = m_a (h_2 - h_1)$

$$m_{a,1} = \frac{\sum q_s + \sum m_w h_w}{h_2 - h_1}$$

$$= \frac{-219{,}620}{23.2 - 33.6} = 21{,}117 \text{ lb}_a/\text{hr}$$

Supply volume $= \dfrac{m_{a,1}(1+\omega_1)v_1}{60}$ cfm

$$= \frac{21{,}117 \times 1.008}{60 \times 0.07}$$

$$= 5068 \text{ cfm}$$

(b) $T_w = T_6^* = T_7^* = 62.3°F$

(c) $m_w = m_{a,6} (\omega_7 - \omega_6)$

$$= 21{,}117 (0.0080 - 0.0054)$$

$$= 54.9 \text{ lb}_w/\text{hr}$$

(d) For the preheat coil, $Q = m_{a,5} (h_6 - h_5)$

$$= 21{,}117\,(23.2 - 18.6)$$

$$= 97{,}138 \text{ Btu/hr}$$

For the reheat coil, $\quad Q = m_{a,7}\,(h_8 - h_7)$

$$= 21{,}117\,(33.6 - 23.2)$$

$$= 219{,}617 \text{ Btu/hr.}$$

Example 5.9

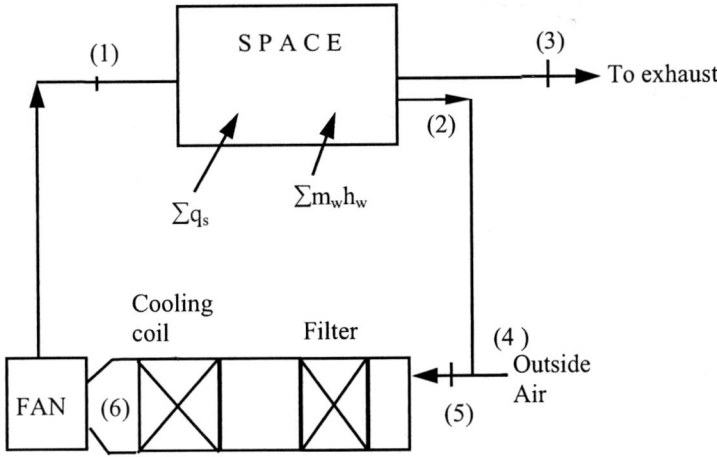

In summer, a space is to be conditioned by a schematic system shown above, to be at 75°F dry-bulb temperature and 62°F wet-bulb temperature. It has a rate of sensible heat gain of 85,000 Btu per hr and a rate of moisture gain (average h_w = 1120 Btu per lb_w) of 18.0 lb_w per hr. Moist air enters the space at a dry-bulb temperature of 64°F. Outdoor air at 92°F dry-bulb temperature and 75°F wet-bulb temperature is supplied for ventilation purposes at a rate of 1200 cu ft per min of standard air. Barometric pressure is 14.696 psia. Determine (a) the dry-bulb temperature and wet-bulb temperature of the air entering the cooling coil, and (b) the tons of refrigeration required.

Solution

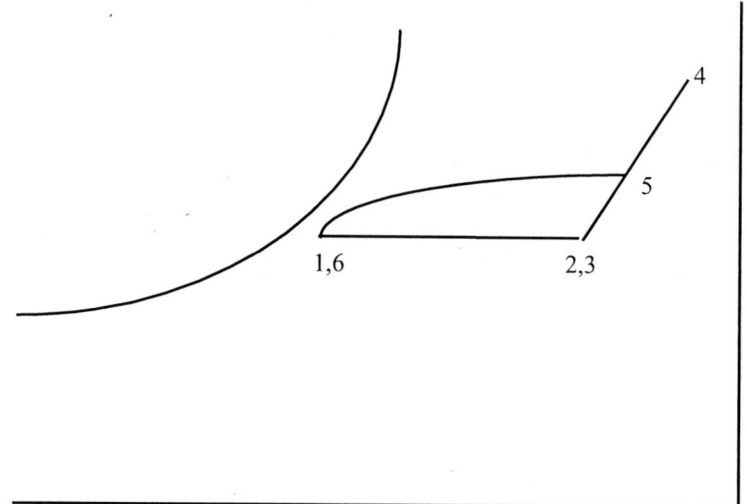

The schematic of the psychrometric chart of the processes are shown above. Locate states 2(3) and 4 from the conditions given.

(a) $\Sigma q_s + \Sigma m_w h_w = 85{,}000 + (18)(1120)$

$$= 105{,}160 \text{ Btu/hr}$$

$$q' = \frac{\text{sensible heat}}{\text{total heat}} = \frac{85{,}000}{105{,}160} = 0.81$$

Draw the space condition line and locate state 1.

$$m_{a,1} = \frac{\Sigma q_s + \Sigma m_w h_w}{h_2 - h_1}$$

$$= \frac{105{,}160}{27.6 - 24.6} = 35{,}053 \text{ lb}_a/\text{hr}$$

$$m_{a,3} = m_{a,4} = \frac{(1200)(60)(0.075)}{1 + \omega_4} = \frac{(1200)(4.5)}{1.0148} = 5321 \text{ lb}_a/\text{hr}$$

Thus, $m_{a,2} = m_{a,1} - m_{a,3} = 29{,}732 \text{ lb}_a/\text{hr}$

Mixing of recirculated and outdoor air,

$$\frac{\overline{25}}{\overline{24}} = \frac{m_{a,4}}{m_{a,5}} = \frac{5321}{35{,}053} = 0.152$$

Locate state 5.

$T_5 = 79.0\ °F$, $T_{5wb} = 66.0°F$

(b) Tons of refrigeration $= \dfrac{m_{a,5}(h_5 - h_6)}{12{,}000} = \dfrac{35{,}053(30.6 - 24.6)}{12{,}000} = 17.53$

Example 5.10

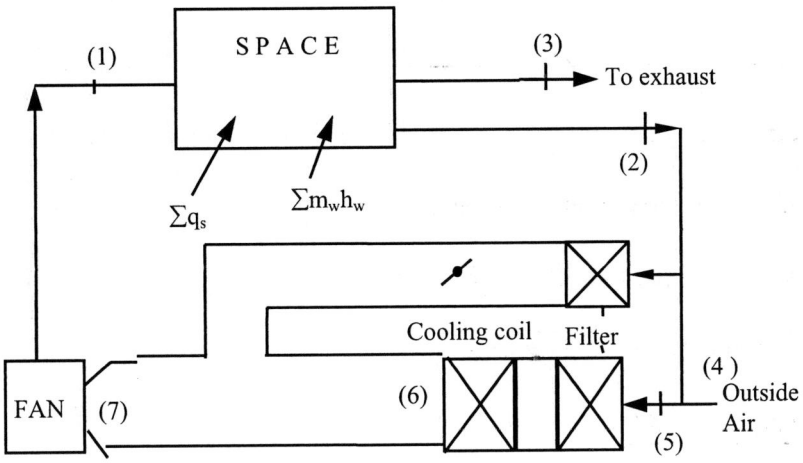

In hot weather, a space is to be maintained at 76°F dry bulb temperature and 50 per cent relative humidity, with a schematic system as shown above. The sensible heat gain is 72,000 Btu per hr and a rate of moisture gain (average h_w = 1050 Btu per lb_w) of 10.0 lb_w per hr. The volume of air supplied to the space is 6,800 cu ft per min of standard air. Outdoor air at 92°F dry-bulb temperature and 76°F wet-bulb temperature is introduced into the system at 1,600 cu ft per min of standard air. The air which passes through the cooling coil is brought to 92% relative humidity. Barometric pressure is 14.696 psia. Find (a) the dry-bulb temperature and thermodynamic wet-bulb temperature of the air supplied to the space, and (b) the volume of recirculated air in cu ft per min (standard air) which should by-pass the cooling coil.

Solution

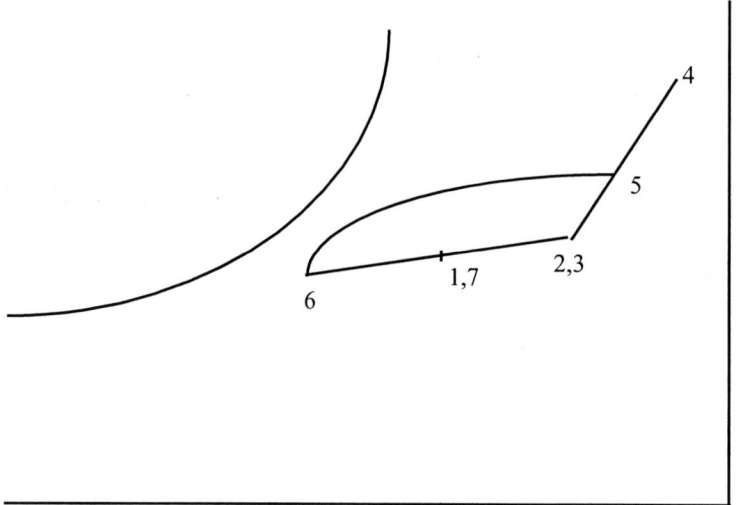

The schematic of the psychrometric chart of the processes are shown above. Locate states 2 and 4 from the conditions given.

(a) $\Sigma q_s + \Sigma m_w h_w = 72{,}000 + (10)(1050)$

$\qquad\qquad\qquad = 82{,}500$ Btu/hr

$q' = \dfrac{\text{sensible heat}}{\text{total heat}} = \dfrac{72{,}000}{82{,}500} = 0.87$

Draw the space condition line and locate state 6.

For the space, $V_1 = \dfrac{m_{a,1}(1+\omega_1)}{(60)(0.075)} = \dfrac{m_{a,1}(1+\omega_1)}{4.50}$ \hfill (i)

But $\sum m_w = m_{a,1}(\omega_2 - \omega_1)$,

so $m_{a,1} = \dfrac{\sum m_w}{\omega_2 - \omega_1}$ \hfill (ii)

From (i) and (ii), $4.5 V_1 = \dfrac{\sum m_w}{\omega_2 - \omega_1}(1+\omega_1)$

$\qquad\qquad 4.5 V_1 \omega_2 - 4.5 V_1 \omega_1 = \sum m_w + \sum m_w \omega_1$

$$\omega_1 = \frac{4.5 V_1 \omega_2 - \sum m_w}{4.5 V_1 + \sum m_w}$$

$$\therefore \omega_1 = \frac{(4.5)(6800)(0.0096) - 10.0}{(4.5)(6800) + 10.0} = 0.0093 \text{ lb}_w/\text{lb}_a$$

State 1 may be located at the intersection of ω_1 with the space condition line.

$T_1 = 67.0°F$, $T_{1wb} = 59.5°F$

For mixing process (by-passed air and air off the coil),

$$\frac{m_{a,bp}}{m_{a,7}} = \frac{\overline{61}}{\overline{62}} = 0.58$$

$$m_{a,7} = m_{a,1} = \frac{4.5 V_1}{1 + \omega_1} = \frac{(4.5)(6800)}{1.0093} = 30{,}318 \text{ lb}_a/\text{hr}$$

$m_{a,bp} = (0.58)(30{,}318) = 17{,}584$ lb$_a$/hr

In terms of standard air,

$$\text{B.P. volume} = \frac{m_{a,bp}(1 + \omega_2)}{(60)(0.075)} = \frac{(17{,}584)(1.0096)}{4.5} = 3945 \text{ cfm.}$$

Example 5.11

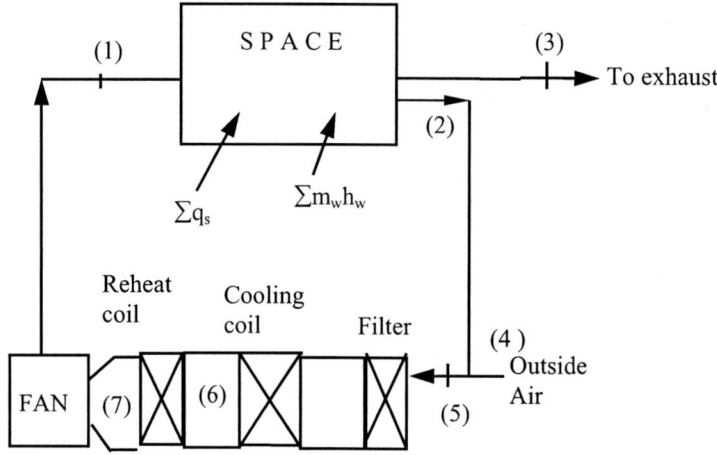

A space in summer is conditioned by a schematic system shown above. It is maintained at 72°F dry-bulb temperature and 60°F wet-bulb temperature. The rate of sensible heat gain is 400,000 Btu per hr and a rate of moisture gain (average h_w = 1150 Btu per lb_w) of 400.0 lb_w per hr. The chilled air leaves the cooling coil at 50°F dry-bulb temperature and 90 % relative humidity. Barometric pressure is atmospheric. Find the (a) dry-bulb and wet-bulb temperatures of the air supplied to the space, and (b) the rate of heat addition by the reheat coil in Btu per hr.

Solution

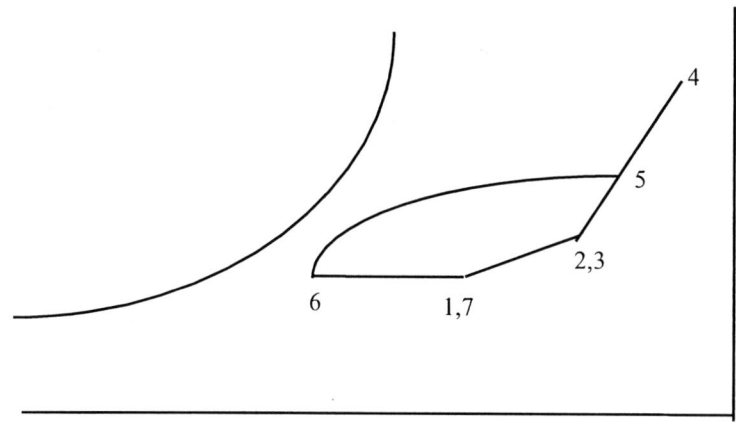

The schematic of the psychrometric chart of the processes are shown above. Locate states 2 and 6 from the conditions given.

$$\Sigma q_s + \Sigma m_w h_w = 400{,}000 + (400)(1150)$$

$$= 860{,}000 \text{ Btu/hr}$$

$$q' = \frac{\text{sensible heat}}{\text{total heat}} = \frac{400{,}000}{860{,}000} = 0.465$$

Draw space condition line, and locate state 1(7).

(a) $T_1 = 67.5°F$, $T_{1wb} = 56°F$

(b) $m_{a,6} = m_{a,1} = \dfrac{\Sigma q_s + \Sigma m_w h_w}{h_2 - h_1} = \dfrac{860{,}000}{27 - 24} = 286{,}667 \text{ lb}_a / \text{hr}$

$_6Q_7 = m_{a,6}(h_7 - h_6) = (286{,}667)(24 - 19.5) = 1{,}290{,}000 \text{ Btu/hr}.$

Example 5.12

A space is to be maintained at 68°F during winter. The space has a rate of sensible heat gain of 72,000 Btu per hr during working hours; moisture gain is negligible. The space is to be cooled by mixing outdoor air with recirculated air. Air is to be supplied to the space at a dry-bulb temperature of 56°F. On a certain day, the outside air is saturated at -10°F. Barometric pressure is atmospheric. (a) Find the volume of supply air required in cu ft per min of standard air. (b) Determine the percentage of the supply air (dry-air mass basis) which is outside air. (c) Assuming one brake horse-power per ton of refrigeration as the compressor power requirement for a mechanical refrigeration system, estimate the daily operational savings of the above system. Assume 12 hr operation and electricity costs of 4.0 cents per kwH.

Solution

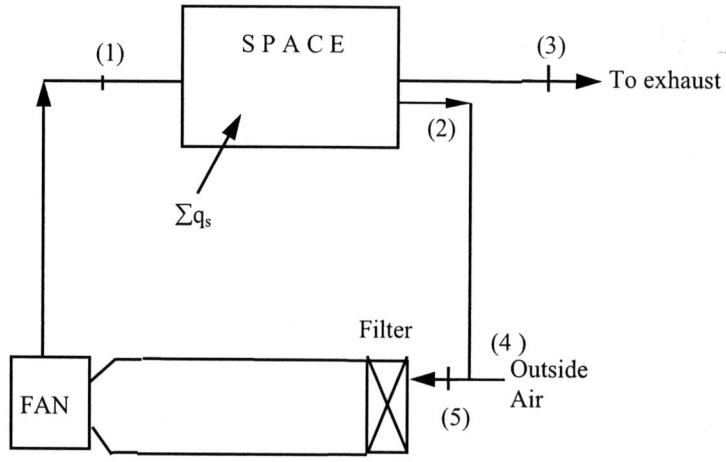

Sketch a simple schematic of the system.

(a) Since $m_w = 0$,

$\omega_1 = \omega_2 = \omega_4 = \omega_5 = 0.00046$ lb$_w$/lb$_a$

$$m_{a,1} = \frac{72,000}{h_2 - h_1} = \frac{72,000}{17.0 - 14.0} = 24,000 \text{ lb}_a / \text{hr}$$

In terms of standard air,

$$\text{Supply volume} = \frac{m_{a,1}(1+\omega_1)}{(60)(0.075)} = \frac{24,000(1.00046)}{4.5} = 5336 \text{ cfm}$$

(b) For the mixing of recirculated air and outdoor air,

$m_{a,2}h_2 + m_{a,4}h_4 = m_{a,5}h_5$ $\qquad\qquad m_{a,4} = m_{a,3}$

$(m_{a,1} - m_{a,4})h_2 + m_{a,4}h_4 = m_{a,5}h_5$ $\qquad m_{a,1} = m_{a,5}$

$m_{a,1}h_2 - m_{a,1}h_5 = m_{a,4}(h_2 - h_4)$

$$\frac{m_{a,4}}{m_{a,1}} = \frac{h_2 - h_5}{h_2 - h_4} = \frac{17.0 - 14.0}{17.0 - (-1.9)} = 0.16$$

Thus, 16% of the supply air is outdoor air.

(c) 72,000 Btu/hr (6 tons of refrigeration) are required.

Assume that the electric motor has an efficiency of 80%.

Power required = $\dfrac{0.746 \times 6}{0.8}$ kW = 5.6 kW

Cost = 5.6 x 12 x 4 = $2.69/day.

Example 5.13

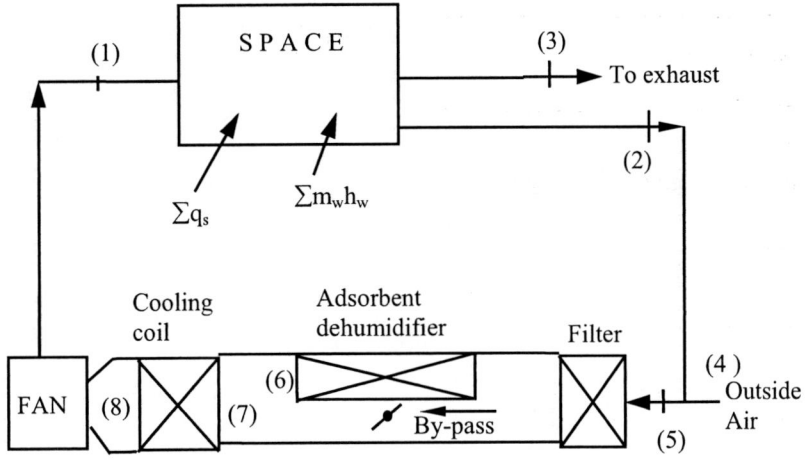

$T_1 = 58°F$
$T_2 = T_3 = 74°F$
$T_{2wb} = T_{3wb} = 58°F$
$T_4 = 88°F$ $\qquad T_{4wb} = 74°F$
$\omega_6 = 0.0028\ lb_w/lb_a$
$m_{a,2} = 0.8\ m_{a,1}$

The figure is a schematic of an industrial air-conditioning system. Barometric pressure is 14.696 psia. All the dehumidification occurs in the adsorbent dehumidifier which is of the ideal adiabatic type ($T_{5wb} = T_{6wb}$). The rate of sensible heat addition is 110,000 Btu per hr and the rate of moisture addition (saturated water vapor at 88°F) is 28 lb per hr. (a) Locate all statepoints on the psychrometric chart and read values of T_{1wb}, T_5, T_{5wb}, T_6, T_{6wb}, and T_7. (b) Find the volume air flowrate in cu ft per min which by-passes the adsorbent dehumidifier.

Solution

Locate states 2(3) and 4.

$\Sigma q_s + \Sigma m_w h_w = 110{,}000 + (28)(1100) = 140{,}800$ Btu/hr

$q' = \dfrac{\text{sensible heat}}{\text{total heat}} = \dfrac{110{,}000}{140{,}800} = 0.78$

Draw space condition line, and locate state 1(8).

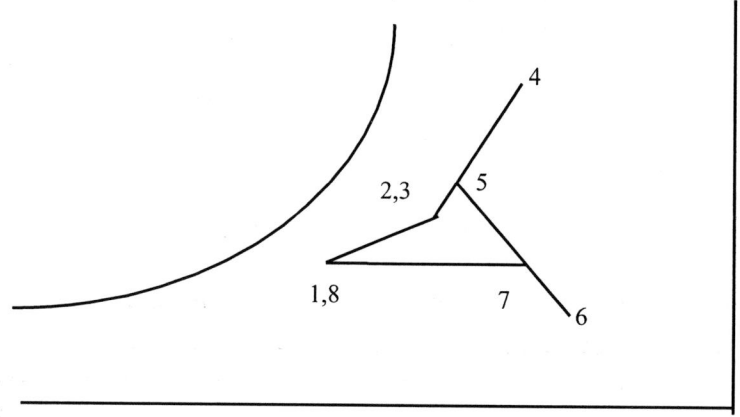

$\dfrac{m_{a,4}}{m_{a,5}} = \dfrac{\overline{25}}{\overline{24}} = 0.2$

Locate state 5. Then, locate states 6 and 7.

$T_{1wb} = 50°F$

$T_5 = 77°F \qquad\qquad T_{5wb} = 62.2°F$

$T_6 = 102°F \qquad\qquad T_{6wb} = 62.2°F$

$T_7 = 88°F$

$$m_{a,5} = m_{a,1} = \frac{\sum q_s + \sum m_w h_w}{h_2 - h_1} = \frac{140{,}800}{25.4 - 20.2} = 27{,}077 \text{ lb}_a/\text{hr}$$

$$m_{a,bp} = m_{a,5}\frac{\overline{76}}{\overline{56}} = 27{,}077\frac{1.625}{2.95} = 14{,}915 \text{ lb}_a/\text{hr}$$

$$\text{Volume by-passed} = \frac{m_{a,bp}v_5}{60} = \frac{(14{,}915)(13.7)}{60} = 3406 \text{ cfm.}$$

Example 5.14

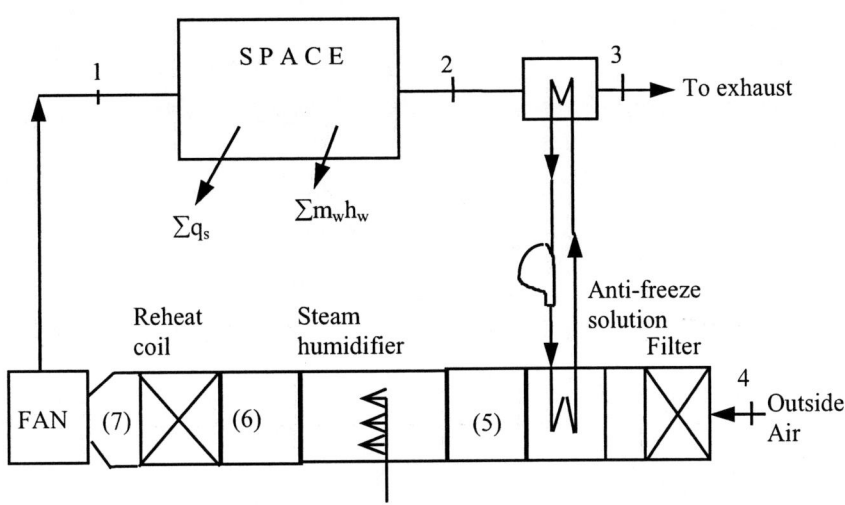

A space is heated by a system shown above. The rate of sensible heat loss $\sum q_s$ from the space is 100,000 Btu per hr and the rate of moisture loss (average h_w = 1090 Btu per lb$_w$) is 10.0 lb per hr. The known state conditions are $T_1 = 95°F$, $T_2 = 72°F$, $T_{2wb} = 55°F$, $T_3 = 60°F$, $T_4 = 35°F$, $\phi_4 = 100\%$, and $\phi_6 = 100\%$. Barometric pressure is 14.696 psia. (a) Locate all statepoints on the psychrometric chart and read values of T_{1wb}, T_{3wb}, T_5, T_{5wb}, and T_6. (b) Determine the required specific enthalpy for the steam sprayed to the air by the humidifier.

Solution

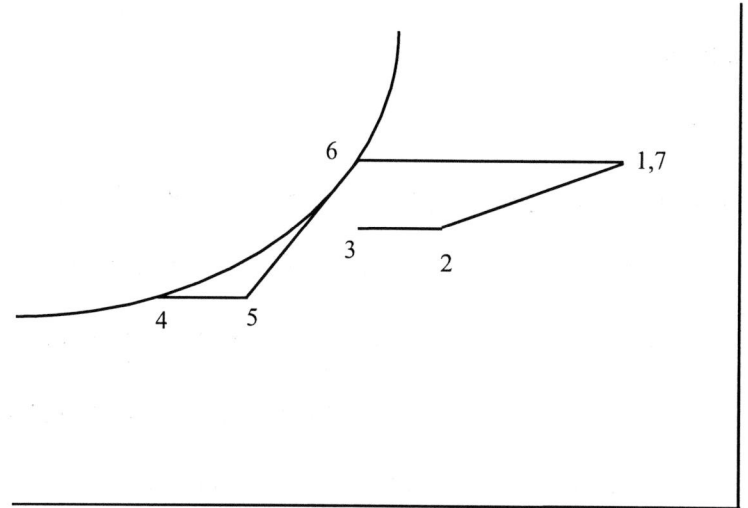

The schematic of the psychrometric chart of the processes are shown above.

(a) First, locate states 2, 3 and 4.

$$\Sigma q_s + \Sigma m_w h_w = -100,000 - (10)(1090)$$

$$= -110,900 \text{ Btu/hr}$$

$$q' = \frac{\text{sensible heat}}{\text{total heat}} = \frac{-100,000}{-110,900} = 0.9.$$

Use the protractor to aid the drawing of the space condition line and locate state 1.

Locate state 6 since $\omega_6 = \omega_1$.

For the heat exchanger, $\quad T_5 - T_4 = T_2 - T_3$

$$T_5 - 35 = 72 - 60$$

$$T_5 = 47°F$$

Since $\omega_5 = \omega_4$, locate state 5.

$T_{1wb} = 74°F$ $\qquad\qquad T_{3wb} = 57°F$

$T_5 = 47°F$ $\qquad\qquad T_{5wb} = 42°F$

$T_6 = 64.5°F$

Use the protractor to find that the specific enthalpy for the steam in the humidifier is

Δh/Δw = 1560 Btu/lb$_a$.

6. Cooling Towers

Large air-conditioning systems, power plants, and some industrial plants produce large quantities of waste heat that is rejected to cooling water from nearby oceans, rivers, or lakes. In many instances, the water supply is limited or thermal pollution prevents this practice. Waste heat then has to be rejected to the atmosphere. Cooling water acts as the working medium to transfer heat between the waste heat source and the sink (the atmosphere). One popular structure used for this purpose is the cooling tower.

A cooling tower is basically an evaporative cooler. An induced-draft counterflow cooling tower is shown schematically in Fig. 5.15. Air from the environment is drawn into the tower from the bottom and leaves through the top. Warm water from the waste heat source is pumped to the top of the tower and sprayed into the airstream. Spraying exposes a large surface area of water to the air, thus improving heat transfer. As the water falls due to gravity, a small percent of the water evaporates and cools the rest of the water. The temperature and the humidity ratio of the air increase during this process. The cooled water collects at the bottom of the tower and is pumped back to the waste heat source; makeup water is necessary for this equipment.

The induced-draft cooling tower makes use of a fan. A natural-draft cooling tower does not, Fig. 5.16. This later makes use of the fact that as the air becomes hotter during the process, it rises. By necessity, since a large volume of air has to be moved, the natural-draft cooling tower is a lot larger than the corresponding induced-draft cooling tower with the same capacity. The natural-draft cooling towers are hyperbolic in profile, principally for structural strength.

Analysis of Fig. 5.15 gives the following mass balances:

$$\dot{m}_{a,1} = \dot{m}_{a,2} = \dot{m}_a \tag{5.31}$$

$$\dot{m}_3 + \dot{m}_{a,1}\omega_1 = \dot{m}_4 + \dot{m}_{a,2}\omega_2$$

or $\quad \dot{m}_3 - \dot{m}_4 = \dot{m}_a(\omega_2 - \omega_1) = \dot{m}_{makeup} \tag{5.32}$

Assuming that the cooling tower is undergoing a steady-state steady-flow process, and neglecting potential energy and kinetic energy terms, the first law of thermodynamics gives

$$\dot{m}_{a,1}h_1 + \dot{m}_3 h_3 = \dot{m}_{a,2} h_2 + \dot{m}_4 h_4 + \dot{W}_{fan}$$

or $\quad \dot{m}_{a,1}h_1 + \dot{m}_3 h_3 = \dot{m}_{a,2} h_2 + (\dot{m}_3 - \dot{m}_{makeup})h_4 + \dot{W}_{fan} \tag{5.33}$

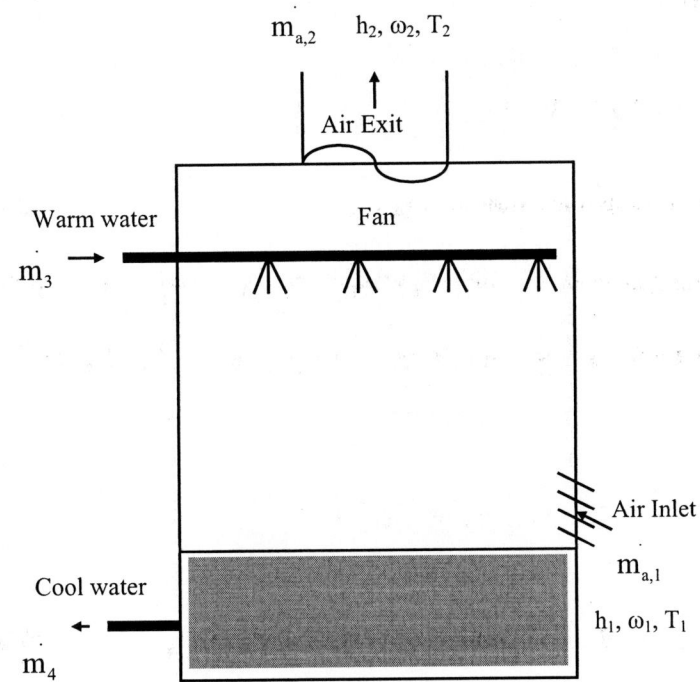

Figure 5.15   Induced-draft counterflow cooling tower.

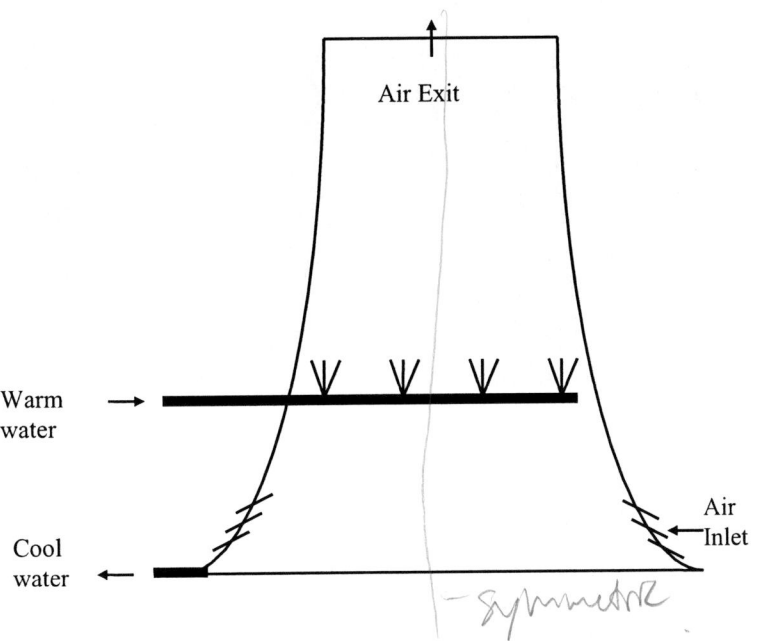

Figure 5.16   Natural-draft cooling tower.

Example 5.15

Air enters the base of a natural-draught cooling tower at the rate of 1200 m³/min with a pressure of 1 bar, a temperature of 18°C (64.4°F), and a relative humidity of 60%. The water enters the tower at 40°C and leaves at 18°C. If the air leaves the tower at 29°C (84.2°F) in a saturated condition, find the mass flow of water entering the tower and the percentage loss of water by evaporation.

Solution

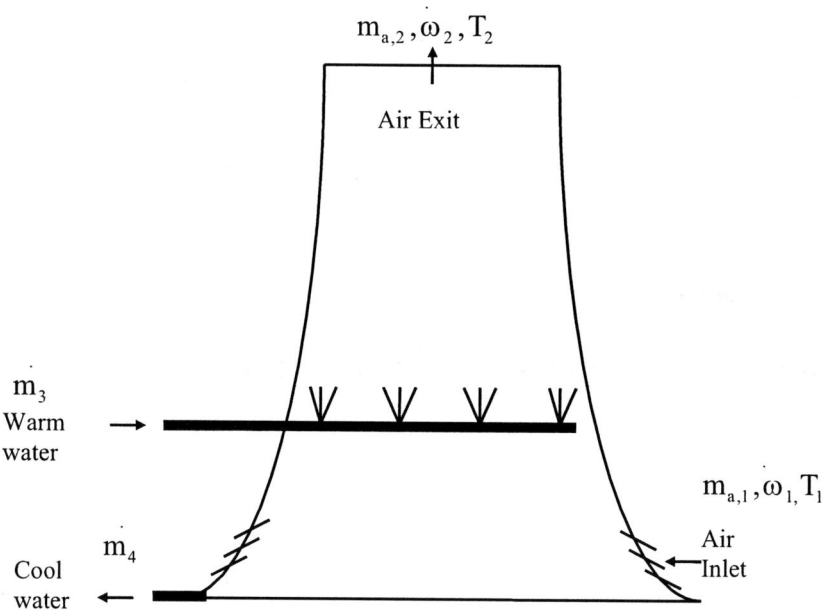

A sketch of the system with the variable quantities is shown. States 1 and 2 are completely specified, so they may be found on the psychrometric chart.

$$v_{a,1} = 13.4 \text{ ft}^3/\text{lb} = \frac{13.4 \times 0.028317}{0.454545} = 0.8348 \text{ m}^3/\text{kg of dry air}$$

$$\dot{m}_{a,1} = \frac{1200}{0.8348} = 1437 \text{ kg/min}$$

From the psychrometric chart, $\omega_1 = 0.0077$ kg/kg of dry air

$$\omega_2 = 0.0256 \text{ kg/kg of dry air}$$

Water lost by evaporation is given by

$$= \dot{m}_{a,1}(\omega_2 - \omega_1)$$
$$= 1437\,(0.0256 - 0.0077) \text{ kg/min}$$
$$= 26 \text{ kg/min}$$

The energy equation is

$$\dot{m}_{a,1} h_1 + \dot{m}_3 h_3 = \dot{m}_{a,2} h_2 + \dot{m}_4 h_4$$

The enthalpies of the water at states 3 and 4 are

$h_3 = 167.57$ kJ/kg and $h_4 = 75.58$ kJ/kg

Thus, $1437(94-38) + (\dot{m}_3 - 26)(75.58) - 167.57\,\dot{m}_3 = 0$

$\dot{m}_3 = 853$ kg/min

The percentage loss by evaporation is $26/853 = 3.0\%$.

PROBLEMS

5.1. Convert supply volume of 10,000 ft^3/min at v_1 = 13.3 ft^3/lb$_a$, ω_1 = 0.0071 lb$_w$/lb$_a$ to standard air.

5.2. Given air at the following conditions:

(a)   75°F, 45% R.H.

(b)   80°F and 60°F w.b.t.

(c)   45°F, 30% R.H.

(d)   85°F, 75°F w.b.t.

For parts (a) and (c), find the w.b.t., v, h, and ω. For parts (b) and (d), find the R.H., v, and h.

5.3. The dry-bulb and wet-bulb temperatures of air at 1 bar are 86°F (30°C) and 55°F (12.8°C). Find the relative humidity, absolute humidity, dew point, and enthalpy.

5.4. Determine the dew point temperature for a sea-level location where the dry-bulb and wet-bulb temperatures are 72 and 55°F (22.2 and 12.8°C), respectively.

5.5. Determine the enthalpy, absolute humidity, and specific volume for saturated air at 41°F(5°C) at sea level.

5.6. Determine the enthalpy, absolute humidity, and specific volume for saturated air at 82°F(27.8°C) at sea level.

5.7. State A is at 100°F and 40% R.H. Find its absolute humidity, enthalpy and wet bulb temperature. State B is at 72°F and 60°F wet-bulb temperature. Find its absolute humidity, enthalpy and R.H. What is the enthalpy difference per lb$_m$ of dry air which undergoes the process AB?

5.8. State A is at 40°C and 50% R.H. Find its absolute humidity, enthalpy and wet bulb temperature. State B is at 22°C and 15°C wet-bulb temperature. Find its absolute humidity, enthalpy and R.H. What is the enthalpy difference per kg of dry air which undergoes the process AB?

5.9. 300 cfm of air at 72°F, 40% R.H. are heated to 110°F. Find the required heat transfer.

5.10. 300 cfm of air at 110°F, 20% R.H. are cooled to 70°F. Find the required heat transfer.

5.11. An air conditioning system is to take in outdoor air at 50°F and 25% relative humidity at a steady rate of 300 cfm and to condition it to 76°F and 65% relative humidity. The outdoor air is sprayed with steam to accomplish this process. Assuming the whole process takes place at atmospheric pressure, calculate (a) the rate of heat added and (b) the mass flow rate of moisture added.

5.12. 300 cfm of air at 75°F, 45% R.H. are cooled to 50°F ideally. Find the lb. of water condensed per hour and the required heat transfer per hour. Do not neglect the energy in the condensate.

5.13. Outside air at 92°F and 15% R.H. is cooled evaporatively to 65% R.H. Determine the dry-bulb temperature of the processed air.

5.14. Outside air at 95°F and 20% R.H. is cooled evaporatively so that its relatively humidity is tripled. Find the corresponding dry bulb temperature.

5.15. Processed air that has been evaporatively cooled is at 65°F and $\omega = 0.010$ lb_w/lb of dry air. Determine its initial dry-bulb temperature if its absolute humidity has been doubled by the cooling process.

5.16. Air that has been processed by an evaporative cooler is at 60°F and 80% R.H. Determine its initial state if its relative humidity has been quadrupled by the process.

5.17. 300 cfm of air at 90°F, 70% R.H. are mixed with 500 cfm of air at 75°F, 50% R.H. Find the dbt, wbt and R.H. of the mixed air. Calculate the cfm of the mixed air from the state of the mixed air.

5.18. Two hundred cfm (5600 L/min) of air are to be humidified by saturated steam at 212°F (100°C). Air at 1 atmosphere enters the steam humidifier at 61°F(16°C) and 41°F(5°C) wet-bulb temperature. What is the steam flow rate if the air is humidified to 70% R.H.? What is the temperature of the humidified air?

5.19. One day in December, outdoor air at 32°F (0°C) and 60% R.H. is heated to 68°F (20°C) in a home. If the required indoor humidity is 65%, calculate the amount of moisture per unit of dry air which must be added to the outdoor air? Assume the air is at 1 atmosphere.

5.20. Air at 36°F and 34°F wet-bulb temperature has to be heated to 70°F, the required temperature of a residence at sea level. The airflow rate is 1000 cfm. What is the heat rate? What is the ratio of sensible heat to the total heat?

5.21. Humidity is added to the outdoor air in Prob. 5.19 by evaporating water sprayed into the air. How much energy must be added to the air to bring it to the required condition?

5.22. Moist air at 68°F (20°C) and 46.5°F (8°C) wet-bulb temperature is humidified to a final dew point temperature of 67.5°F (19.7°C) by addition of saturated steam.

What is the temperature of the saturated steam used? If the airflow rate is 180 lb$_m$/min (81 kg/min), what is the required rate of steam flow?

5.23. Outside air at 41°F (5°C) and 55% R.H. is heated and humidified by steam at 212°F (100°C). The airflow rate is 360 ft^3/s (10,080 L/s), and heat is added to the air at the rate of 108,000 Btu/h (31.7 kW) while it absorbs 172.6 lb$_m$/h (78.29 kg/h) of steam. What are the dry- and wet-bulb temperatures at the exit of this heater-humidifier if it is located at sea level?

5.24. Outdoor air at 95°F and 75°F wet-bulb temperature mixes with 75°F and 48% R.H. return air from the building in the mass flow ratio of 1:4. What are the absolute humidity, R.H., enthalpy, and temperature of the mixed air?

5.25. Cold air at 8°C and 3°C wet-bulb temperature is mixed with warm air at 24°C and 18°C wet-bulb temperature in a ratio of 1:2.5 respectively. Find for the resultant mixture at atmospheric pressure: temperature and wet-bulb temperature, relative humidity, absolute humidity, and enthalpy.

5.26. An evaporative cooler has been tested to be capable of cooling air by 90% of the difference between the entering air dry- and wet-bulb temperatures. If the inlet air is at 102°F (39°C) and 30% R.H., what is the outlet condition temperature, relative humidity and absolute humidity? How much water is evaporated if the airflow is 10,800 cfm (5,040 L/s)? Assume sea-level atmospheric pressure.

5.27. An evaporative cooler has been designed to cool air by 75% of the difference between the entering air dry- and wet-bulb temperatures. If the inlet air is at 89.5°F (32°C) and 20% R.H., what is the outlet condition temperature, relative humidity and absolute humidity? How much water is evaporated if the airflow is 21,600 cfm (10,080 L/s)? Assume the air pressure is 1 bar or 101 kPa.

5.28. At sea-level, air is cooled from 82.5°F (28°C) and 73.5°F (23°C) wet-bulb temperature to saturation at the 60°F (15.5°C) outlet of a cooling coil. How much water is removed? How much latent heat is removed, and how much sensible heat? What is the sensible heat ratio (SHR)?

5.29. For a location at 1 bar pressure, air is cooled from 88°F (31°C) and 68°F (20°C) wet-bulb temperature to saturation at the 54°F (12°C) outlet of a cooling coil. How much water is removed? How much latent heat is removed, and how much sensible heat? What is the SHR?

5.30. A commercial space is occupied by 20 persons who each produce 200 Btu/h (58W) of sensible heat and 0.25 lb/h (0.1 kg/h) of moisture. The space is to be maintained at 70°F (21°C) and 55% R.H. Conditioned air is supplied at 61°F (16°C) to handle the sensible and latent heat loads. What is the SHR? To handle the loads, what must the absolute humidity and mass flow rate of the supply air be? Assume sea-level conditions.

5.31. An ideal evaporative cooler cools inlet air to the inlet air wet-bulb temperature. What is the inlet absolute humidity to such an ideal evaporative cooler that produces saturated outlet air at 68°F (20°C) from 89.5°F (32°C) inlet air? The pressure is atmospheric.

5.32. An adiabatic saturator operating at sea level with entering air of 82.5°F (28°C) has air leaving at a temperature of 60°F (15.5°C). Determine the absolute humidity and relative humidity of the entering air.

5.33. Summer time heat gain for a space is 80,000 Btu/hr. 15,000 Btu/hr of this total heat gain is latent heat. If the air leaving the apparatus has a relative humidity of 95%, determine the temperature of the air leaving the apparatus and the cfm of the cooled air needed to maintain the design conditions for the space which is at 75°F, 50% R.H. Determine the lb. of water condensed per hour by the apparatus.

5.34. With the data of Problem 5.33, outside air is required for ventilation. Consider ventilation air is 20% (by mass of dry air) of the apparatus air. Determine the total refrigeration now required including the ventilation air. Outside air is at 90°F, 70% R.H., also determine the total weight of water condensed. (Hint: visualize the outside air is cooled to the same state as the recirculated air before mixing).

5.35. With the same data as Problems 5.33 and 5.34, assume that the recirculated air is mixed with the outside air before cooling. Determine the state (dbt and R.H.) of the mixed air and show on a sketch of the psychrometric chart, the processes of the system. Determine the refrigeration heat transfer required in the cooling process and the mass of water removed also. Discuss the effect of this change on the results calculated in the previous problem.

5.36. Air at 65°F, 60% R.H. is supplied to a factory where the conditions are maintained at 75°F, 50% R.H. Determine the heat load and the SHR.

5.37. Apparatus air for winter conditioning is based only on sensible heat lost from the space of 200,000 Btu/hr. Heated air is delivered to the space at 115°F. Design condition for the space is 75°F, 50% R.H. Outside air is 40°F, 30% R.H. 100%

of the apparatus air is outside air for ventilation. Determine the total heat requirements and the weight of water added per hour.

5.38. For Problem 5.37, assume that the incoming air is heated to an appropriate temperature, then humidified in an ideal adiabatic saturation process, then heated again. Find that portion of heat required in each stage of heating and the air temperature after the first heater.

5.39. Repeat the same types of solutions required in both Problems 5.37 and 5.38, if outside air only represents 25% of the apparatus air. Alter the problem according to the following information. 30,000 Btu/hr of the 200,000 Btu/hr is due to latent heat loss. The adiabatic saturation process terminates at 80% R.H. instead of saturated air. Two solutions are required. The heating and moisture requirements are to be determined by analysis of the total system and also by analysis of the processes.

5.40.

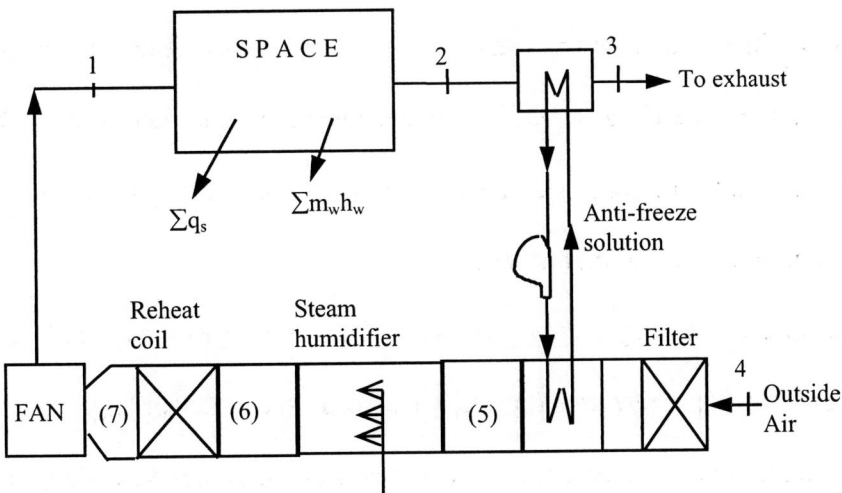

A space is heated by a system shown above. The rate of sensible heat loss Σq_s from the space is 200,000 Btu per hr and the rate of moisture loss (average h_w = 1095 Btu per lb_w) is 20.0 lb per hr. The known state conditions are $T_1 = 105°F$, $T_2 = 75°F$, $T_{2wb} = 60°F$, $T_3 = 60°F$, $T_4 = 37°F$, $\phi_4 = 100\%$, and $\phi_6 = 100\%$. Barometric pressure is 14.696 psia. (a) Locate all statepoints on the psychrometric chart and read values of T_{1wb}, T_{3wb}, T_5, T_{5wb}, and T_6. (b) Determine the required specific enthalpy for the steam sprayed to the air by the humidifier.

5.41.

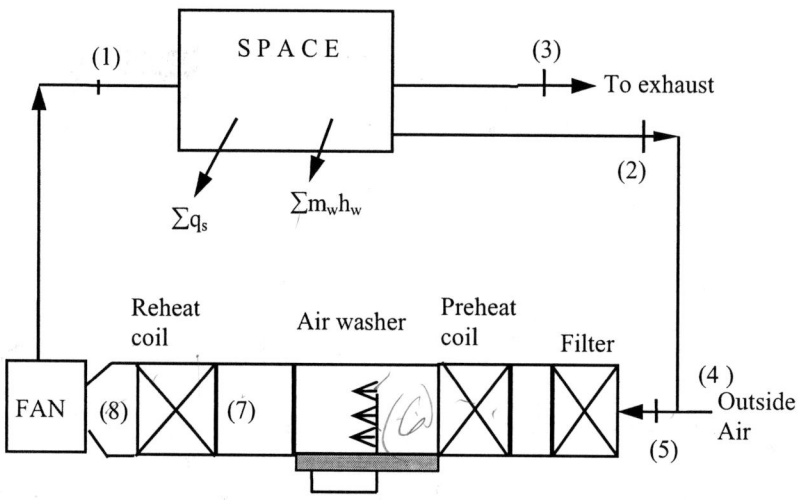

In winter, a space is conditioned as shown. The sensible heat loss is 175,000 Btu per hr and the rate of moisture loss (average h_w = 1092 Btu per lb_w) of 20 lb_w per hr. Moist air is withdrawn from the space at 72°F dry-bulb temperature and 57.5°F wet-bulb temperature. Barometric pressure is 14.696 psia. Moist air is supplied to the space at 98 °F dry-bulb temperature. Outdoor air is saturated at 35°F. The dry-air flow rate of outdoor air let into the system is 50% of the dry-air flow rate of the air supplied to the space. The air washer has an efficiency of 52%. Find (a) the volume of air supplied to the space in cu ft per min of standard air, (b) the spray water temperature, (c) the lb per hr of make-up water required for the air washer, and (d) the rate of heat added to the air by each heating coil in Btu per hr.

5.42.

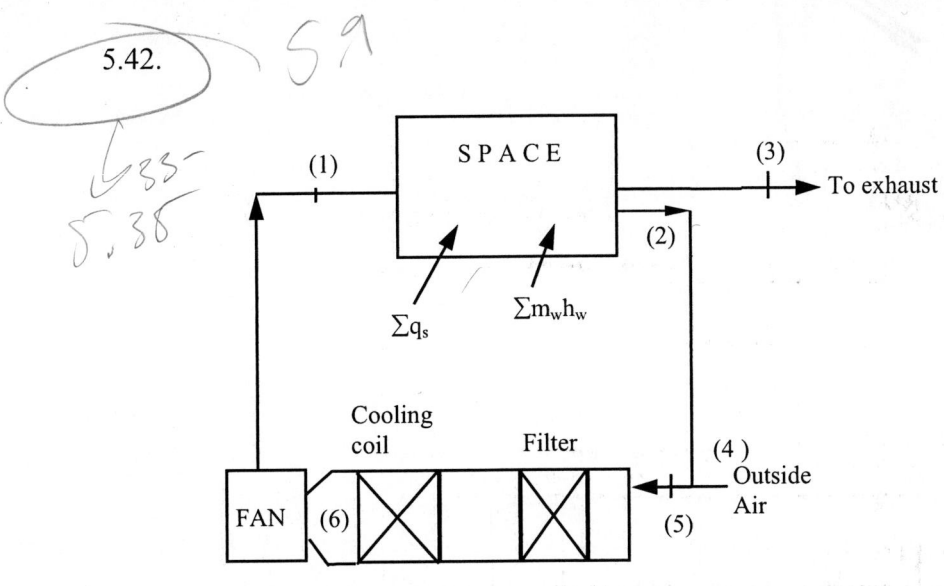

In summer, a space is to be conditioned by a schematic system shown above, to be at 75°F dry-bulb temperature and 64°F wet-bulb temperature. It has a rate of sensible heat gain of 82,000 Btu per hr and a rate of moisture gain (average h_w = 1120 Btu per lb_w) of 18.0 lb_w per hr. Moist air enters the space at a dry-bulb temperature of 62°F. Outdoor air at 94°F dry-bulb temperature and 77°F wet-bulb temperature is supplied for ventilation purposes at a rate of 800 cu ft per min of standard air. Barometric pressure is 14.696 psia. Determine (a) the dry-bulb temperature and wet-bulb temperature of the air entering the cooling coil, and (b) the tons of refrigeration required.

5.43.

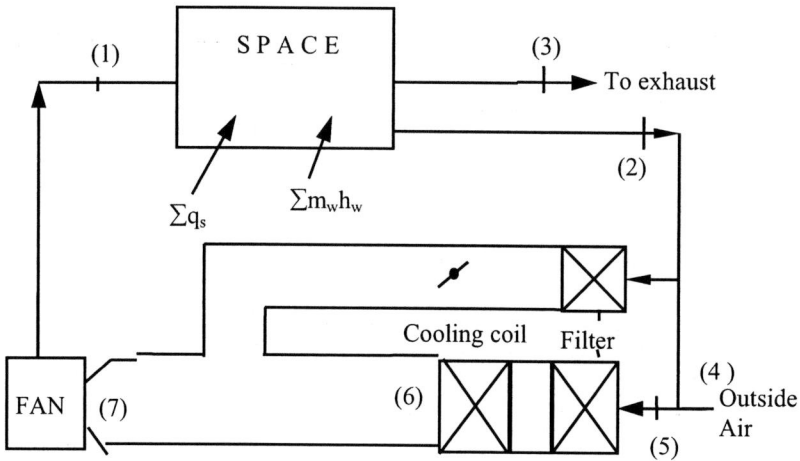

In hot weather, a space is to be maintained at 78°F dry bulb temperature and 50 per cent relative humidity, with a schematic system as shown above. The sensible heat gain is 73,000 Btu per hr and a rate of moisture gain (average $h_w = 1050$ Btu per lb_w) of 12.0 lb_w per hr. The volume of air supplied to the space is 7,000 cu ft per min of standard air. Outdoor air at 97°F dry-bulb temperature and 77°F wet-bulb temperature is introduced into the system at 1,500 cu ft per min of standard air. The air which passes through the cooling coil is brought to 88% relative humidity. Barometric pressure is 14.696 psia. Find (a) the dry-bulb temperature and thermodynamic wet-bulb temperature of the air supplied to the space, and (b) the volume of recirculated air in cu ft per min (standard air) which should by-pass the cooling coil.

5.44.

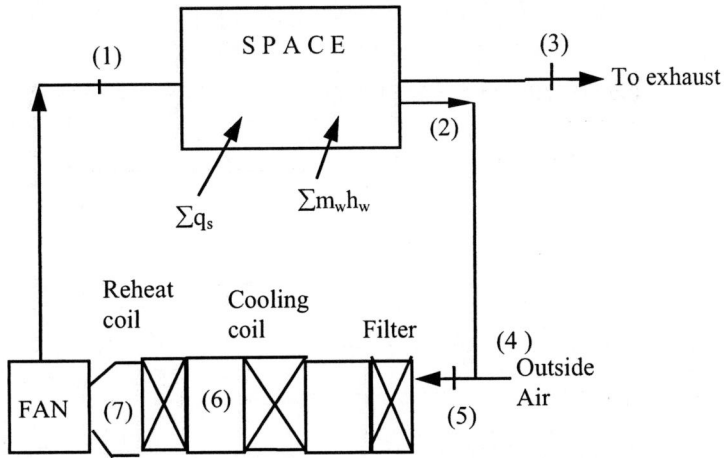

A space in summer is conditioned by a schematic system shown above. It is maintained at 76°F dry-bulb temperature and 62°F wet-bulb temperature. The rate of sensible heat gain is 360,000 Btu per hr and a rate of moisture gain (average h_w = 1050 Btu per lb_w) of 320.0 lb_w per hr. The chilled air leaves the cooling coil at 52°F dry-bulb temperature and 90 % relative humidity. Barometric pressure is atmospheric. Find the (a) dry-bulb and wet-bulb temperatures of the air supplied to the space, and (b) the rate of heat addition by the reheat coil in Btu per hr.

5.45. A space is to be maintained at 70°F during winter. The space has a rate of sensible heat gain of 84,000 Btu per hr during working hours; moisture gain is negligible. The space is to be cooled by mixing outdoor air with recirculated air. Air is to be supplied to the space at a dry-bulb temperature of 54°F. On a certain day, the outside air is saturated at -10°F. Barometric pressure is atmospheric. (a) Find the volume of supply air required in cu ft per min of standard air. (b) Determine the percentage of the supply air (dry-air mass basis) which is outside air. (c) Assuming one brake horse-power per ton of refrigeration as the compressor power requirement for a mechanical refrigeration system, estimate the daily operational savings of the above system. Assume 8 hr operation and electricity costs of 2.0 cents per kwH.

5.46.

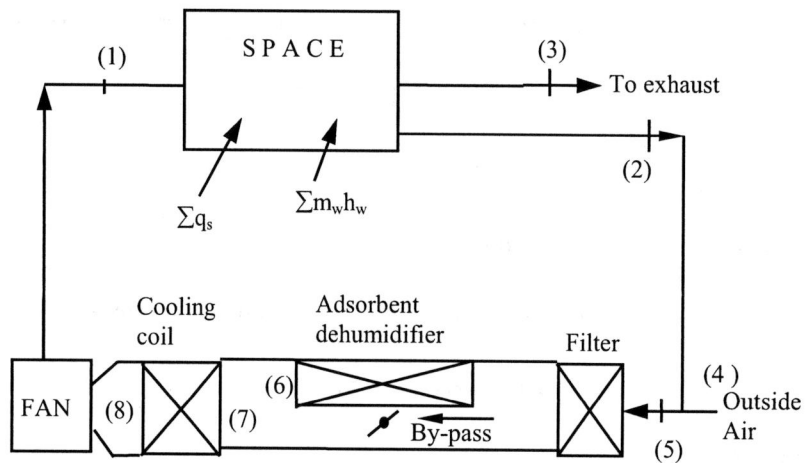

$T_1 = 54°F$
$T_2 = T_3 = 76°F$
$T_{2wb} = T_{3wb} = 60°F$
$T_4 = 92°F$ $\quad T_{4wb} = 72°F$
$\omega_6 = 0.003 \, lb_w/lb_a$
$m_{a,2} = 0.85 \, m_{a,1}$

The figure is a schematic of an industrial air-conditioning system. Barometric pressure is 14.696 psia. All the dehumidification occurs in the adsorbent dehumidifier which is of the ideal adiabatic type ($T_{5wb} = T_{6wb}$). The rate of sensible heat addition is 120,000 Btu per hr and the rate of moisture addition (saturated water vapor at 92°F) is 32 lb per hr. (a) Locate all statepoints on the psychrometric chart and read values of T_{1wb}, T_5, T_{5wb}, T_6, T_{6wb}, and T_7. (b) Find the volume air flowrate in cu ft per min which by-passes the adsorbent dehumidifier.

5.47.

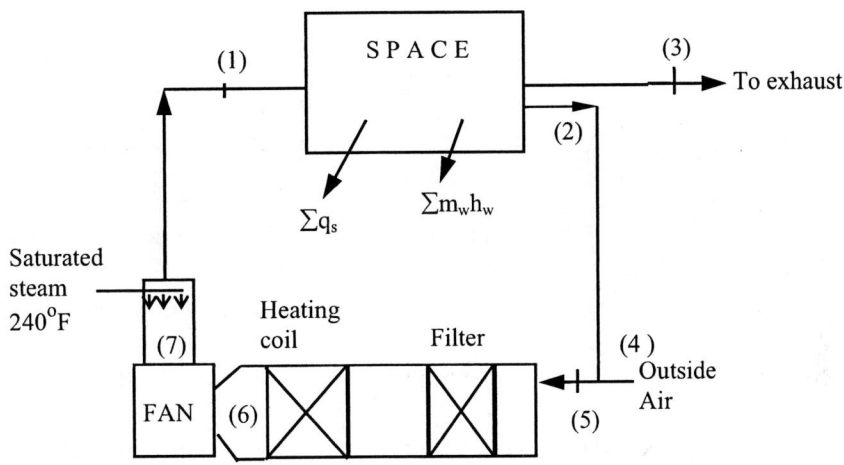

$T_1 = 115°F$
$T_2 = T_3 = 72°F$
$T_{2wb} = T_{3wb} = 62°F$
$T_4 = 30°F \qquad \phi_4 = 100\%$
$T_5 = 60°F$

In winter, an indoor space is conditioned by a system with schematic as shown. The rate of sensible heat loss from the space is 132,000 Btu per hr and the rate of moisture loss (average $h_w = 1100$ Btu per lb_w) is 14.0 lb per hr. The pressure is atmospheric. (a) Locate all statepoints on the psychrometric chart and read values of T_{1wb}, T_{5wb}, T_7, and T_{7wb}. (b) Find the required volume of air supplied to the space in cu ft per min. (c) Calculate the lb per hr of steam required for the humidifier.

5.48. Each of the situations listed provides the dry-bulb temperature and relative humidity of the moist-air stream entering an air-conditioning system: (a) 32°C,

40%, (b) 15°C, 60%, (c) 25°C, 65%, (d) 12°C, 40%, (e) 25°C, 30%. The condition of the moist-air stream exiting the system should satisfy the following constraints for comfort: $20 \leq T \leq 27°C$, $40 \leq \phi \leq 60\%$. In each case, develop the processes and a schematic of the equipment required to achieve the desired state. Sketch the processes on a psychrometric chart.

5.49. On one day in July, the air has a temperature of 32°C and a relative humidity of 85%. An air-conditioning equipment is to deliver 35 m³/min at a temperature of 19°C and a relative humidity of 60%. This is done by cooling the air to the dew-point of the delivery air and reheating it. An axial-flow fan, situated before the cooler, absorbs 1.5 kW. Calculate the temperature to which the air must be cooled by the cooling coils, and the heat transfer rates required in the cooler and heater. Assume that the pressure is atmospheric.

5.50. In a tropical island, the temperature on a particular day is 92°F and a relative humidity of 92%. The air-conditioner is to deliver 1000 ft³/min at a temperature 68°F and a relative humidity of 45%. The air-conditioner cools the air to the dew-point of the delivery air and reheats it. Neglect the power absorbed by the fan. Calculate the heat transfer rates in the cooler and the reheater.

5.51. Air enters the base of a natural-draught cooling tower at the rate of 1400 m³/min with a pressure of 1 bar, a temperature of 16°C (60.8°F), and a relative humidity of 55%. The water enters the tower at 42°C and leaves at 19°C. If the air leaves the tower at 30°C (86°F) in a saturated condition, find the mass flow of water entering the tower and the percentage loss of water by evaporation.

COMPUTER, DESIGN AND GENERAL PROBLEMS

5.52. Identify the major sources of heat gain in your college building in summer. Suggest methods of minimizing the heat gain and thus reduce the cooling load.

5.53. Identify the major sources of heat loss in your house in winter. Suggest methods of minimizing the heat loss and thus reduce the heating load.

5.54. Research the different devices used for measuring humidity. Discuss the advantages and disadvantages of each of them.

5.55. Consider an older home in Florida that has 4 rooms and 4 window air-conditioning units. The utility company has a program to assist in the conversion to a single large central air-conditioning system. List all the important factors which should be considered before applying to the utility company for aid.

5.56. Ice-storage is used to store "coolness" by manufacturing ice during periods when electricity rates are lower, e.g., from midnight to dawn. The ice is then used to cool the air during the daylight hours, when the heat load on a building is greater than at night, and the electricity rates are also higher. Discuss this method of energy storage, taking into account both economical and thermodynamic factors.

5.57. Dehumidification can be achieved by the use of desiccants. Research the properties of commonly used desiccants. Discuss the uses of desiccants in various applications.

5.58. Write computer programs that allow specific entropy and enthalpy to be determined at vapor states for the cases listed below.

(a) Water

(b) Refrigerant 134a

(c) Oxygen

(d) Nitrogen.

5.59. Write a user-friendly computer program to determine the properties of atmospheric air at any pressure when the dry-bulb temperature and relative humidity are provided.

5.60. Write a user-friendly computer program to determine the properties of atmospheric air at 1 bar when the dry-bulb temperature and relative humidity are provided.

6. CHEMICAL REACTIONS

6.1 Introduction

This chapter discusses chemical reactions, and in particular, combustion. The analysis of reactive systems is an extension of the principles introduced thus far. The concepts are all the same, namely, mass conservation, the first and the second law of thermodynamics. Only a departure is going to be made in the evaluation of specific enthalpy, internal energy, and entropy. With the appropriate values thus determined, they are used as in earlier chapters in the energy and entropy balances for the reactive system.

6.2 Combustion Process

Combustion processes are important in engineering, because often they are used as heat sources. In combustion, rapid oxidation of combustible elements of the fuel allows energy to be released as combustion products are created. The two major combustible elements in most common fuels are carbon and hydrogen. A fuel is said to have undergone complete combustion if all the carbon in the fuel is burned to carbon dioxide, and all the hydrogen in the fuel is burned to water. Otherwise, the combustion is incomplete. Sulfur is another element present in fuels, though it does not contribute much to the energy released. However, it is significant because of pollution and corrosion problems.

Consider a simple example of the complete combustion of carbon with oxygen

$$1C + 1O_2 \rightarrow 1CO_2 \tag{6.1}$$

Carbon dioxide is the only product of the reaction. The numerical coefficients in the equation, which precede the chemical symbols to give equal amounts of each chemical element on both sides of the equation, are called **stoichiometric** coefficients. Equation (6.1) may be expressed as follows in S.I. and English units:

$$1 \text{ kmol C} + 1 \text{ kmol O}_2 \rightarrow 1 \text{ kmol CO}_2$$

$$1 \text{ lbmol C} + 1 \text{ lbmol O}_2 \rightarrow 1 \text{ lbmol CO}_2$$

Though the total numbers of moles on the left and right sides of Eq. (6.1) are not equal, mass is conserved, that is, the total mass of reactants must equal to the total mass of products. Since 1 kmol of C equals 12 kg, 1 kmol of O_2 equals 32 kg and 1 kmol of CO_2 equals 44 kg, Eq. (6.1) can be interpreted as

$$12 \text{ kg C} + 32 \text{ kg O}_2 \rightarrow 44 \text{ kg CO}_2$$

or in English units

$$12 \text{ lb C} + 32 \text{ lb O}_2 \rightarrow 44 \text{ lb CO}_2$$

6.2.1 Fuels

A fuel is a substance that undergoes combustion. We emphasize hydrocarbon fuels, that is, substances that contain hydrogen and carbon. Sulfur and other chemical substances may also be present.

Gaseous hydrocarbon fuels are obtained from natural gas wells or are produced in chemical processes. Generally, methane CH_4 is the major component of natural gas, with several other different hydrocarbons. Compositions of gaseous fuels are generally given in terms of mole fractions.

Liquid hydrocarbon fuels are generally derived from crude oil through distillation and cracking processes. Gasoline, kerosene and diesel fuel are examples. Most liquid fuels are mixtures of hydrocarbons for which compositions are normally given in terms of mass fractions. For simplicity, diesel fuel is considered to be dodecane, $C_{12}H_{26}$, and gasoline to be octane, C_8H_{18}. Liquid and gaseous hydrocarbons may be synthesized from coal, tar sands, and oil shale.

Coal is a solid fuel. Its composition varies with the location of its place of origin. The composition of coal is normally expressed as an ultimate analysis. This analysis gives the composition on a mass basis in terms of the relative amounts of chemical elements (carbon, sulfur, hydrogen, nitrogen, oxygen) and ash.

6.2.2 Combustion Air

Generally, air is used to provide the needed oxygen. For the combustion calculations, components of dry air other than oxygen are lumped together with nitrogen to simplify matters. Air is considered to be 21% oxygen and 79% nitrogen on a molar basis. The molar ratio of nitrogen to oxygen is 0.79/0.21 = 3.76. When air is used to supply the oxygen, every mole of oxygen is accompanied by 3.76 moles of nitrogen.

It is also assumed that nitrogen in the air used for combustion does not undergo any chemical reaction. The nitrogen is at the same temperature as the other products of combustion, so its change of state has to be considered in the calculations. If temperatures reach about 1810 K, oxides of nitrogen are formed such as nitric oxide and nitrogen dioxide. These are significant air pollutants, and should not be ignored.

Two important parameters used to describe the quantities of fuel and air in a combustion process are the air-fuel ratio and its reciprocal, the fuel-air ratio. The air-fuel ratio is the quantity of air to the quantity of fuel. The ratio may be written on a molar basis or on a mass basis. Conversion between these ratios is achieved by multiplying appropriately by the molecular weights of air, M_{air}, and fuel, M_{fuel},

$$\frac{\text{mass of air}}{\text{mass of fuel}} = \frac{\text{moles of air} \times M_{air}}{\text{moles of fuel} \times M_{fuel}}$$

$$= \frac{\text{moles of air}}{\text{moles of fuel}} \left(\frac{M_{air}}{M_{fuel}}\right)$$

or $\quad AF = \overline{AF}\left(\dfrac{M_{air}}{M_{fuel}}\right)$ (6.2)

where AF is the ratio on a mass basis and $\overline{AF}$ is the air-fuel ratio on a molar basis. For the combustion calculations, the molecular weight of air is taken to be 28.97. This is consistent with the previous assumption that dry air is 21% oxygen and 79% nitrogen. Note that AF and $\overline{AF}$ are without dimensions, and thus independent of the units used.

The minimum amount of air needed for the complete combustion of a fuel is called the **stoichiometric** or **theoretical air**. When a fuel is completely burned with theoretical air, no uncombined oxygen will be present in the products of combustion. Consider the theoretical combustion of octane, C_8H_{18},

$$C_8H_{18} + 12.5O_2 + 12.5(3.76)N_2 \rightarrow 8CO_2 + 9H_2O + 47.0N_2 \quad (6.3)$$

Observe that the products of the theoretical combustion contain no unburned octane, and no C, H_2, CO, or free O_2.

In practice, the amount of air actually supplied is expressed in terms of the percent of theoretical air. For instance, 120% of theoretical air means that the air supplied is 1.2 times the theoretical amount of air. In addition, the quantity of air supplied can be expressed as a percent excess or a percent deficiency of air. For instance, 120% of theoretical air is equivalent to 20% excess air, and 90% of theoretical air is the same as 10% deficiency of air. The quantity of air used in combustion processes can also be expressed in terms of the equivalence ratio, which is the ratio of the actual fuel-air ratio to the stoichiometric or theoretical fuel-air ratio.

6.2.3 Products of Combustion

In the complete combustion of hydrocarbons, the final products are carbon dioxide, water, and nitrogen. Oxygen may also be present if excess air is used. The amount of the products can be determined by applying the conservation of mass to the chemical equation.

In actual situations where the combustion is incomplete, the analysis is much more complicated. Even when the amount of air supplied may exceed the theoretical amount needed, some carbon monoxide and unburned oxygen may appear in the products. This is due to the degree of mixing of the fuel and the air, or insufficient time for complete combustion. When less than theoretical air is supplied, one should expect both carbon monoxide and carbon dioxide in the products, together with unburned oxygen. The products of combustion of actual combustion processes and their relative amounts can best be determined by experiment.

Equipment used for determination of the products of combustion include the Orsat apparatus, gas chromatograph, flame ionization detector, and infrared analyzer. The analyses are normally reported on a *dry* basis, that is, the mole fractions are given for all gaseous products except the water vapor. The water vapor in the gaseous products of combustion can be significant, as water is formed in the combustion of hydrocarbons.

Example 6.1

Problem

Methane (CH_4) is burned with 35% excess air. Assuming complete combustion and a total pressure of 100 kPa, calculate the air-fuel ratio. What is the dew-point temperature of the products of combustion?

Solution

Since the combustion is complete, the products will comprise CO_2, H_2O, N_2, and the unreacted O_2. The combustion reaction may be represented by

$$CH_4 + 1.35(2)(O_2 + 3.76\, N_2) \rightarrow$$

$$CO_2 + 2H_2O + 0.7O_2 + (1.35 \times 2 \times 3.76)\, N_2$$

In the combustion reactions of hydrocarbons, use one molecule of the fuel and first balance the carbon atoms on either side of the equation. Secondly, balance the hydrogen atoms, and thirdly, balance the oxygen atoms. The nitrogen atoms are then balanced. It has been mentally observed that the stoichiometric amount of oxygen is $2O_2$ to completely burn CH_4. The coefficient "2" is used in front of the components of air. On the left-hand side, the ratio of oxygen to nitrogen is 1:3.76, as it is in the air. Since there is 35% excess air, the multiplying factor 1.35 is used in front of the components of air.

Simplifying,

$$CH_4 + 2.7(O_2 + 3.76\, N_2) \rightarrow$$

$$CO_2 + 2H_2O + 0.7O_2 + 10.152\, N_2$$

The air-fuel ratio is found as

$$AF = \frac{m_{air}}{m_{fuel}} = \frac{(2.7 \times 4.76\, kmol)(28.97\, kg/kmol)}{(1\, kmol)(16\, kg/kmol)} = 23.27$$

In other words, 23.27 kg of air is used per kilogram of fuel.

The products of combustion start to condense when the temparture drops to the dew-point temperature. The dew-point temperature of a gas-vapor mixture is the saturation temperature of the water vapor corresponding to its partial pressure. Assuming ideal gas behavior for the products of combustion,

$$P_v = \left(\frac{N_v}{N_{prod}}\right)(P_{prod}) = \left(\frac{2 \text{ kmol}}{13.852 \text{ kmol}}\right)(100 \text{ kPa}) = 14.438 \text{ kPa}$$

Hence, $T_{dp} = T_{sat@14.438 \text{ kPa}} = 53.18°C$.

Example 6.2

Problem

Consider the combustion of propane (C_3H_8) in dry air. The volumetric analysis of the products of combustion on a dry basis is CO_2, 12%; CO, 1%; O_2, 1.5%; N_2, 85.5%. Find (a) the air-fuel ratio, (b) the percentage of theoretical air utilized, and (c) the fraction of the water which condenses as the products are cooled to 20°C at 100 kPa.

Solution

If we assume that the combustion gases behave ideally, the volume fractions stated are equivalent to mole fractions. Consider 100 kmol of dry products for convenience. The combustion equation may be represented as

$aC_3H_8 + b(O_2 + 3.76 N_2) \rightarrow$

$12 CO_2 + CO + 1.5 O_2 + 85.5 N_2 + c H_2O$

Use mass balances to find the unknowns a, b and c.

N: $(2 \times 3.76)b = (2 \times 85.5)$, thus $b = 22.74$

C: $3a = 13$ thus $a = 4.33$

H: $8a = 2c$ thus $c = 4a = 17.33$

O: $2b = 24 + 1 + 3 + c$ thus   LHS = 45.48, RHS = 45.33;

close enough to accept the previous calculations.

The combustion equation for 1 kmol of fuel is obtained by substituting the values for a, b and c, and dividing the whole equation by a,

$$C_3H_8 + 5.25(O_2 + 3.76 N_2) \rightarrow$$

$$2.77 CO_2 + 0.23 CO + 0.35 O_2 + 19.4 N_2 + 4.0 H_2O$$

(a)   The air fuel ratio is

$$AF = \frac{m_{air}}{m_{fuel}} = \frac{(5.25 \times 4.76 \text{ kmol})(28.97 \text{ kg/kmol})}{(1 \text{ kmol})(44 \text{ kmol})} = 16.45 \text{ kg air/kg fuel}$$

(b)   The theoretical combustion equation is

$$C_3H_8 + 5(O_2 + 3.76 N_2) \rightarrow$$

$$3 CO_2 + 4.0 H_2O + (5 \times 3.76) N_2$$

$$\text{Percentage of theoretical air} = \frac{m_{air,act}}{m_{air,th}}$$

$$= \frac{N_{air,act}}{N_{air,th}}$$

$$= \frac{(5.25)(4.76) \text{kmol}}{(5)(4.76) \text{kmol}} = 105\%$$

In other words, 5% excess air was used. In practice, because of poor mixing, carbon monoxide is formed even when some of the oxygen go unreacted.

(c)   Assuming that the dew-point temperature of the products of combustion is above 20°C, some of the water vapor will condense as the products are cooled to 20°C. For each kind of fuel burned, there are (2.77+0.23+0.35+19.40+4.00) = 26.75 kmol of products.

When N_{cond} kmol of water condenses, ($4-N_{cond}$) kmol of water vapor remains. The products remaining in the gas phase decrease to ($26.75-N_{cond}$) kmols. Assuming ideal gas behavior, the unknown N_{cond} can be found by equating the mole fraction of water vapor to its pressure fraction;

$$\frac{N_{cond}}{N_{prod,gas}} = \frac{P_v}{P_{prod}}$$

$$\frac{4-N_{cond}}{26.75-N_{cond}} = \frac{P_{sat@20°C}}{100\,kPa} = \frac{2.339\,kPa}{100\,kPa}$$

$N_{cond} = 3.46$ kmol

Hence, 3.46 kmol of the water vapor in the products (or 86.5%) will condense as the product gases are cooled.

Example 6.3

Problem

A gas mixture is made up of the following volumetric percentages:- 71% octane, 24% nitrogen, 3% oxygen, and 2% carbon dioxide. The mixture is burned with the theoretical amount of air, which enters the combustion process at 25°C, 1 atm, and 60% relative humidity. Find the dew-point temperature of the products of combustion, if the complete combustion takes place at 1 atm.

Solution

The water in the air does not react in the combustion process. It adds to the water produced in the process. The combustion equation is written with dry air, then water is added to both sides of the equation.

Consider 1 kmol of fuel.

0.71 C_8H_{18} + 0.24 N_2 + 0.03 O_2 + 0.02 CO_2 + a (O_2 + 3.76 N_2)

$$\rightarrow b\ CO_2 + c\ H_2O + d\ N_2 \qquad (a)$$

Use mass balances to find the unknowns a, b, c and d.

C: $5.68 + 0.02 = b$,   thus $b = 5.70$

H: $0.71 \times 18 = 2c$,   thus $c = 6.39$

O: $0.06 + 0.04 + 2a = 2b + c$, thus $a = 8.845$

N: $0.48 + 7.52\ a = 2\ d$,   thus $d = 33.4972$

There are $4.76a = 4.76(8.845) = 42.1022$ kmol of dry air used. The partial pressure of the moisture in the air is

$$P_{v,air} = \phi_{air}\ P_{sat\,@\,25°C} = (0.60)(3.169\ kPa) = 1.9014\ kPa$$

Assume ideal-gas behavior, the number of moles of water in the air is

$$N_{v,air} = \left(\frac{P_{v,air}}{P_{total}}\right) N_{total}$$

$$= \left(\frac{1.9014\ kPa}{101.3\ kPa}\right)(42.1022 + N_{v,air})$$

Thus, $N_{v,air} = 0.805$ kmol

The correct representation of the combustion process is obtained by substituting the values of the coefficients in Eq. (a) and adding the appropriate amount of water to both sides of the equation.

$$0.71\ C_8H_{18} + 0.24\ N_2 + 0.03\ O_2 + 0.02\ CO_2 + 8.845\ (O_2 + 3.76\ N_2) + 0.805\ H_2O$$

$$\rightarrow 5.70\ CO_2 + 7.195\ H_2O + 33.497\ N_2$$

The partial pressure of water vapor in the products of combustion, assuming ideal gas behavior, is

$$P_{v,prod} = \left(\frac{N_{v,prod}}{N_{prod}}\right) P_{prod}$$

$$= \left(\frac{7.195}{46.392}\right)(101.3 \text{ kPa}) = 15.711 \text{ kPa}$$

Hence, the dew point temperature is

$$T_{dp} = T_{sat@15.711kPa} = 54.94°C.$$

6.3   First-Law Analysis of Reacting Systems

This section discusses the use of the first law of thermodynamics (conservation of energy) for the analysis of reacting systems. The methods used for evaluating the properties of reacting systems differ somewhat from the methods used thus far.

6.3.1 Enthalpy of Formation and Enthalpy of Combustion

The molecules of a system possess energy in different forms such as sensible and latent energy (associated with phase change), chemical energy (associated with molecular structure) and nuclear energy (associated with atomic structure). The property that describes the amount of chemical energy of a substance is the enthalpy of formation. The enthalpy of formation $\overline{h}_f$ is the enthalpy of a substance at a specified state due to its chemical composition.

As a beginning point, the enthalpy of formation of all stable elements (such as N_2, H_2, O_2, and C) are assigned a value of zero at the standard reference state of 25°C and 1 atm. In other words, $\overline{h}_f^\circ = 0$ for all stable elements. The stable form of an element is the chemically stable form of that element at 25°C and 1 atm. The stable form of oxygen at the standard reference state is diatomic oxygen O_2, not monatomic oxygen O. If an element exists in more than one stable form at 25°C and 1 atm., one of the forms is specified as the stable form. For example, graphite, not diamond, is specified to be the stable form of carbon.

Consider the formation of CO_2 from its elements C and O_2, during a steady-flow combustion process. Both the carbon and the oxygen enter the combustion chamber at 25°C and 1 atm. The combustion of carbon releases heat, i.e., it is an exothermic reaction. This process involves no work. Thus, from the steady-state steady-flow energy balance, the heat transfer during this process must be equal to the difference between the enthalpy of the products and the enthalpy of the reactants. In other words,

$$Q = H_{prod} - H_{react}$$

Since both the reactants and the products are at the same state, the enthalpy of change during this process is only due to the changes in the chemical composition of the system. This enthalpy change is called the **enthalpy of reaction**, h_R. It is defined as the difference between the enthalpy of the products at a specified state and the enthalpy of the reactants at the same state for a complete reaction.

For combustion processes, the enthalpy of reaction is called the **enthalpy of combustion** h_C. This is the quantity of heat released during a steady-flow combustion process when 1 kmol (or 1 kg) of fuel is burned completely at a specified temperature and pressure. It is defined as

$$h_C = H_{prod} - H_{react} \qquad (6.4)$$

where H_{prod} is the enthalpy of the products at a specified state, and H_{react} is the enthalpy of the reactants at the same state.

Consider again the formation of CO_2 from its elements C and O_2 at 25°C and 1 atm. during a steady-state steady-flow process. The enthalpy of change during this process is experimentally found to be

$$H_{prod} - H_{react} = -393{,}520 \text{ kJ/kmol}$$

But $H_{react} = 0$ since both reactants are elements at the standard reference state, and the products comprise 1 kmol of CO_2 at the same state. Thus, the enthalpy of formation of CO_2 at the standard reference state is -393,520 kJ/kmol. In other words,

$$\overline{h}^{\circ}_{f,CO_2} = -393{,}520 \text{ kJ/kmol}$$

The negative sign means that the enthalpy of 1 kmol of CO_2 at 25°C and 1 atm. is 393,520 kJ less than the enthalpy of 1 kmol of C and 1 kmol of O_2 at the same state. Energy is leaving the system as heat when C and O_2 combine to form 1 kmol of CO_2. In other words, a negative enthalpy of formation for a compound shows that heat is released during the formation of that compound from its stable elements. A positive value indicates heat is absorbed by the reacting system.

There is a difference in the enthalpy of formation of liquid water, for instance, and that of water vapor at 25°C and 1 atm. This is called the enthalpy of vaporization of water at 25°C and 1 atm. Similar differences can be seen for the enthalpies of formation of the liquid form and of the vapor form of various other substances existing as liquid and as vapor at 25°C and 1 atm. These differences are the enthalpies of vaporization of those substances at the standard reference state.

Another popular term is the **heating value** of the fuel, which is defined as the quantity of heat released when a fuel is burned completely in a steady-flow process and the products are returned to the state of the reactants. The heating value of a fuel is equal to the absolute value of the enthalpy of combustion of the fuel,

$$\text{Heating value} = |h_C| \qquad \text{(kJ/kg fuel)}$$

The heating value is dependent on the phase of the water in the products of combustion. The heating value is the **higher heating value** (HHV) when the water in the products is in the liquid form, and it is the **lower heating value** (LHV) when the water in the products is in the vapor form. The two heating values are related by

$$\text{HHV} = \text{LHV} + (N\overline{h_{fg}})_{H_2O} \qquad \text{(kJ/kg fuel)} \qquad (6.4)$$

where N is the number of moles of water in the products and $\overline{h_{fg}}$ is the enthalpy of vaporization of water at the specified temperature.

Example 6.4

Problem

Find the higher heating value of gaseous methane at 25°C and 1 atm, using the enthalpy of formation data.

Solution

The stoichiometric equation for the combustion of methane is

$$CH_4 + 2(O_2 + 3.76N_2) \rightarrow CO_2 + 2H_2O_{(l)} + (2 \times 3.76) N_2$$

N_2 and O_2 are stable elements, and so their enthalpy of formation is zero at the stated conditions. Products are also at the standard state of 25°C and 1 atm. To obtain the higher heating value of methane, the water in the products of combustion has to be in the liquid state.

$$\text{HHV} = \overline{h_C}$$

$$= H_{prod} - H_{react}$$

$$= \left(N\overline{h}_f^o\right)_{CO_2} + \left(N\overline{h}_f^o\right)_{H_2O} - \left(N\overline{h}_f^o\right)_{CH_4}$$

Using the values of the enthalpy of formation,

HHV = (1 kmol)(-393,520 kJ/kmol) + (2 kmol)(-285,830 kJ/kmol) - (1 kmol)

(-74,850 kJ/kmol)

= -890,330 kJ

This value is practically the same as the value listed for the HHV of methane.

6.3.2 Energy Balances for Reacting Systems

In chemically reacting systems, we can use the conservation equations, but the changes in chemical energies should be explicitly expressed. The steady-flow system is more general than the closed system, so we consider it first.

Steady-Flow Systems

The enthalpy of a component on a unit-mole basis can be expressed as

$$\text{Enthalpy} = \overline{h}_f^o + (\overline{h} - \overline{h}^o) \quad \text{(kJ/kmol)}$$

where the term within brackets is the sensible enthalpy relative to the standard reference state. This term is the difference between $\overline{h}$ and $\overline{h}^o$ (the sensible enthalpy at the standard reference state of 25°C and 1atm). We can thus use values from several tables even though the tables have been constructed using different reference states.

When we neglect kinetic and potential energy terms, the steady-flow first law equation for chemically reacting steady-flow system is

$$\dot{Q}_{in} + \dot{W}_{in} + \sum n_r (\overline{h}_f^o + \overline{h} - \overline{h}^o)_r = \dot{Q}_{out} + \dot{W}_{out} + \sum n_p (\overline{h}_f^o + \overline{h}_T - \overline{h}^o)_p \quad (6.5)$$

where $\dot{n}_r$ and $\dot{n}_p$ represent the molal flow rates of the reactant r and the product p, respectively.

Generally, the quantities are expressed per mole of fuel. Thus,

$$Q_{in} + W_{in} + \sum N_r (\overline{h_f^o} + \overline{h} - \overline{h^o})_r = Q_{out} + W_{out} + \sum N_p (\overline{h_f^o} + \overline{h_T} - \overline{h^o})_p \quad (6.6)$$

where N_p and N_r are the number of moles of the product p and the reactant r, respectively, per mole of fuel. Observe that $N_r = 1$ for the fuel, and the other N_p and N_r values can be seen directly from the balanced combustion equation. Using the conventional signs for heat and work quantities, the energy conservation equation may be written as

$$Q - W = \sum N_p (\overline{h_f^o} + \overline{h_T} - \overline{h^o})_p - \sum N_r (\overline{h_f^o} + \overline{h} - \overline{h^o})_r \quad (6.7)$$

Since $\quad Q - W = H_{prod} - H_{react} \qquad$ (kJ/kmol fuel) $\qquad (6.8)$

where $\quad H_{react} = \sum N_r (\overline{h_f^o} + \overline{h} - \overline{h^o})_r \qquad$ (kJ/kmol fuel) $\qquad (6.9a)$

$\qquad H_{prod} = \sum N_p (\overline{h_f^o} + \overline{h_T} - \overline{h^o})_p \qquad$ (kJ/kmol fuel) $\qquad (6.9b)$

If the enthalpy of combustion $\overline{h_C^o}$ is known for a specific reaction, the steady-flow first law equation per mole of fuel can be expressed as

$$Q - W = \overline{h_C^o} + \sum N_p (\overline{h} - \overline{h^o})_p - \sum N_r (\overline{h} - \overline{h^o})_r \quad (6.10)$$

The first law equation above is sometimes written without the work term since this quantity is mostly absent in steady-flow combustion processes.

There is normally no heat input, and only heat output in a combustion process. Then the first law equation for a typical steady-flow combustion process is

$$Q_{out} = \sum N_r (\overline{h_f^o} + \overline{h} - \overline{h^o})_r - \sum N_p (\overline{h_f^o} + \overline{h_T} - \overline{h^o})_p \quad (6.11)$$

This simply means that the heat output during a combustion process is the difference between the enthalpy of the reactants entering and the enthalpy of the products of combustion exiting the chamber.

Closed Systems

For closed systems, we have from the first law that

$$(Q_{in} - Q_{out}) + (W_{in} - W_{out}) = U_{prod} - U_{react} \quad \text{(kJ/kmol fuel)} \quad (6.12)$$

where U represents the internal energy. We can use the definition of enthalpy to substitute $\bar{u} = \bar{h} - P\bar{v}$ or $\bar{u}_f^\circ + \bar{u} - \bar{u}^\circ = \bar{h}_f^\circ + \bar{h} - \bar{h}^\circ - P\bar{v}$. So

$$Q - W = \sum N_p (\bar{h}_f^\circ + \bar{h} - \bar{h}^\circ - P\bar{v})_p - \sum N_r (\bar{h}_f^\circ + \bar{h} - \bar{h}^\circ - P\bar{v})_r \quad (6.13)$$

The $P\bar{v}$ terms are negligible for solids and liquids, and may be replaced by $R_u T$ for gases that behave ideally.

The work term in Eq. (6.13) represents all forms of work, including the boundary work. It has been shown previously that $\Delta U + W_{boundary} = \Delta H$ for nonreacting closed systems undergoing a P = constant process. This is also true in the corresponding case for chemically reacting systems.

6.4 Adiabatic Flame Temperature

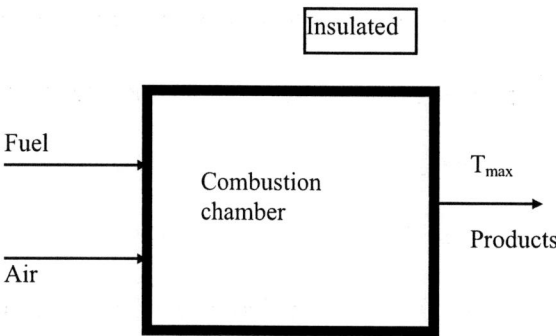

Figure 6.1   Temperature of the products of combustion is a maximum when no heat is lost to the surroundings.

When there are no work interactions and any changes in kinetic or potential energies may be neglected, the chemical energy released in a combustion process may be lost to the surroundings or used to raise the temperature of the combustion products. If no heat is lost to the surroundings, the products of combustion will reach a maximum temperature. This is called the **adiabatic flame** or **adiabatic combustion temperature** of the reaction.

The adiabatic flame temperature of a steady-flow combustion process is calculated by setting $Q = 0$ and $W = 0$ in Eq. (6.8),

$$H_{prod} = H_{react} \tag{6.14}$$

or $\quad \sum N_p (\overline{h}_f^\circ + \overline{h}_T - \overline{h}^\circ)_p = \sum N_r (\overline{h}_f^\circ + \overline{h} - \overline{h}^\circ)_r \tag{6.15}$

The enthalpy of the reactants H_{react} are known from their states. The temperature of the products is the unknown that has to be found. This is done by a trial-and-error method. A temperature is assumed for the products of combustion, and the H_{prod} is calculated for this temperature. If it is not equal to H_{react}, the computations are repeated with another temperature. The adiabatic flame temperature is found from these two results by interpolation. When air is used to supply oxygen, the products of combustion comprise mostly of nitrogen, and a good first approximation for the adiabatic flame temperature is obtained by treating all the product gases as nitrogen.

The highest temperature to which the material in the combustion chamber should be exposed is limited by metallurgical considerations. Hence, the adiabatic flame temperature is an important parameter in the design of combustion chambers, internal combustion engines, nozzles and gas turbines. The maximum temperatures in these devices are much lower in practice than the adiabatic flame temperature. Combustion is normally incomplete, and some heat loss does take place. The maximum temperature in a combustion chamber may be adjusted by controlling the amount of excess air, which also serves as a coolant in the combustion process.

Example 6.5

Problem

Acetylene (C_2H_2) enters a combustion chamber steadily at 1 atm and 25°C, and is burned with air at the same state. Neglect changes in K.E. and P.E. Find the adiabatic flame temperature for (a) complete combustion with 100% theoretical air, (b) complete combustion with 200% theoretical air, and (c) incomplete combustion (CO produced) with 75% theoretical air.

Solution

Assumptions: (1) There is no work interactions.

(2) The process considered is adiabatic.

(3) Air and the products of combustion are ideal gases.

Analysis

The equation for the combustion of acetylene with theoretical air is

$$C_2H_2 + 2.5(O_2 + 3.76 N_2) \rightarrow 2 CO_2 + H_2O + 9.4 N_2$$

The first law equation gives

$$H_{prod} = H_{react}$$

$$\sum N_p \left(\bar{h}_f^o + \bar{h} - \bar{h}^o \right)_p = \left(N \bar{h}_f^o \right)_{C_2H_2}$$

The $\bar{h}_f^o$ and $\bar{h}$ values of the various gases at 298.15 K are

Substance	$\bar{h}_f^o$ kJ/kmol	$C_p \Delta T$
C_2H_2	+226,730	0
O_2	0	0
N_2	0	0
$H_2O_{(g)}$	-241,820	0
CO_2	-393,520	0

Substituting the values,

$$(2 \text{ kmol})\{(-393,520 + \bar{h}_{CO_2}) \text{kJ/kmol}\}$$
$$+ (1 \text{ kmol})[(-241,820 + \bar{h}_{H_2O}) \text{kJ/kmol}]$$
$$+ (9.4 \text{ kmol})[(0 + \bar{h}_{N_2}) \text{kJ/kmol}]$$
$$= (1 \text{ kmol})(+226,730 \text{ kJ/kmol})$$

which gives

$$\{2\bar{h}_{CO_2} + \bar{h}_{H_2O}\} + 9.4\bar{h}_{N_2} = 1,255,590 \text{ kJ}$$

An initial guess is obtained by dividing the RHS of the equation by the total number of moles, which gives (1,255,590)/(2+1+9.4) = 101,257 kJ/kmol. Since nitrogen is the major component, we will use nitrogen as a guide. From the ideal gas property-tables for nitrogen, it can be seen that this value of enthalpy corresponds to about 3240 K, but somewhat less. Thus, a good first guess is 3000 K.

The table below provides a summary of the iterative procedure for three trial values of T_{prod}. The specific heat values for the ideal gases are evaluated at a convenient average temperature, say 1500 K. These values are 2.6 kJ/(kg.K) for water vapor and 1.33 kJ/(kg.K) for carbon dioxide. The values of $\bar{h}_{N_2}$ may be read directly from the ideal gas tables for nitrogen at 1 atmosphere. Since the summation of the enthalpies of the products equal 1,255,590 kJ, the actual value of T_{prod} is in between 2500 K and 3000 K. Interpolation gives $T_{prod} = 2900$ K.

	3000 K	2000 K	2500 K
$2\,\bar{h}_{CO_2}$	316,225	199,185	257,705
$\bar{h}_{H_2O_{(g)}}$	126,447	84,327	103,047
$9.4\,\bar{h}_{N_2}$	871,521	527,688	698,434
$\sum N_p \bar{h}_{prod}$	1,314,193	811,200	1,059,186

Hence, the adiabatic flame temperature is about 2900 K. Since the ideal-gas enthalpy is not really a linear function of temperature, the actual value of the temperature will not be exactly the same as this value.

(b)   For complete combustion of acetylene with 200% theoretical air, the combustion equation is

$$C_2H_2 + 5(O_2 + 3.76\,N_2) \rightarrow 2\,CO_2 + H_2O + 2.5\,O_2 + 18.8\,N_2$$

The first law equation gives

$(2\text{ kmol})\{(-393,520 + \bar{h}_{CO_2})\text{kJ/kmol}\}$
$+(1\text{ kmol})[(-241,820 + \bar{h}_{H_2O})\text{kJ/kmol}]$
$+(2.5\text{ kmol})[(0 + \bar{h}_{O_2})\text{kJ/kmol}]$
$+(18.8\text{ kmol})[(0 + \bar{h}_{N_2})\text{kJ/kmol}]$
$= (1\text{ kmol})(+226,730\text{ kJ/kmol})$

which reduces to

$$\{2\bar{h}_{CO_2} + \bar{h}_{H_2O}\} + 2.5\bar{h}_{O_2} + 18.8\bar{h}_{N_2} = 1{,}255{,}590 \text{ kJ}$$

Using the same procedure as before, it is found that $T_{prod} = 1750$ K. Note that this temperature is less than that with 100% theoretical air. The excess air acts as a coolant to the products of combustion.

(c)   The incomplete combustion with 75% theoretical air is

$$C_2H_2 + 1.875\,(O_2 + 3.76\,N_2) \rightarrow 0.75\,CO_2 + 1.25\,CO + H_2O + 7.05\,N_2$$

The first law equation gives

$$(0.75 \text{ kmol})\{(-393{,}520 + \bar{h}_{CO_2})\text{kJ / kmol}\}$$
$$+(1.25 \text{ kmol})[(-110{,}530 + \bar{h}_{CO})\text{kJ / kmol}]$$
$$+(1 \text{ kmol})[(-241{,}820 + \bar{h}_{H_2O})\text{kJ / kmol}]$$
$$+(7.05 \text{ kmol})[(0 + \bar{h}_{N_2})\text{kJ / kmol}]$$
$$= (1 \text{ kmol})(+226{,}730 \text{ kJ / kmol})$$

which reduces to

$$\{0.75\bar{h}_{CO_2} + \bar{h}_{H_2O}\} + 1.25\bar{h}_{CO} + 7.05\bar{h}_{N_2} = 901{,}853 \text{ kJ}$$

Using the same procedure as before, it is found that $T_{prod} = 2920$ K. Note that this temperature is less than that with 100% theoretical air. The adiabatic flame temperature decreases because of the incomplete combustion, as it did with excess air. It should be noted that the maximum adiabatic flame temperature is obtained with complete combustion at the theoretical quantity of air.

6.5   Third Law of Thermodynamics and Absolute Entropy

The examination of reacting systems and combustion processes is not complete without the second-law analysis. This later involves exergy (availability), and entropy production. The entropy balance equations and the availability balance equations are equally applicable to both reacting and nonreacting systems provided that the entropies of individual components are evaluated properly using a common basis.

This is accomplished by using the third law of thermodynamics and the concept of absolute entropy. The third law addresses the entropy of substances at the absolute zero of temperature. Based on experimental observations, the **third law** states that the entropy of a pure crystalline substance is zero at the absolute zero of temperature, 0 K or 0°R. If a substance does not have a pure crystalline structure at absolute zero, it will have a nonzero value of entropy at absolute zero. The significance of the third law is that it provides a datum relative to which the entropy of each substance in a chemical reaction can be evaluated so that no ambiguities arise. Entropy values relative to this datum are called the **absolute entropy**. The $\bar{s}^o$ values are listed for various gases such as N_2, O_2, CO, CO_2, H_2, and H_2O, and these are the ideal-gas absolute entropy values at the specified temperature and at a pressure of 1 atm. The absolute entropy values for various fuels are also listed together with the $\bar{h}_f^o$ values at the standard reference state of 25°C and 1 atm.

When computing the entropy of a component of an ideal-gas mixture, we have to use the temperature and the partial pressure of the component. Recall that the temperature of a component is the same as that of the mixture, and the partial pressure of a component is equal to the mixture pressure multiplied by the component mole fraction.

Absolute entropy values at pressures other than P_o = 1 atm for any temperature T can be obtained from the ideal-gas entropy change relation written for a fictitious isothermal process between states (T, P_o) and (T, P),

$$\bar{s}(T,P) = \bar{s}°(T,P_0) - R_u \ln \frac{P}{P_0} \qquad \{kJ/(kmol.K)]\qquad (6.16)$$

For the component i of an ideal-gas mixture, this equation may be written as

$$\bar{s}_i(T,P_i) = \bar{s}_i°(T,P_0) - R_u \ln \frac{y_i P_m}{P_0} \qquad \{kJ/(kmol.K)]\qquad (6.17)$$

where $P_0 = 1$ atm, P_i is the partial pressure, y_i is the mole fraction of the component, and P_m is the total pressure of the mixture. When a gas mixture is not ideal, a more accurate equation of state should be used.

6.6 Second-Law Analysis of Reacting Systems

The entropy balance for any system (reacting or nonreacting) undergoing a process is

$$S_{in} - S_{out} + S_{gen} = \Delta S \qquad (kJ/K) \qquad (6.18)$$

When the total entropy change or the entropy generated has been calculated, the irreversibility I or the exergy destroyed $X_{destroyed}$ associated with a chemical reaction can be computed from

$$I = X_{destroyed} = T_o S_{gen} \qquad (kJ) \qquad (6.19)$$

where T_o is the absolute temperature of the surroundings.

Recall from a previous chapter that the reversible work W_{rev} is the maximum work that can be done during a process. Neglecting the kinetic and potential energy terms, the reversible work for a steady-flow combustion process that involves heat transfer only with the surroundings at T_o is

$$W_{rev} = \sum N_r (\overline{h_f°} + \overline{h} - \overline{h°} - T_o \bar{s})_r - \sum N_p (\overline{h_f°} + \overline{h} - \overline{h°} - T_o \bar{s})_p \qquad (6.20)$$

Consider the case when both the reactants and the products are at the temperature of the surroundings T_0. In this case, $\overline{h} - T_0 \overline{s} = (\overline{h} - T_0 \overline{s})_{T_0} = \overline{g_0}$, which by definition, is the **Gibbs function** of a unit mole of a substance at temperature T_0. The W_{rev} equation can be written as

$$W_{rev} = \sum N_r \overline{g_{0,r}} - \sum N_p \overline{g_{0,p}} \qquad (6.21)$$

or

$$W_{rev} = \sum N_r (\overline{g_f^o} + \overline{g_{T_0}} - \overline{g^o})_r - \sum N_p (\overline{g_f^o} + \overline{g_{T_0}} - \overline{g^o})_p \qquad (6.22)$$

where $\overline{g_f^o}$ is the Gibbs function of formation ($\overline{g_f^o} = 0$ for stable elements like O_2 and N_2 at the standard reference state of 25°C and 1 atm, just like the enthalpy of formation) and $\overline{g_{T_0}} - \overline{g^o}$ is the value of the sensible Gibbs function of a substance at temperature T_0 relative to the standard reference state.

For the special case of $T_{react} = T_{prod} = T_0 = 25°C$, and the partial pressure $P_i = 1$ atm for each component of the reactants and the products, Eq. (6.22) reduces to

$$W_{rev} = \sum N_r \overline{g_{f,r}^o} - \sum N_p \overline{g_{f,p}^o} \qquad (kJ) \qquad (6.23)$$

We can see that the $-\overline{g_f^o}$ value (the negative of the Gibbs function of formation at 25°C and 1 atm) of a compound is the reversible work associated with the formation of that compound from its stable elements at 25°C and 1 atm in an environment at 25°C and 1 atm. The $\overline{g_f^o}$ values of several substances are listed.

Example 6.6

Problem

Acetylene (C_2H_2) gas enters steadily a combustion chamber at 25°C and 1 atm and is burned with 80% excess air, which also enters at the same conditions. After the combustion, the products loose heat to the surroundings until the temperature falls to 25°C. Find (a) the heat transfer per kmol of acetylene, (b) the entropy generation, and (c) the irreversibility of the process. The surrounding temperature is $T_o = 298.15$ K, and the combustion products leave the chamber at 1 atm pressure.

Solution

Assumptions: (1) Neglect K.E. and P.E. changes.

(2) Combustion is complete, since 80% excess air is used.

(3) All gaseous reactants and combustion products are treated as ideal gases.

Analysis:

The complete combustion equation with theoretical air is

$$C_2H_2(g) + 2.5\,(O_2 + 3.76\,N_2) \rightarrow 2\,CO_2 + H_2O + 9.4\,N_2$$

When 80% excess air is used, the complete combustion equation is

$$C_2H_2(g) + 4.5\,(O_2 + 3.76\,N_2) \rightarrow 2\,CO_2 + H_2O + 2\,O_2 + 16.92\,N_2$$

At 25°C part of the water will condense, and the amount of water vapor in the combustion products is

$$\frac{N_v}{N_{gas}} = \frac{P_v}{P_{total}} = \frac{3.169\,\text{kPa}}{101.3\,\text{kPa}} = 0.0313$$

and $\quad N_v = \left(\dfrac{P_v}{P_{total}}\right) N_{gas} = (0.0313)(20.92 + N_v)$

$N_v = 0.68$ kmol

Hence, 0.32 kmol of the water formed will be in liquid form. For the steady-flow combustion process, the first law equation is

$$Q = \sum N_p \bar{h}_{f,p}^{\circ} - \sum N_r \bar{h}_{f,r}^{\circ}$$

as all the reactants and components are at the standard reference of 25°C and the enthalpy of ideal gases depends on temperature only. Substituting for the $\bar{h}_f^{\circ}$ values, for 1 kmol of fuel,

$$\begin{aligned}
Q &= (2 \text{ kmol})(-393{,}520 \text{ kJ/kmol}) \\
&\quad + (0.68 \text{ kmol } H_2O_{(g)})(-241{,}820 \text{ kJ/kmol } H_2O_{(g)}) \\
&\quad + (0.32 \text{ kmol } H_2O_{(l)})(-285{,}830 \text{ kJ/kmol } H_2O_{(l)}) \\
&\quad - (1 \text{ kmol})(+226{,}730 \text{ kJ/kmol}) \\
&= -1{,}269{,}673 \text{ kJ}
\end{aligned}$$

(b) The entropy values listed in the ideal gas tables are for a 1-atm pressure. Both the air and the gaseous combustion products are at a total pressure of 1 atm. The entropies are calculated at the partial pressure of the components which is $P_i = y_i P_{total}$, where y_i is the mole fraction of component i.

$$S_i = N_i \bar{s}_i(T, P_i) = N_i \left(\bar{s}_i^{\circ}(T, P_o) - R_u \ln y_i P_m \right)$$

The entropy calculations are shown in tabular form.

	N_i	y_i	$\bar{s}_i^{\circ}$ (T,1 atm)	$-R_u \ln y_i P_m$	$N_i \bar{s}_i$
C_2H_2	1	1.00	200.85	—	200.85
O_2	4.5	0.21	205.04	12.98	981.09
N_2	16.92	0.79	191.61	1.96	3275.2
				$S_{react} =$	4457.1
CO_2	2	0.093	213.80	19.75	467.10

$H_2O_{(g)}$	0.68	0.031	188.83	28.88	148.10
O_2	2	0.093	205.04	19.75	449.58
N_2	16.92	0.783	191.61	2.03	3276.39
$H_2O_{(l)}$	0.32	1.000	69.92	—	22.37
				S_{prod} =	4363.48

Thus, $\Delta S_{sys} = S_{prod} - S_{react}$

$= (4363.48 - 4457.1) = -93.62 \text{ kJ/(kmol.K)}$

$$\Delta S_{surr} = \frac{Q_{surr}}{T_o} = \frac{1,269,673 \text{ kJ/kmol}}{298 \text{ K}} = 4260.6 \frac{\text{kJ}}{\text{kmol.K}}$$

$S_{gen} = \Delta S_{sys} + \Delta S_{surr}$

$= -93.62 + 4260.6 \frac{\text{kJ}}{\text{kmol.K}} = 4167.0 \frac{\text{kJ}}{\text{K.kmol } C_2H_2}$

(c) The irreversibility of the process is given by

$I = T_o S_{gen}$

$= (298.15 \text{ K})(4167.0 \text{ kJ/(kmol.K)})$

$= 1,242,391 \text{ kJ/(kmol } C_2H_2)$

PROBLEMS

Combustion Process

6.1. Ethane (C_2H_6) is burned with 15% excess air. Assuming complete combustion and a total pressure of 100 kPa, calculate the air-fuel ratio. What is the dew-point temperature of the products of combustion?

6.2. Octane (C_8H_{18}) is burned with 25% excess air. Assuming complete combustion and a total pressure of 100 kPa, calculate the air-fuel ratio. What is the dew-point temperature of the products of combustion?

6.3. Consider the combustion of propane (C_3H_8) in dry air. The volumetric analysis of the products of combustion on a dry basis is CO_2, 11%; CO, 0.5%; O_2, 3.5%; N_2, 85%. Find (a) the air-fuel ratio, (b) the percentage of theoretical air utilized, and (c) the fraction of the water which condenses as the products are cooled to 20°C at 100 kPa.

6.4. A gas mixture is made up of the following volumetric percentages:-

60% octane, 11% hydrogen, 24% nitrogen, 3% oxygen, and 2% carbon dioxide. The mixture is burned with the theoretical amount of air, which enters the combustion process at 25°C, 1 atm, and 70% relative humidity. Find the dew-point temperature of the products of combustion, if the complete combustion takes place at 1 atm.

First-Law Analysis of Reacting Systems

6.5. Find the higher heating value of gaseous ethane at 25°C and 1 atm, using the enthalpy of formation data.

6.6. Find the higher heating value of gaseous propane at 25°C and 1 atm, using the enthalpy of formation data.

6.7. Find the higher heating value of gaseous propylene at 25°C and 1 atm, using the enthalpy of formation data.

Adiabatic Flame Temperature

6.8. Ethylene (C_2H_4) enters a combustion chamber steadily at 1 atm and 25°C, and is burned with air at the same state. Neglect changes in K.E. and P.E. Find the adiabatic flame temperature for (a) complete combustion with 100% theoretical air, (b) complete combustion with 200% theoretical air, and (c) incomplete combustion (CO produced) with 75% theoretical air.

Second-Law Analysis of Reacting Systems

6.9. Ethylene (C_2H_4) gas enters steadily a combustion chamber at 25°C and 1 atm and is burned with 80% excess air, which also enters at the same conditions. After the combustion, the products loose heat to the surroundings until the temperature falls to 25°C. Find (a) the heat transfer per kmol of ethylene, (b) the entropy generation, and (c) the irreversibility of the process. The surrounding temperature is T_o = 298 K, and the combustion products leave the chamber at 1 atm pressure.

6.10. Ethane (C_2H_6) gas enters steadily a combustion chamber at 25°C and 1 atm and is burned with 60% excess air, which also enters at the same conditions. Calculate the adiabatic flame temperature for complete combustion with the 60% excess air. After the combustion, the products loose heat to the surroundings until the temperature falls to 25°C. Find (a) the heat transfer per kmol of ethane, (b) the entropy generation, and (c) the irreversibility of the process. The surrounding temperature is T_o = 298 K, and the combustion products leave the chamber at 1 atm pressure.

7. THERMODYNAMICS OF COMPRESSIBLE FLUID FLOW

7.1 Stagnation Properties

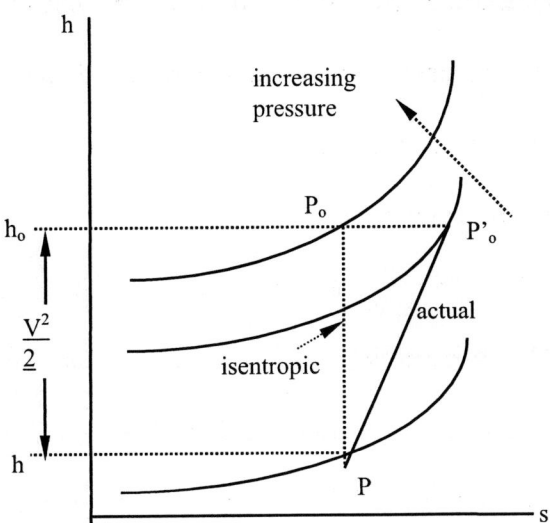

P' = Actual stagnation pressure
P_o = Isentropic stagnation pressure
P = Pressure at actual state

Figure 7.1 Enthalpy-entropy diagram illustrating stagnation state.

From the first law for a steady-state, steady flow process we conclude that

$$h + \frac{V^2}{2} = h_o \qquad (7.1)$$

The actual and isentropic stagnation states for a typical gas or vapor are shown on the h-s diagram of Fig. 7.1. The actual stagnation state is the state reached after an actual deceleration to zero velocity, and there may be irreversibilities involved in the deceleration process. Thus, the term stagnation property is sometimes reserved for the properties associated with the actual state, and the term total property is used for the isentropic stagnation state.

Example 7.1

Problem

Steam in a pipeline is at 300°C and 1.5 MPa, and flowing at 500 m/s. Determine the stagnation enthalpy, temperature, pressure, and specific volume of the steam.

Solution

Assumption: (1) The deceleration process is isentropic.

Analysis:

From the thermodynamic tables,

$$h = 3038 \text{ kJ/kg}, \qquad s = 6.918 \text{ kJ/(kg.K)}$$

The stagnation enthalpy of the steam is

$$h_o = h + \frac{V^2}{2}$$

$$= 3038 \frac{\text{kJ}}{\text{kg}} + \frac{(500 \text{ m/s})^2}{2}\left(\frac{1 \text{ kJ/kg}}{1000 \text{ m}^2/\text{s}^2}\right)$$

$$= 3038 \frac{\text{kJ}}{\text{kg}} + 125 \frac{\text{kJ}}{\text{kg}} = 3163 \frac{\text{kJ}}{\text{kg}}$$

Since the deceleration process is isentropic, the stagnation entropy is equal to the entropy.

$$s_o = s = 6.918 \text{ kJ/(kg.K)}$$

These two stagnation properties define the stagnation state. Hence, the stagnation temperature, pressure, and specific volume may be found from the tables.

$$T_o = 365°C$$

$$P_o = 2.389 \text{ MPa}$$

$$v_o = 0.11838 \text{ m}^3/\text{kg}.$$

7.2 Adiabatic, One-Dimensional, Steady-State, Steady Flow of an Incompressible Fluid through a Nozzle.

A nozzle is a device in which the kinetic energy of a fluid is increased in an adiabatic process. This involves a decrease in pressure. A diffuser is a device in which the kinetic energy of a fluid is decreased in an adiabatic process. This involves an increase in pressure.

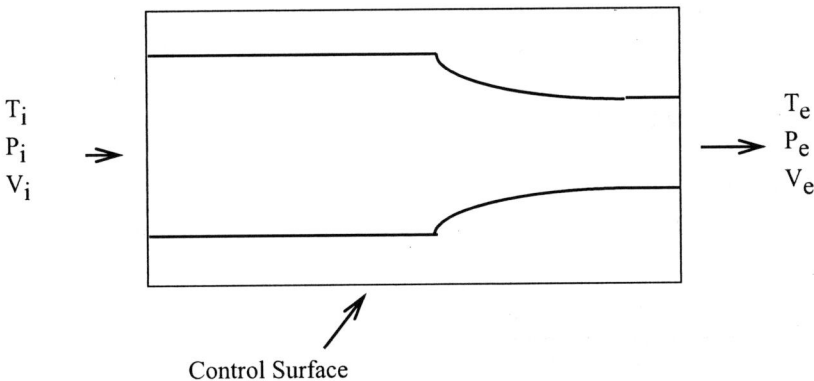

Figure 7.2 Schematic sketch of a nozzle.

Assume an adiabatic, one-dimensional, steady-state, steady-flow process of an incompressible fluid. From the continuity equation,

$$\dot{m}_e = \dot{m}_i = \rho A_i V_i = \rho A_e V_e \qquad (7.2)$$

$$\frac{A_i}{A_e} = \frac{V_i}{V_e} \qquad (7.3)$$

The first law for this process is

$$h_e - h_i + \left(\frac{V^2}{2}\right)_e - \left(\frac{V^2}{2}\right)_i + g(z_e - z_i) = 0 \qquad (7.4)$$

The second law requires that $s_e \geq s_i$, and the equality holds for a reversible process. Since

$$Tds = dh - vdP$$

for the reversible process,

$$h_e - h_i = \int_i^e v\, dP \tag{7.5}$$

If the fluid is incompressible, the equation can be integrated to give

$$h_e - h_i = v(P_e - P_i) \tag{7.6}$$

Substituting in the above, we obtain the Bernoulli equation,

$$v(P_e - P_i) + \left(\frac{V^2}{2}\right)_e - \left(\frac{V^2}{2}\right)_i + g(z_e - z_i) = 0 \tag{7.7}$$

The Bernoulli equation represents a combination of the first and second law of thermodynamics.

Example 7.2

Problem

Water enters a nozzle at a velocity of 20 m/s, a pressure of 300 kPa and a temperature of 30°C. It leaves the nozzle with a velocity of 25 m/s and a pressure of 101 kPa. Determine the exit pressure for a reversible nozzle with the same inlet state and outlet velocity. Calculate the increase in enthalpy, internal energy, and the entropy for the actual nozzle.

Solution

Assumption: (1) The nozzle is adiabatic.

Analysis:

Consider a control volume around the reversible nozzle. Since there is no change in elevation, Bernoulli's equation gives

$$v\left(P_e\big|_s - P_i\right) + \frac{V_e^2 - V_i^2}{2} = 0$$

From the thermodynamic tables, $v = 0.001004 \text{ m}^3/\text{kg}$

$$P_e\big|_s - P_i = \frac{(20)^2 - (25)^2}{0.001004 \times 2 \times 1000} \frac{\text{m}^2 \cdot \text{kg}}{\text{s}^2 \cdot \text{m}^3} \cdot \frac{1 \text{ kPa}}{1000 \text{ Pa}}$$
$$= -112 \text{ kPa}$$
$$P_e\big|_s = 188 \text{ kPa}$$

Now consider a control volume around the actual nozzle. From the first law,

$$h_e - h_i = \frac{V_i^2 - V_e^2}{2} = \frac{(20)^2 - (25)^2}{2 \times 1000} = -0.1125 \frac{\text{kJ}}{\text{kg}}$$

The change in internal energy is found from this change in enthalpy and the definition of enthalpy.

$$h_e - h_i = (u_e - u_i) + (P_e v_e - P_i v_i)$$

$$u_e - u_i = h_e - h_i - v(P_e - P_i) \quad \text{for an incompressible fluid}$$
$$= -0.1125 - 0.001004(101 - 300) \qquad = 0.08730 \text{ kJ/kg}.$$

The change in entropy can be approximated using the relation $Tds = du + Pdv$

Assume the temperature is constant (which is approximately true). Since $dv = 0$ for an incompressible fluid,

$$s_e - s_i = (u_e - u_i)/T = 0.08730/303 = 0.000288 \text{ kJ/(kg·K)}$$

The calculation shows that the entropy increases, as it should since the actual nozzle generates an irreversible process.

7.3 Velocity of Sound in an Ideal Gas

Properties after   Wave   Properties before

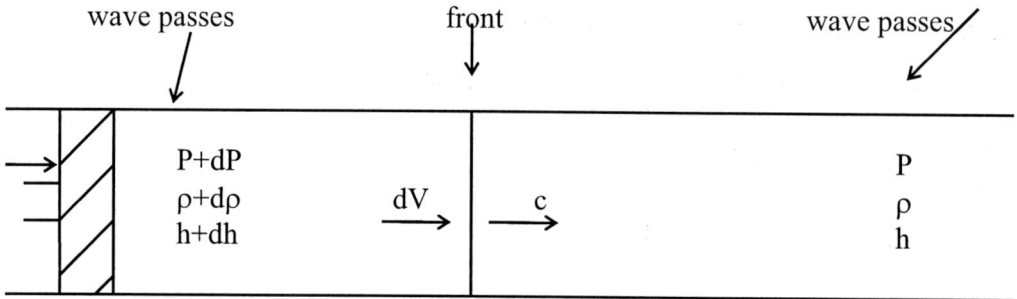

Figure 7.3 (a) Stationary observer - wave front traveling at velocity c.

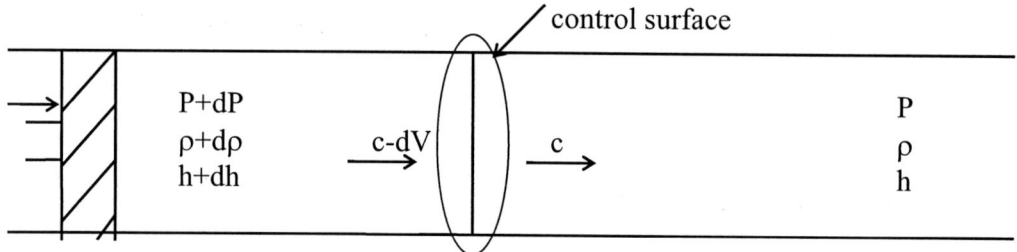

Figure 7.3 (b) Observer traveling with wave front - wave front stationary.

First law for S.S.S.F.,

$$h + \frac{c^2}{2} = (h+dh) + \frac{(c-dV)^2}{2} \qquad (7.8)$$

dh - cdV = 0

Continuity : $\rho Ac = (\rho + d\rho)A(c - dV)$ $\qquad (7.9)$

$\qquad\qquad c d\rho - \rho dV = 0$

Relation between properties: $Tds = dh - \frac{dP}{\rho}$

Isentropic :   ds = 0

Combined with Eq. (7.8) to give

$$\frac{dP}{\rho} - cdV = 0 \qquad (7.10)$$

Combined with Eq. (7.9) to give

$$\frac{dP}{\rho} = c^2$$

Since the process is assumed isentropic,

$$\left(\frac{\partial P}{\partial \rho}\right)_s = c^2 \qquad (7.11)$$

268

An alternate derivation of the above is as follows:-

For the control volume, the momentum equation is

$$PA - (P + dP)A = \dot{m}(c - dV - c) = \rho A c(c - dV - c)$$

$$dV = \rho c\, dP \qquad (7.12)$$

Combining with Eq. (7.10),

$$\left(\frac{\partial P}{\partial \rho}\right)_s = c^2$$

For an ideal gas undergoing an isentropic change of state, assuming a specific heat ratio of k,

$$\frac{dP}{P} - k\frac{d\rho}{\rho} = 0 \quad \text{or} \quad \left(\frac{\partial P}{\partial \rho}\right)_s = \frac{kP}{\rho}$$

Thus, $\quad c^2 = \dfrac{kP}{\rho}$

But $\dfrac{P}{\rho} = RT$, $\quad \boxed{c^2 = kRT} \qquad (7.13)$

Example 7.3

Problem

Determine the speed of sound in air at 298 K and 500 K.

Solution

Speed of sound $c = \sqrt{kRT} = \sqrt{1.4 \times 0.287 \times 298 \times 1000} = 346\, m/s$

At 500 K, $\quad c = \sqrt{1.4 \times 0.287 \times 500 \times 1000} = 448\, m/s$

There is a significant increase in the speed of sound with the temperature increase.

7.4 Entropy Connection to Vorticity

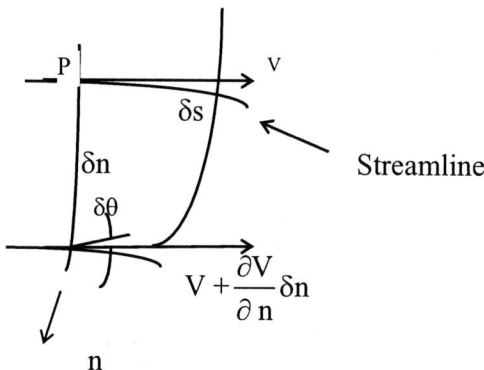

Figure 7.4 Streamline coordinates.

Consider two streamlines as shown in Fig. 7.4, separated by a distance δn. At a point P on the streamline, the normal velocity component v_n is zero. On the adjacent streamline, there is a small normal velocity, δv_n, because the two streamlines differ in direction by $\delta\theta$. In going in the direction s, the distance increases because of this directional difference. The incremental variation of streamline spacing over a distance δs is $\delta s \delta\theta$. It follows that

$$\left[\frac{\partial}{\partial s}(\delta n)\right]\delta s = \delta s \delta\theta = \delta s\left[\frac{\partial \theta}{\partial n}\delta n\right]$$

$$\frac{\partial}{\partial s}(\delta n) = \frac{\partial \theta}{\partial n}\delta n$$

Since steady flow is considered, the mass flow rate is constant between the two streamlines. So

$$\frac{\partial}{\partial s}(\rho V \delta n) = \rho V \frac{\partial}{\partial s}(\delta n) + \delta n \frac{\partial}{\partial s}(\rho V) = 0$$

which gives the continuity equation in two-dimensional streamline coordinates for steady compressible flow,

$$\rho V \frac{\partial \theta}{\partial n} + \frac{\partial}{\partial s}(\rho V) = 0 \qquad (7.14)$$

The circulation about the element in Fig. 7.4 is

$$\delta \Gamma = V \delta s + \delta V_n \delta n - (V + \delta V) \delta s = \delta V_n \delta n - \delta V \delta s$$

Since $\delta A = \delta n \delta s$, $\zeta = \dfrac{\delta \Gamma}{\delta A} = \dfrac{\delta V_n}{\delta s} - \dfrac{\delta V}{\delta n}$

As $\delta A \to 0$, vorticity $\zeta = \dfrac{V}{r} - \dfrac{\partial V}{\partial n}$ \qquad (7.15)

where r = radius of curvature of the streamline at point P.

For perfect gases, Gibbs equation gives $TdS = dh - \dfrac{dP}{\rho}$

$$T \frac{\partial S}{\partial s} = \frac{\partial h}{\partial s} - \frac{1}{\rho} \frac{\partial P}{\partial s} \Rightarrow T \frac{\partial S}{\partial s} = \frac{\partial h_o}{\partial s} - \left(V \frac{\partial V}{\partial s} + \frac{1}{\rho} \frac{\partial P}{\partial s} \right) \qquad (7.16)$$

$$T \frac{\partial S}{\partial n} = \frac{\partial h}{\partial n} - \frac{1}{\rho} \frac{\partial P}{\partial n} \Rightarrow T \frac{\partial S}{\partial n} = \frac{\partial h_o}{\partial n} - \left(V \frac{\partial V}{\partial n} + \frac{1}{\rho} \frac{\partial P}{\partial n} \right)$$

$$T \frac{\partial S}{\partial n} = \frac{\partial h_o}{\partial n} - \left(\frac{V^2}{r} + \frac{1}{\rho} \frac{\partial P}{\partial n} \right) + V \zeta$$

$$(7.17)$$

The above equations relate the change in entropy along and across the streamlines to the stagnation enthalpy. Under adiabatic conditions, the stagnation enthalpy change is zero. When friction is neglected, the terms within brackets are also zero (deduced from the Euler equation in streamline coordinates).

For isentropic flows,

$$\frac{P}{\rho^k} = \text{constant} \Rightarrow \frac{\partial P}{\partial s} = k \frac{P}{\rho} \frac{\partial \rho}{\partial s} = c^2 \frac{\partial \rho}{\partial s} \qquad (7.18)$$

Streamwise component of the Euler equation is

$$\rho V \frac{\partial V}{\partial s} = -c^2 \frac{\partial \rho}{\partial s} \quad \text{or} \quad \frac{V}{\rho} \frac{\partial \rho}{\partial s} = -M^2 \frac{\partial V}{\partial s}$$

Combining with continuity, Eq. (7.14), we have

$$V\frac{\partial \theta}{\partial n} + (1-M^2)\frac{\partial V}{\partial s} = 0 \qquad (7.19)$$

When velocity increases in the streamline direction, $\frac{\partial V}{\partial s}$ is positive. If the flow is subsonic, $(1-M^2)$ is positive, Eq. (7.19) can hold only if $\frac{\partial \theta}{\partial n}$ is negative; this implies that the streamlines must converge, as in incompressible flow.

If the flow is supersonic and accelerating, the streamlines must diverge. This is directly opposite to the expectation for incompressible flow. If the flow were decelerating along streamlines, the spacing between them would grow in subsonic flow but decrease in supersonic flow.

Putting $\frac{1}{r} = \frac{\partial \theta}{\partial s}$ in Eq. (7.15), and setting vorticity to zero,

$$V\frac{\partial \theta}{\partial s} - \frac{\partial V}{\partial n} = 0 \qquad (7.20)$$

Equations (7.19) and (7.20) are two independent relationships for the magnitude and direction of the velocity of two-dimensional ideal compressible flows.

7.5 Reversible, Adiabatic, One-Dimensional Steady Flow of an Ideal Gas through a Nozzle

A nozzle or diffuser with both a converging and diverging section is shown in Fig. 7.5. The smallest cross-sectional area is called the throat, like the throat of a human body.

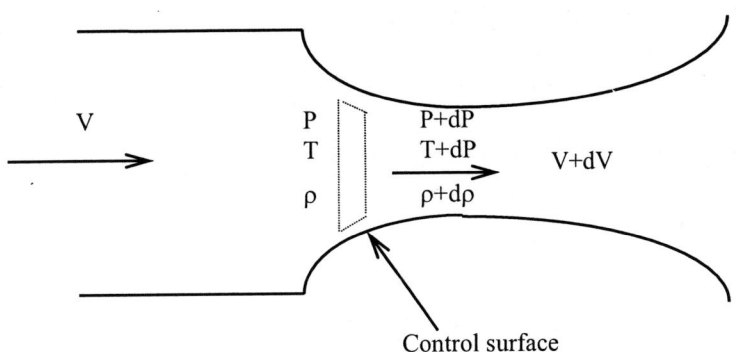

Figure 7.5 One-dimensional, reversible, adiabatic steady flow through a nozzle.

Consider the control volume. The first law gives

$$dh + VdV = 0 \qquad (7.21)$$

and the property relation is

$$Tds = dh - \frac{dP}{\rho} = 0 \qquad (7.22)$$

Continuity gives $\rho AV = \dot{m} = $ constant

Thus $\dfrac{d\rho}{\rho} + \dfrac{dA}{A} + \dfrac{dV}{V} = 0 \qquad (7.23)$

Combining Eqs. (7.21) and (7.22),

$$dh = \frac{dP}{\rho} = -VdV$$

$$dV = -\frac{1}{\rho V} dP$$

Substituting this in Eq. (7.23),

$$\frac{dA}{A} = -\frac{d\rho}{\rho} - \frac{dV}{V} = -\frac{d\rho}{\rho}\left(\frac{dP}{dP}\right) + \frac{1}{\rho V^2} dP$$

$$= -\frac{dP}{\rho}\left(\frac{d\rho}{dP} - \frac{1}{V^2}\right) = \frac{dP}{\rho}\left(-\frac{1}{\frac{dP}{d\rho}} + \frac{1}{V^2}\right)$$

Since the flow is isentropic,

$$\frac{dP}{d\rho} = c^2 = \frac{V^2}{M^2}$$

Thus, $\dfrac{dA}{A} = \dfrac{dP}{\rho V^2}(1 - M^2)$ \hfill (7.24)

From Eq. (7.24), the following conclusions are drawn about the proper shape for nozzles and diffusers:

For a nozzle, $dP < 0$

    subsonic $M < 1$, $dA < 0$ i.e. converging

    supersonic $M > 1$, $dA > 0$ i.e. diverging

For a diffuser, $dP > 0$

    subsonic $M < 1$, $dA > 0$ i.e. diverging

    supersonic $M > 1$, $dA < 0$ i.e. converging

When $M = 1$, $dA = 0$ which means sonic velocity can be achieved only at the throat of the nozzle or diffuser.

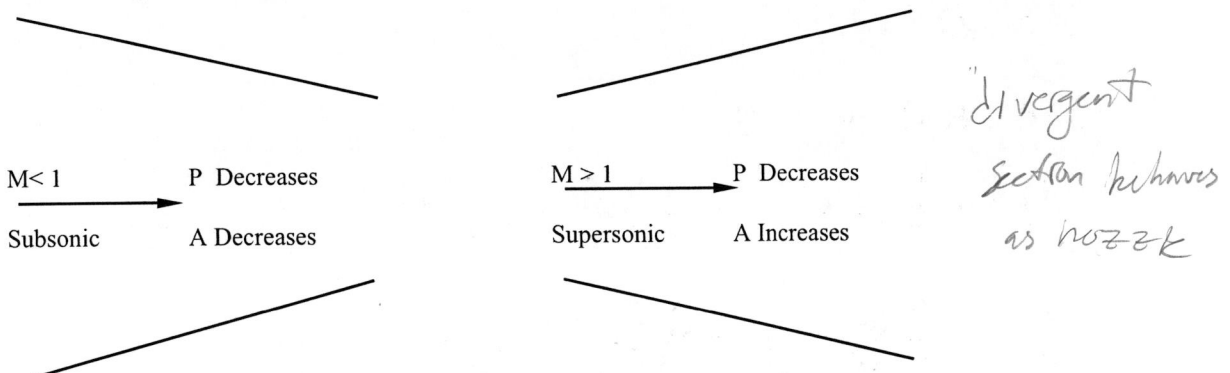

Figure 7.6 Required area changes for nozzles.

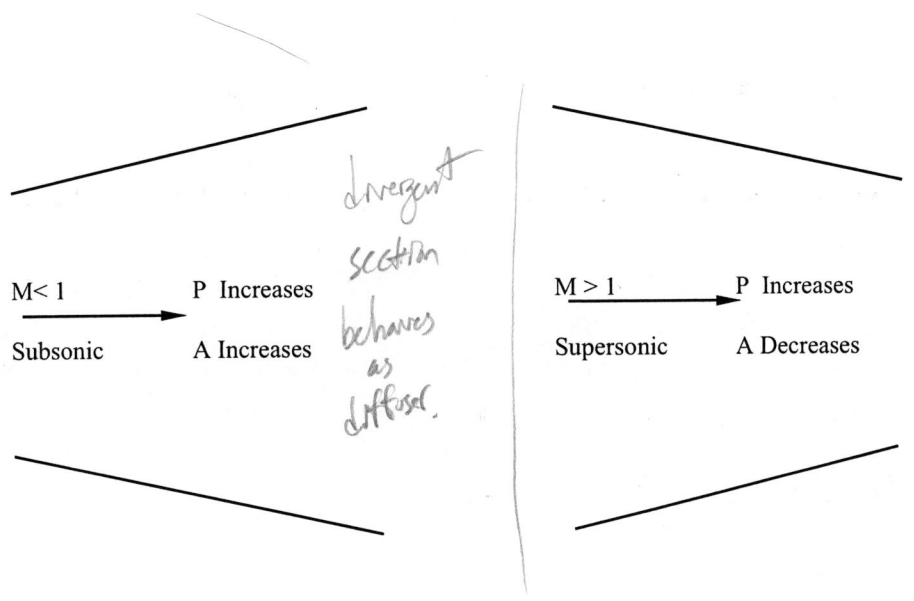

Figure 7.7 Required area changes for diffusers.

Table 7.1 Differences in behavior between subsonic and supersonic one-dimensional reversible adiabatic flow.

Variation	Subsonic		Supersonic	
	Convergent	Divergent	Convergent	Divergent
Area	−	+	−	+
Velocity	+	−	−	+
Mach No.	+	−	−	+
Pressure	−	+	+	−
Temperature	−	+	+	−
Density	−	+	+	−

The relation between enthalpy, stagnation enthalpy, and kinetic energy is

$$h + \frac{V^2}{2} = h_o$$

For an ideal gas with constant specific heat,

$$V^2 = 2(h_o - h) = 2c_{po}(T_o - T) = \frac{2kRT}{k-1}(T_o - 1)$$

Since $c^2 = kRT$

$$V^2 = \frac{2c^2}{k-1}\left(\frac{T_o}{T} - 1\right)$$

$$\frac{T_o}{T} = 1 + \frac{(k-1)}{2}M^2 \tag{7.25}$$

For an isentropic process,

$$\left(\frac{T_o}{T}\right)^{k/(k-1)} = \frac{P_o}{P}, \quad \left(\frac{T_o}{T}\right)^{1/(k-1)} = \frac{\rho_o}{\rho}; \text{ so,}$$

$$\frac{P_o}{P} = \left[1 + \frac{(k-1)}{2}M^2\right]^{k/(k-1)} \tag{7.26}$$

$$\frac{\rho_o}{\rho} = \left[1 + \frac{(k-1)}{2}M^2\right]^{1/(k-1)} \tag{7.27}$$

The conditions at the throat of the nozzle are at M = 1. The properties at the throat when M = 1, are referred to as the critical pressure, the critical temperature, and the critical density.

Critical temperature ratio
$$\frac{T^*}{T_o} = \frac{2}{k+1} \tag{7.28}$$

Critical pressure ratio
$$\frac{P^*}{P_o} = \left(\frac{2}{k+1}\right)^{k/(k-1)} \tag{7.29}$$

Critical density ratio
$$\frac{\rho^*}{\rho_o} = \left(\frac{2}{k+1}\right)^{1/(k-1)} \tag{7.30}$$

7.6 Mass Rate of Flow of an Ideal Gas through an Isentropic Nozzle

From the continuity equation,

$$\frac{\dot{M}}{A} = \rho V = \frac{PV}{RT}\sqrt{\frac{kT_o}{kT_o}} = \frac{PV}{\sqrt{kRT}}\sqrt{\frac{k}{R}}\sqrt{\frac{T_o}{T}}\sqrt{\frac{1}{T_o}} = \frac{PM}{\sqrt{T_o}}\sqrt{\frac{k}{R}}\sqrt{1+\frac{k-1}{2}M^2} \tag{7.31}$$

Subst. $\dfrac{P_o}{P} = \left[1+\dfrac{(k-1)}{2}M^2\right]^{\frac{k}{(k-1)}}$ into (7.31), the flow for the unit area can be expressed in terms of stagnation pressure, stagnation temperature, mach number, and gas properties.

$$\frac{\dot{M}}{A} = \frac{P_o}{\sqrt{T_o}}\sqrt{\frac{k}{R}} \times \frac{M}{\left(1+\frac{k-1}{2}M^2\right)^{\frac{k+1}{2(k-1)}}} \tag{7.32}$$

At the throat, M = 1

$$\frac{\dot{M}}{A^*} = \frac{P_o}{\sqrt{T_o}}\sqrt{\frac{k}{R}} \times \frac{1}{\left(\frac{k+1}{2}\right)^{\frac{k+1}{2(k-1)}}} \tag{7.33}$$

Dividing Eq. (7.33) by Eq. (7.32),

$$\frac{A}{A^*} = \frac{1}{M}\left[\left(\frac{2}{k+1}\right)\left(1 + \frac{k-1}{2}M^2\right)\right]^{\frac{k+1}{2(k-1)}} \quad (7.34)$$

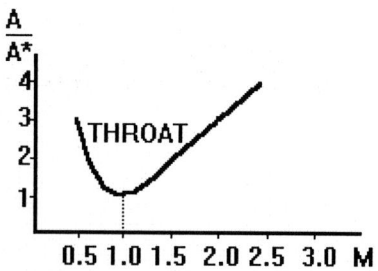

Figure 7.8 Area ratio as a function of Mach No. for a reversible adiabatic nozzle.

The figure is in accordance with the previous conclusion that a subsonic nozzle is converging and a supersonic nozzle is diverging.

The ratio of the velocity to the velocity of sound at the throat is given by

$$M^* = \frac{V}{c^*} \quad (7.35)$$

$$M^* = \frac{Mc}{c^*} = \frac{M\sqrt{kRT}}{\sqrt{kRT^*}} = M\sqrt{\frac{T}{T^*}}$$

Hence, $M^* = M\sqrt{\dfrac{k+1}{2 + (k-1)M^2}} \quad (7.36)$

Example 7.4

Problem

A convergent nozzle has an outlet area of 25 cm.² The inlet air has stagnation conditions of 2000 kPa pressure and 380 K. Calculate the mass flow rate if the back pressure is (a) 1600 kPa, (b) 1056 kPa and (c) 500 kPa.

Solution

Assumption: (1) The flow is isentropic.

Analysis:

For air, k = 1.4. The critical pressure ratio is

$$\frac{P^*}{P_o} = \left(\frac{2}{k+1}\right)^{k/(k-1)} = 0.528$$

When back pressure = 0.528(2000 kPa) = 1056 kPa, the nozzle is choked and M = 1 at the nozzle outlet.

(b) When back pressure = 1056 kPa,

$$\frac{T^*}{T_o} = 0.8333, \quad T^* = 316K$$

At the outlet, $V = c = \sqrt{kRT} = \sqrt{1.4 \times 0.287 \times 316 \times 1000} = 356.3 \text{ m/s}$

$$\rho^* = \frac{P^*}{RT^*} = \frac{1056}{0.287 \times 316} = 11.64 \text{ kg/m}^3$$

Mass flow rate $\dot{m} = \rho A V$

At the throat (outlet), $\dot{m} = 11.64 \times 25 \times 10^{-4} \times 356.3 = 10.37 \text{ kg/s}$.

(a) When back pressure = 1600 kPa,

$$\frac{P_e}{P_o} = 0.8 \quad \text{(subscript e denotes exiting, or at the outlet)}$$

From the tables,

$$M_e = 0.573, \qquad \frac{T_e}{T_o} = 0.9381$$

$T_e = 356.5 \text{ K}$

$c_e = \sqrt{kRT_e} = \sqrt{1.4 \times 0.287 \times 356.5 \times 1000} = 378.5 \text{ m/s}$

$V_e = M_e c_e = 216.9 \text{ m/s}$

$$\rho_e = \frac{P_e}{RT_e} = \frac{1600}{0.287 \times 356.5} = 15.64 \text{ kg/m}^3$$

At the throat (outlet), $\dot{m} = 15.64 \times 25 \times 10^{-4} \times 216.9 = 8.48$ kg/s.

(c) When back pressure = 500 kPa < P* = 1056 kPa,

the nozzle is choked and the mass flow rate is the same as when the outlet is at the critical pressure.

Thus, $\dot{m} = 10.37$ kg/s.

Example 7.5

Problem

A convergent-divergent nozzle has an outlet area to throat area ratio of 1.5. Air enters the nozzle at stagnation conditions of 1800 kPa and 370 K. The throat area is 10 cm². Determine the Mach number, pressure, temperature, velocity at the outlet, and the mass flow rate for the two cases:

(a) choked at the throat, divergent section behaves as a nozzle;

(b) choked at the throat, divergent section behaves as a diffuser.

Solution

From the tables, when A/A* = 1.5, the Mach number is either 0.4360 or 1.8525. Case (a) corresponds to M > 1 and case (b) corresponds to M < 1.

(a) From the tables,

$$\frac{A_e}{A^*} = 1.5, \qquad M_e = 1.8525$$

$$\frac{P_e}{P_o} = 0.1610, \qquad \frac{T_e}{T_o} = 0.59258$$

Thus, $P_e = 0.1610(1800) = 289.8$ kPa.

$T_e = 0.59258(370) = 219.3$ K

$$c_e = \sqrt{kRT_e} = \sqrt{1.4 \times 0.287 \times 219.3 \times 1000} = 293.2 \, m/s$$

$$V_e = M_e c_e = 1.8525(293.2) = 543.1 \, m/s$$

Flow at the throat is choked, or $M = 1$ at the throat.

$$\frac{P^*}{P_o} = 0.528, \quad P^* = 950.4 \, kPa$$

$$\frac{T^*}{T_o} = 0.8333, \quad T^* = 308 K$$

At the throat, $V = c = \sqrt{kRT} = \sqrt{1.4 \times 0.287 \times 308 \times 1000} = 351.8 \, m/s$

$$\rho^* = \frac{P^*}{RT^*} = \frac{950.4}{0.287 \times 308} = 10.75 \, kg/m^3$$

At the throat, $\dot{m} = 10.75 \times 10 \times 10^{-4} \times 351.8 = 3.78 \, kg/s$.

(b) From the tables,

$$\frac{A_e}{A^*} = 1.5, \quad M_e = 0.4360$$

$$\frac{P_e}{P_o} = 0.8767, \quad \frac{T_e}{T_o} = 0.9630$$

Thus, $P_e = 0.8767(1800) = 1578 \, kPa$.

$T_e = 0.9630(370) = 356.3 \, K$

$$c_e = \sqrt{kRT_e} = \sqrt{1.4 \times 0.287 \times 356.3 \times 1000} = 378.4 \, m/s$$

$V_e = M_e c_e = 0.4360(378.4) = 165 \, m/s$

Since the throat is choked, the mass flow rate is the same as in case (a). Hence, mass flow rate is 3.78 kg/s.

7.7 Nozzles

7.7.1 Convergent Nozzles

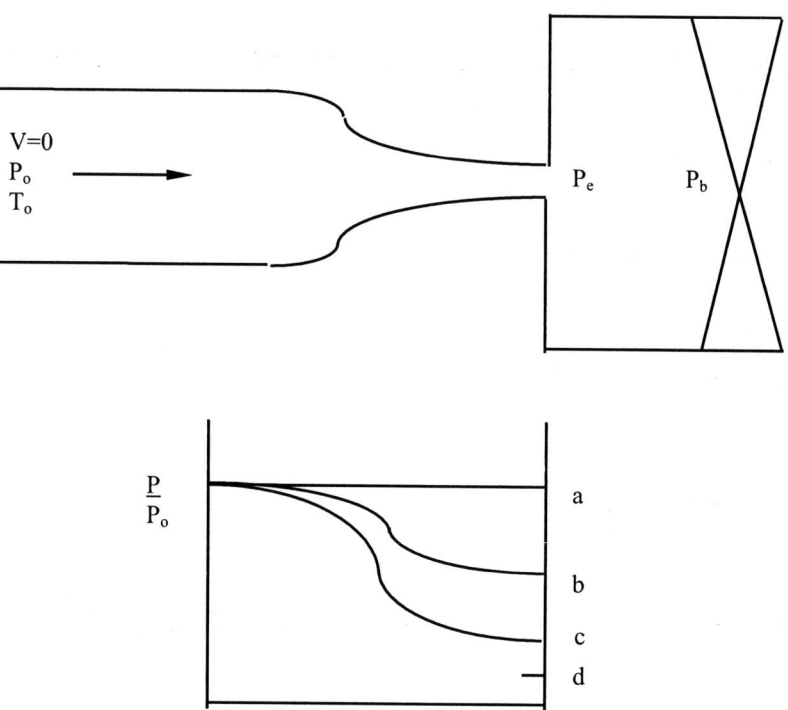

Figure 7.9 Pressure ratio as a function of back pressure for a convergent nozzle.

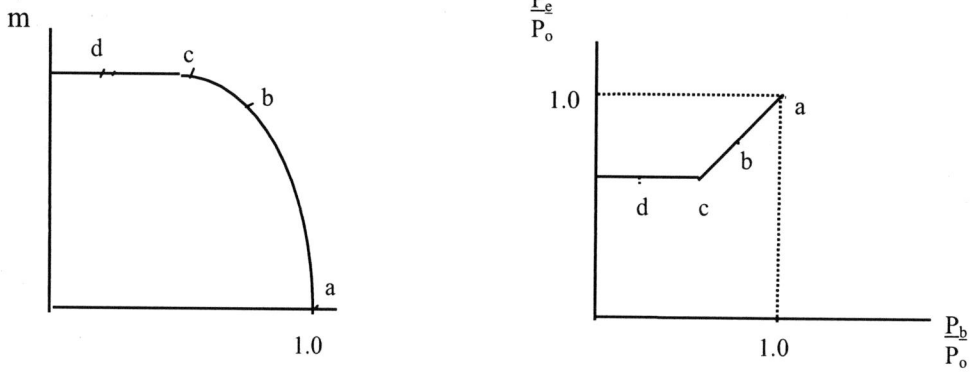

Figure 7.10 Mass rate of flow and exit pressure as a function of back pressure for a convergent nozzle.

Figure 7.9 is the plot of the pressure ratio P/Po along the length of a convergent nozzle. Figure 7.10 is a plot of the mass flow rate and the exit pressure as a function of back pressure for a convergent nozzle. The stagnation conditions upstream are shown, and assumed to be constant. The back pressure P_b is controlled by a valve, and the pressure at the exit plane is P_e.

When $\dfrac{P_b}{P_o} = 1$, $\dfrac{P_e}{P_o} = 1$, there is no flow.

When $\dfrac{P_b}{P_o} >$ critical pressure ratio, $P_e = P_b$, $M < 1$.

When $\dfrac{P_b}{P_o} =$ critical pressure ratio, $P_e = P_b$, $M = 1$.

When $\dfrac{P_b}{P_o} <$ critical pressure ratio, $P_e =$ critical pressure, $M = 1$; the drop of pressure from P_e to P_b takes place outside the nozzle exit. The nozzle is choked, which means that for given stagnation conditions, the nozzle is passing the maximum possible mass flow. It follows that supersonic flow cannot be obtained with only a convergent nozzle.

7.7.2 Convergent-Divergent Nozzles

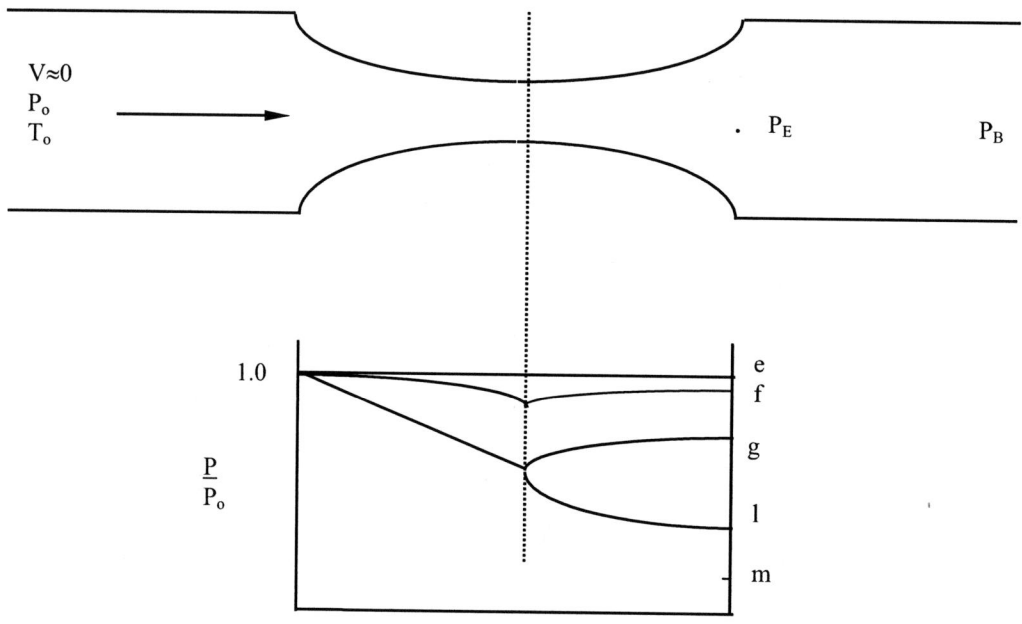

Figure 7.11 Nozzle pressure ratio as a function of back pressure for a reversible convergent-divergent nozzle.

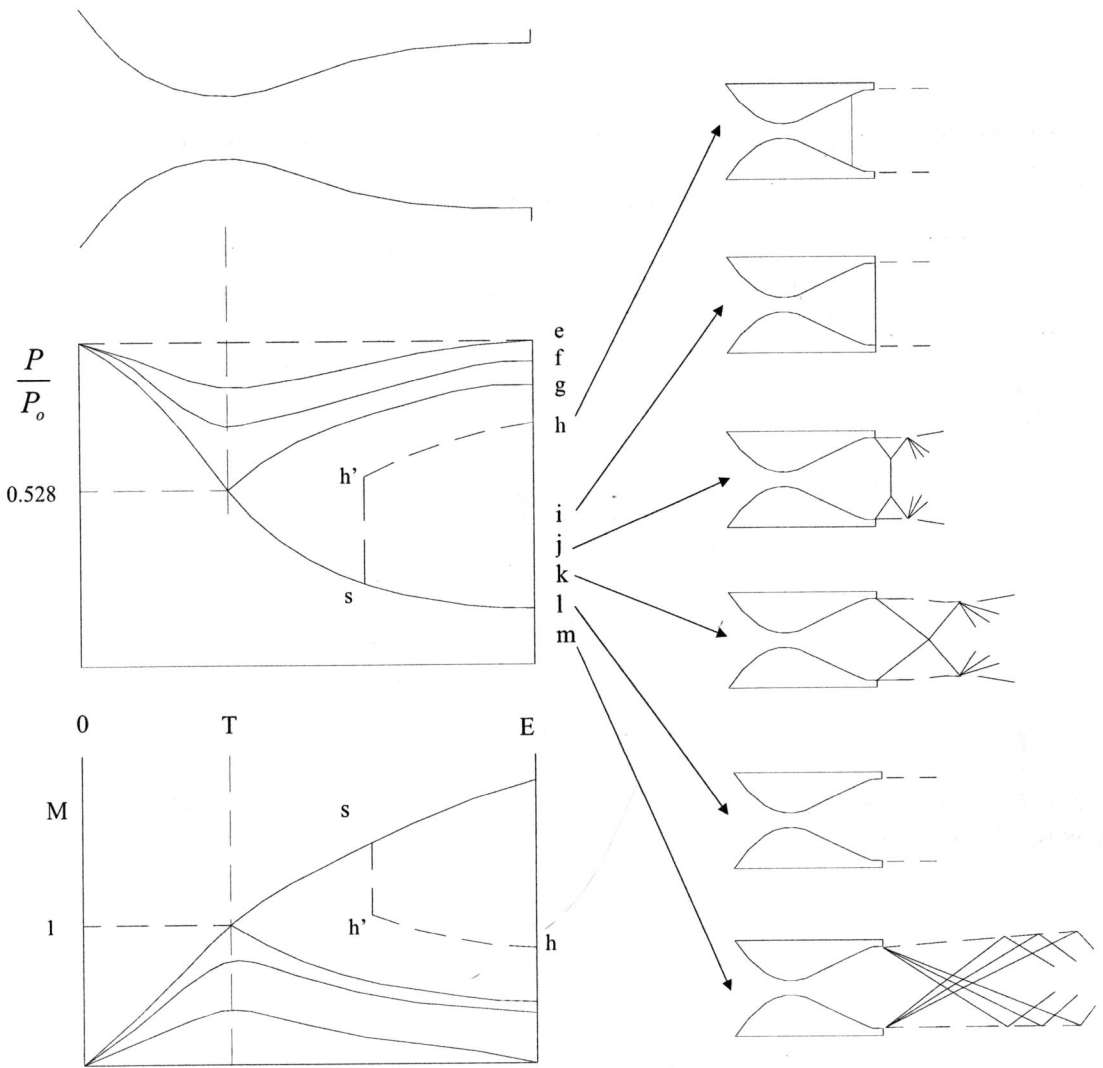

Figure 7.11a Nozzle pressure ratio and Mach number as a function of back pressure for a reversible convergent-divergent nozzle.

For a convergent-divergent nozzle,

Point e   There is no flow.

Point f   The velocity increases in the convergent section but M<1 at the throat.

Point g   M=1 at the throat, but the diverging section acts as a subsonic diffuser in which the pressure increases and velocity decreases.

Point l   This designates one other back pressure that permits isentropic flow, and in this case the diverging section acts as a supersonic nozzle, with a decrease in pressure and an increase in velocity. Between the back pressures designated by points c and d, an isentropic solution is not possible, and shock waves will be present.

Point m   The drop in pressure from P_e to P_b takes place outside the nozzle.

7.8 Normal Shocks

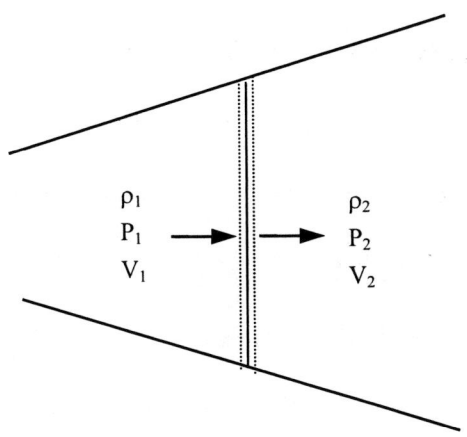

Figure 7.12 Normal compression shock wave.

Consider the control volume around the shock. The governing equations are as follows:-

Continuity: $\dfrac{\dot{m}}{A} = \rho_1 V_1 = \rho_2 V_2$ \hfill (7.37)

Energy: $\dfrac{V_1^2}{2} + h_1 = \dfrac{V_2^2}{2} + h_2 = h_0 = \dfrac{V^2}{2} + \dfrac{k}{k-1}\dfrac{P}{\rho}$ \hfill (7.38)

Momentum: $(P_1 - P_2)A = \rho_2 A V_2^2 - \rho_1 A V_1^2 \therefore P_1 + \rho_1 V_1^2 = P_2 + \rho_2 V_2^2$ \hfill (7.39)

In addition, $P = \rho\, RT$

$$\therefore P_2 = \dfrac{1}{k+1}\left[2\rho_1 V_1^2 - (k-1)P_1\right] \quad (7.40)$$

Combining continuity and momentum equations,

$P_1 + \rho_1 V_1^2 = P_2 + \rho_2 V_1 V_2$ \hfill (7.41)

V_2 can be obtained.

With $M_1 > 1$, values of P_2, V_2, ρ_2 and $M_2 = \dfrac{V_2}{(kP_2/\rho_2)^{0.5}}$ exists. M_2 is less than 1.

Eliminate V_1 & V_2 between Eqs.(7.37), (7.38), & (7.39), to obtain the Rankine-Hugoniot equations

$$\frac{P_2}{P_1} = \frac{[(k+1)/(k-1)](\rho_2/\rho_1) - 1}{[(k+1)/(k-1)] - \rho_2/\rho_1} \qquad (7.42)$$

and $\dfrac{\rho_2}{\rho_1} = \dfrac{1 + [(k+1)/(k-1)]P_2/P_1}{[(k+1)/(k-1)] + P_2/P_1} = \dfrac{V_1}{V_2}$ (7.43)

These relate conditions on either side of the shock wave.

From Eq.(13.36),

$$\frac{V^2}{2} + \frac{k}{k-1} \cdot \frac{P}{\rho} = \frac{C^{*2}}{2} + \frac{C^{*2}}{k-1} = \frac{k+1}{k-1} \cdot \frac{C^{*2}}{2} \qquad (7.44)$$

Since $C^* = \sqrt{\dfrac{k \cdot P^*}{\rho^*}}$

$$V_1 - V_2 = \frac{P_2}{\rho_2 \cdot V_2} - \frac{P_1}{\rho_1 \cdot V_1}$$

Eliminate $\dfrac{P_2}{\rho_2}$ and $\dfrac{P_1}{\rho_1}$,

$$V_1 - V_2 = (V_1 - V_2)\left[\frac{C^{*2}(k+1)}{2kV_1V_2} + \frac{k-1}{2k}\right] \qquad (7.45)$$

which is satisfied by $V_1 = V_2$ (no shock) or by $V_1 V_2 = C^{*2}$

So $\dfrac{V_1}{C^*} \cdot \dfrac{V_2}{C^*} = 1$.

If $V_1 > C^*$, $V_2 < C^*$.

If $V_1 < C^*$, $V_2 > C^*$.

From Eq.(7.38)

$$\frac{P_2}{P_1} = \frac{1}{k+1}\left[\frac{2k\rho_2 V_1^2}{kP_1} - (k-1)\right] \qquad (7.46)$$

Since $C_1^2 = \frac{kP_1}{\rho_1}$ and $M_1 = \frac{V_1}{C_1}$,

$$\frac{P_2}{P_1} = \frac{2kM_1^2 - (k-1)}{k+1}$$

Placing this value of $\frac{P_2}{P_1}$ in Eq.(7.41),

$$\frac{\rho_2}{\rho_1} = \frac{M_1^2(k+1)}{2+M_1^2(k-1)} \qquad (7.47)$$

Substitute these ratios into the expression for entropy,

$$S_2 - S_1 = C_v \cdot \ln\left\{\frac{2kM_1^2 - k + 1}{k+1}\left[\frac{2 + M_1^2(k+1)}{M_1^2(k+1)}\right]^k\right\}$$

If we substitute $M_1 > 1$, $S_2 - S_1 > 0$. This confirms that the entropy increases for a shock wave, or it is an irreversible process.

Example 7.6

Problem

A convergent-divergent nozzle has an outlet area to throat area ratio of 2.64. Air enters with stagnation conditions of 1500 kPa and 380 K. The flow conditions are such that a normal shock stands in the outlet plane of the nozzle. Calculate the static temperature, pressure and the stagnation pressure just downstream of the normal shock.

Solution

From the tables for isentropic flow functions, with $A/A^* = 2.64$,

$M = 2.50$, $\qquad \frac{P_e}{P_o} = 0.058528$, $\qquad \frac{T_e}{T_o} = 0.44444$

Hence, $\qquad P_e = 87.79$ kPa, $\qquad T_e = 168.9$ K

From the tables for normal shock functions, when $M_x = 2.50$, $M_y = 0.51299$.

$$\frac{P_y}{P_x} = 7.1250, \qquad \frac{T_y}{T_x} = 2.1375, \qquad \frac{P_{oy}}{P_{ox}} = 0.49901$$

$P_y = 7.1250 P_x = 7.1250 P_e = 7.1250(87.79) = 625.5$ kPa

$T_y = 2.1375 T_x = 2.1375 T_e = 2.1375(168.9) = 361$ K

$P_{oy} = 0.49901 P_{ox} = 0.49901(1500) = 748.5$ kPa.

Example 7.7

Problem

The flow in the nozzle of Example 7.6 is such that a normal shock stands at the point where $M = 2.0$. Determine the outlet plane pressure, temperature and Mach number.

Solution

Assumption: (1) The flow is isentropic except for the normal shock.

Analysis:

From the tables for isentropic flow functions, when $M_x = 2.0$,

$$\frac{P_x}{P_{ox}} = 0.12780, \qquad \frac{T_x}{T_{ox}} = 0.55556, \qquad \frac{A_x}{A_x^*} = 1.68750$$

Thus, $P_x = 0.12780(1500) = 191.7$ kPa

$T_x = 0.55556(380) = 211.1$ K

The properties after the shock, at point y, can be computed from the normal shock functions.

From the tables for normal shock functions, $M_y = 0.57735$

$$\frac{P_y}{P_x} = 4.500, \qquad \frac{T_y}{T_x} = 1.6875, \qquad \frac{P_{oy}}{P_{ox}} = 0.72087$$

$P_y = 4.500 P_x = 4.500(191.7) = 862.7$ kPa

$T_y = 1.6875 T_x = 1.6875(211.1) = 356.2$ K

$P_{oy} = 0.72087 P_{ox} = 0.72087(1500) = 1081$ kPa.

The stagnation temperature across a normal shock remains constant, so

$T_{oy} = T_{ox} = 380$ K.

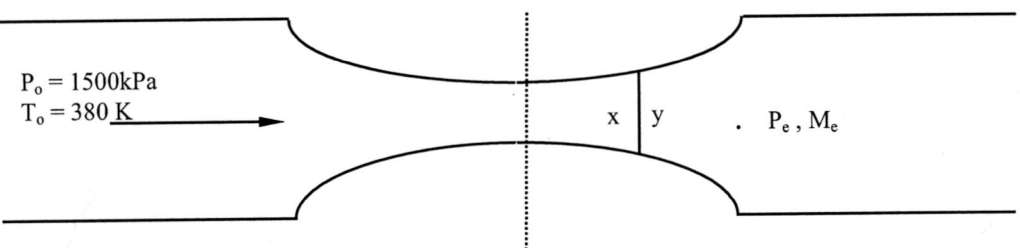

Sketch for Ex. 7.7.

From point y to the exit e, the divergent section behaves as a subsonic diffuser. We can consider the flow at y as originating from an isentropic nozzle with a throat area $A_y{}^*$. We can use the table of isentropic flow functions to find that corresponding to $M_y = 0.57735$,

$$\frac{P_y}{P_{oy}} = 0.79737, \qquad \frac{T_y}{T_{oy}} = 0.93727, \qquad \frac{A_y}{A_y{}^*} = 1.2225$$

It was given that $\dfrac{A_e}{A_x{}^*} = 2.64$.

Hence,
$$\frac{A_e}{A_c{}^*} = \frac{A_e}{A_y{}^*} = \frac{A_e}{A_x{}^*} \times \frac{A_x{}^*}{A_x} \times \frac{A_x}{A_y} \times \frac{A_y}{A_y{}^*}$$

$$= \frac{A_e}{A_y{}^*} = 2.64 \times \frac{1}{1.68750} \times 1 \times 1.2225 = 1.913.$$

From the isentropic flow functions table, corresponding to $A/A^* = 1.913$ and $M < 1$,

$$M_e = 0.327, \qquad \frac{P_e}{P_{oe}} = 0.9276, \qquad \frac{T_e}{T_{oe}} = 0.9787$$

So, $\dfrac{P_e}{P_{oe}} = \dfrac{P_e}{P_{oy}} = 0.9276$

$P_e = 0.9276(P_{oy}) = 0.9276(1081) = 1002.7$ kPa.

$T_e = 0.9797(T_{oe}) = 0.9787(380) = 371.9$ K.

7.9 Supersonic Flow Past Wedges and Cones

Supersonic flow past wedges and cones creates shock waves which are generally attached to the tip and inclined at an angle which varies with the incident Mach number. In the case of the wedge, the shock wave is in the form of two inclined planes; for the cone, the shock wave has the form of a concentric outer cone.

7.9.1 Wedges

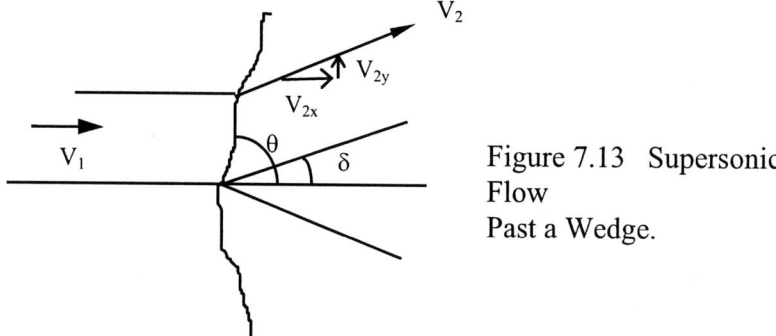

Figure 7.13 Supersonic Flow Past a Wedge.

If the bow shock is attached to the wedge, as it will be if the semivertex angle, δ, is less than the critical angle, the shock wave is straight and the flow downstream of the shock is parallel to the wedge surface, Fig. 7.13. The conditions on either side of the shock can be found from the normal shock tables if $M_1 \sin\theta$ is used in place of M_x in the first column. If the shock is not attached, the shock tables cannot be used.

For small values, $\sin\theta \approx \dfrac{1}{M_1}$ (7.48)

It is given exactly by the formula

$$\tan\theta = \dfrac{V_1 - V_2 \cos\delta}{V_2 \sin\delta} \qquad (7.49)$$

Unfortunately, there is no convenient exact formula for finding θ from M_1 and δ, although cubic solutions and iterative processes exist.

7.9.2 Cones

There are also difficult to handle by exact methods. For small semi-vertex angles, the shock angle is also given by Eq.(7.48). If θ is known, conditions behind the shock wave may also be determined from the shock tables using $M_1 \sin\theta$ for the first column value.

Example 7.8

Problem

The uniform free stream Mach number before a wedge of semi-vertex angle 9° is 1.6. The upstream stagnation conditions are 120 kPa and 288 K. Find the deflection angle θ, and the velocity after the inclined shock wave caused by the wedge.

Solution

From the shock relations tables, when $M_1 = 1.6$,

$M_2 = 0.66844$ $\qquad\qquad \dfrac{T_2}{T_1} = 1.3880$

From the isentropic flow relations tables, when $M_1 = 1.6$,

$\dfrac{T_1}{T_{o1}} = 0.66138$

Thus, $T_1 = 0.66138(288) = 190$ K

$T_2 = 1.3880\, T_1 = 264.4$ K

The speed of sound after the shock is

$$c_2 = \sqrt{kRT_2} = \sqrt{1.4 \times 0.287 \times 264.4 \times 1000} = 325.9 \text{ m/s}$$

Velocity after the shock is $V_2 = 0.66844 c_2 = 218$ m/s.

Velocity before the shock is

$$V_1 = 1.6 c_1 = 1.6\sqrt{1.4 \times 0.287 \times 190 \times 1000} = 442 \text{ m/s}.$$

$$\tan\theta = \frac{V_1 - V_2 \cos\delta}{V_2 \sin\delta} = \frac{442 - 218\cos 9^o}{218 \sin 9^o} = 8.12$$

$\theta = 83^o$.

Table 7.2 Approximate maximum semi-vertex angles for attached shock waves for wedges and cones.

M_1	Wedge	Cone
1.0	0°	0°
1.2	4	19
1.4	9	27.5
1.6	14.5	33
1.8	19	37.5
2.0	23	41
2.2	26	43
2.4	28.5	45
2.6	31	47
2.8	32.5	48
3.0	34	49
3.2	35.5	50
3.4	36.5	51
3.6	37.5	51.7
3.8	38	52.2
4.0	39	52.7
∞	45	

7.10 Oblique Shocks

Normal shocks are a special case of a more general family of oblique waves in supersonic flow. As shown in Fig. 7.13, oblique shocks can occur when supersonic flow is turned into itself. At point P, the solid surface which bounds the flow on one side, is bent upward at an angle θ. The streamlines are deflected upward, all at the same deflection angle θ at the shock. The flow downstream of the shock is uniform and parallel to the wall downstream of point P. The flow direction changes across a shock wave which is oblique to the original free-stream direction. The Mach number decreases, and the pressure, temperature, and density increase across the shock.

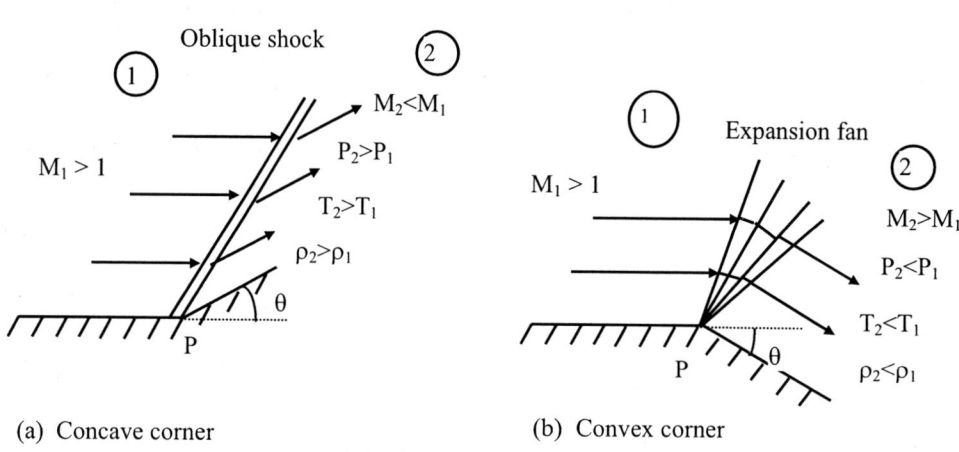

(a) Concave corner   (b) Convex corner

Figure 7.13   Supersonic flow over a corner.

For case (b) in Fig. 7.13, at point P, the solid surface which bounds the flow on one side, is bent downward at an angle θ. The streamlines are deflected downward; this change in flow direction occurs across an expansion wave, centered at point P. The flow downstream of the shock is uniform and parallel to the wall downstream of point P. The flow properties vary smoothly and continuously through an expansion wave, unlike the case of a shock. The wall streamline does have a discontinuity at the point P. The Mach number increases, and the pressure, temperature, and density decrease through the expansion wave.

Oblique shock and expansion waves are common in two- and three- dimensional supersonic flows. The waves are two-dimensional in nature, as compared to normal shocks which are one-dimensional. Oblique waves are caused by the same physical mechanism that cause normal shocks. The source of these waves are disturbances which spread by molecular collisions at the speed of sound, some of which join into shocks, and others disperse in the form of expansion waves.

Consider the oblique shock, with geometry as shown in Fig. 7.14. Upstream of the shock, the velocity is W_1 which is horizontal, and the Mach number is M_1. The oblique shock makes a wave angle β with the horizontal. After the shock, the flow is turned toward the shock by the flow-deflection angle θ. The velocity and Mach number after the shock are W_2, and the corresponding Mach number is M_2. The components of W_1 normal and parallel to the shock are respectively, u_1 and v_1; the corresponding components of W_2 are u_2 and v_2. The normal and tangential Mach numbers are M_{n1} and M_{t1} before the shock, and M_{n2} and M_{t2} behind the shock.

When M_{n1} is known, all other properties may be obtained from the normal shock tables. Since $M_{n1} = M_1 \sin \beta$, the problem becomes one of finding the wave angle β. From Fig. 7.14, we see that

$$M_{n1} = M_1 \sin \beta \qquad M_{n2} = M_2 \sin (\beta-\theta) \qquad (7.50)$$

$$u_1 = v_1 \tan \beta \qquad u_2 = v_2 \tan (\beta-\theta) \qquad (7.51)$$

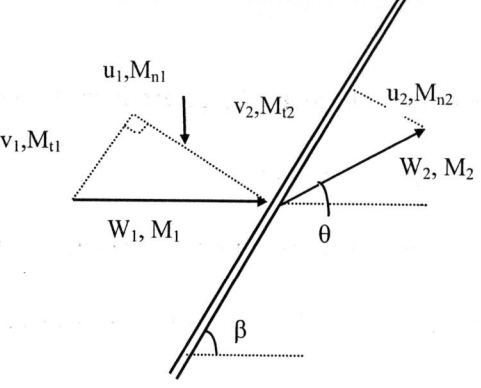

Figure 7.15   Oblique shock geometry.

The pressure changes from one side of the oblique shock to the other. The flows on both sides of the shock are uniform, and momentum considerations does not allow accelerations tangent to the wave. The assumption of no friction is still being held. Thus,

$$v_1 = v_2 \tag{7.52}$$

Mass continuity gives

$$\rho_1 v_1 = \rho_2 v_2 \tag{7.53}$$

So

$$\frac{v_2}{v_1} = \frac{\tan(\beta - \theta)}{\tan \beta} = \frac{\rho_1}{\rho_2} \tag{7.54}$$

From the normal shock relations, after a lot of algebra,

$$\frac{\rho_y}{\rho_x} = \frac{P_y}{P_x}\frac{T_x}{T_y} = \frac{(k+1)M_x^2}{(k-1)M_x^2 + 2} \tag{7.55}$$

For the oblique shock, putting $M_1 \sin\beta$ instead of M_x,

$$\frac{\rho_2}{\rho_1} = \frac{(k+1)M_1^2 \sin^2\beta}{(k-1)M_1^2 \sin^2\beta + 2} \tag{7.56}$$

Eliminating the density ratio between Eqs. (7.54) and (7.56), we obtain

$$\frac{\tan(\beta - \theta)}{\tan \beta} = \frac{(k-1)M_1^2 \sin^2\beta + 2}{(k+1)M_1^2 \sin^2\beta} \tag{7.57}$$

The Mach number M_1 and the deflection angle θ, determines the wave angle β. The normal component of the Mach number is given by $M_{n1} = M_1 \sin\beta$, with which the properties after the shock are determined from the normal shock tables. With the value of M_{n2}, the Mach number after the shock is found from $M_2 = M_{n2}/\sin(\beta-\theta)$. After much manipulation of Eq.(7.57), the deflection angle θ may be found from

$$\tan\theta = 2\cot\beta \left[\frac{M_1^2 \sin^2\beta - 1}{M_1^2(k + \cos 2\beta) + 2} \right] \qquad (7.58)$$

Tangent θ is zero for $\beta = \pi/2$, and $\beta = \sin^{-1}(1/M_1)$. The first corresponds to the normal shock. The second case corresponds to a very weak (isentropic) disturbance that results in Mach waves in supersonic flows. The array of solutions is displayed in Fig. 7.15.

The following facts are important to note about the solutions in Fig. 7.15:-

(1) When $\theta = 0$, then $\beta = \pi/2$ corresponding to a normal shock, or $\beta = \sin^{-1}(1/M)$ corresponding to a Mach wave.

(2) For any M_1, there is a maximum deflection angle θ_{max}. If the actual geometry is such that $\theta > \theta_{max}$, a straight oblique shock does not exist. The shock will be curved and detached.

(3) For any given $\theta < \theta_{max}$, there are two possible values of β. Since the changes across a shock are greater as β increases, the large value of β is called the strong shock solution, and the other value is called the weak shock solution. In actuality, the weak solution usually occurs. M_2 is subsonic in the strong shock solution, while M_2 is supersonic in the weak shock solution except for a small region near θ_{max}.

(4) For any deflection angle θ, the Mach number decreases from high to low supersonic values, the wave angle increases (for the weak shock solution). Solutions

only exist for values of the Mach number above a certain value; at this value of Mach number,

$\theta = \theta_{max}$. For values of Mach number lower than this, the shock becomes detached.

Example 7.9

Problem

A supersonic stream with $M_1 = 2.0$, $P_1 = 1$ atm., and $T_1 = 283$ K meets a compression corner (similar to Fig. 7.14a). The stream is deflected by $\theta = 15°$. Calculate the shock wave angle β, and P_2, T_2, M_2, P_{o2}, and T_{o2} after the shock.

Solution

Assumptions: (1) The flow is uniform before and after the shock.

Analysis:

From the oblique shock properties in Fig.7.15, $\beta = 46°$.

$M_{n1} = M_1 \sin \beta = 2 \sin 46° = 1.4387$

From the normal shock relations tables, when $M_{n1} = 1.4387$,

$\dfrac{P_2}{P_1} = 2.2466$ $\dfrac{T_2}{T_1} = 1.2799$

$M_{n2} = 0.7241$ $\dfrac{P_{o2}}{P_{o1}} = 0.9479$

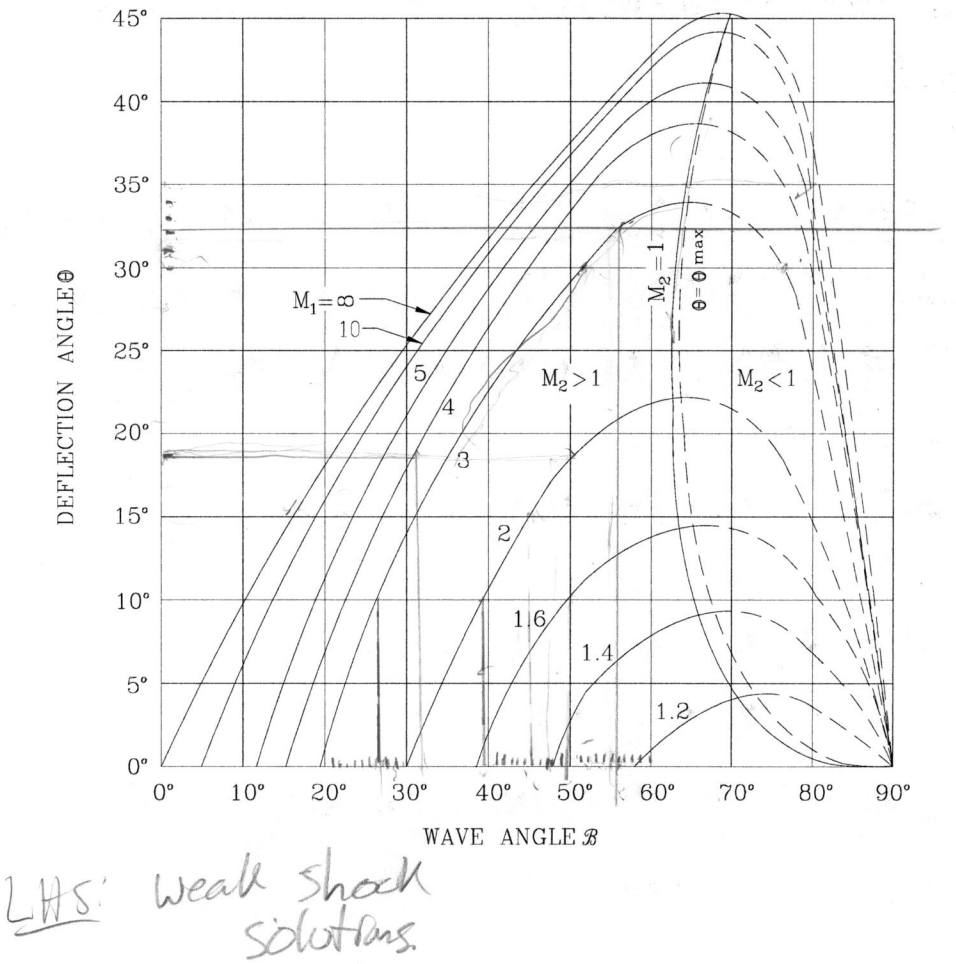

Figure 7.15 Oblique shock properties.

Thus, $P_2 = \dfrac{P_2}{P_1} P_1 = (2.2466)1 = 2.2466$ atm.

$$T_2 = \dfrac{T_2}{T_1} T_1 = (1.2799)(283) = 362.2 \text{ K}$$

$$M_2 = \dfrac{M_{n2}}{\sin(\beta - \theta)} = \dfrac{0.7241}{\sin 31°} = 1.406$$

From the tables for isentropic flow relations, when $M_1 = 2$,

$$\dfrac{P_1}{P_{o1}} = 0.12780, \qquad \dfrac{T_1}{T_{o1}} = 0.55556$$

Thus, $P_{o2} = \dfrac{P_{o2}}{P_{o1}} \dfrac{P_{o1}}{P_1} P_1 = (0.9479)\dfrac{1}{0.12780} = 7.417$ atm.

$$T_{o2} = T_{o1} = \dfrac{T_{o1}}{T_1} T_1 = \dfrac{1}{0.55556}(283) = 509.4 \text{ K}$$

only shocks are nonisentropic

Example 7.9

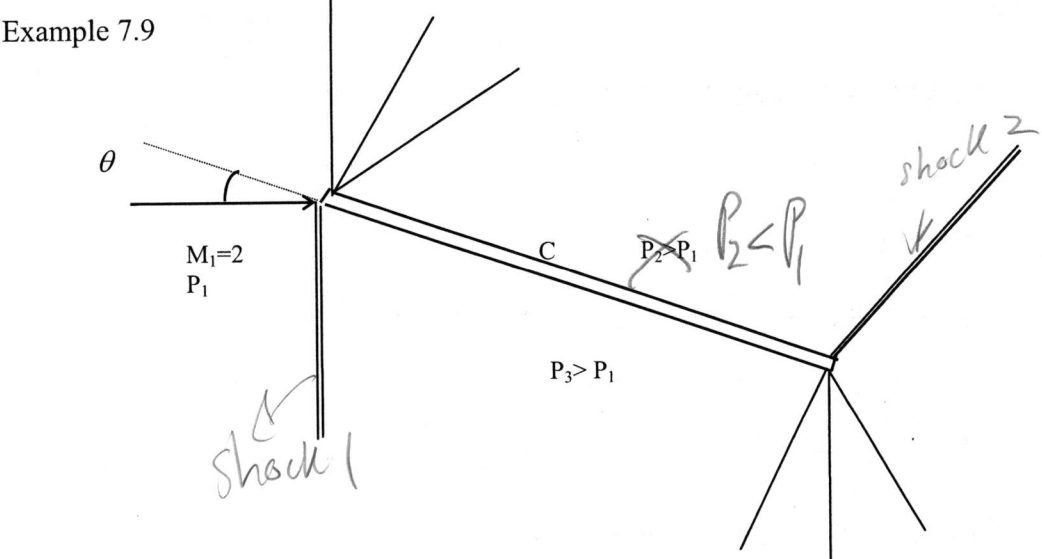

Sketch for Ex. 7.9.

Problem

An airplane wing in supersonic flight may be approximated by a flat plate with an angle of attack of θ.

Given:
$\delta_2 = \delta_1 + \theta$
Mach no. before first shock wave, $M_1 = 2$, $\delta_1 = 26.380°$
$\delta_2 = 26.380 + 10 = 36.380°$
Mach no. before last shock wave, $M_2 = 2.385$

Find the pressure ratios P_2/P_1, P_3/P_1, and hence the lift and drag coefficients.

Solution

From the isentropic flow relations table,

$M_1 = 2, \dfrac{P_{01}}{P_1} = 7.825$

$M_2 = 2.385, \dfrac{P_{02}}{P_2} = 14.281$

Since $P_{01} = P_{02}$,

$\dfrac{P_2}{P_1} = \dfrac{P_{01}}{P_1} \bigg/ \dfrac{P_{02}}{P_2} = \dfrac{7.825}{14.281} = 0.548$

The next step is to calculate $\dfrac{P_3}{P_1}$.

From θ-β-M diagram of Fig. 7.15,

when $M_1 = 2$ and $\theta = 10°$, $\beta = 39°$

$M_{n1} = M_1 \cdot \sin\beta = 2 \cdot \sin 39° = 1.2586$

From the table of normal shock relations,

when $M_{n1} = 1.2586, \dfrac{P_3}{P_1} = 1.68143$

Lift $L' = (P_3 - P_2) \cdot c \cdot \cos\theta$

Lift coeff. $c_l = \dfrac{L'}{q_1 S} = \dfrac{L'}{\left(\dfrac{\gamma}{2}\right) \cdot P_1 \cdot M_1^2 \cdot c} = \dfrac{2}{\gamma \cdot M_1^2}\left(\dfrac{P_3}{P_1} - \dfrac{P_2}{P_1}\right)\cos\theta$

$= \dfrac{2}{(1.4)(2)^2}(1.6143 - .548) \cdot \cos 10°$

$= 0.399$

Drag $D' = (P_3 - P_2) \cdot c \cdot \cos\theta$

Drag coeff. $c_d = \dfrac{D'}{g_1 \cdot S} = \dfrac{2}{\gamma \cdot M_1^2}\left(\dfrac{P_3}{P_1} - \dfrac{P_2}{P_1}\right)\sin\theta$

$= \dfrac{2}{(1.4)(2)^2}(1.6143 - .548) \cdot \sin 10°$

$= 0.0703$

PROBLEMS

Stagnation Properties

7.1. Steam in a pipeline is at 350°C and 0.5 MPa, and flowing at 400 m/s. Determine the stagnation enthalpy, temperature, pressure, and specific volume of the steam.

7.2. Steam in a pipeline is at 320°C and 1.2 MPa, and flowing at 550 m/s. Determine the stagnation enthalpy, temperature, pressure, and specific volume of the steam.

7.3. Steam in a pipeline is at 630°F and 75 $lb_f/in.^2$, and flowing at 1200 ft/s. Determine the stagnation enthalpy, temperature, pressure, and specific volume of the steam.

7.4. Steam in a pipeline is at 610°F and 180 $lb_f/in.^2$, and flowing at 1650 ft/s. Determine the stagnation enthalpy, temperature, pressure, and specific volume of the steam.

7.5. Air in a pipeline is at 300°C and 1.5 MPa, and flowing at 500 m/s. Determine the stagnation enthalpy, temperature, and pressure of the air.

7.6. Air in a pipeline is at 572°F and 220 $lb_f/in.^2$, and flowing at 1200 ft/s. Determine the stagnation enthalpy, temperature, and pressure of the air.

Adiabatic, One-Dimensional, Steady-state, Steady Flow

7.7. Water enters a nozzle at a velocity of 20 m/s, a pressure of 400 kPa and a temperature of 30°C. It leaves the nozzle with a velocity of 30 m/s and a pressure of 101 kPa. Determine the exit pressure for a reversible nozzle with the same inlet state and outlet velocity. Calculate the increase in enthalpy, internal energy, and the entropy for the actual nozzle.

7.8. Water enters a nozzle at a velocity of 60 ft/s, a pressure of 60 $lb_f/in.^2$ and a temperature of 60°F. It leaves the nozzle with a velocity of 90 ft/s and a pressure of 14.7 $lb_f/in.^2$ Determine the exit pressure for a reversible nozzle with the same inlet state and outlet velocity. Calculate the increase in enthalpy, internal energy, and the entropy for the actual nozzle.

Speed of Sound

7.9. Determine the speed of sound in air at 303 K and 600 K.
7.10. Determine the speed of sound in steam at 310 K and 650 K.
7.11. Determine the speed of sound in air at 86°F and 620.6°F.
7.12. Determine the speed of sound in steam at 98.6°F and 710.6°F.

Mass Rate of Flow through an Isentropic Nozzle

7.13. A convergent nozzle has an outlet area of 10 $cm.^2$ The inlet air has stagnation conditions of 1500 kPa pressure and 380 K. Calculate the mass flow rate if the back pressure is (a) 1200 kPa, (b) 792 kPa and (c) 101 kPa.

7.14. A convergent nozzle has an outlet area of 2 $in.^2$ The inlet air has stagnation conditions of 220 lb_f/in^2. pressure and 690°F. Calculate the mass flow rate if the back pressure is (a) 176 lb_f/in^2, (b) 116.16 lb_f/in^2 and (c) 14.7 lb_f/in^2.

7.15. A convergent-divergent nozzle has an outlet area to throat area ratio of 1.25. Air enters the nozzle at stagnation conditions of 1600 kPa and 360 K. The throat area is 15 cm^2. Determine the Mach number, pressure, temperature, velocity at the outlet, and the mass flow rate for the two cases:

(a) choked at the throat, divergent section behaves as a nozzle;

(b) choked at the throat, divergent section behaves as a diffuser.

7.16. A convergent-divergent nozzle has an outlet area to throat area ratio of 3.0. Air enters the nozzle at stagnation conditions of 2200 kPa and 390 K. The throat area is 30 cm². Determine the Mach number, pressure, temperature, velocity at the outlet, and the mass flow rate for the two cases:

(a) choked at the throat, divergent section behaves as a nozzle;

(b) choked at the throat, divergent section behaves as a diffuser.

Normal Shocks

7.17. A convergent-divergent nozzle has an outlet area to throat area ratio of 1.555. Air enters with stagnation conditions of 1000 kPa and 350 K. The flow conditions are such that a normal shock stands in the outlet plane of the nozzle. Calculate the static temperature, pressure and the stagnation pressure just downstream of the normal shock.

7.18. The flow in the nozzle of Problem 7.17 is such that a normal shock stands at the point where M = 1.4. Determine the outlet plane pressure, temperature and Mach number.

7.19. A convergent-divergent nozzle has an outlet area to throat area ratio of 2.00. Air enters with stagnation conditions of 1150 kPa and 373 K. The flow conditions are such that a normal shock stands in the outlet plane of the nozzle. Calculate the static temperature, pressure and the stagnation pressure just downstream of the normal shock.

7.20. The flow in the nozzle of Problem 7.19 is such that a normal shock stands at the point where M = 1.8. Determine the outlet plane pressure, temperature and Mach number.

Oblique Shocks

7.21. A supersonic stream with $M_1 = 2.2$, $P_1 = 1.1$ atm., and $T_1 = 300$ K meets a compression corner. The stream is deflected by $\theta = 18°$. Calculate the shock wave angle β, and P_2, T_2, M_2, P_{o2}, and T_{o2} after the shock.

7.22. A supersonic stream with $M_1 = 3.0$, $P_1 = 1$ atm., and $T_1 = 303$ K meets a compression corner. The stream is deflected by $\theta = 32°$. Calculate the shock wave angle β, and P_2, T_2, M_2, P_{o2}, and T_{o2} after the shock.

7.23. A supersonic stream with $M_1 = 1.6$, $P_1 = 1.2$ atm., and $T_1 = 283$ K meets a compression corner. The stream is deflected by $\theta = 10°$. Calculate the shock wave angle β, and P_2, T_2, M_2, P_{o2}, and T_{o2} after the shock.

7.24. A supersonic stream with $M_1 = 4.0$, $P_1 = 1.3$ atm., and $T_1 = 293$ K meets a compression corner. The stream is deflected by $\theta = 18°$. Calculate the shock wave angle β, and P_2, T_2, M_2, P_{o2}, and T_{o2} after the shock.

COMPUTER, DESIGN AND GENERAL PROBLEMS

7.25. From the isentropic flow relations given by Eqs. (7.25-27), (7.34) and (7.36), write a computer program to give the one-dimensional compressible flow relations for an ideal gas with k = 1.33.

7.26. From the normal shock relations given by Eqs. (7.40), (7.41), etc., write a computer program to give the one-dimensional normal shock relations for an ideal gas with k = 1.33.

7.27. From the θ-β-M relation, write a computer program to generate the values of θ or β given two of the other parameters.

7.28. Design the shape of a convergent-divergent nozzle for air for a mass flow rate of 1 kg/s and inlet stagnation conditions of 150°C and 1000 kPa. Do the procedure many times for 25-kPa increments of pressure drops. Compute and plot the Mach number along the nozzle, which should be drawn to scale.

7.29. You do not have a wind tunnel that goes up to 150 mph. However, you need to test a wind-impact measuring device you have invented at 150 mph. Discuss at least one way in which this can be done, without too much difficulty.

7.30. Design a supersonic wind-tunnel for a Mach number of 1.5 at the test-section. Show the detailed calculations, and any cooling that may be required for the wind-tunnel system.

Chapter 8   Sustainable Energy Sources and Applications

8.1 Fuel Cells
8.1.1   Introduction

One popular fuel cell is the hydrogen fuel cell. One way of describing how it works is to say that the hydrogen fuel is being burnt or combusted in the simple reaction:

$$H_2 + \frac{1}{2}O_2 \rightarrow H_2O \tag{8.1}$$

Instead of heat energy being produced, electrical energy is generated.

The different fuel cell types are usually identified by the electrolyte that is used, although there are always other important differences as well. Currently, five broad classes of fuel cells are recognized as viable systems for the present and immediate future.

Table 8.1   Types of Fuel Cells

Fuel Cell Type	Mobile Ion	Operating Temp.	Applications and details
Alkaline - AFC	OH^-	50-200°C	Space vehicles
Proton exchange membrane - PEM	H^+	50-100°C	Good for vehicles and mobiles applications. Used for lower combined heat and power (CHP) systems.
Phosphoric acid - PAFC	H^+	-220°C	Many 200 kW CHP systems in use.
Molten carbonate - MCFC	CO_3^{2-}	-650°C	Good for medium to large scale CHP systems, up to MW capacity.
Solid oxide - SOFC	O^{2-}	500-1000 °C	Good for all sizes of CHP systems, 2kW to multi MW.

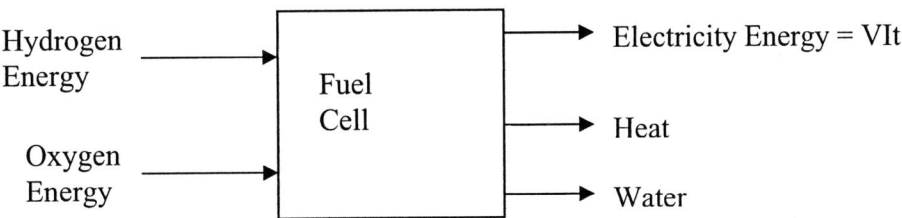

Figure 8.1 Fuel cell inputs and outputs.

For a hydrogen fuel cell as an example, the inputs and outputs are shown in Fig. 8.1. Energy carried by the hydrogen and the oxygen enter the cell. Water is produced in the reaction and leaves with its energy; electricity is produced and so is heat. For fuel cells, the Gibbs free energy is a significant property. Gibbs free energy may be defined as the energy available to do external work, not including any work done by changes in pressure and/or volume. In the fuel cell the external work involves moving electrons round an external circuit. Any work done by a change in volume between the input and output is not harnessed by the fuel cell.

8.1.2 Hydrogen Fuel Cell

This section describes the evaluation of the molar Gibbs energy of formation, $\Delta \bar{g}_f$, for the reaction

$$H_2 + \frac{1}{2}O_2 \rightarrow H_2O \tag{8.1}$$

The Gibbs function of system can be defined in terms of the entropy and the enthalpy:

$$G = H - TS \tag{8.2}$$

The change in energy is the interesting factor. In a fuel cell, the temperature is constant. Hence,

$$\Delta \bar{g}_f = \Delta \bar{h}_f - T\Delta \bar{s} \tag{8.3}$$

The value of $\Delta \bar{h}_f$ is the difference between $\bar{h}_f$ of the products and $\bar{h}_f$ for the reactants. Thus, for the reaction expressed in Eq. (8.1):

$$\Delta \bar{h}_f = \left(\bar{h}_f\right)_{H_2O} - \left(\bar{h}_f\right)_{H_2} - \frac{1}{2}\left(\bar{h}_f\right)_{O_2} \tag{8.4}$$

In addition, $\Delta \bar{s}$ is the difference between $\bar{s}$ of the products and $\bar{s}$ of the reactants. In this case:

$$\Delta \bar{s} = \left(\bar{s}\right)_{H_2O} - \left(\bar{s}\right)_{H_2} - \frac{1}{2}\left(\bar{s}\right)_{O_2} \tag{8.5}$$

The values of $\bar{h}_f$ and $\bar{s}$ are dependent upon temperature according to the equations provided below. These standard equations are derived using thermodynamic theory, and their proof can be found in some books on engineering thermodynamics (e.g. Balmer, 1990). In the equations following, the subscript to $\bar{h}_f$ and $\bar{s}$ is the temperature, and $\bar{c}_p$ is the molar heat capacity at constant pressure, and 298.15 K is the standard temperature.

The molar enthalpy of formation at temperature T is given by:

$$\bar{h}_T = \bar{h}_{298.15} + \int_{298.15}^{T} \bar{c}_p \, dT \tag{8.6}$$

The molar entropy is given by:

$$\bar{s}_T = \bar{s}_{298.15} + \int_{298.15}^{T} \frac{1}{T} \bar{c}_p \, dT \tag{8.7}$$

The values for the molar entropy and enthalpy of formation at 298.15 K are obtainable from thermodynamics tables (e.g. Keenan and Kaye, 1948), and are given in Table 8.2 below. These values are at standard pressure.

Table 8.2 Values of $\bar{h}_f$ in J.mol^{-1} and $\bar{s}$ in J.mol^{-1}.K^{-1}, at 298.15 K, for the hydrogen fuel cell.

	$\bar{h}_f$	$\bar{s}$
H$_2$O (steam)	-241827	188.83
H$_2$O (liquid)	-285838	70.05
H$_2$	0	130.59
O$_2$	0	205.14

For Eqs. (8.6) and (8.7), the values of the molar heat capacity at constant pressure $\bar{c}_p$ are needed. The empirical equations for $\bar{c}_p$ are obtainable and provided in some thermodynamics texts (e.g. Van Wylen, 1986), and the equations below are good to within 0.6% over the range 300 to 3500K.

For steam:

$$\overline{c}_p = 143.05 - 58.040 T^{0.25} + 8.275 T^{0.5} - 0.036989 T \qquad (8.8)$$

For hydrogen:

$$\overline{c}_p = 56.505 - 22222.6 T^{-0.75} + 116500 T^{-1} - 560700 T^{-1.5} \qquad (8.9)$$

For oxygen:

$$\overline{c}_p = 37.432 + 2.0102 \times 10^{-5} T^{1.5} - 178570 T^{-1} + 2368800 T^{-2} \qquad (8.10)$$

The three equations for $\overline{c}_p$ are in J/gmole K. They may be substituted into Eqs. (8.6,7), integrated rather readily and evaluated at any temperature T. This is done to obtain values for $\overline{h}_f$ and $\overline{s}$ for steam, hydrogen and oxygen. These values can then be substituted into Eqs. (8.4,5), giving values for $\Delta \overline{h}_f$ and $\Delta \overline{s}$, which are finally substituted into Eq. (8.3), giving the change in molar Gibbs energy of formation $\Delta \overline{g}_f$. Sample values are shown in Table 8.2.

For the case of liquid water, standard values from Table 8.1 for $\overline{h}_f$ and $\overline{s}$ are used for 25°C. At 80°C Eqs.(8.6,7) are used to find $\overline{h}_f$ and $\overline{s}$, but it can be assumed that $\overline{c}_p$ is constant, since the temperature range is small.

Table 8.3 Sample values for $\Delta \overline{h}_f$, $\Delta \overline{s}$ and $\Delta \overline{g}_f$, for the reaction Eq. (8.1). Temperatures are in Celsius, $\Delta \overline{h}_f$ in kJ.mol^{-1}, other two in kJ.mol^{-1}.K^{-1}.

Temperature	$\Delta \overline{h}_f$	$\Delta \overline{s}$	$\Delta \overline{g}_f$
900	-248.8	-0.0561	-183.1
700	-247.6	-0.0549	-194.2
500	-246.2	-0.0533	-205.0
300	-244.5	-0.0507	-215.4
100	-242.6	-0.0466	-225.2

If there are no losses in the fuel cell, or the process is reversible, all the Gibbs free energy is converted into electrical energy. (In practical situations, some is also released as heat.) This Gibbs free energy will be employed to find the reversible open circuit voltage of a fuel cell.

For the hydrogen fuel cell, whose basic reaction is represented by Eq. (8.1), it can be seen that two electrons pass round the external circuit for each water molecule produced and each molecule of hydrogen used. So, for one mole of hydrogen used 2N electrons pass round the external circuit; N is the Avagadro's number. If $-e$ is the charge on one electron, then the charge that flows is

$$-2Ne = -2F \text{ Coulombs} \qquad (8.11)$$

F being the Faraday constant, or the charge on one mole of electrons.

If E is the voltage of the fuel cell, then the electrical work done moving this charge round the circuit is:

$$\text{Electrical work done} = \text{charge} \times \text{voltage} = -2FE \text{ Joules} \qquad (8.12)$$

If the system is reversible (or has no losses) then this electrical work done will be equal to the Gibbs free energy released $\Delta \bar{g}_f$. So

$$\Delta \bar{g}_f = -2FE \qquad (8.13)$$

Thus,
$$E = \frac{-\Delta \bar{g}_f}{2F} \qquad (8.14)$$

This basic equation gives the EMF or reversible open circuit voltage of the hydrogen fuel cell.

8.1.3 The Carbon Monoxide Fuel Cell

It is possible that in the higher temperature fuel cells, the carbon monoxide gas generated from steam reforming of fuel such as methane is directly oxidized. The reaction is:

$$CO + \frac{1}{2}O_2 \rightarrow CO_2 \qquad (8.15)$$

The procedure used, and the theory employed, for evaluating the Gibbs free energy change is exactly the same as for the hydrogen fuel cell, but the equations have to fit the new reaction. The values of the molar specific heat capacity for carbon monoxide and carbon dioxide are given by:

For CO,

$$\bar{c_p} = 69.145 - 0.022282T^{-0.75} - 2007.7T^{-0.5} + 5589.64T^{-0.75} \tag{8.16}$$

For CO_2,

$$\bar{c_p} = -3.7357 + 3.0529T^{0.5} - 0.041034T + 2.4198 \times 10^{-6} T^2 \tag{8.17}$$

With values from Table 8.4 below, these equations are used with Eqs.(8.6,7) to find the molar enthalpies and entropies for the three gases under discussion.

Table 8.4 Values of $\bar{h}_f$ in J.mol^{-1} and $\bar{s}$ in J.mol^{-1}.K^{-1}, at 298.15 K, for the carbon monoxide fuel cell.

	$\bar{h}_f$	$\bar{s}$
CO	-110529	197.65
CO_2	-393522	213.80
O_2	0	205.14

The change in the molar enthalpy and molar entropy are then calculated using these two equations:

$$\Delta \bar{h}_f = \left(\bar{h}_f\right)_{CO_2} - \left(\bar{h}_f\right)_{CO} - \frac{1}{2}\left(\bar{h}_f\right)_{O_2} \tag{8.18}$$

$$\Delta \bar{s} = \left(\bar{s}\right)_{CO_2} - \left(\bar{s}\right)_{CO} - \frac{1}{2}\left(\bar{s}\right)_{O_2} \tag{8.19}$$

The change in molar Gibbs free energy of formation is then computed, as with the hydrogen fuel cell, using Eq.(8.3). Example values are given in Table 8.5.

Table 8.5 Sample values for $\Delta \bar{h}_f$, $\Delta \bar{s}$ and $\Delta \bar{g}_f$, for the reaction Eq. (8.15). Temperatures are in Celsius, $\Delta \bar{h}_f$ in kJ.mol^{-1}, other two in kJ.mol^{-1}.K^{-1}.

Temperature	$\Delta \bar{h}_f$	$\Delta \bar{s}$	$\Delta \bar{g}_f$
900	-282.0	-0.0883	-178.5
700	-282.8	-0.0887	-196.5
500	-283.4	-0.0890	-214.6
300	-283.7	-0.0888	-232.7
100	-283.4	-0.0877	-250.7

8.1.4 Efficiency and Open Circuit Voltage

The ideal open circuit voltage for a hydrogen fuel cell (derived previously) is given by the equation:

$$E = \frac{-\Delta \bar{g}_f}{2F} \tag{8.14}$$

In theory, for a reaction where z electrons are transferred for each molecule of fuel the ideal open circuit voltage is:

$$E = \frac{-\Delta \bar{g}_f}{zF} \tag{8.20}$$

Nonetheless, $\Delta \bar{g}_f$ varies with temperature and other factors. The maximum efficiency is given by the expression:

$$\eta_{max} = \frac{-\Delta \bar{g}_f}{\Delta \bar{h}_f} x 100\% \tag{8.21}$$

The efficiency of a working hydrogen fuel cell can be calculated from the formula:

$$\eta = \mu_f \frac{V_c}{1.48} 100\% \tag{8.22}$$

where μ_f is the fuel utilization (normally about 0.95) and V is the voltage of a single cell within the fuel cell stack. The efficiency is given relative to the higher heating value of hydrogen.

The pressure and concentration of the reactants affects the Gibbs free energy, and hence the voltage. This is expressed in the Nernst equation, which can be expressed in many ways. For instance if the pressures of the reactants and products are in bars, and the water product is in the steam state, then:

$$E = E^0 + \frac{RT}{2F} \ln\left(\frac{P_{H_2} \cdot P^{1/2}_{O_2}}{P_{H_2O}}\right) \qquad (8.23)$$

In practical situations the operating voltage is less than what is given by these equations, and in some cases much less. This is the consequence of losses or irreversibilities.

Example 8.1   Hydrogen partial pressure

From Eq.(8.23), separating out the pressure of hydrogen term,

$$E = E^0 + \frac{RT}{2F} \ln\left(\frac{P^{1/2}_{O_2}}{P_{H_2O}}\right) + \frac{RT}{2F} \ln(P_{H_2})$$

If the hydrogen partial pressure changes from P_1 to P_2 bars, with the partial pressures of oxygen and water unchanged, find the relationship between voltage change and P_1 to P_2. The use of H_2 mixed with CO_2 occurs particularly in phosphoric acid fuel cells, operating at about 200°C. By substituting the values for R,T and F, compare the result with the experimental result of

$$\Delta V = 0.024 \ln\left(\frac{P_2}{P_1}\right) \text{ volts}$$

Solution:

The voltage change dependency on P_1 to P_2 is given by

$$\Delta V = \frac{RT}{2F} \ln(P_2) - \frac{RT}{2F} \ln(P_1)$$

$$\Delta V = \frac{RT}{2F} \ln\left(\frac{P_2}{P_1}\right)$$

By substituting the values for R,T and F,

$$\Delta V = 0.02 \ln\left(\frac{P_2}{P_1}\right) \text{ volts}$$

In addition, when using 50% hydrogen/carbon dioxide mixture instead of pure hydrogen, the voltage is reduced by 0.015 volt per cell.

8.1.5 Fuel Cell Equations

To increase the usefulness of the equations, they are given in terms of the electrical power of the whole fuel cell stack P_e, and the average voltage of each cell in the stack V_e. Since the electrical power is the most basic and important information about a fuel cell system, it will almost always be a known quantity. If V_e is not known, it can be assumed to be between 0.6 and 0.7 volt, since most fuel cells operate at this range of voltage. An estimate of 0.65 volt is acceptable. Estimate somewhat higher if the fuel cell is pressurized.

8.1.5.1 Oxygen and Air Usage

From the reaction equation describing the fundamental operation of the fuel cell, we know that

$$\text{Charge} = 4F \times \text{amount of } O_2 \tag{8.24}$$

Rearranging and dividing by time,

$$O_2 \text{ usage} = \frac{I}{4F} \text{ moles.s}^{-1} \tag{8.25}$$

This is a single cell. For a stack of n cells:

$$O_2 \text{ usage} = \frac{In}{4F} \text{ moles.s}^{-1} \tag{8.26}$$

The equation would be useful if the number of cells is not needed and the units in kg/s, and in terms of power, rather than current. Since $P_e = V_e \times I \times n$, $I = P_e/(nV_e)$. Hence,

$$O_2 \text{ usage} = \frac{P_e}{4V_e F} \text{ moles.s}^{-1} \tag{8.28}$$

Changing from moles/s to kg/s:

$$O_2 \text{ usage} = \frac{32 \times 10^{-3} P_e}{4V_e F} \text{ kg/s} = 8.29 \times 10^{-8} \times \frac{P_e}{V_e} \text{ kg/s} \tag{8.29}$$

If V_e is not given, it may be calculated from the efficiency. If efficiency is also not known, the figure of 0.65 volt may be used as a good estimate.

The oxygen supplied will normally be from air, so Eq. (8.29) needs to reflect that. The molar proportion of air that is oxygen is 0.21, and the molar mass of air is 28.97 x 10^{-3} kg/mole. Hence, Eq. (8.29) becomes:

$$\text{Air usage} = \frac{28.97 \times 10^{-3} \times P_e}{0.21 \times 4 \times V_e \times F} \text{ kg/s} = 3.57 \times 10^{-7} \frac{P_e}{V_e} \text{ kg/s} \quad (8.30)$$

If the air was supplied at this rate, then as it left the cell it would not have any oxygen – it would be all used up. In practice, the air is typically supplied twice as much as stoichiometric. If the stoichiometry is β, then the equation for air usage becomes:

$$\text{Air usage} = 3.57 \times 10^{-7} \times \beta \times \frac{P_e}{V_e} \text{ kg/s} \quad (8.31)$$

The kg/s is not, in practice, a very commonly used unit of mass flow. The following conversions to "volume at standard conditions related" mass flow units should be used. The mass flowrate from Eq.(8.31) should be multiplied by:

- 5.1 x 10^4 to give slm (standard L/min)
- 847 to give sls (standard L/sec)
- 3050 to give standard m^3/hr
- 1795 to give SCFM (standard ft^3/min).

8.1.5.2 Flowrate of Exit Air

We need to distinguish between the inlet flowrate of the air, which is given by Eq.(8.31), and the exit flowrate which is quite different. This is important for humidity calculations, which is an important issue in certain types of fuel cells, like PEM fuel cells. The difference is because of consumption of oxygen. There will usually be more water vapor in the exit air, but we are considering dry air at this time. Water production is treated in section 8.5.4. It is clear that:

Exit air flowrate = Air inlet flowrate – oxygen usage

Using Eqs.(8.29,31), this becomes

$$\text{Exit air flowrate} = \left(3.57 \times 10^{-7} \times \beta - 8.28 \times 10^{-8}\right) \frac{P_e}{V_e} \text{ kg/s}. \quad (8.32)$$

8.1.5.3 Usage of Hydrogen

The rate of usage of hydrogen is derived in a similar way to oxygen, except that there are two electrons from each mole of hydrogen. The hydrogen usage for a stack of n cells, is:

$$H_2 \text{ usage} = \frac{In}{4F} \text{ moles.s}^{-1} \qquad (8.33)$$

and

$$H_2 \text{ usage} = \frac{P_e}{2V_e F} \text{ moles.s}^{-1} \qquad (8.34)$$

The molar mass of hydrogen is 2.02×10^{-3} kg/mole. This equation becomes:

$$H_2 \text{ usage} = \frac{2.02 \times 10^{-3} P_e}{2V_e F} = 1.05 \times 10^{-8} \times \frac{P_e}{V_e} \text{ kg/s} \qquad (8.35)$$

at stoichiometric operation. This equation only applies to a hydrogen-fed fuel cell. In the situation with a hydrogen/carbon monoxide mixture derived from a reformed hydrocarbon, the equation has to be appropriately modified for the proportion of carbon monoxide present. The answer can be converted to a volume rate using the density of hydrogen, which is 0.084 kg/m³ at NTP.

In addition to the rate of hydrogen usage, it is useful to know the electrical energy that could be produced from a given mass or volume of hydrogen. The table below lists the energy in kWh since this is the more usual measure used for electrical power systems. The "raw" energy per kilogram and standard liter is given, together with an "effective" energy, taking into consideration the efficiency of the cell. This is given in terms of V_e, the mean voltage of each cell. If an equation with the efficiency is needed, then use Eq. (8.22).

Table 8.6 "Raw" and effective energy content of hydrogen fuel.

Form	Energy content
Specific enthalpy (HHV)	39.3 kWh/kg
Specific enthalpy (HHV)	1.42 j/kg
Effective specific electrical energy	26.6 x V_e kWh/kg
Energy density at NTP (HHV)	3.29 kWh/m³ = 3.29 Wh.SL^{-1}
Energy density at STP (HHV)	3.20 kWh/m³ = 3.20 Wh.SL^{-1}

STP is standard temperature at 273.15 K and pressure at 1 atmosphere.
NTP is normal temperature at 298.15K and pressure at 1 atmosphere.

8.1.5.4 Production of Water

In a hydrogen-fed fuel cell water is produced at the rate of one mole for every two electrons. Modifying Eq.(8.28) for water, we obtain:

$$\text{Water production} = \frac{P_e}{2V_e F} \text{ moles.s}^{-1} \tag{8.36}$$

The molecular mass of water is 18.02×10^{-3} kg/mole, hence:

$$\text{Water production} = 9.34 \times 10^{-8} \frac{P_e}{V_e} \text{ kg/s} \tag{8.37}$$

In the hydrogen-fed fuel cell the rate of production of water has to be more or less stoichiometric. But if the fuel cell is a mixture of carbon monoxide with hydrogen, then the water production would be less - in proportion to the percentage of hydrogen in the mixture of carbon monoxide and hydrogen. If the fuel were a hydrocarbon internally reformed then some of the product water would be used in the reformation process. For instance, if methane is internally reformed, then half the product water is used in the reformation process, thus halving the rate of production.

Example 8.2. Consider a 1 kW fuel cell operating for 1 hour, at a cell voltage of 0.7 volt. (This corresponds to an efficiency of 47%.) Find the rate of water production, and hence the amount of water produced in 1 hour.

$$\text{Rate of water production} = 9.34 \times 10^{-8} \frac{1000}{0.7} \text{ kg/s} = 1.33 \times 10^{-4} \text{ kg/s}$$

Mass of water produced in one hour = $1.33 \times 10^{-4} \times 60 \times 60 = 0.48$ kg

From this example, about 480 cc of water or 1 pint of water is generated. As a rule of thumb, 1 kWh of fuel cell generated electricity produced about 1 pint or 0.5 liter of water in an hour.

8.1.5.5 Production of Heat

Heat is produced when a fuel cell runs. If all the enthalpy of reaction of a hydrogen fuel cell were converted into electrical energy, it can be shown that the output voltage would be:
 1.48 volts if the water product were in liquid form
 1.25 volts if the water product were in vapor form.

The difference between the actual cell voltages and these calculated voltages, is energy that is converted into heat.

It is not often that the water finally ends up in the liquid state. Let us then consider the vapor case only. This means that the energy is leaving the fuel cell in three forms, electricity, ordinary "sensible" heat, and in the latent heat of the water vapor.

For a stack of n cells at current I, the heat generated is:

Heating rate = $nI(1.25 - V_e)$ Watts (8.38)

In terms of electrical power, this is:

Heating rate = $P_e\left(\dfrac{1.25}{V_e} - 1\right)$ Watts (8.39)

8.2 Wind Turbines
8.2.1 Introduction

Several wind turbine configurations have been tested, including:
1. lift-type (with vertical or horizontal axes)
2. drag-type
3. Vortex wind plants
4. Magnus effect wind plants.

In practice, almost all wind turbines are of the lift type and, over 90% of these are of the horizontal axis type. Types 3 and 4 have not been proven to be effective in practice.

The ideal wind turbine would be custom designed to the wind conditions of each location. With steady unvarying winds the rated power of the generator should be the same as that of the turbine. However, since steady winds are not common, the most economical combination has to be determined by taking many factors into account.

The Boeing Model 2 wind turbine was of the horizontal-axis (propeller) type. It has a variable pitch which allowed the control of start-up and shutdown as well as the adjustment of its rotating speed. The performance of this turbine is shown in Fig. 8.2. At wind speeds less than 3.9 m/s, the propeller does not rotate; at 6.3 m/s the machine reaches 17.5 rpm and its output is synchronized with the power grid. The power generated increases up to wind velocities of 12.5 m/s and then remains constant up to 26.8 m/s. Greater than this wind speed, the machine shuts itself down to avoid destructive stresses.

Wind turbines often deliver their energy to a utility-operated network and must do so with alternating current of the correct frequency. There are two general methods to the synchronization process:

1. Letting the turbine to rotate at the speed determined by load and wind velocity. For this situation, dc is generated and electronically inverted to ac. Such variable-speed machines are rather more expensive but are more efficient and have a greater service life.
2. Rotating the turbine at a constant rate (by varying the blade pitch, for example).

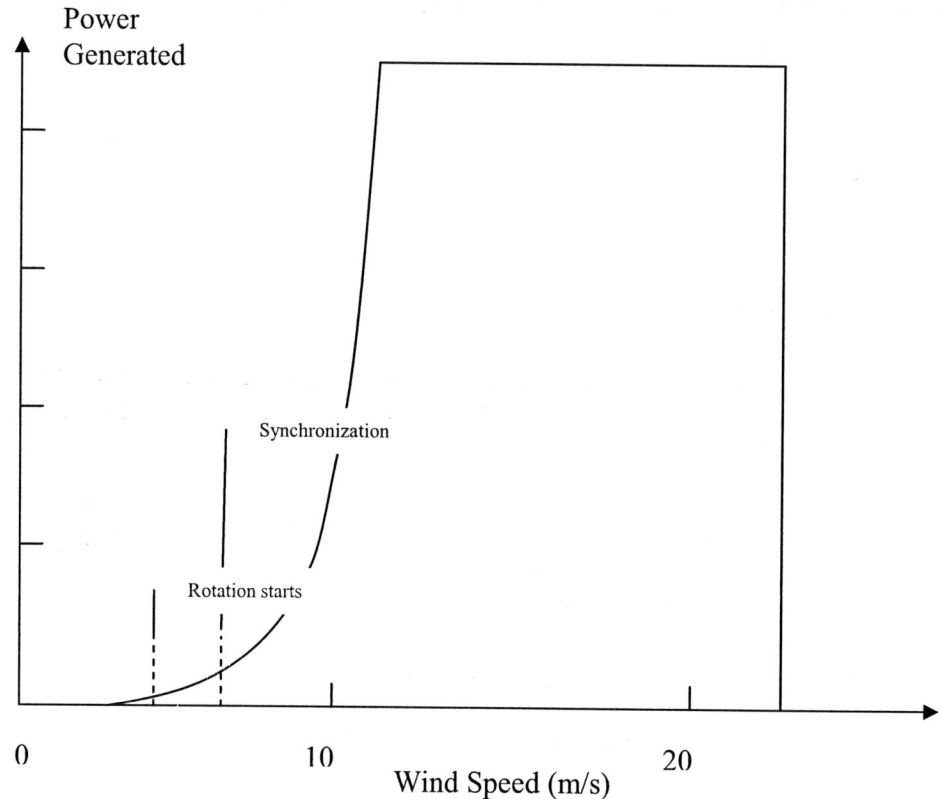

Figure 8.2 Power output of the Boeing Model 2 wind turbine as a function of the wind velocity.

8.2.1.1 Wind Data Analysis

Wind data is very variable. Different probability functions have been fitted with field data to find suitable statistical distributions for representing wind regimes. It has been determined that the Weibull and Rayleigh distributions can be used to describe the wind variations in a particular mode with acceptable precision. The Weibull distribution are characterized by two functions; (1) The probability density function and (2) The cumulative distribution function.

The cumulative distribution function can be used for calculating the time for which wind is within a certain velocity interval. The probability of wind velocity falling between V_1 and V_2 is calculated by the difference of cumulative probabilities corresponding to V_2 and V_1. Hence

$$P(V_1 < V < V_2) = F(V_2) - F(V_1)$$
$$= e^{-\left(\frac{V_1}{c}\right)^k} - e^{-\left(\frac{V_2}{c}\right)^k} \tag{8.40}$$

It is also interesting to know the probabilities of extreme wind at a particular location because the system should be designed to withstand the maximum probable loads. The probability for the wind velocity going above V_x is given by

$$P(V>V_x) = 1 - \left[1 - e^{-\left(\frac{V_x}{c}\right)^k}\right] = e^{-\left(\frac{V_x}{c}\right)^k} \qquad (8.41)$$

8.2.2 Principles of Aerodynamics

The symbol, P, in this section is reserved for both power and power density – that is, power per unit area, depending on the context. The lower case, p, stands for pressure. The following subscripts are used:

$P_W = \frac{1}{2}\rho v^2$ "Power density in the wind." This is the amount of energy transported across a unit area in unit time.

$P_A = \frac{16}{27}\frac{1}{2}\rho v^3$ "Available power density." This is the theoretical maximum amount of power that can be obtained from the wind.

$P_A = \frac{16}{27}\frac{1}{2}\rho v^3 A \eta$ "Power delivered." This is the power that a wind turbine delivers to its load.

8.2.2.1 Flux

The flux of a fluid is defined as the number of molecules that cross a unit area (normal to the flow) in unit time. If n is the concentration of the molecules (number per unit volume) and v is the bulk velocity of the flow, then the flux, φ, is:

$$\varphi = nv \quad m^{-2}s^{-1} \qquad (8.42)$$

The total flow across an area, A, is thus:

$$\phi = \varphi A \quad s^{-1} \qquad (8.43)$$

8.2.2.2 Power in the Wind

Let the mean mass of the gas molecules be m. Then the mean energy of a molecule owing to its bulk motion (not thermal motion) is ½ mv². The power density of the wind is the amount of energy being transported across a unit area in unit time:

$$P_W = \frac{1}{2}mv^2\varphi = \frac{1}{2}mnv^3 = \frac{1}{2}\rho v^3 \text{ Wm}^{-2} \qquad (8.44)$$

Please note that the power density is proportional to the cube of the wind velocity. The quantity, ρ, is the gas density, that is, $\rho = mn$ kgm^{-3}. At standard temperature and pressure (STP), the density of air is

$$\rho = \frac{0.2 \times 32 + 0.8 \times 28}{22.4} = 1.29 \text{ kgm}^{-3}. \qquad (8.45)$$

In the expression above, the numerator is the average molecular mass of air containing 20% oxygen and 80% nitrogen, by volume, and the denominator is the number of cubic meters per kilomole at STP. By the ideal gas law, at STP,

$$V = \frac{RT}{p} = \frac{8314 \times 273.3}{1.013 \times 10^5} = 22.4 \text{m}^3 \qquad (8.46)$$

8.2.2.3 Dynamic Pressure

Since 1 m^3 of gas comprises n molecules and each molecule carries ½ mv^2 joules of energy owing to its bulk motion, the total energy density – that is, the total energy per unit volume is

$$W_d = \frac{1}{2}nmv^2 = \frac{1}{2}\rho v^2 \text{ Jm}^{-3} \text{ or Nm}^{-2}. \qquad (8.47)$$

Energy per unit volume has the dimensions of force per unit area or the dimensions of pressure. Hence, W_d is called the dynamic pressure.

8.2.2.4 Power Available

The question about wind power is what is the maximum power available to be extracted from the wind. When the surface that interacts with the wind is not moving, it extracts no power because there is no motion. If the surface is allowed to drift downwind without any resistance, then again no power is extracted because the wind will not exert any force on it. It is reasonable to deduce that there is velocity such that maximum power is extracted from the wind.

The power density, P, extracted from the wind is the product of the pressure, p, on the surface and the velocity, w, with which the surface drifts downwind. The wind pressure, and the power density equations are then

$$p = \frac{1}{2}\rho C_D(v-w)^2 \qquad (8.48)$$

$$P = pw = \frac{1}{2}\rho C_D(v-w)^2 w \qquad (8.49)$$

Letting ∂P/∂w be equal to zero, an extremum of P is found. This is a maximum and occurs for w = v/3 independently of the value of C_D. In most texts, C_D is called the drag coefficient.

$$P_{max} = \frac{2}{27}\rho C_D v^3 \text{ Wm}^{-2} \qquad (8.50)$$

The ratio of maximum extractable power to power in the wind is

$$\frac{P_{max}}{P_w} = \frac{\frac{2}{27}\rho C_D v^3}{\frac{1}{2}\rho v^3} = \frac{4}{27}C_D \qquad (8.51)$$

The maximum value of C_D is that predicted by our simple formula, by stating that $p = \frac{1}{2}\rho v^2$, implies that $C_D = 4$. Therefore, it is possible to extract a maximum of 16/27 or 59.3% of the "power in the wind". This is the available power density from the wind:

$$P_A = \frac{16}{27}\frac{1}{2}\rho v^3 \qquad (8.52)$$

8.2.2.5 Wind Turbine Efficiency

The efficiency of a wind turbine is the ratio of the power, P_D, supplied to the load, to a reference power. There is a little arbitrariness in this definition. Some authors select the "power in the wind" ($\frac{1}{2}\rho v^2$) as reference. In this text, we use the available power (P_A):

$$\eta = \frac{P_D}{P_A} \qquad (8.53)$$

It is possible for the efficiency of a good wind turbine to reach 0.7.

8.2.3 Wind Turbine Analysis

A gyromill or the Darrieus type wind turbine is used for the wind turbine analysis in this section because it is much simpler than that of propeller-type machines. It highlights the important conclusions that, with suitable modifications, are also applicable to other lift-type devices.

Consider a vertical-axis wind turbine of either the Darrieus type or the McDonnell-Douglas type. A right-handed orthogonal coordinate system is chosen with the z-axis coinciding with the vertical axis of the machine. The system is so oriented that the horizontal component of the wind velocity, V, is parallel to the x-axis.

Let us consider an airfoil, whose cross section lies in the x-y plane, has a chord that makes an angle, ξ, with the normal to the radius vector. This is the setup angle selected by the manufacturer of the wind turbine. It may be adjustable, but it is considered constant in this example.

Figure 8.3. Angles and forces on a wing. For clarity, $\vec{V}$ has been about equal to $\vec{U}$. Generally, $\vec{U}$ is much larger.

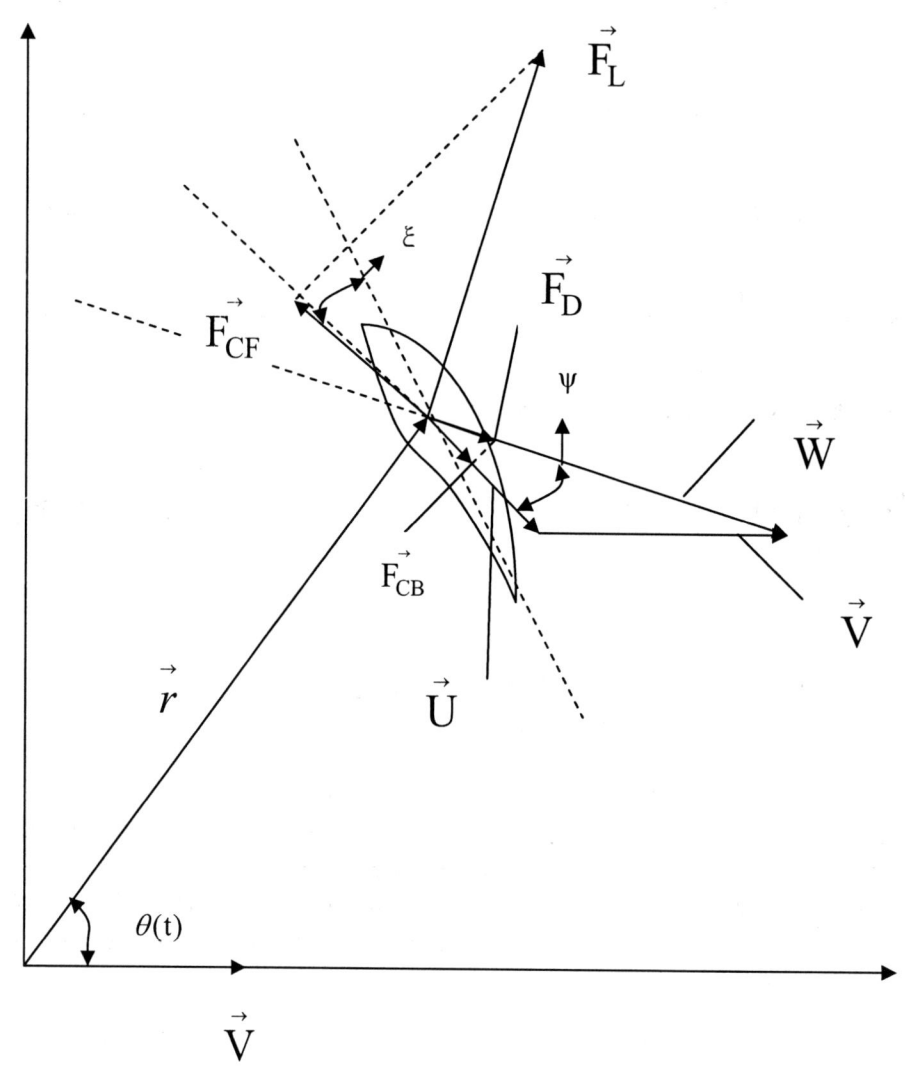

The radius vector makes an angle, θ(t), with the x-axis. Figure 8.3 displays the vectors and angles used in this derivation. The wind velocity, V, and the velocity, U (due to the rotation), combine to produce an induced velocity, W, which is the velocity perceived by the wing. If there is no wind, U is the velocity perceived by the wing.

From Fig. 8.3, the angle of attack is $\alpha = \psi + \xi$.

$$\vec{\omega} = \vec{k}\,\omega \tag{8.54}$$

$$\vec{r} = r(\vec{i}\cos\theta + \vec{j}\sin\theta) \tag{8.55}$$

$$\vec{U} = -\vec{\omega}\times\vec{r} = U(\vec{i}\cos\theta - \vec{j}\sin\theta) \tag{8.56}$$

$$\vec{W} = \vec{U} + \vec{V} = \vec{i}(V + U\sin\theta) - \vec{j}\,U\cos\theta \tag{8.57}$$

$$W = \sqrt{V^2 + U^2 + 2UV\sin\theta} \equiv \Gamma V \tag{8.58}$$

$$\vec{U}\bullet\vec{W} = (U\sin\theta)(V + U\sin\theta) + U^2\cos^2\theta$$

$$\vec{U}\bullet\vec{W} = U^2 + UV\sin\theta = UW\cos\psi \tag{8.59}$$

From which

$$\cos\psi = \frac{U^2 + UV\sin\theta}{UW} = \frac{U + V\sin\theta}{\sqrt{V^2 + U^2 + 2UV\sin\theta}} = \frac{U/V + \sin\theta}{\Gamma} \tag{8.60}$$

Given a wind speed V and an angular velocity ω of the wind turbine, the ratio, U/V, is constant. The quantity Γ, and the angle ψ, vary with the angular position of the wing, thus they vary throughout the revolution. Therefore, the angle of attack also changes. If there is no wind, α is constant. If there is a high U/V ratio (i.e. the wind speed is much smaller than that of the rotating wing), then α changes only a little throughout the revolution.

Given a U/V ratio and a wind velocity, it is possible to calculate both α and W for any wing position, θ. For a given W and α, and A_P is the area of the wing, the wing will generate a lift and a drag of:

$$F_L = \frac{1}{2}\rho W^2 A_P C_L \tag{8.61}$$

$$F_D = \frac{1}{2}\rho W^2 A_P C_D \qquad (8.62)$$

Observe that $\vec{F}_L$ is normal to $\vec{W}$ in the x-y plane and that $\vec{F}_D$ is parallel to $\vec{W}$. The lift force, $\vec{F}_L$, has a component, F_{CF}, normal to the radius vector, causing a forward torque. The drag force, $\vec{F}_D$, has a component, F_{CB}, also normal to the radius vector, effecting a retarding torque. The resulting torque is:

$$\gamma = r(F_{CF} - F_{CB}) \qquad (8.63)$$

From Figure 8.3,

$$F_{CF} - F_{CB} = F_L \sin\psi - F_D \cos\psi = \frac{1}{2}\rho W^2 A_P (C_L \sin\psi - C_D \cos\psi) \qquad (8.64)$$

Thus, $\gamma = \frac{1}{2}\rho V^2 A_P r \left[\Gamma^2 (C_L \sin\psi - C_D \cos\psi)\right] \qquad (8.65)$

The average torque taken over a complete revolution is

$$<\gamma> = \frac{1}{2\pi}\int_0^{2\pi}\gamma(\theta)d\theta \qquad (8.66)$$

In the expression for γ only the portion in brackets is a function of θ. Define a quantity D such that:

$$D \equiv \Gamma^2 (C_L \sin\psi - C_D \cos\psi) \qquad (8.67)$$

$$<D> = \frac{1}{2\pi}\int_0^{2\pi} D\,d\theta \qquad (8.68)$$

is the average D. The average torque is terms of the average D is thus

$$<\gamma> = \frac{1}{2}\rho V^2 A_P r <D> \qquad (8.69)$$

The turbine power produced is:

$$P_D = \omega <\gamma> N \qquad (8.70)$$

N is the number of wings on the wind turbine. The swept area is :
$$A_v = 2rH \tag{8.71}$$

and the area of each wing is:

$$A_p = KH \tag{8.72}$$

where H is the vertical length of the wing and K is the chord (assumed uniform).

A solidity, S, is defined:

$$S = \frac{NA_p}{A_v} = N\frac{K}{2r} \tag{8.73}$$

The available power from the wind is:

$$P_A = \frac{16}{27}\frac{1}{2}\rho V^3 A_v \tag{8.74}$$

The efficiency is:

$$\eta = \frac{P_D}{P_A} = \frac{\frac{1}{2}\rho V^2 NA_p r\omega <D>}{\frac{1}{2}\rho V^3 A_v \, 16/27} = \frac{27}{16}\frac{U}{V}<D>S \tag{8.75}$$

The efficiency formula above is correct only to first order. It neglects losses due to friction and to the generation of vortices; it ignores the reduction in wind velocity caused by the wind turbine itself; it does not consider the interference of one wing blade on the next. With large values of solidities, equation (8.75) predicts the efficiency can be greater than one, which can never happen.

The U/V<D> product is a function of the parameter U/V. <D> has to be obtained from numerical analysis looking up values of C_L and C_D for the various α values that occur during one revolution. To get a better understanding of the shape of the U/V<D> vs U/V graph, look at the case when U = 0. It is clear that when U/V = 0, and since D cannot take on an infinite value, U/V<D> must necessarily be 0 also.

When U approaches infinity, $W \to U$ and $\psi \to 0$. From Eq. (8.67),
$$D = \Gamma^2\left(C_L \sin\psi - C_D \cos\psi\right) \to -\Gamma^2 C_D$$

For large values of U/V, D< 0 and thus, U/V<D> is less than zero. This means that at high rpm, the wind turbine has a negative torque and tends to slow down. Therefore, one can expect that the efficiency has a maximum at some value of U/V in the range 0<U/V<∞.

For an illustration, consider the G_O-420 airfoil. The calculations of U/V<D> for various values of U/V have been done with a number of setup angles, ξ. Figure 8.4 displays the results. Note that the optimum setup angle is -6°. Symmetric airfoils work best with $\xi = 0$. For $\xi = -6°$, the airfoil reaches a U/V<D> value of 4.38 (nondimensional) at a U/V value of 6.5. In this particular case, the efficiency formula gives:

$$\eta_{max} = 7.39S \tag{8.76}$$

If one follows Eq.(8.74), efficiencies greater than 1 could be obtained by using solidities, S, larger than 0.135. It is logical that there must be some value of solidity above which the formula fails. In Fig. 8.5, the efficiency of a wind turbine is plotted versus solidity. The linear dependence predicted by Eq. (8.76) is represented by the dashed line with the 7.39 slope of the example. Using a more complicated aerodynamical model, Sandia Laboratory produced the results shown in the solid line. Note that increasing the solidity to greater than 0.1 does not change the efficiency much. It is possible to distinguish two regions in the efficiency versus solidity curve. As predicted by the simple derivation, one region is where the efficiency is proportional to the solidity. The second region is where the efficiency is approximately independent of the solidity.

Points in Fig. 8.5 show values of efficiency measured by Sandia using small models of the wind turbines. Measured efficiencies are about half of the calculated ones. See the discussion later on for explanation of this discrepancy.

The main reason for the behavior depicted in Fig. 8.5 is that the simple analysis did not take into account the interference of one wing with the next. The larger the solidity, the farther the disturbance trails behind the wing and the more serious the interference thus counteracting the efficiency gain from a larger S. Therefore, the optimum U/V decreases as S increases.

It is shown in Fig. 8.6 the experimentally observed effect of solidity on the optimum U/V. If the straight line were extrapolated, it would be found that for $S = 1$, the optimum U/V would be equal to approximately 0.7.

In the range of solidities that have a minor effect on the efficiency, increasing S results in a wind turbine that rotates more slowly (due to the smaller optimum U/V) and has more torque (due to the efficiency – and hence the power – is the same). Increasing S has the result of gearing down the wind turbine. Because the cost of a wind turbine is approximately proportional to its mass, and hence to its solidity, one should favor machines with S in the lower end of the range if the efficiency is not affected. For this reason, propellers are employed rather than vanes for large machines. In small wind turbines, the ease of vane construction may offset the greater amount of material used.

Figure 8.4. Performance of the G_O-420 airfoil in a vertical-axis turbine.

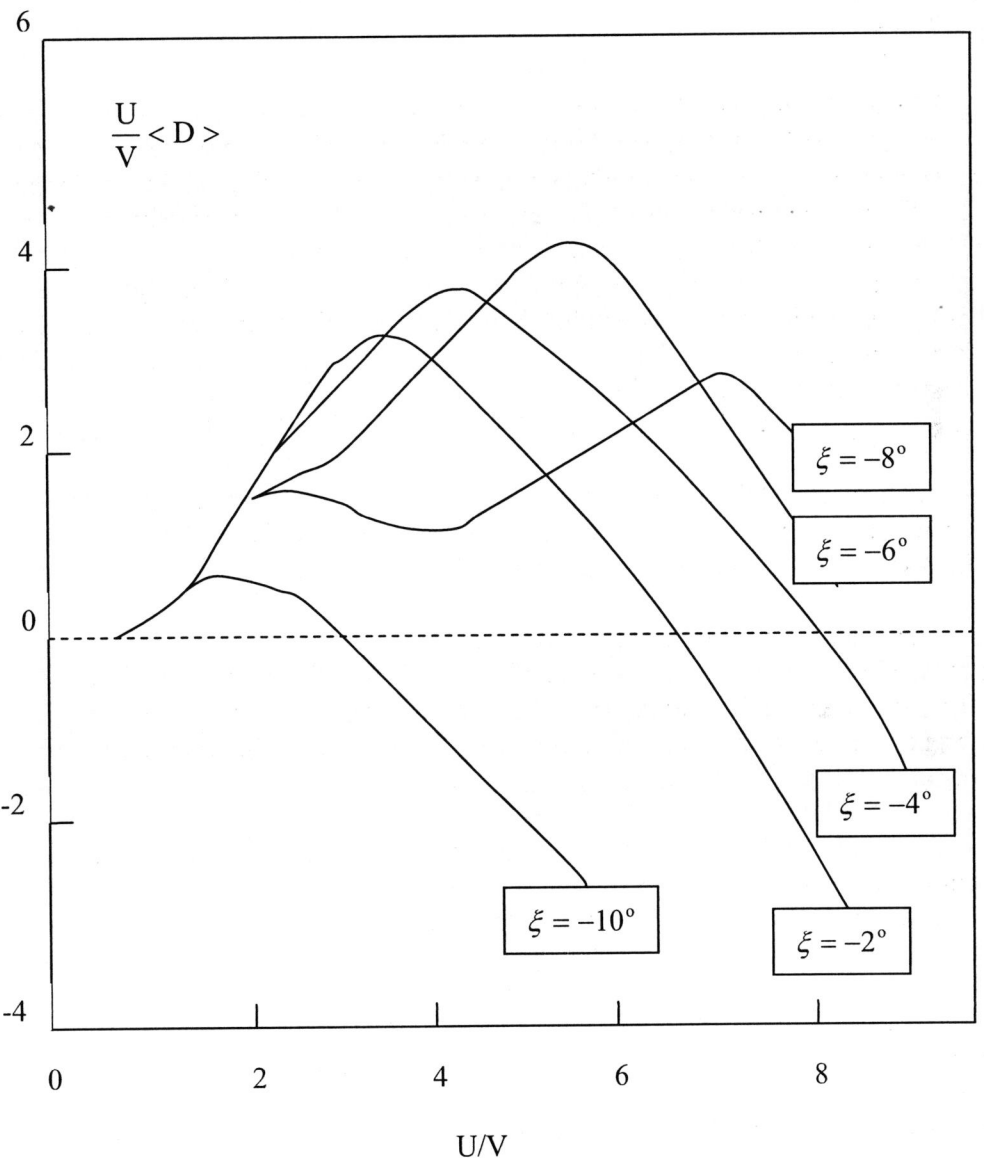

The preceding discussion helps in the understanding of the basic wind turbine processes. However, they are not precise in predicting performance. Many refinements are needed. These are listed below.

1. The wind, having delivered part of its energy to the turbine, will slow down. The average wind velocity experienced by the blades is less than the free stream velocity and the power is, hence less than that calculated by the formulae.
2. The rotating wings generate vortices; these non-useful conversion of wind energy into whirling motion of air have to be taken into account.
3. One must take into account frictional losses in bearings.
4. The accuracy of the calculation is better if the appropriate Reynolds number (Re), is used. The value of Re varies throughout the revolution, in practice. Sandia Laboratory has shown that the larger the Re, the better the performance.

Figure 8.5. Effect of solidity on efficiency of a vertical-axis wind turbine.

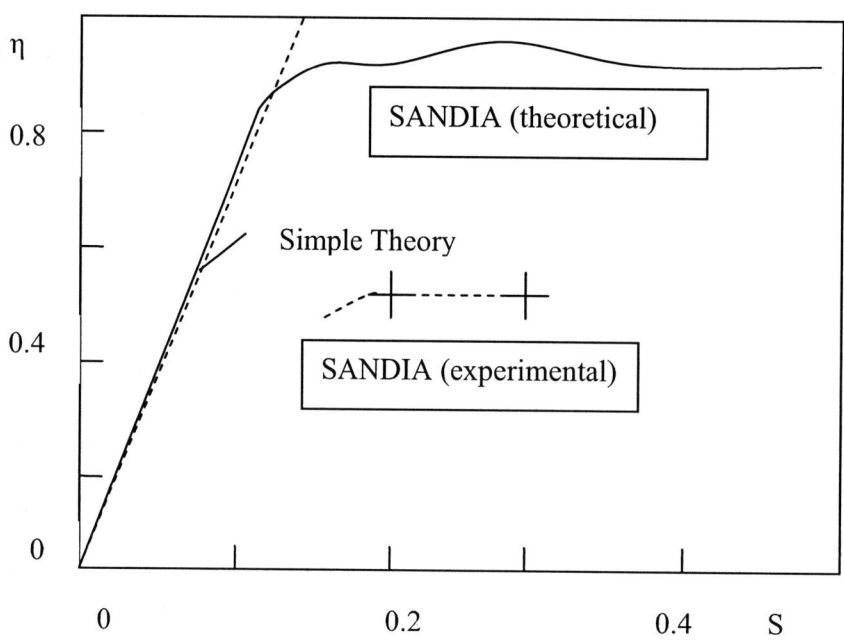

Figure 8.6. Dependence of the optimum U/V on solidity. Experimental data from the Sandia 2-m diameter Darrieus turbine.

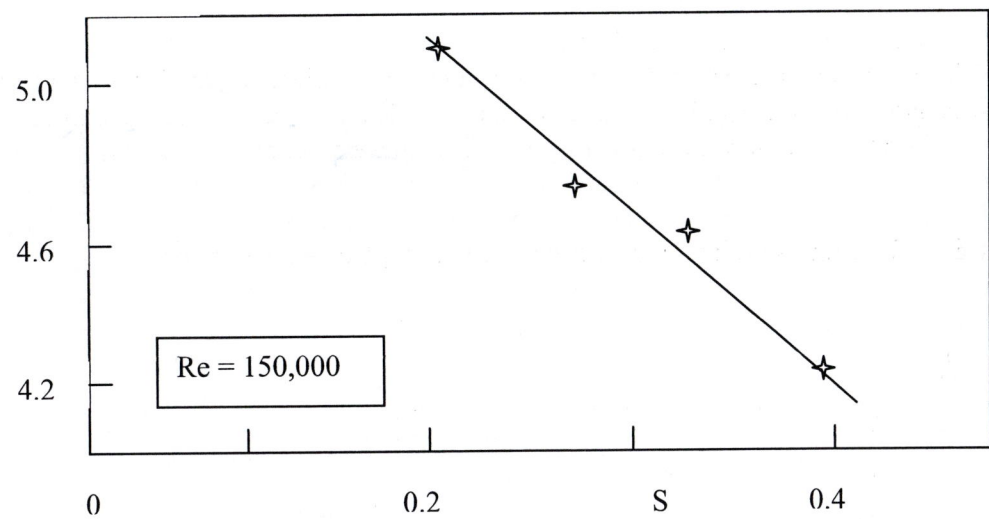

8.3 Tidal Turbines
8.3.1 Introduction

The source of marine current or tidal stream energy is the tide. Marine current is a moving mass of water with a speed and direction. Tides and tidal currents are caused by gravitational forces of the sun and moon on the earth's waters. Owing to its proximity of the earth, the moon exerts roughly twice the tidal raising force of the sun. The gravitational forces of the sun and the moon create two bulges in the earth's oceans: one closest to the moon, and the other on the opposite side of the globe. These bulges are the two tides (high water to low water sequence) a day – the dominant tidal pattern in most of the world's oceans. As the axis of the earth is tilted at 23.5 degrees to the moon's orbit, the two bulges are not equal unless the moon is over the equator. This difference in tidal height between the two daily tides is called the diurnal (or declinational) inequality. The phenomenon occurs regularly on a 14 day cycle as the moon orbits around the earth. One cycle of high water to low water takes an average of 12.4 hours, although there are some fluctuations resulting in a lengthening or shortening of this time.

8.3.1.1 Tidal Patterns

Spring tide is the very highest and very lowest timed (that is, largest tidal range) which occurs twice a month (every 14/15 days) when the moon is either new or full when the gravitational pull of the sun and the moon is aligned. Neap tides are opposite of the spring tide. The tidal range between high and low water is smallest and occurs nearest the time of the first and last lunar quarters. The ratio of springs to neaps can be as large as 2. The combination of the spring to neaps cycle and the 14 day diurnal tidal cycle results in a fluctuation of the tides through the months of the year. There are more than a hundred harmonic components (cyclic constituents) of the tide, each with a different cycle time. These components coalesce so that tides only repeat themselves exactly every 18.6 years.

8.3.1.2 Tidal Currents

Many of the strongest tidal currents are located in shallow waters or through narrow channels that connect large areas of water – hence the coastline and islands of South Korea are a good location for exploiting tidal currents. In North America areas considered suitable include the coastline and islands of Maine in the U.S., and those of New Brunswick and Nova Scotia in Canada. In Europe, those of the West of Scotland are considered ideal. The oldest tidal power generation plant, however, is on the Rance river in France.

Halfway between high water and low water is usually where the speed is at its highest. The water is more or less stationary during the slack water at high and low water (the peaks and troughs in the diagram.) In open water, the flow depends on the direction of the tidal wave. In channels, the current is constrained to flow either up or down the channel.

8.3.1.2 Current Variations

The predicted tidal pattern can be affected by two factors:

* Wind acting on the sea surface - only has an impact to a certain depth below the surface.
* Atmospheric pressure causing storm surges.

Under exceptional conditions, these factors can raise tidal height by 2 or 3 meters, having a subsequent impact on tidal current velocities.

The wind action on the sea surface may be an important consideration in exposed areas in winter months (depending upon turbine depth and the corresponding barometric pressure). If possible, turbines need to be located below the area of influence of the wind component of the current.

Another factor to be considered is slack water. This is the period of quiet water when the tide reverses from flood to ebb or vice versa. The duration of slack water will vary, depending upon the site and time of the year. The tidal change from flood (tide in) to ebb (tide out) is known as high water slack, the tidal change from ebb to flood is known as low water slack.

8.3.1.3 Power Output

In Fig.8.7 and 8, the potential power out from the flood and the ebb is shown. The flood stream is usually stronger than the ebb, although the difference is less severe at neaps. If the turbine only operated in one direction, one would only be able to exploit power from the flood component of the tide. However, most practical turbines have full-pitch control which enables it to reverse the blades, the power from both components can be harnessed as shown in Fig. 8.8.

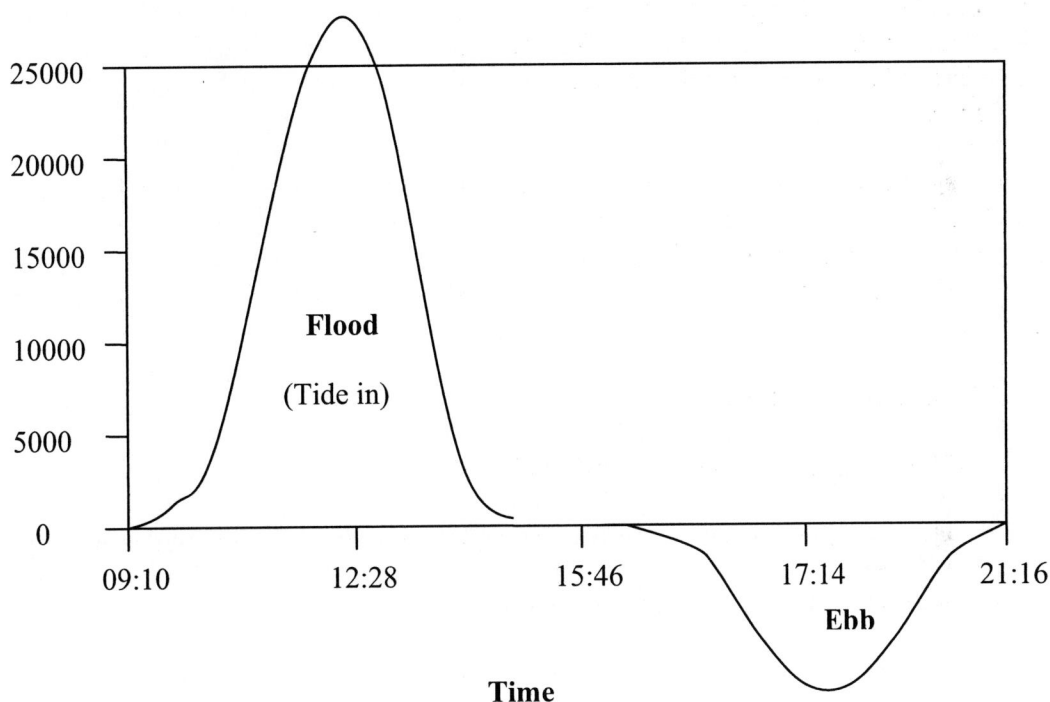

Figure 8.7. Available power in flood and ebb tides, if turbine can only operate in one direction.

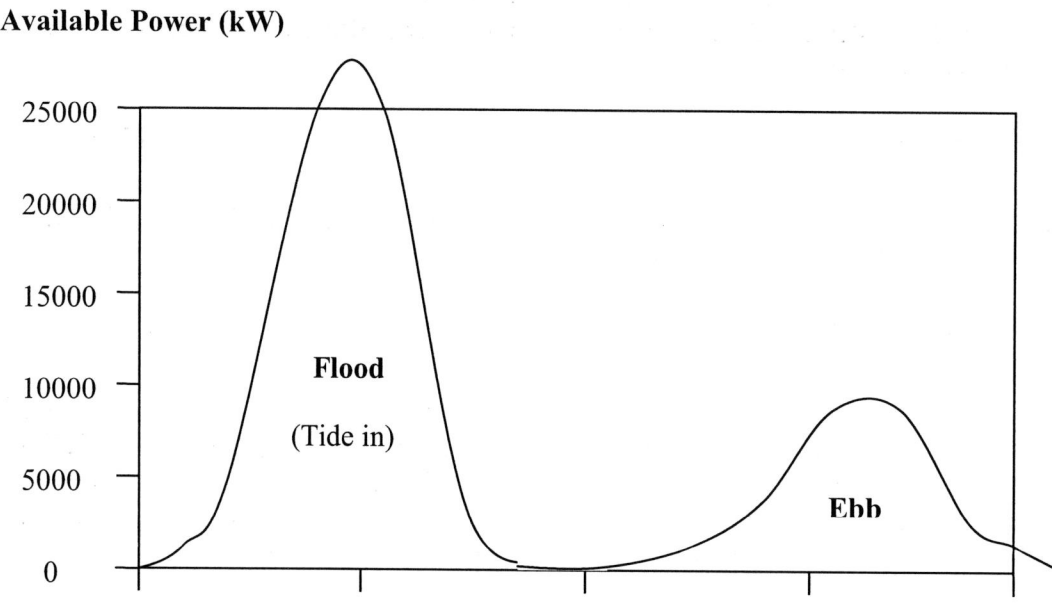

Figure 8.8. Available power in flood and ebb tides, if turbine can operate in both directions.

The "Rule of Twelfths" describes the varying power of the tide throughout its cycle. Assuming a semi-diurnal tidal cycle and a period of approximately 6 hours between low water (LW) and high water (HW), then the rule states that in the :

* 1st hour after LW, one twelfth of the total water displaced travels.
* 2nd hour after LW, two twelfths of the total water displaced flows in.
* 3rd hour after, three twelfths of the total water displaced flows in.
* 4th hour after, three twelfths of the total water displaced flows in.
* 5th hour after, two twelfths of the total water travel in.
* 6th hour after, one twelfth of the total water travel in.

Hence, the fastest streams take place during the 3rd and 4th hour after slack water (LW or HW) when the greatest amount of water travels (six twelfths or one half of the total water displaced). These facts are the same for the tide going out from HW to LW.

Despite the inherent predictability of tidal currents, a number of factors have been identified which will cause the behavior of the tidal currents to deviate from the standard sinusoidal model. Wherever possible, such factors should be included to make the results relate to the practical situation better.

8.3.2 Energy Conversion

Water that moves has kinetic energy similar to wind. The energy per second intercepted by a device of frontal area A_o (m²) in water of density ρ, and current velocity V (m/s) is given by:

$$P_e(t) = 0.5 \rho A_o V^3(t) \tag{8.77}$$

The power that can be converted to a useable mechanical form is limited for a device in an open water flow to:

$$P_m(t) = 0.5 C_p \rho A_o V^3(t) \tag{8.78}$$

where Cp is the power coefficient. The value of Cp for a turbine exposed to the flow of incompressible fluid is limited to a theoretical maximum value of approximately 0.593 according to Betz law. For a device the power coefficient is generally a function of the tip speed ratio (ratio between the speed of the turbine blade tip and the fluid flow speed), which is a function of the blade form and the number of the blades.

Assuming a gearbox transmission efficiency of η_1 and generator efficiency of η_2 then the electrical power output is given as:

$$P(t) = \eta_1 \eta_2 0.5 C_p \rho A_o V^3(t) \tag{8.79}$$

Tidal currents are not constant. Generally they are a combination of quasi-steady marine currents and flows induced by the tides. Estimation of energy capture therefore becomes a fairly complex procedure. However for most sites the flows are purely tidal, making it possible to characterize the tidal currents as series of simple sinusoidal waves. Assuming the current velocity V(t) follows a cyclic pattern then:

$$V(t) = V_{max} \sin \omega t \quad \text{and} \quad \omega = \frac{2\pi}{T} \tag{8.80}$$

where Vmax is the maximum current speed at the surface,
ω is the angular velocity of the tide
T is the period of the cycle, typically 12h 25 min or 745 minutes.

In Figure 8.9 is shown the power available and the predicted power output of a marine current turbine over a typical cycle. The turbine power coefficient was assumed to be 0.4, a cut-in speed of 0.7 m/s (14 kW) was dictated, and rated speed of 2.4 m/s, thereby limiting the maximum power (rated) to a value of 500 kW. Since tidal flows are predictable, it should not be necessary to design a cut-out condition for the turbine during normal operation.

The times at which cut-in and rated power take place (relative to the start of the cycle) are indicated by T_1 and T_2 in the figure.

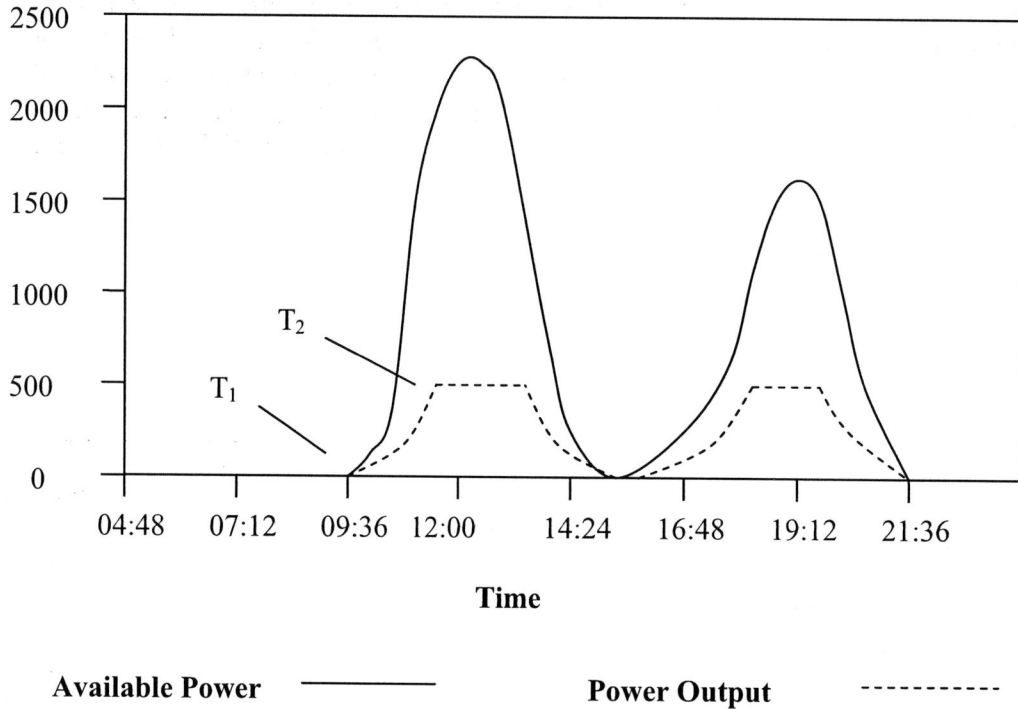

Figure 8.9. Power Profile

A practical tidal turbine will generate power for both flow (flood and ebb) directions, so its power characteristic (as a function of time) will be similar for each half of the cycle, however the speeds for the flood flow are generally higher than that for the ebb flow. The energy harnessed is given by the area under the power curve. So the energy harnessed during one half of each half tidal cycle is:

$$\int P(t)dt = \int_{T_1}^{T_2} \left(\eta_1 \eta_2 0.5 C_p \rho A_o V_{max}^3 \sin^3 \omega t \right) dt + P_{rated}(T_m - T_2) \qquad (8.81)$$

using units for time in minutes. T_m is the mid-point for each half-cycle shown in Fig. 8.9. The mean power output and capacity coefficient (same definition as for wind turbines) may be then be evaluated. Observe that the turbine produces no power for a period equal to $2T_1$, spanning the end of one half-cycle and the beginning of the next.

8.3.3. Trapezium Rule for Area Estimation

The trapeziuim rule provides a means of estimating the area under a curve. It becomes very useful if the curve cannot be represented by an equation. It works by splitting the area under the curve into a number of trapezia. The areas of the various trapezia are then summed up giving an approximate area under the curve. Look at the curve in Fig.8.10. The area under the curve between a and b is given by the sum of trapezia A, B, C and D of equal widths. Increasing the number of divisions increases the precision of the results.

Figure 8.10. Curve showing the trapezium rule.

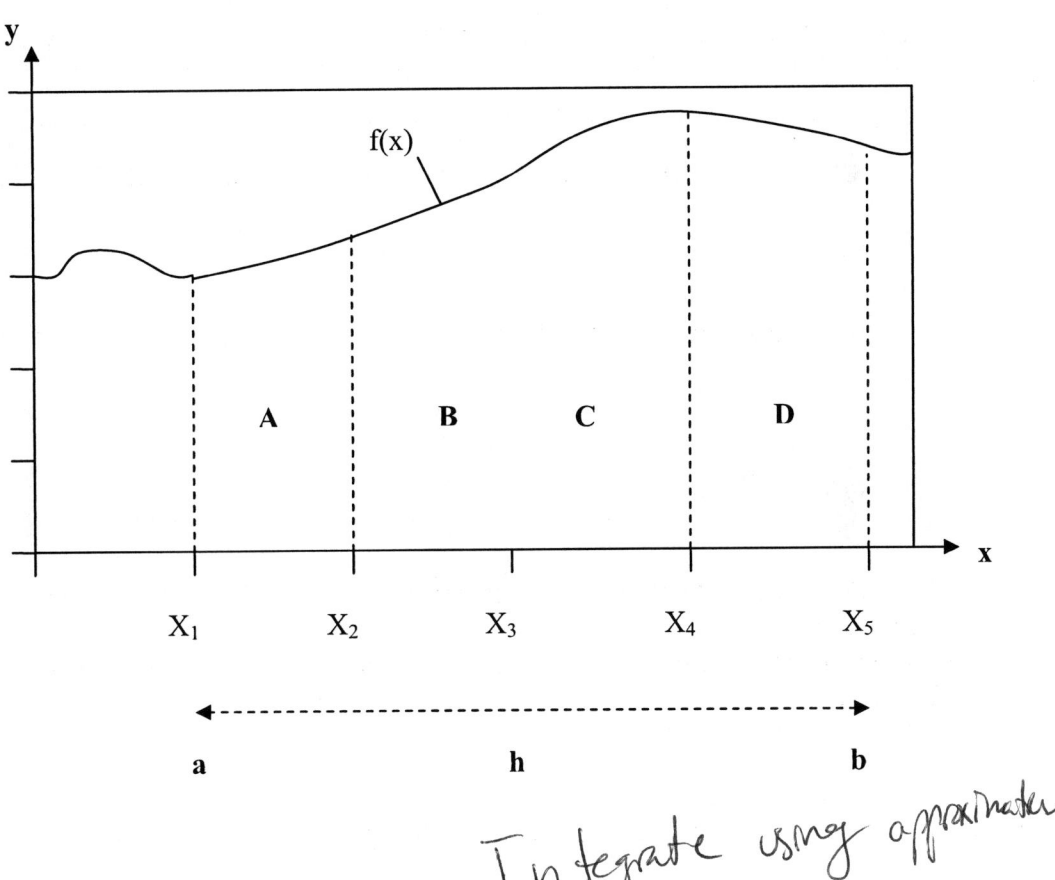

That is,

$$\int_a^b f(x)dx = \frac{1}{2}h(f_1 + f_2) + \frac{1}{2}h(f_2 + f_3) + \frac{1}{2}h(f_3 + f_4) + \frac{1}{2}h(f_4 + f_5) \qquad (8.82)$$

This becomes:

$$\int_a^b f(x)dx = h(\tfrac{1}{2}(f_1 + f_5) + (f_2 + f_3 + f_4)) \qquad (8.83)$$

Generalising for n points:

$$\int_{x_1}^{x_n} f(x)dx = h(\tfrac{1}{2}(f_1 + f_n) + (f_2 + f_3 + ... + f_{n-1})) \qquad (8.84)$$

PROBLEMS

8.1. For a SOFC operating at 1000°C, calculate the voltage change due to pressure changing from P_1 to P_2. This should be in good agreement with reported results (Bevc, 1997 and Hirschenhofer, 1995) for high temperature cells.

8.2. For a phosphoric acid fuel cell working at 200°C, calculate the effect of pressure change on the voltage. Compare this with that reported (by Hirschenhofer, 1995) of

$$\Delta V = 0.063 \ln\left(\frac{P_2}{P_1}\right).$$

8.3. Consider a PEM fuel cell at 80°C. Determine the change in voltage if the fuel is fed with oxygen instead of air.

8.4. With the data in Table 8.5 and Eq.(8.21), sketch the efficiency limit in percentage versus temperature in degrees Celsius. On the same sketch, plot the efficiency limit for the Carnot engine, using a 50°C exhaust temperature.

8.5. At a location with Weibull shape factor 2.4 and scale factor 9.8 m/s, a wind turbine is installed. The turbine has a cut-in velocity of 4 m/s and a cut-out velocity of 25 m/s. In a day, for how many hours will the turbine generate electricity? Calculate the probability of wind velocity going beyond 35 m/s.

8.6. Calculate the area under the sine curve sin2t in the interval 0 to $\pi/2$, by integration, and also by the trapezium rule, using (a) 4 slices, (b) 8 slices.

REFERENCES

1. Balmer R., "Thermodynamics", 1990, West.
2. Bevc F., "Advances in solid oxide fuel cells and integrated power plants", Proc. Instn. Mech Engrs, Vol.211, Part A, 1997, pp359-366.
3. Hirschenhofer J.H., Stauffer D.B., Engleman R.R., "Fuel Cells: A Handbook", Business/Technology books, 1995, pp3-7 and pp5-23.
4. Keenan J.H. and Kaye J., "Gas Tables", 1948, Wiley.
5. Van Wylen G.J. and Sonntag R.E., "Fundamentals of Classical Thermodynamics", 3rd Ed, 1986, p 688, Wiley.

Appendix Table 1 Critical Constants

Substance	Formula	Molec. Mass	Vol. m³/kmol	Temp. K	Pressure MPa
Ammonia	NH_3	17.031	0.0725	405.5	11.35
Argon	Ar	39.948	0.0749	150.8	4.87
Bromine	Br_2	159.808	0.1272	588	10.3
Carbon dioxide	CO_2	44.01	0.0939	304.1	7.38
Carbon monoxide	CO	28.01	0.0932	132.9	3.5
Chlorine	Cl_2	70.906	0.1238	416.9	7.98
Fluorine	F_2	37.997	0.0663	144.3	5.22
Helium	He	4.003	0.0574	5.19	0.227
Hydrogen	H_2	2.016	0.0651	33.2	1.3
Krypton	Kr	83.8	0.0912	209.4	5.5
Neon	Ne	20.183	0.0416	44.4	2.76
Nitrogen	N_2	28.013	0.0898	126.2	3.39
Nitric Oxide	NO	30.006	0.0577	180	6.48
Nitrogen Dioxide	NO_2	46.006	0.1678	431	10.1
Nitrous Oxide	N_2O	44.013	0.0974	309.6	7.24
Oxygen	O_2	31.999	0.0734	154.6	5.04
Sulfur dioxide	SO_2	64.063	0.1222	430.8	7.88
Water	H_2O	18.015	0.0571	647.3	22.12
Xenon	Xe	131.3	0.1184	289.7	5.84
Benzene	C_6H_6	78.114	0.259	562.2	4.89
Chlorodifluoromethane (r-22)	$CHClF_2$	86.469	0.1656	369.3	4.97
Dichlorodifluoromethane (r-12)	CCl_2F_2	120.914	0.2167	385	4.14
Ethane	C_2H_6	30.07	0.1483	305.4	4.88
Ethyl Alcohol	C_2H_5OH	46.069	0.1671	513.9	6.14
Ehylene	C_2H_4	28.054	0.1304	282.4	5.04
n-Heptane	C_7H1_6	100.205	0.432	540.3	2.74
n-Hexane	C_6H_{14}	86.178	0.37	507.5	3.01
Methane	CH_4	16.043	0.0992	190.4	4.6
Methyl Alcohol	CH_3OH	32.042	0.118	512.6	8.09
n-Octane	C_8H_{18}	114.232	0.492	568.8	2.49
n-Pentane	C_5H_{12}	72.151	0.304	469.7	3.37
Propane	C_3H_8	44.094	0.203	369.8	4.25
Tetrafluoroethane (r-134a)	CF_3CH_2F	102.03	0.2008	374.2	4.06

Appendix Table 2 Properties of Selected Ideal Gases at 25°C, 0.1 MPa (or saturation pressure if it is < 0.1 MPa)

Gas	Formula	Molecular Mass	R kJ/(kg.K)	v m³/kg	C_{vo} kJ/(kg.K)	C_{po} kJ/(kg.K)	k
Air	-	28.97	0.287	0.855432	0.717	1.004	1.400
Ammonia	NH_3	17.031	0.4882	1.440922	1.642	2.130	1.297
Argon	Ar	39.948	0.2081	0.619963	0.312	0.520	1.667
Carbon monoxide	CO	28.01	0.2968	0.884956	0.744	1.041	1.399
Carbon dioxide	CO_2	44.01	0.1889	0.563380	0.653	0.842	1.289
Ethane	C_2H_6	30.07	0.2765	0.818331	1.490	1.766	1.186
Ethanol	C_2H_5OH	46.069	0.1805	0.531067	1.246	1.427	1.145
Ethylene	C_2H_4	28.054	0.2964	0.878735	1.252	1.548	1.237
Helium	He	4.003	2.0071	6.191950	3.116	5.193	1.667
Hydrogen	H_2	2.016	4.1243	12.300123	1.008	14.209	1.409
Methane	CH_4	16.043	0.5183	1.543210	1.736	2.254	1.299
Methanol	CH_3OH	32.042	0.2595	0.763359	1.146	1.405	1.227
Neon	Ne	20.183	0.412	1.228501	0.618	1.030	1.667
Nitric oxide	NO	30.006	0.2771	0.826446	0.716	0.993	1.387
Nitrous oxide	N_2O	44.013	0.1889	0.563380	0.690	0.879	1.274
Nitrogen	N_2	28.013	0.2968	0.884956	0.745	1.042	1.400
n-Octane	C_8H_{18}	114.23	0.07279	10.869565	1.638	1.711	1.044
Oxygen	O_2	31.999	0.2598	0.773994	0.662	0.922	1.393
Propane	C_3H_8	44.094	0.1886	0.553097	1.490	1.679	1.126
R-12	CCl_2F_2	120.914	0.06876	0.200803	0.547	0.616	1.126
R-134a	CF_3CH_2F	102.03	0.08149	0.238095	0.771	0.852	1.106
Steam	H_2O	18.015	0.4615	43.290043	1.410	1.872	1.327

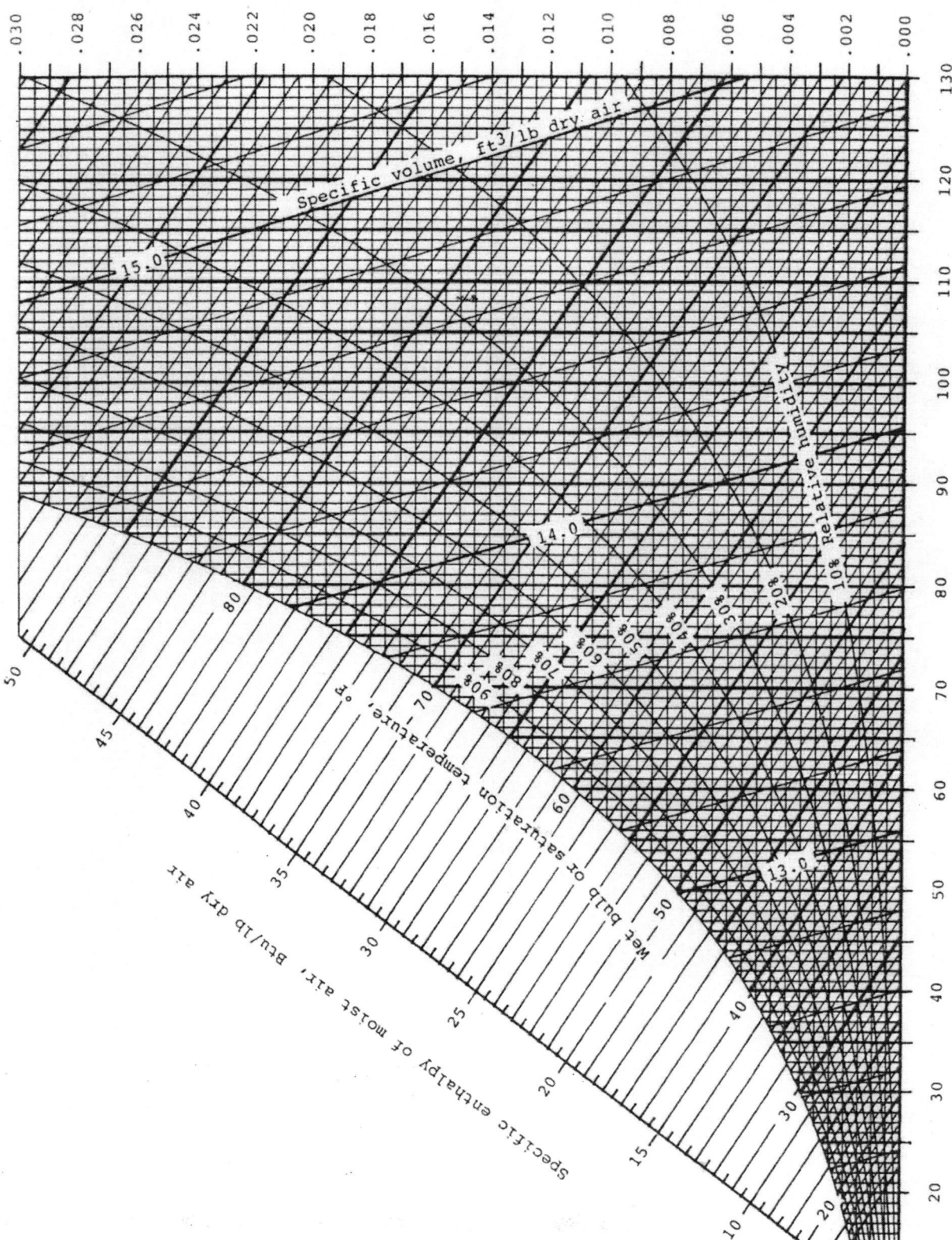

Appendix Figure 1. Psychrometric chart for atmospheric pressure in English units.
Source: Z. Zhang and M.B. Pate, "A Methodology for Implementing a Psychrometric Chart in a Computer Graphics System," ASHRAE Transactions, Vol.94, Pt. 1, 1988.

THERMODYNAMICS FOR ENGINEERS II

Kau-Fui Vincent Wong Ph.D., P.E.

University of Miami

Linus
Publications, Inc.

Published by Linus Publications, Inc.

Deer Park, NY 11729

Copyright © 2007 Kau-Fui Vincent Wong Ph.D., P.E.

All Right Reserved.

ISBN 1-934188-21-2

No part of this publications may be reproduced, stored in a retrieval system, or transmitted, in any form or by any means, electronic, mechanical, photocopying, recording, or otherwise, without the prior permission of the publisher.

Printed in the United States of America.

10 9 8 7 6 5 4 3 2 1

THERMODYNAMICS FOR ENGINEERS II

© 2007   Kau-Fui Vincent Wong, Ph.D., P.E.

PREFACE

In this third edition, the main objective is to present a comprehensive treatment of engineering thermodynamics from the classical aspect, so as to provide a foundation for all engineering students to prepare them to use thermodynamics in professional practice. The book is written for the second course in thermodynamics for undergraduates in engineering.

A prime difficulty of engineering undergraduates in studying thermodynamics is the use of thermodynamic tables, and finding the right properties of substances. This difficulty is removed by emphasizing the use of computer-aided thermodynamic tables from the onset.

In the spirit of simplicity, various thermodynamic systems are introduced; first, the refrigeration cycle, then the gas cycle, followed by thermodynamic relations and gas mixtures. After the gas mixtures, a detailed chapter on psychrometrics, a chapter on chemical reactions and combustion, a chapter on compressible fluid flow, ending with a chapter on sustainable energy systems.

The special features of the book are as follows:-

* It is a print-on-demand book.

* Lengthy treatise and unnecessary details have not been included. Only important facts and methods have been treated to make the work of the student easier.

* Limit the manual interpolation of thermodynamic tables. Support the use of computer-aided thermodynamic tables. These tables are downloadable from the author's website.

* Allow expansion of the property tables by the reader.

* Minimize the differences between the ideal gas treatment and the vapor treatment, by referring to computer-aided thermodynamic tables for all properties.

* Unify the treatment of the conservation of energy, the creation of entropy, and the destruction of availability, by using a balance equation for each of them.

* The chapter on psychrometrics will give a very strong background for the student of air conditioning. If the student wants to develop an expertise in air conditioning, the material covered will be ideal. If the student just wants to have a general education in various thermodynamic systems, the chapter is more than adequate.

· The chapter on compressible flow will give an excellent introduction of the topic to the student. If the student intends to acquire an expertise in compressible flow, the topics covered will be ideal. If the student prefers to obtain a general education in compressible flow, the material covered is more than sufficient.

* The chapter on sustainable energy sources and applications focuses on fuel cells, wind turbines and tidal turbines. These topics are essential for the modern energy engineer.

The special features of the book are geared towards making thermodynamics a less difficult field for undergraduates in engineering. An electronic version of the thermodynamic tables is available at the author's website. One special feature is that students can add to the thermodynamic tables, either by using smaller intervals in the existing databases or increasing the ranges in the databases. This participatory nature of the textbook can be accomplished by any reader with excess to Excel. Adding to the databases is not only a good learning process but also provides a sense of accomplishment to students on completion.

As an assistance to the reader, an introductory section is provided to review the laws of thermodynamics.

THERMODYNAMICS FOR ENGINEERS II

© 2007, Kau-Fui Vincent Wong, Ph.D., P.E.

TABLE OF CONTENTS

Introduction	Laws of Thermodynamics		
Chapter 1	Refrigeration and Heat Pump Systems		
	1.1	The Reversed Carnot Vapor Cycle	1
	1.2	The Vapor-Compression Refrigeration Cycle	3
	1.3	Actual Vapor-Compression Refrigeration Cycle	6
	1.4	Heat Pump Systems	10
	1.5	Refrigerant Considerations	14
	1.6	Other Refrigeration Systems	15
	1.7	Gas Refrigeration Cycles	25
	1.8	Absorption Refrigeration System	30
Chapter 2	Gas Power Cycles		
	2.1	Basic Considerations	47
	2.2	Air Standard Cycles	48
	2.3	Preliminaries on Reciprocating Engines	49
	2.4	Air-Standard Otto Cycle	51
	2.5	Air-Standard Diesel Cycle	61
	2.6	Air-Standard Dual Cycle	68
	2.7	Stirling and Ericsson Cycles	74
	2.8	Gas Brayton Cycle	78
	2.9	Brayton Cycle with Regeneration	89
	2.10	Regenerative Gas Cycle with Reheat and Intercooling	93
	2.11	Jet Propulsion Cycles	99
	2.12	Second Law Analysis of Gas Power Cycles	105
Chapter 3	Thermodynamic Property Relations		
	3.1	The Maxwell Relations	111
	3.2	The Clapeyron Equation	117
	3.3	General Relations for Thermodynamic Properties	121
	3.4	The Joule-Thomson Coefficient	132
	3.5	The Enthalpy, Internal Energy, and Entropy Changes of Real Gases	137
Chapter 4	Gas Mixtures		
	4.1	Composition of a Gas Mixture	147
	4.2	P-v-T Relationships for Ideal and Real Gas Mixtures	149
	4.3	Properties of Ideal and Real Gas Mixtures	155

Chapter 5	Gas-Vapor Mixtures and Psychrometrics		
	5.1	Atmospheric Air and Dry Air	167
	5.2	Specific and Relative Humidity of Air	168
	5.3	Dew-Point Temperature	170
	5.4	Adiabatic Saturation Process and Wet-Bulb Temperatures	171
	5.5	The Psychrometric Chart	176
	5.6	Psychrometric Processes	179
Chapter 6	Chemical Reactions		
	6.1	Introduction	233
	6.2	Combustion Process	233
	6.3	First-Law Analysis of Reacting Systems	243
	6.4	Adiabatic Flame Temperature	250
	6.5	Third Law of Thermodynamics and Absolute Entropy	255
Chapter 7	Thermodynamics of Compressible Fluid Flow		
	7.1	Stagnation Properties	263
	7.2	Adiabatic, One-Dimensional, Steady-State, Steady Flow of an Incompressible Fluid through a Nozzle	265
	7.3	Velocity of Sound in an Ideal Gas	268
	7.4	Entropy Connection to Vorticity	270
	7.5.	Reversible, Adiabatic, One-Dimensional Steady Flow of an Ideal Gas through a Nozzle	273
	7.6.	Mass Rate of Flow of an Ideal Gas through an Isentropic Nozzle	277
	7.7.	Nozzles	282
	7.8.	Normal Shocks	287
	7.9.	Supersonic Flow past Wedges and Cones	292
	7.10.	Oblique Shocks	296
Chapter 8	Sustainable Energy Sources and Applications		
	8.1	Fuel Cells	311
	8.2	Wind Turbines	323
	8.3	Tidal Turbines	335

Appendices

DIMENSIONS	S.I./ENGLISH	ENGLISH/S.I.
Length	1 cm = 0.3937 in. 1 m = 3.2808 ft	1 in. = 2.54 cm 1 ft = 0.3048 m
Volume	1 c.c. = 0.061024 in.^{3} 1 m^3 = 35.315 ft^3 1 L = 10^{-3} m^3 1 L = 0.0353 ft^3	1 in.^{3} = 16.387 c.c. 1 ft^3 = 0.028317 m^3 1 gal = 0.13368 ft^3 1 gal = 0.0037854 m^3
Velocity	1 m/s = 3.2808 ft/s 1 km/h = 0.62137 mph	1 ft/s = 0.3048 m/s 1 mph = 1.6093 km/h
Mass and Density	1 kg = 2.2046 lb$_m$ 1 g/cm^3 = 62.428 lb/ft^3	1 lb$_m$ = 0.4536 kg 1 lb$_m$/ft^3 = 0.016018 g/cm^3 1 lb$_m$/ft^3 = 1.6018 kg/m^3
Force	1 N = 1 kg.m/s^2 1 N = 0.22481 lb$_f$	1 lb$_f$ = 32.174 lb$_m$.ft/s^2 1 lb$_f$ = 4.4482 N
Pressure	1 Pa = 1 N/m^2 = 1.4504x10^{-4} lb$_f$/in.^{2} 1 bar = 100 kPa = 10^5 N/m^2 1 atm = 1.01325 bars	1 lb$_f$/in.^{2} = 6894.8 Pa 1 atm = 14.696 lb$_f$/in.^{2} 1 lb$_f$/in.^{2} = 144 lb$_f$/ft^2
Energy and Specific Energy	1 J = 1 N.m = 0.73756 ft.lb$_f$ 1 kJ = 737.56 ft.lb$_f$ 1 kJ = 0.9478 Btu 1 kJ/kg = 0.42992 Btu/lb$_m$ 1 kcal = 4.1868 kJ	1 ft.lb$_f$ = 1.35582 J 1 Btu = 778.17 ft.lb$_f$ 1 Btu = 1.0551 kJ 1 Btu/lb$_m$ = 2.326 kJ/kg
Specific Heat	1 kJ/(kg.K) = 0.238846 Btu/(lb$_m$.°R) 1 kcal/(kg.K) = 1 Btu/(lb$_m$.°R)	1 Btu/(lb$_m$.°R) = 4.1868 kJ/(kg.K)
Rate of Energy Transfer	1 W = 1 J/s = 3.413 Btu/h 1 kW = 1.341 hp	1 Btu/h = 0.293 W 1 hp = 0.7457 kW 1 hp = 2545 Btu/h 1 hp = 550 ft.lb$_f$/s

Temperature Conversions

$T(°R) = 1.8 T(K)$
$T(K) = T(°C) + 273.15$
$T(°R) = T(°F) + 459.67$

Universal Gas Constant

$\bar{R} = 8.314 \text{ kJ/(kmol·K)}$
$= 1.986 \text{ Btu/(lbmol·°R)}$
$= 1545 \text{ (ft·lb}_f\text{)/(lbmol·°R)}$

Standard Atmospheric Pressure

$1 \text{ atm} = 1.01325 \text{ bars}$
$= 14.696 \text{ lb}_f/\text{in.}^2$

Standard Acceleration of Gravity

$g = 32.174 \text{ ft/s}^2$
$= 9.80665 \text{ m/s}^2$

INTRODUCTION. LAWS OF THERMODYNAMICS

There are four laws of thermodynamics, from the zeroth to the third law. All the laws are empirical, that is, they have been deduced from observations and practice. The zeroth law stipulates that if two bodies are in thermal equilibrium with a third, they are in thermal equilibrium with each other and therefore at the same temperature. This law forms the foundation of the temperature scale. One of the three bodies can be a thermometer. Hence, because of this law, the thermometer can be used to compare the temperatures of two bodies without the bodies being in touch with each other.

The first law of thermodynamics is the conservation of energy. It states that energy can neither be created nor destroyed. For the practice of engineering, it often means that whatever amount of energy one has at the beginning, one ends up with the same amount of energy, maybe transformed or distributed differently, but the same amount.

The second law of thermodynamics is also known as the creation of entropy. It states that entropy can be created, but not destroyed. In practice, it usually means that whatever amount of entropy one has at the beginning, one ends up with the same amount or more entropy.

The third law of thermodynamics states that the entropy of a pure crystalline substance is zero at the absolute zero temperature. This law forms the foundation of the absolute temperature scale.

The four laws of termodynamics are often used with the conservation of mass principle. This principle states that mass is neither created nor destroyed. For the engineer in the field, it generally means that whatever amount of mass one has at the beginning, one ends up with the exact amount of mass.

1. REFRIGERATION AND HEAT PUMP SYSTEMS

1.1 The Reversed Carnot Vapor Cycle

A T-s diagram of a reversed Carnot cycle operating as a heat pump or refrigerator is shown in Fig. 1.1. In the case of the refrigerator, a quantity of heat Q_L is transferred reversibly from a low temperature T_L to the cycle. The reversed Carnot cycle operates in a cycle during which net work W is added to the system and a quantity of heat is transferred reversibly to a higher temperature. From the first law, $Q_L + W = Q_H$. From the second law for a reversible process, $T_H / T_L = Q_H / Q_L$. The reverse Carnot vapor cycle is represented by a rectangle on a T-s diagram. It is a useful standard because it requires the minimum net work input for a given refrigeration effect.

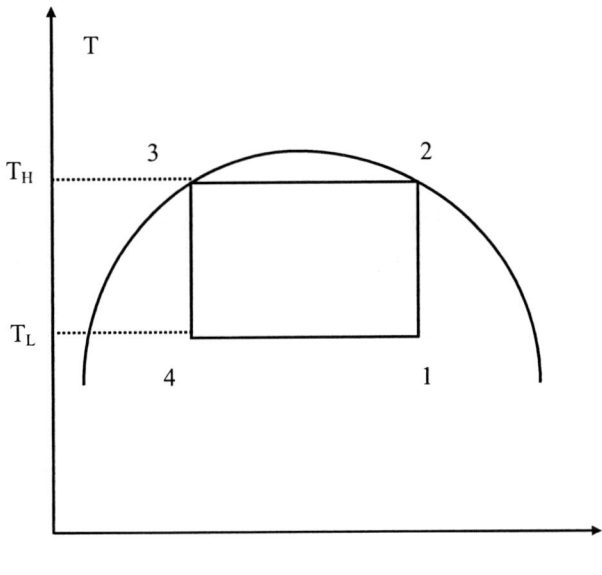

Figure 1.1 Reversed carnot cycle.

The performance of refrigeration processes is the coefficient of performance. The performance standard is defined as the ratio of the desired output to the costly input. The objective of the refrigerator is to remove heat from the low temperature space, and this is done by doing net work on the cycle. So the coefficient of performance (COP) for a refrigerator is defined as

$$\beta = \frac{Q_L}{W_{in}} \qquad (1.1)$$

Recall that the areas under the T_H and T_L lines in Fig. 1.1 represent Q_H and Q_L, respectively. Thus for a Carnot refrigerator,

$$\beta_{Carnot} = \frac{T_L}{T_H - T_L} \qquad (1.2)$$

Note that the value of the COP can exceed unity. The COP of the Carnot refrigerator is represented by the area under T_L divided by the area enclosed by the cycle. The performance is improved by increasing T_L and decreasing T_H. However, T_H cannot be lower than the environmental temperature because heat is rejected to it, and T_L cannot be higher than the temperature of the cold space from which heat is removed.

The objective of the heat pump is to add heat to the high temperature space from the low temperature space, and this is done by doing net work on the cycle. So the coefficient of performance (COP) for a heat pump is defined as

$$\gamma = \frac{Q_H}{W_{in}} \qquad (1.3)$$

Thus for a Carnot heat pump,

$$\gamma_{Carnot} = \frac{T_H}{T_H - T_L} \qquad (1.4)$$

The COP of the Carnot heat pump is represented by the area under T_H divided by the area enclosed by the cycle. The performance is improved by decreasing T_H and increasing T_L. However, T_L cannot be higher than the environmental temperature because heat is extracted from the environment, and T_H cannot be lower than the temperature of the warm space to which heat is added.

As before for the forward Carnot cycle, there are some impracticalities in the reversed Carnot cycle as described:

1. The isentropic compression process in the compressor is a problem because it is not practical to engineer a compressor that will handle two phases.

2. The expansion can be done easily in practice using an expansion valve, but the process will not be isentropic.

1.2 The Vapor-Compression Refrigeration Cycle

The impracticalities of the reversed Carnot cycle can be eliminated by compressing the working fluid entirely in the vapor region, and expanding the working fluid after the condenser through a valve or a capillary tube. The vapor-compression refrigeration cycle, shown in Fig. 1.2, does not have any internal irreversibilities except for the valve or capillary tube, and comprises the following processes:

1-2   Isentropic compression in a compressor

2-3   Heat is removed at constant pressure in the condenser

3-4   Adiabatic expansion in an expansion valve or capillary

4-1   Heat enters the evaporator at constant pressure.

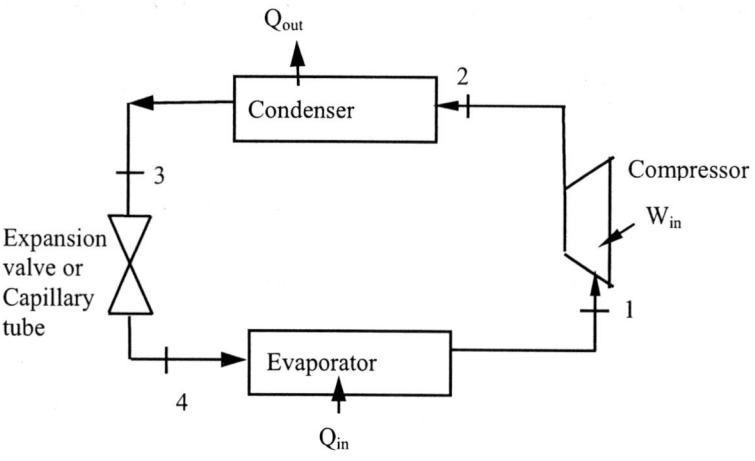

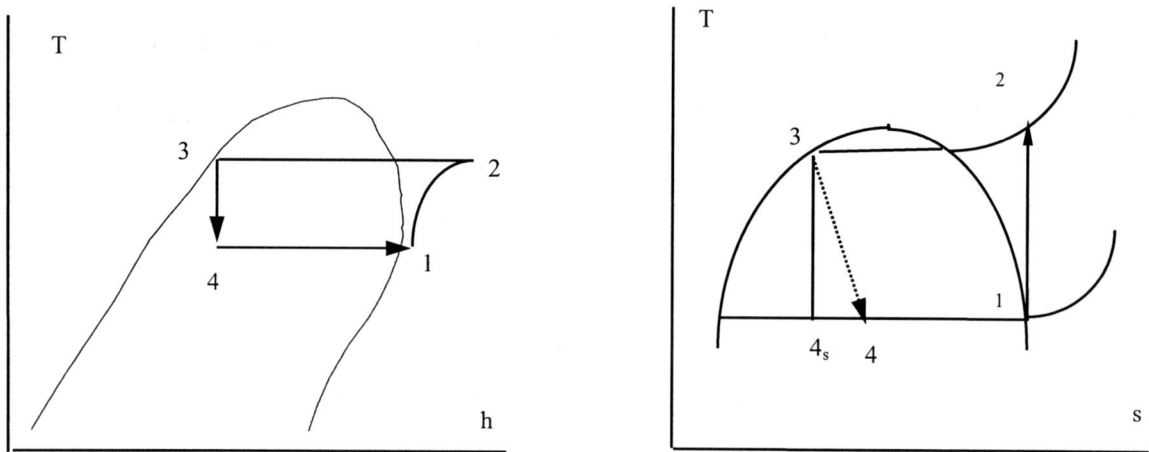

Figure 1.2 Vapor-compression refrigeration cycle.

Both the T-s diagram and the P-h diagram of the ideal vapor-compression refrigeration cycle are shown in Fig. 1.2. In the ideal cycle the working fluid leaves the evaporator at the saturated vapor state, and it leaves the condenser at the saturated liquid state. In the T-s diagram, the COP of the refrigeration cycle is represented by the area under process 4-1, divided by the area enclosed by the cycle. This can be expressed as

$$\beta = \frac{Q_L}{W_{in}} = \frac{h_1 - h_4}{h_2 - h_1} \qquad (1.5)$$

The P-h diagram is useful because three of the four processes appear as straight lines. In addition, the heat transfer in the evaporator and the condenser is proportional to the lengths of the corresponding process lines. The COP is the ratio of the length of the process 4-1 and the horizontal distance corresponding to the process curve 1-2.

Example 1.1

Problem

A refrigerator operates on an ideal vapor-compression refrigeration cycle between 0.15 and 0.6 MPa. Refrigerant-134a is the working fluid, and its flow rate in the cycle is 0.1 kg/s. Determine (i) the heat transfer rate from the refrigerated space, (ii) the power input, and (iii) the COP of the refrigerator.

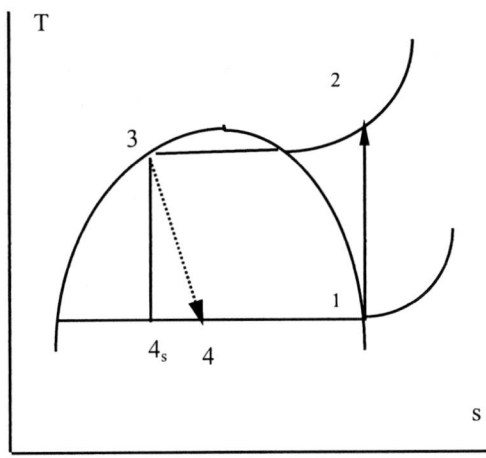

Solution

Assumptions: (i) K.E. and P.E. changes are negligible.

Analysis:

From $P_1 = 0.15$ MPa, $x_1 = 1.0$,

$$h_1 = 387.8 \text{ kJ/kg}, \qquad s_1 = 1.7372 \text{ kJ/(kg.K)}$$

From $P_2 = 0.6$ MPa, $s_2 = s_1$, $\qquad h_2 = 416.4$ kJ/kg,

From $P_3 = 0.6$ MPa, $x_3 = 0.0$, $\quad h_3 = 229.6$ kJ/kg, $\qquad s_3 = 1.1035$ kJ/(kg.K)

From $P_4 = 0.15$ MPa, $h_4 = h_3$, $\qquad s_4 = 1.119$ kJ/(kg.K)

(i) From the first law applied to the evaporator,

$$\dot{Q}_L = \dot{m}(h_1 - h_4)$$

Hence, heat transfer rate from the refrigerated space is

$$(0.1 \text{ kg/s})(158.2 \text{ kJ/kg}) = 15.82 \text{ kW}$$

(ii) From the first law applied to the compressor,

$$\dot{W}_{in} = \dot{m}(h_2 - h_1)$$

Hence, the power input is

$$(0.1 \text{ kg/s})(28.6 \text{ kJ/kg}) = 2.86 \text{ kW}$$

(iii) The COP of the refrigerator is

$$\beta = \frac{\dot{Q}_L}{\dot{W}_{in}} = \frac{15.82}{2.86} = 5.53.$$

1.3 Actual Vapor-Compression Refrigeration Cycle

The actual vapor-compression refrigeration cycle differs from the ideal one in several ways because of the irreversibilities in the various components. Two of these irreversibilities are the viscosity of the working fluid, and heat interactions with the surroundings. The T-s diagram of the actual vapor-compression refrigeration cycle is shown in Fig. 1.3.

In the ideal cycle, the working fluid leaves the evaporator as a saturated vapor. Since it is not easy to control the state of the refrigerant , it is expedient to design the system so that the refrigerant is slightly superheated at the evaporator outlet. In addition, the pressure drop due to fluid viscosity and heat transfer from the surroundings to the refrigerant can be significant. The result of this is an increase in specific volume, thus an increase in the work input to the compressor because steady-flow work is proportional to the specific volume.

The actual compression process involves frictional effects, which increase the entropy, and heat interactions with the surroundings, which may increase or decrease the entropy, depending on the direction. Thus, the entropy of the refrigerant may increase (process 1-2) or decrease (process 1-3) during an actual compression process. The compression process 1-3 may be more desirable than the isentropic compression process (1-2_s) since the specific volume of the refrigerant and thus the work input are smaller for process 1-3. For this reason, the refrigerant is cooled during the compression process whenever practical.

In practice, some pressure drop does occur in the condenser and in the lines connecting the condenser to the other equipment. This is shown by state 4 being at a different pressure from state 3 in Fig.1.3. The condensation process cannot be controlled so precisely that the refrigerant leaves as a saturated liquid. Since it is undesirable to let the refrigerant enter the throttling valve as a two-phase fluid, the refrigerant is subcooled before it enters the throttling valve, state 4. This is desirable since the refrigerant enters the evaporator with a lower enthalpy and thus can absorb more heat from the refrigerated space. From state 4 to state 5, there are frictional losses in the connecting line.

Throttling lowers the pressure at state 5 to the pressure at state 6. The throttling valve is situated close to the evaporator to minimize the pressure drop in the connecting line.

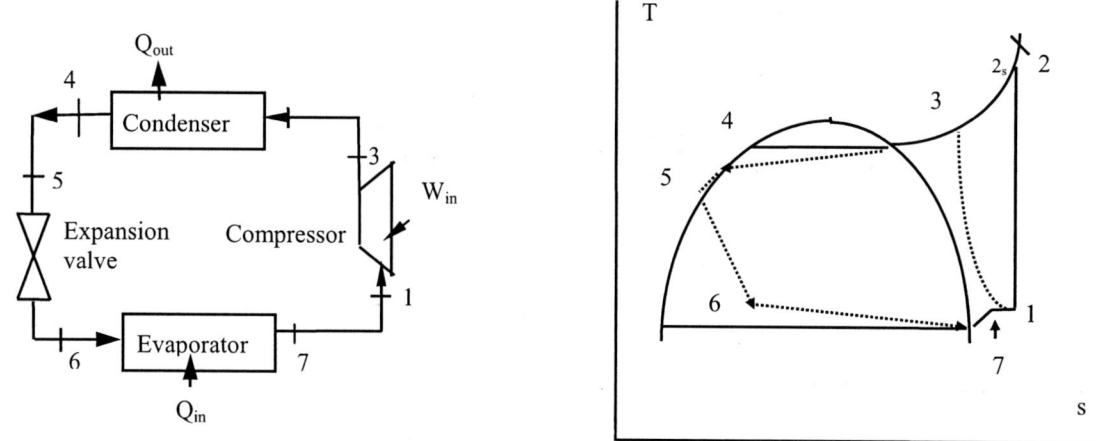

Figure 1.3 Actual vapor-compression refrigeration cycle.

Example 1.2

Problem

The inlet and outlet conditions of refrigerant-134a in the compressor of a refrigeration system are 0.15 MPa and -15°C and 0.6 MPa and 48°C, respectively. The mass flow rate is 0.1 kg/s. The refrigerant-134a is cooled to 18°C and 0.57 MPa in the condenser, and then throttled to 0.16 MPa. Calculate (a) the rate of heat transferred from the refrigerated space, (b) the isentropic efficiency of the compressor, (c) the compressor power input, and (d) the COP of the refrigeration system.

Solution

Assumptions: (i) Heat transfer in the connecting lines between the components are negligible.

(ii) Pressure drops in the connecting lines between the components are negligible.

Analysis:

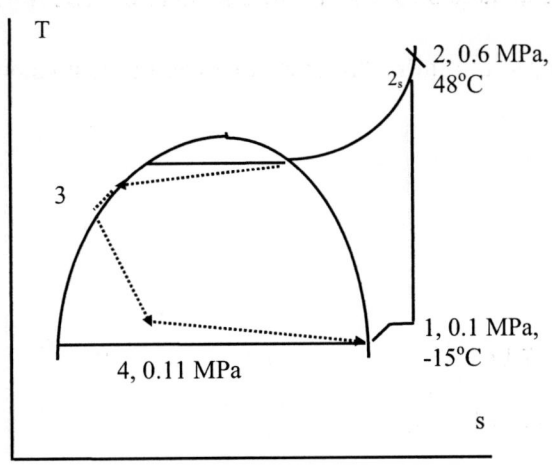

From $P_1 = 0.15$ MPa, $T_1 = -15°C$,

$\quad h_1 = 389.7$ kJ/kg $\qquad s_1 = 1.7446$ kJ/(kg.K)

From $P_2 = 0.6$ MPa, $T_2 = 48°C$,

$\quad h_2 = 436.7$ kJ/kg $\qquad s_2 = 1.8024$ kJ/(kg.K)

From $P_3 = 0.57$ MPa, $T_3 = 18°C$,

$\quad h_3 = 224.7$ kJ/kg

$\quad h_4 = h_3$

(a) From the first law equation applied to the evaporator,

$$\dot{Q}_L = \dot{m}(h_1 - h_4)$$

Rate of heat transferred from the refrigerated space is

$\quad (0.1 \text{ kg/s})(165 \text{ kJ/kg}) = 16.5$ kW

(b) Isentropic efficiency of the compressor is

$$\eta_c = \frac{h_{2s} - h_1}{h_2 - h_1}$$

$P_{2s} = 0.6$ MPa, $s_{2s} = s_1 = 1.7446$ kJ/(kg.K)

From the thermodynamic tables,

$h_{2s} = 418.6$ kJ/kg

Thus, $\eta_c = \dfrac{28.9}{47} = 0.615$

(c) From the first law equation applied to the compressor,

$$\dot{W}_{in} = \dot{m}(h_2 - h_1)$$

The compressor power input is

(0.1 kg/s) (47 kJ/kg) = 4.7 kW

(d) For the refrigeration system

$$\beta = \dfrac{\dot{Q}_L}{\dot{W}_{in}} = \dfrac{16.5}{4.7} = 3.51.$$

This example could be the actual cycle corresponding to the ideal cycle of Ex. 1.1. The heat transferred from the refrigerated space increases (by 4.3%), but the compressor power input increases by a larger percentage (64%). Hence, the COP of the refrigeration system decreases.

1.4 Heat Pump Systems

In spite of their relatively higher capital costs, heat pumps are increasingly popular. The most common energy source for heat pumps is atmospheric air, although water and soil have been used. The most serious problem is frost formation on the evaporator coils in humid climates (eastern U.S.A.) , when the temperature falls below about 5°C. The frost may be removed by reversing the heat pump cycle, that is, using it as an air conditioner. This obviously reduces the efficiency of the system.

Heat pumps and air conditioners have the same equipment. Thus, one system can be used as a heat pump in winter and an air conditioner in summer. This is done by adding a reversing valve to the cycle, Fig.1.4. The evaporator of the heat pump (located outdoors) acts as the condenser of the air conditioner in summer. The condenser of the heat pump (located indoors) acts as the evaporator of the air conditioner. Window units using this reversing principle are used in motels.

Heat pumps are most appropriate in regions that have a large cooling load in the summer and a relatively small heating load during the winter, as in the southern U.S.A. In these areas, the reversible heat pump systems can meet the entire heating and cooling requirements of the residential or commercial buildings. Heat pumps are less appropriate in areas where the heating load is significant and the cooling load is small, as in the northern U.S.A. Most air-source heat pumps need a supplementary heating system, such as electric resistance heaters when the heating load is large. This may not be needed for water-source or soil-source systems.

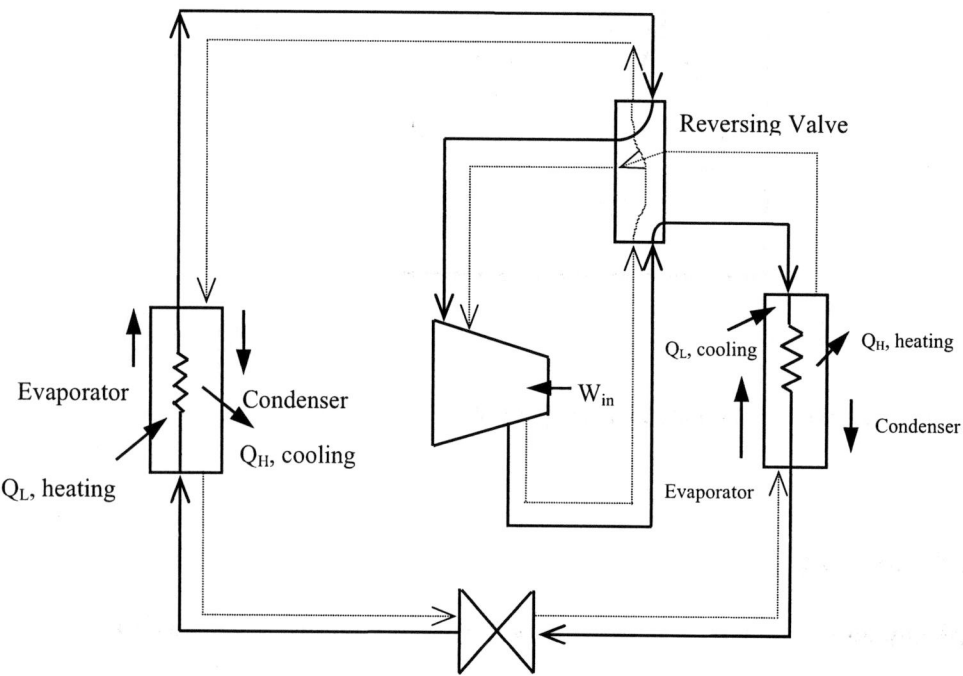

Figure 1.4 Heat pump system with reversing valve in heating mode (solid line) and cooling mode (dashed line)

Example 1.3

Problem

A refrigerant-134a heat pump is used for a residence with a design heating load of 200 Btu/s. The evaporator operates at 10°F and the condenser at 150 lb$_f$/in^2. Assume an ideal cycle. Determine (i) the mass flow rate of the refrigerant, (ii) the power input to the compressor, (iii) the COP of the heat pump.

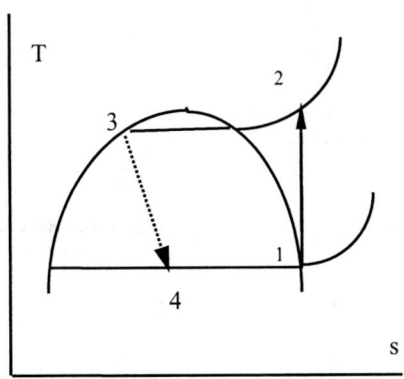

Solution

Assumptions: (I) K.E. and P.E. changes are negligible.

Analysis:

From $T_1 = 10°F$, $x_1 = 1.0$,

$\quad\quad P_1 = 26.79$ psia $\quad\quad h_1 = 168.06$ Btu/lb$_m$, $\quad\quad s_1 = 0.414$ Btu/(lb$_m$·°R)

From $P_2 = 150$ psia, $s_2 = s_1$, $\quad\quad h_2 = 183.5$ Btu/lb$_m$,

From $P_3 = 150$ psia, $x_3 = 0.0$, $h_3 = 110.7$ Btu/lb$_m$

(i) From the first law applied to the condenser,

$$\dot{Q}_H = \dot{m}(h_2 - h_3)$$

Hence, the heating load is

$$\dot{m}(72.8 \text{ Btu/lbm}) = 200 \text{ Btu/s}$$

Mass flow rate of the refrigerant is 2.747 lb$_m$/s.

(ii) From the first law applied to the compressor,

$$\dot{W}_{in} = \dot{m}(h_2 - h_1)$$

Hence, the power input is

$\quad\quad (2.747$ lb$_m$/s$)(15.44$ Btu/lb$_m) = 42.41$ Btu/s

(iii) The COP of the heat pump is

$$\gamma = \frac{\dot{Q}_H}{\dot{W}_{in}} = \frac{200}{42.41} = 4.72.$$

1.5 Refrigerant Considerations

There are several refrigerants from which to select, such as chlorofluorocarbons (CFCs), ammonia, hydrocarbons (propane, ethane, ethylene,etc.), carbon dioxide, air (aircraft air-conditioning), and water (for applications above its freezing point). Of these, the CFCs make up the largest family of refrigerants.

Because of the concern about the effects of halogenated refrigerants on the earth's protective ozone layer, international agreements have been made to phase out their use. The halogenated refrigerants destroy the protective ozone layer, which regulates the ultraviolet radiation into the earth's atmosphere. The halogenated refrigerants also prevent the infrared radiation from escaping the earth and thus contribute to the greenhouse effects that causes global warming. Fully halogenated CFCs (such as R-11, R-12, and R-115) do the most damage to the ozone layer. The non-fully halogenated refrigerants such as R-22 have only a small percentage of the ozone-depleting capability of R-12. CFCs that do not deplete the ozone-layer and do not contribute to the greenhouse effect have been developed. At present, the chlorine-free R-134a is being used to replace R-12.

Ammonia is used in the industrial and commercial sectors with large loads. The advantages ammonia have over some of the other refrigerants are its low cost, the higher COPs of its absorption cycle, better transport properties, better heat transfer characteristics, greater detectability in the event of a leak, and no effect on the ozone layer. The major disadvantage of ammonia is its toxicity, which makes it unsuitable for domestic use.

The temperatures of the refrigerant in the evaporator and the condenser are respectively determined by the temperatures of the cold refrigerated space and the warm environment to which heat is rejected. Therefore, the choice of the refrigerant is in part based on its suitability of its pressure-temperature relationship in the range of the particular application. Because of leakage problems, it is best to avoid excessively high condenser pressures, and excessively low evaporator pressures. Other considerations in refrigerant choice include toxicity, chemical stability, corrosiveness, and cost. The compressor used also contributes to the selection of the refrigerant. Reciprocating compressors perform well over large pressure ranges and are suitable for handling low specific volume refrigerants. The centrifugal compressors are better for low evaporator pressures and refrigerants with large specific volumes.

1.6 Other Refrigeration Systems

For some large industrial applications, the simple vapor-compression refrigeration cycle is inadequate. A few modifications and improvements are discussed in the following sections.

1 Cascade Refrigeration Systems

A large temperature range requirement also means a large pressure range in the cycle and poor performance for a reciprocating compressor. One modification is to perform the refrigeration process in stages. In other words, two or more refrigeration cycles are made to operate in series. These refrigeration cycles are called cascade refrigeration cycles.

A two-stage cascade refrigeration cycle is shown in Fig. 1.4. The heat exchanger acts as the evaporator for the topping cycle and the condenser for the bottoming cycle. Under ideal conditions, the heat loss from the fluid in the topping cycle should equal the heat gain by the fluid in the bottoming cycle. The relationship of the mass flow rates in the cycles is obtained from this fact, that is

$$\dot{m}_a (h_5 - h_8) = \dot{m}_b (h_2 - h_3)$$

$$\dot{m}_a / \dot{m}_b = (h_2 - h_3) / (h_5 - h_8) \qquad (1.6)$$

Then,
$$\beta_{cascade} = \dot{Q}_{in} / \dot{W}_{net,in}$$

$$= \frac{\dot{m}_b (h_1 - h_4)}{\dot{m}_a (h_6 - h_5) + \dot{m}_b (h_2 - h_1)} \qquad (1.7)$$

In the cascade system shown in Figure 1.5, the refrigerant in the topping cycle is assumed to be the same as that in the bottoming cycle. However, this is not necessary since the heat exchanger is a closed kind and no mixing occurs. The refrigerants with more desirable characteristics can be used in each cycle. The saturation dome for each of the refrigerants will then be different.

From the T-s diagram of the figure, the compressor work decreases and the amount of heat removed from the refrigerated space increases as a result of cascading, as shown by the shaded areas in Fig 1.5. Thus the COP of the system is improved by cascading. Sometimes, three or four stages of cascading are used.

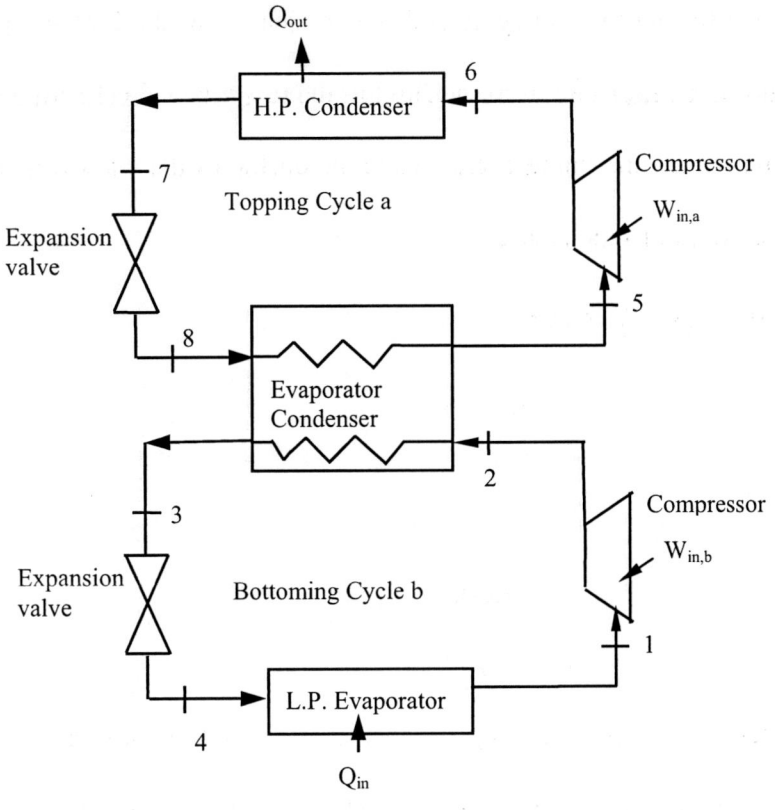

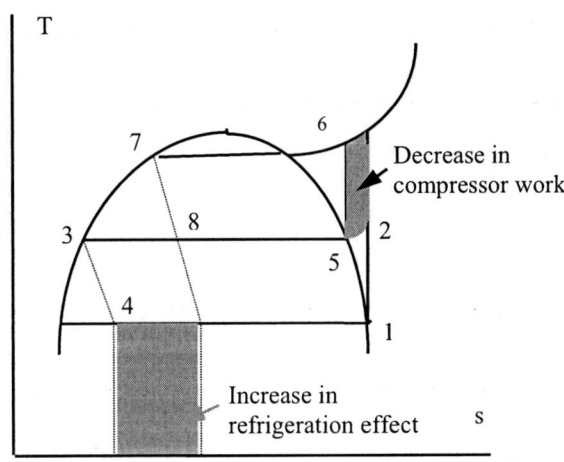

Figure 1.5 Cascade refrigeration cycle.

Example 1.4

Problem

A refrigerator operates on a two-stage cascade system between 0.15 MPa and 0.6 MPa. Refrigerant-134a is the working fluid in both cycles, and its flow rate in the topping cycle is 0.1 kg/s. The intermediate pressure of the adiabatic counterflow heat exchanger is 0.3 MPa, where heat is transferred from the bottoming cycle to the topping cycle. (Actually, the refrigerant in the bottoming cycle will be at a higher pressure and temperature in the heat exchanger for the heat transfer to take place.) Determine (i) the rate of heat transferred from the refrigerated space, (ii) the power input to the compressors, and (iii) the COP of the cascade refrigeration system.

Solution

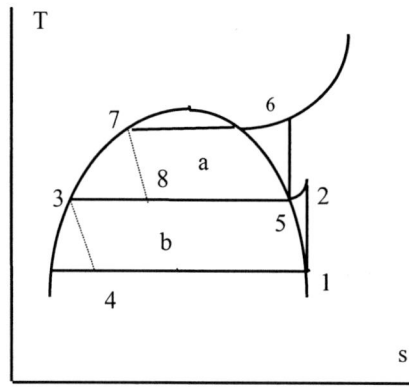

Assumptions: (i) The changes in K.E. and P.E. can be neglected.

(ii) Both compressors are isentropic.

(iii) The refrigerant enters both compressors as saturated vapor.

(iv) The refrigerant leaves both condensers as saturated liquid.

Analysis:

Cycle a is the topping cycle, and cycle b is the bottoming cycle.

From $P_5 = 0.3$ MPa, $x_5 = 1.0$,

$$h_5 = 398.7 \text{ kJ/kg}, \qquad s_5 = 1.7259 \text{ kJ/(kg.K)}$$

From $P_6 = 0.6$ MPa, $s_6 = s_5$, $\qquad h_6 = 413$ kJ/kg

From $P_7 = 0.6$ MPa, $x_7 = 0.0$, $\qquad h_7 = 229.6$ kJ/kg

$$P_8 = 0.3 \text{ MPa and } h_8 = h_7$$

From $P_1 = 0.15$ MPa, $x_1 = 1.0$,

$$h_1 = 387.8 \text{ kJ/kg}, \qquad s_1 = 1.7372 \text{ kJ/(kg.K)}$$

From $P_2 = 0.3$ MPa, $s_2 = s_1$, $\qquad h_2 = 401.8$ kJ/kg

From $P_3 = 0.3$ MPa, $x_3 = 0.0$, $\qquad h_3 = 200.8$ kJ/kg

$$P_4 = 0.15 \text{ MPa and } h_4 = h_3$$

(i) To obtain the mass flow rate of the refrigerant in the bottoming cycle, the first law equation is applied to the counterflow heat exchanger.

$$\dot{m}_a (h_5 - h_8) = \dot{m}_b (h_2 - h_3)$$

$$(0.1 \text{ kg/s})(169.1 \text{ kJ/kg}) = \dot{m}_b (201 \text{ kJ/kg})$$

Hence, the mass of refrigerant flow in the bottoming cycle is 0.08413 kg/s.

From the first law equation applied to the evaporator,

$$\dot{Q}_L = \dot{m}_b (h_1 - h_4)$$

Rate of heat transferred from the refrigerated space is

$$(0.08413 \text{ kg/s})(187 \text{ kJ/kg}) = 15.73 \text{ kJ/s}.$$

(ii) Power input to the compressors is

$$\dot{m}_a (h_6 - h_5) + \dot{m}_b (h_2 - h_1)$$

$$= 1.43 + 1.178 = 2.608 \text{ kW}$$

(iii) The COP of the cascade refrigeration system is

$$\beta = \frac{\dot{Q}_L}{\dot{W}_{in}} = \frac{15.73}{2.608} = 6.03.$$

2 Multistage Compression Refrigeration Systems

A multistage compression refrigeration system is one where there is more than one stage of compression and the working fluid in all the stages are the same. Since the refrigerant is the same, the heat exchanger in the cascade system can be replaced by a mixing chamber (called a flash chamber) which has better heat transfer characteristics. A two-stage compression refrigeration system is shown in Fig. 1.6.

In Fig. 1.6, it can be seen that the saturated refrigerant vapor at state 1 is first compressed to the interstage pressure at state 2. Here, it is mixed with the saturated vapor leaving the flash chamber at state 3 to produce a mixture at state 9. The second stage of compression brings the pressure of the refrigerant up to the condenser pressure at state 4. After giving up heat to the warm environment in the condenser, the liquid refrigerant expands in the first expansion valve to the flash chamber pressure, which is at the compressor interstage pressure. Part of the liquid vaporizes and at state 3, is mixed with the superheated vapor from state 2 as stated above. The saturated liquid at state 7 expands through the second expansion valve into the evaporator, where it removes heat from the refrigerated space.

The compression process in this system is essentially a two-stage compression with intercooling, since the superheated vapor at state 2 is cooled to state 9 before the next stage of compression. As such, the specific volume of the vapor is decreased and the overall compressor work decreases. The mass flow rates are not the same in all parts of the cycle.

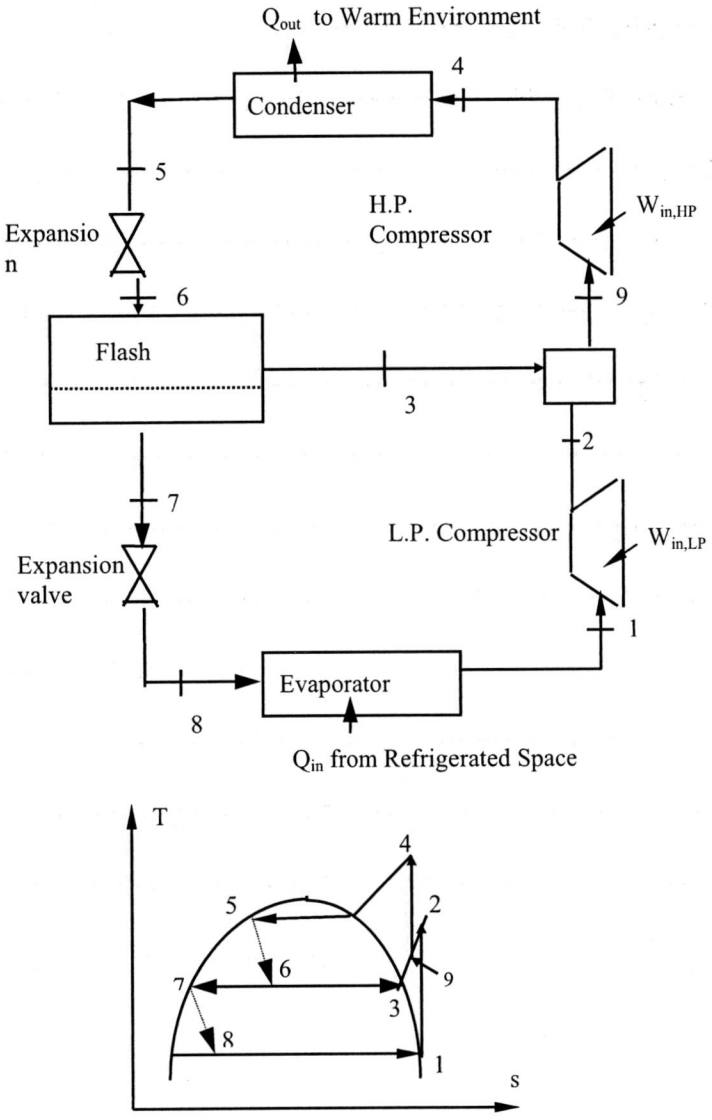

Figure 1.6 Two-stage compression refrigeration system with a flash chamber.

3 Multievaporators with One Compressor

One compressor may be used to compress the refrigerant from several evaporators operating at different pressures, hence temperatures. A cycle with a compressor with two evaporators is shown in Fig. 1.7.

An example of the two-evaporator refrigeration cycle is the household refrigerator-freezer unit. Such units are mostly used for foods, which generally have a high water content. The refrigerated space must be maintained above the ice point to prevent freezing. The freezer compartment, on the other hand, is maintained at about -18°C. This means that the refrigerant should enter the freezer at about -25°C to facilitate heat transfer. If a single evaporator were used, the refrigerant would have to circulate in both the refrigerated space and the freezer at about -25°C, which would cause ice formation near and around the evaporator coils and dehydration of the produce. This is not acceptable. This problem is overcome by throttling the refrigerant to a higher pressure (hence temperature) for use in the refrigerated space and then throttling it to the minimum pressure for use in the freezer. A single compressor is used to compress the refrigerant to the condenser pressure.

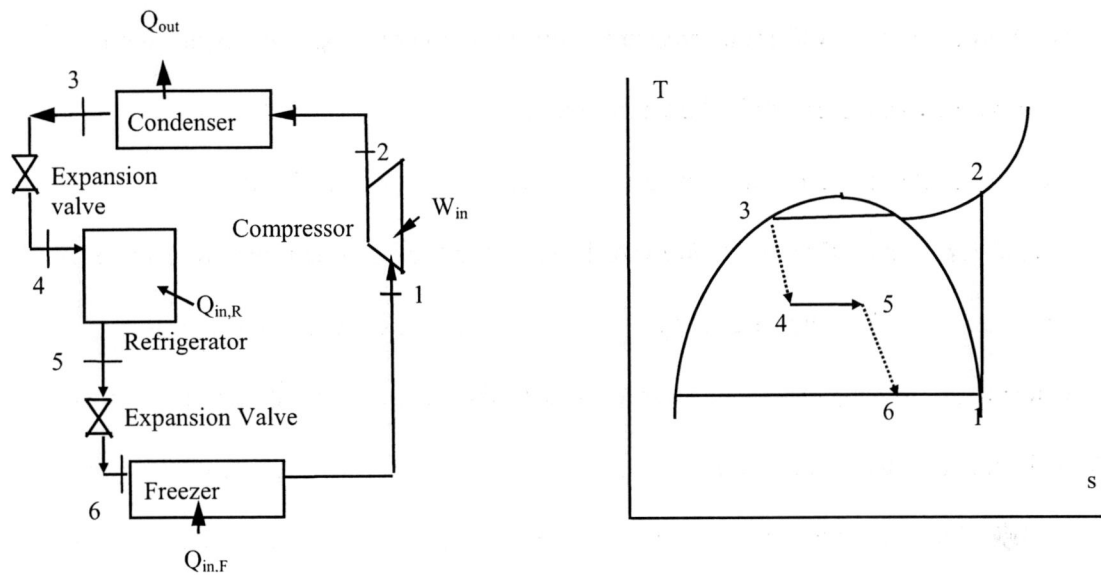

Figure 1.7 Two-evaporator with one compressor refrigeration cycle.

Example 1.5

Problem

A refrigerator operates on a two-evaporator with one compressor cycle, using refrigerant-134a as the working fluid. The flow rate of the refrigerant is 0.1 kg/s. The pressure of the freezer evaporator is 0.15 MPa, and that of the refrigerator evaporator is 0.3 MPa; the condenser pressure is 0.6 MPa. The rate of heat transfer from the refrigerator space is 10 kJ/s. Determine (i) the rate of heat transferred from the freezer space, (ii) the power input to the compressor, and (iii) the COP of the system.

Solution

Assumptions: (i) The changes in K.E. and P.E. can be neglected.

(ii) The compressor is isentropic.

(iii) The refrigerant enters the compressor as saturated vapor.

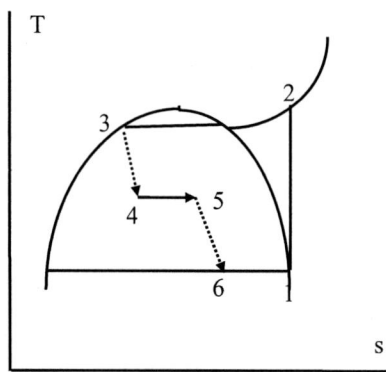

(iv) The refrigerant leaves the condenser as saturated liquid.

Analysis:

From $P_1 = 0.15$ MPa, $x_1 = 1.0$,

$$h_1 = 387.8 \text{ kJ/kg}, \quad s_1 = 1.7372 \text{ kJ/(kg.K)}$$

From $P_2 = 0.6$ MPa, $s_2 = s_1$, $\quad h_2 = 416.4$ kJ/kg

From $P_3 = 0.6$ MPa, $x_3 = 0.0$,

$$h_3 = 229.6 \text{ kJ/kg}, \quad s_3 = 1.1035 \text{ kJ/(kg.K)}$$

Also, $P_4 = 0.3$ MPa, $h_4 = h_3$

Apply the first law to the refrigerator evaporator,

$$\dot{Q} + \dot{m}h_4 = \dot{m}h_5$$

$$10 + (0.1)(229.6) = 0.1 h_5$$

Thus, $h_5 = 329.6$ kJ/kg.

Also, $P_6 = 0.15$ MPa, $h_6 = h_5$

(i) Apply the first law to the freezer evaporator,

$$\dot{Q} + \dot{m}h_6 = \dot{m}h_1$$

$$\dot{Q} = \dot{m}(h_1 - h_6)$$

The rate of heat transfer from the freezer evaporator is

$(0.1 \text{ kg/s})(58.2 \text{ kJ/kg}) = 5.82 \text{ kW}.$

(ii) Apply first law to the compressor,

$$\dot{m}h_1 = \dot{m}h_2 - \dot{W}_c$$

$$\dot{W}_c = -\dot{m}(h_2 - h_1)$$

The power input to the compressor is

$(0.1 \text{ kg/s})(28.6 \text{ kJ/kg}) = 2.86 \text{ kW}.$

(iii) COP of the system is

$$\beta = \frac{\text{Rate of heat removed by both evaporators}}{\dot{W}_c} = \frac{10 + 5.82}{2.86} = 5.53.$$

Note that the COP of the system does not change from that of the corresponding ideal refrigeration cycle with one evaporator, as worked out in Ex. 1.1.

1.7 Gas Refrigeration Cycles

The vapor compression cycles considered this far involve changes in phase. This allowed the heat transfer at the evaporator and at the condenser to take place at constant temperature, as in the reversed Carnot cycle. In gas refrigeration cycles, the working fluid remains a gas throughout the cycle. Since the heat transfer at the evaporator and at the condenser then do not take place at constant temperature, the cycle deviates more than the vapor compression cycle from the reversed Carnot cycle, thus giving up performance. However, gas cycles are used for a number of important applications. They are used for specialized applications like aircraft cabin cooling, and for the liquefaction of air and other gases where very low temperatures are required.

The simple gas refrigeration cycle is shown in Fig. 1.8. The gas is compressed during process 1-2_s. The high-temperature gas then rejects heat to the surroundings in process 2_s-3. The gas is then expanded in a turbine, where the pressure drops to P_4. The cool gas removes heat from the refrigerated space in process 4_s-1. The ideal cycle is shown by 1-2_s-3-4_s-1. The actual cycle would be 1-2-3-4-1, which takes into account the irreversibilities during adiabatic compression and expansion. Pressure drops due to fluid viscosity have not been considered.

The coefficient of performance for the gas refrigeration cycle is

$$\beta = \frac{q_L}{W_{net,in}} \tag{1.8}$$

where $\quad q_L = h_1 - h_4$

$W_{net,in} = W_{compressor,in} - W_{turbine,out} = (h_2 - h_1) - (h_3 - h_4)$

Even though they have relatively low COPs, the gas refrigeration cycles have two desirable characteristics. They involve simple, lighter components, which is a good feature for aircraft cooling. Gas cycles can include regeneration, which makes them suitable for liquefaction of gases and cryogenic applications.

The regenerative gas cycle is shown in Fig. 1.9. In the cycle, a counterflow heat exchanger is added. Without regeneration, the lowest turbine inlet temperature is T_o, the temperature of the surroundings or any other cooling medium. With regeneration, the high-pressure gas is cooled further to T_4 before expanding in the turbine. By lowering the turbine inlet temperature, the turbine exit temperature is correspondingly lowered. The turbine exit temperature is the lowest temperature in the cycle. Very low temperatures can be obtained by repeating this process.

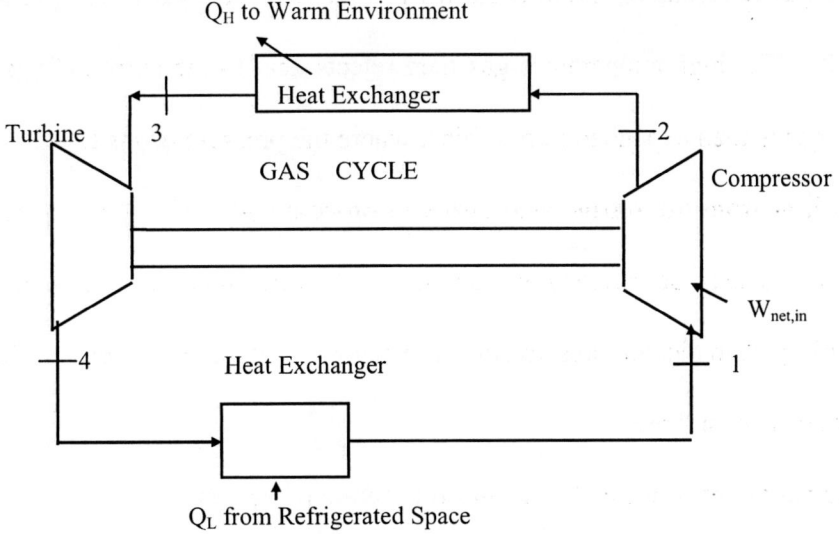

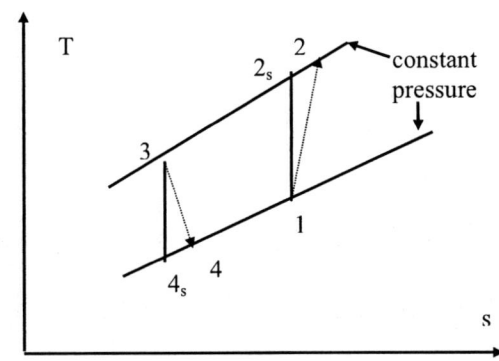

Figure 1.8 Simple gas refrigeration cycle.

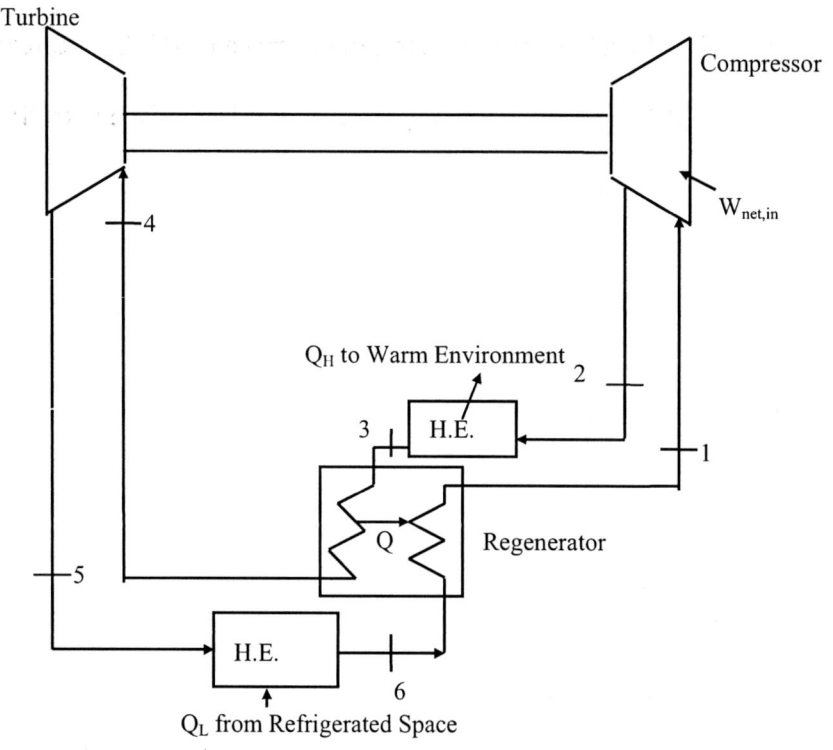
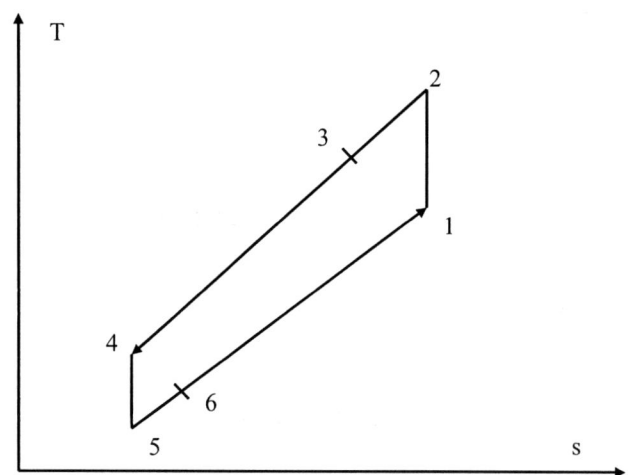

Figure 1.9 Gas refrigeration cycle with regeneration.

Example 1.6

Problem

An air-refrigeration ideal cycle keeps the refrigerated space at -13°C, and rejects heat to the environment at 22°C. The compressor pressure ratio is 3. Calculate (i) the temperature range of the cycle, (ii) the COP.

Solution

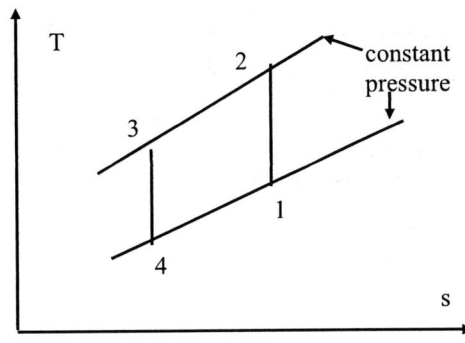

Assumptions: (i) Neglect K.E. and P.E. changes.

(ii) Both turbine and compressor are isentropic.

Analysis:

(i) From the tables,

$T_1 = 260$ K $\qquad h_1 = 260.09$ kJ/kg $\qquad$ and $\qquad P_{r1} = 0.8405$

$$P_{r2} = \frac{P_2}{P_1} P_{r1} = (3)(0.8405) = 2.5215$$

Hence, $\qquad h_2 = 356.5$ kJ/kg $\qquad$ and $\qquad T_2 = 356$ K

$T_3 = 295$ K $\qquad h_3 = 295.17$ kJ/kg $\qquad$ and $\qquad P_{r3} = 1.3068$

$$P_{r4} = \frac{P_4}{P_3} P_{r3} = \left(\frac{1}{3}\right)(1.3068) = 0.4356$$

Hence, $\qquad h_4 = 214.97$ kJ/kg $\qquad$ and $\qquad T_4 = 215$ K

The temperature range of the cycle is (356 - 215) K = 141 K.

(ii) Apply first law equation to the evaporator,

$$q_L = h_1 - h_4 = 45.12 \text{kJ/kg}$$

Apply first law equation to the turbine,

$$w_t = h_3 - h_4 = 80.2 \text{kJ/kg}$$

Apply first law equation to the compressor,

$$w_c = h_1 - h_2 = -96.4 \text{kJ/kg}$$

$$COP = \frac{q_L}{\text{net work input}} = \frac{45.12}{16.2} = 2.79.$$

1.8 Absorption Refrigeration System

Absorption refrigeration is a form of refrigeration that becomes financially attractive when there is a rather inexpensive source of energy at about 100 to 200°C. These sources include solar energy, geothermal energy, waste heat from process heat or cogeneration, and inexpensive natural gas.

Absorption refrigeration cycles are similar to vapor compression cycles, except in two aspects. The first is that instead of the refrigerant being compressed between the evaporator and the condenser, the refrigerant of an absorption system is absorbed by a secondary fluid (called an absorbent) to form a liquid solution. The liquid solution is pumped to the higher pressure. Since the average specific volume of the liquid solution is a lot less than that of the refrigerant vapor, much less work is required. Consequently, there is a relatively small work input in such cycles compared to vapor-compression cycles.

The second difference is that an energy source mentioned above is needed as input to a means that retrieves the refrigerant vapor from the liquid solution before the refrigerant enters the condenser.

The schematic of the simple ammonia-water absorption refrigeration system is shown in Fig. 1.10. After picking up heat from the cold refrigerated space in the evaporator, the ammonia vapor enters the absorber where it dissolves and reacts with water. The formation of this liquid solution is exothermic. Since the quantity of ammonia that is soluble in water increases as the solution temperature decreases, it is necessary to cool the absorber to maintain its temperature as low as possible, hence to maximize the amount of ammonia dissolved in water. The strong ammonia-water solution leaves the absorber and enters the pump, where its pressure is increased to that of the generator. Heat is transferred to the solution from a source to vaporize some of the solution. The vapor, which is rich in ammonia, passes through a rectifier where the water is separated and returned to the generator. The high-pressure pure ammonia vapor then continues through the rest of the cycle , by next entering the condenser. The hot ammonia and water solution, which is weak in ammonia, then goes through a regenerator, where it gives up some heat to the rich solution leaving the pump, and is throttled to the absorber pressure.

Absorption refrigeration systems are more complex and thus more expensive than vapor-compression systems. They occupy more space,and tend to be less efficient thus requiring much larger cooling towers to reject the waste heat. They are less popular and thus it is more difficult to find help to service them. However, interests in ammonia as a refrigerant has grown with the awareness of the poor environmental qualities of refrigerants like the chlorofluorocarbons (CFCs). Absorption refrigeration systems are primarily used in large commercial and industrial installations.

The COP of absorption refrigeration systems is defined as

$$\beta = \frac{\text{Desired output}}{\text{Required input}}$$

$$= \frac{Q_{in}}{Q_{gen} + W_{pump,in}} \cong \frac{Q_{in}}{Q_{gen}} \qquad (1.9)$$

Another kind of absorption system uses lithium bromide as the absorbent and water as the refrigerant. Basically, the operation principle is the same as the ammonia-water systems. To improve the low temperature characteristics of the lithium-water absorption system, it may be combined with an ammonia cycle to form a cascade refrigeration system.

The maximum COP of an absorption refrigeration system will be lower than the COP of the corresponding heat operated Carnot refrigeration cycle shown in Fig. 1.11. In such a system, the heat from the source is transferred to a Carnot heat engine, and the work output of this heat engine ($W = \eta_{th,rev} Q_{gen}$) is used to power a Carnot refrigerator to remove heat from the refrigerated space. Since $Q_L = W \times \beta_{rev} = \eta_{th,rev} Q_{gen} \beta_{rev}$, then the overall COP of the reversible absorption refrigeration system is

$$\beta_{\text{Heated Carnot}} = \frac{Q_{in}}{Q_{gen}} = \eta_{th,rev} \beta_{rev} = \left(1 - \frac{T_o}{T_s}\right)\left(\frac{T_L}{T_o - T_L}\right). \qquad (1.10)$$

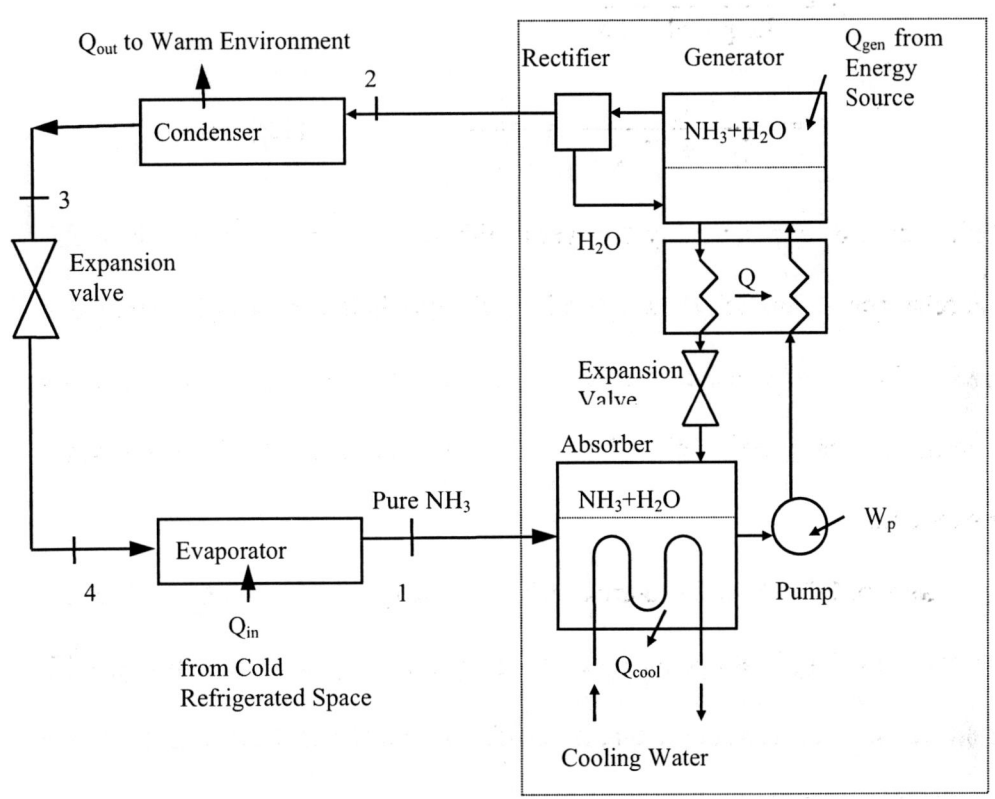

Figure 1.10 Ammonia absorption refrigeration cycle.

T_s, T_o, and T_L are the absolute temperatures of the heat source, environment, and refrigerated space, respectively. Any absorption refrigeration system operating between a temperature of T_s and T_L, in an environment of T_o, will not have a COP higher than that given by Eq. (1.10).

$$W = \eta_{th,rev} Q_{gen} = (1 - \frac{T_o}{T_s}) Q_{gen}$$

$$Q_L = \beta_{rev} W = (\frac{T_L}{T_o - T_L}) W$$

$$\beta_{\text{Heated Carnot}} = \frac{Q_{in}}{Q_{gen}} = (1 - \frac{T_o}{T_s})(\frac{T_L}{T_o - T_L})$$

Figure 1.11 Maximum COP of an heat operated Carnot refrigeration system.

Example 1.7

Problem

An absorption refrigeration system requires 40 Btu/s from a geothermal source at 260°F to remove heat at 25 Btu/s from the refrigerated space. The condenser rejects heat at 20 Btu/s to the environment at 80°F, and the cooling water removes heat at 35 Btu/s from the absorber. Determine the power supplied to the pump. Determine the temperature of the refrigerated space.

```
ERROR: timeout
OFFENDING COMMAND: timeout

STACK:

0.98232
0.97355
0.96482
0.95614
0.94751
0.93892
0.93038
0.92189
0.91343
0.90503
0.89666
0.88835
0.88007
0.87185
0.86367
0.85554
0.84744
0.8394
0.83139
0.82343
0.81552
0.80765
0.79983
0.79206
0.78433
0.77663
0.76899
0.76138
0.75383
0.74632
0.73885
0.73142
0.72404
0.71669
0.7094
0.70215
0.69495
0.68778
0.68066
0.67357
0.66654
0.65955
0.6526
0.6457
0.63884
0.63201
0.62524
0.61849
0.6118
0.60515
0.59855
0.59198
0.58545
0.57897
0.57253
0.56613
0.55979
0.55347
0.54719
0.54097
0.53477
0.52863
0.52253
0.51646
0.51043
```